Awakening Verse

Awakening Verse

The Poetics of Early American Evangelicalism

WENDY RAPHAEL ROBERTS

OXFORD
UNIVERSITY PRESS

OXFORD
UNIVERSITY PRESS

Oxford University Press is a department of the University of Oxford. It furthers
the University's objective of excellence in research, scholarship, and education
by publishing worldwide. Oxford is a registered trade mark of Oxford University
Press in the UK and certain other countries.

Published in the United States of America by Oxford University Press
198 Madison Avenue, New York, NY 10016, United States of America.

Library of Congress Cataloging-in-Publication Data
Names: Roberts, Wendy Raphael, author.
Title: Awakening verse : the poetics of early American evangelicalism /
Wendy Raphael Roberts.
Other titles: Poetics of early American evangelicalism
Description: New York, NY : Oxford University Press, [2020] |
Includes bibliographical references and index.
Identifiers: LCCN 2019058174 | ISBN 9780197510278 (hardback) |
ISBN 9780197510292 (epub) | ISBN 9780197510308 (online)
Subjects: LCSH: Religious poetry, American—History and criticism. |
American poetry—18th century—History and criticism. | American
poetry—19th century—History and criticism. | Evangelicalism in
literature. | Religion in literature. | Evangelicalism—United
States—History—18th century.
Classification: LCC PS310.R4 R63 | DDC 811/.009382—dc23
LC record available at https://lccn.loc.gov/2019058174

1 3 5 7 9 8 6 4 2

Printed by Integrated Books International, United States of America

To Maia and Sage

Contents

Illustrations

Acknowledgments

It is a joy to remember that writers do not write alone and to celebrate the generous mentors and friends who have given so much of themselves to see this book written. I count myself among the most fortunate to have completed my graduate work in the English Department at Northwestern University and to call myself a student of both Betsy Erkkilä and Robert Orsi. Betsy is the epitome of what it means to be, in her very soul, a feminist scholar and teacher. I am grateful for her intellectual acumen, curiosity, and trust. I will always be humbled by Bob's kind and generous welcome into religious studies—a scholar that has transformed the entire field to the extent that few can claim—and thankful not only for his poignant guidance but for his belief in my work. This project would not be what it is without him. I am additionally grateful to him for bringing David Hall on board as a reader who graciously provided timely feedback. Julia Stern and Jay Grossman also helped shape the first version of this project and both provided insightful criticism and encouragement at just the right times. Other Northwestern faculty who influenced my thinking include Ivy Wilson, Carl Smith, Brian Edwards, Barbara Newman, Vivasvan Soni, Helen Thompson, Regina Schwartz, Jules Law, and Reginald Gibbons. Many fellow colleagues enriched my work and my life and made my time in Evanston one of my dearest memories, including Nathan Hedman, Abram Van Engen, Katy Chiles, Peter Jaros, Hunt Howell, Sarah Blackwood, Sarah Mesle, Janaka Brown Lewis, Liz McCabe, Josh Smith, Lora Walsh, Gayle Rogers, Brodie Austin, Greg Laski, Jenny Lee, Sarah Turner Lahey, Patrick Leahy, Melissa Daniels-Rauterkus, Wanalee Romero, Carissa Harris, Emily Izenstein Algranati, Jason Malikow, Matthew John Cressler, Brian Clites, Tina Howe Clites, Hugh McIntosh, Vanessa Corredera, Rachel Blumenthal, Whitney Taylor, Michael Slater, Laura Passin, and Nathan Mead. I continue to be humbled by the scholarly work that my cohort and those before and after me have produced. I am proud to be counted among you. My graduate work began at the University of Arizona. I would be remiss not to acknowledge the early direction of Tenney Nathanson, Greg Jackson, Roxanne Mountford, Eric Hayot, and Charlie Bertsch on my thinking, and the colleagues that I gained there,

especially Amanda Gradisek. Thank you also to my earliest professors, Paul
Buchanan and Brian Ingraffia, who encouraged graduate school, and Nancy
Takacs who suggested I be an English major in the first place.

After leaving Northwestern, I was again blessed to find myself surrounded
by supportive colleagues at the University at Albany, SUNY. Laura Wilder,
Bret Benjamin, Paul Stasi, and Erica Fretwell have not only supported my
scholarly endeavors, but created a new home for me (along with Megan
Ingalls and Todd Carmody). A special thank you to Paul Stasi, Helene Scheck,
James Lilley, Erica Fretwell, and Michael Leong for generously reading
chapters. I am also grateful for the intellectual engagement and support of
Jennifer Greiman, Derik Smith, Eric Keenaghan, Ineke Murakami, Ronald
Bosco, Kori Graves, Laura Tetreault, Edward Schwarzchild, Kir Kuiken,
Vesna Kuiken, Rick Barney, Mary Valentis, Aashish Kaul, Helen Elam, Jeffrey
Berman, and Liz Lauenstein. Thank you to my department chairs Randy
Craig, Glyne Griffith, and Charles Shepherdson for clear direction and kind-
ness. I would also like to thank the English Department for a semester of
writing leave and United University Professionals for the Drescher Award
to support a subsequent writing semester. Thank you also to the department
and the Dean of the College of Arts and Sciences for making it possible for
me to take leave for outside research grants.

Several editors and readers helped craft early versions of this project.
Sandra Gustafson, Justine Murison, and Jordan Stein sharpened my ideas
about evangelical poetry and religious methods, which appeared in *Early
American Literature*. Thank you to Elizabeth Maddock Dillon and Tracy
Fessenden for their insightful responses. Sandra Gustafson and Vincent
Carretta supported and refined my work on Phillis Wheatley and Ruth Barrell
Andrews, which also appeared in *Early American Literature*. Paul Erickson,
ever an early supporter of my work for which I cannot express enough grat-
itude, invited me to speak on Sarah Moorhead and Phillis Wheatley at the
American Antiquarian Society, which was subsequently published in *Papers
of the Bibliographic Society of America*. Kimberly Johnson offered insightful
critique of my work on espousal poetics for her special issue of *Christianity
and Literature*. Theresa Strouth Gaul supported and edited my work on
evangelical print culture for the first volume of the *Blackwell Companion
to American Literature*, while Jonathan Yeager has supported and provided
feedback for my work on evangelical poetry for his volume, *The Oxford
Handbook of Early Evangelicalism*. All of these readers and editors refined
my writing and thinking for which I am grateful. I am particularly grateful

to the anonymous Oxford readers who provided the final impetus and guidance to make the book closer to what I knew it should be, for the support of my Oxford editor Cynthia Read, and for the development editing of Brandon Proia.

Many organizations have provided the space and the funding for this project to grow. In addition to those already listed, I would like to thank the American Antiquarian Society, whose generous support both at the dissertation stage and at the book stage anchored this project. Thank you to Elizabeth Pope for confirming that Sarah Moorhead's Whitefield poem was printed as a stand-alone poem and for Meredith Neuman and her research assistant Tony Armstrong for hunting down clues. The Charlotte Newcombe Dissertation Fellowship supported the first version of this project, as did the McNeil Center for Early American Studies. Both of these organizations deserve special recognition for being progressive supporters of women scholars by making room for motherhood in the academy. I am grateful to have met McNeil Center Director Daniel Richter and other cohort fellows, especially Brian Connolly, Carrie Hyde, and Joseph Rezek. Thank you also to the Newberry Library and the Huntington Library for funding research at the dissertation stage. The Massachusetts Historical Society generously funded research and writing for an academic year, for which I am grateful. Thank you especially to Conrad Wright and Kate Viens for friendship and for accommodating my schedule, and to the many librarians and fellows there. I am also grateful for the New England Regional Consortium Fellowship, which supported a separate project, but from which some of the research trickled into these pages during the final revisions. Thank you especially to Marjorie Strong at the Vermont Historical Society, who suggested I look at the Royall Tyler Papers.

There are people across the field who have taken me under their wing or provided encouragement or an insightful critique. I cannot name them all. I especially thank those who have given constant support, mentorship, and generously read chapters: Meredith Neuman, Chris Phillips, Claudia Stokes, and Abram Van Engen. And a special thank you to David Shields for generously sharing his microfilm and files of transcribed poetry with me. The Society of Early Americanists has been a constant home for me, and I am particularly grateful for the many scholars there who welcomed me as a graduate student and junior scholar, including Laura Stevens, Kristina Bross, Hilary Wyss, Susan Imbarrato, Patrick Erben, Lisa Gordis, and Kelly Wisecup. Thank you to Sarah Rivett, Kathryn Lofton, Michael Warner, Max

Cavitch, Stephen Marini, Sally Promey, Harry Stout, Catherine Brekus, Joanna Brooks, Eric Slauter, Janet Lindman, Christopher Looby, Edward Cahill, Michael Cohen, Colin Jager, Honorée Jeffers, and Vincent Carretta for support or critique at various stages. Finally, thank you to my virtual (and virtuous) writing group, who patiently read drafts (and then read them again) and whose own manuscripts in process and in print taught me so much: Angela Calcaterra, Travis Foster, Greta LaFleur, Michele Navakas, Kacy Tillman, Abram Van Engen, and Caroline Wigginton. It is an honor to count myself one of your colleagues.

Last of all, this book would have never been finished without my family. The godparents of my children, Meg and Emiyah, are a constant source of rest and belonging. My mother, Susan Orth, traveled across the country to help while I was away on research. She, my father Frank Miller, and my sister Angela Poliquin always believed I would finish, and their pride in my work has given it extra significance. Charlene DeForest and Dale Orth, my grandparents, passed away during the early stages of this project, yet I thrive on their love and support even now. This book is dedicated to my daughters, Maia and Sage, who are bibliophiles in their own right. For their entire lives, mama has been writing this book. And for their entire lives they have brought joy, balance, and meaning to my days. Finally, I met my life partner, most devoted editor, and ardent supporter, Jesse, my freshman year in college. At the deepest level, this project, like all else in my life, is equal parts his.

Introduction

Revival Poetry

A Verse may find him who a Sermon flies,
Saith Herbert well. Great Truth to dress in Meeter;
Becomes a Preacher who Mens Souls do prize,
That Truth in Sugar roll'd may taste the sweeter.
> —James Mitchell, "On the Following Work, and Its Author,"
> in Michael Wigglesworth's *Day of Doom* (1666)

When shall the Divine Fires of Poetry and Devotion flame unitedly to
Heaven, and diffuse celestial Fervour through the World!
> —Samuel Davies, *Miscellaneous Poems, Chiefly*
> *on Divine Subjects* (1752)

In 1824, an American sailor aboard a cargo ship rummaged through his collection of novels and romances to occupy a vacant hour. To his surprise he found a New Testament. Inside he discovered a poem by the popular British poet Felicia Hemans, enclosed with care by his wife "to arrest" his attention. It worked. Unable to put the poem down, he read it "again and again" as thoughts of his own mortality began to overtake him. Immediately, his desire for novels and romances ceased; a voracious appetite for the Bible and other devotional texts ensued. The first line of Hemans's "The Hour of Death"—"Thou hast all seasons for thine own, O death!"—filled his mind, ushering in a time of conviction for his sins, and soon, his salvation.[1] The sailor, Joseph Bates, would become integral to the birth of Seventh-day Adventism, a church formed out of the explosive religious activity of the early nineteenth century typically designated the Second Great Awakening. What initiated this chain of events that ignited a unique feature of the religious landscape of America? According to Bates, a single poem thrust him, a

Awakening Verse. Wendy Raphael Roberts, Oxford University Press (2020). © Oxford University Press.
DOI: 10.1093/oso/9780197510278.001.0001

lapsed Presbyterian, into the revival fire of the early nineteenth century, significantly altering American religious history.

Bates's conversion through a poem was not a singular event, nor was the faith his wife placed in the potential of exchanging poetry an unusual phenomenon. Their story exemplifies a pervasive revival poetic culture that began in the early eighteenth century and privileged the interventionist work of poetry both in individual salvation and in the progress of history. *Awakening Verse: The Poetics of Early American Evangelicalism* is the backstory to the monumental encounter with verse of Bates, his wife, and many others of their time. By Bates's conversion in 1824, large swaths of itinerant ministers and laypeople wrote and exchanged verse with the belief that their words directly participated in and facilitated the purposes of God in history.

This poetry crossed denominational and national affiliations and appeared in various periodicals, tracts, books, and manuscript forms. Notable poems written by revivalists and printed in the early nineteenth century include, among many others, the Methodist turned Independent itinerant and fervent abolitionist Thomas Branagan's *Avenia: or, A Tragical Poem, on the Oppression of the Human Species* (1805) and *The Penitential Tyrant; or, Slave Trader Reformed: A Pathetic Poem, in Four Cantos* (1807); the Baptist turned Universalist minister Elhanan Winchester's *The Process and Empire of Christ* (1805); the Universalist Lucy Barns's *The Female Christian* (1809); the Shaker itinerant William Scales's *The Quintessence of Universal History; or, An Epitomial History of the Christian Era* (1806); the British Baptist Samuel Deacon's *An Attempt to Answer the Important Question, What Must I Do to Be Saved?* (1807); Methodist itinerant William Thacher's *Battle between Truth and Error* (1808); transatlantic Methodist Joshua Marsden's *Leisure Hours; or, Poems, Moral, Religious, & Descriptive* (1812); the Presbyterian (later turned Episcopal minister) Benjamin Allen's *Urania, or The True Use of Poesy* (1814); the "Sweet Singer of Hartford" and "American Hemans," Lydia Huntley Sigourney's *Moral Pieces in Prose and Verse* (1815); Christian Connexion itinerant Joseph Thomas's *The Pilgrim's Muse* (1816); Methodist Harriett Muzzy's *Poems, Moral and Sentimental* (1821); Methodist itinerant John N. Maffitt's *Tears of Contrition* (1821) and *Poems* (1839); and the combative Calvinist poems of John Peck, including *A Poem, Containing a Descant on the Universal Plan* (1801), *The Devil's Shaving Mill* (1815), *The Spirit of Methodism* (1829), and *The Dagon of Calvinism, or The Moloch of Decrees* (1827).[2] While we have a great deal of scholarly work on evangelical culture and the rise of early evangelicalism, the vast majority of these poetic works have never been discussed.

And the neglect of such writings grows even larger when we expand into and beyond the nineteenth century and include the many influential named and anonymous women revival poets, or begin to consider the prolific revival verse circulating in periodicals and manuscript.[3] Revivalists, in short, were deeply invested in poetic production.[4] And for good reason. As this book argues, poetry was not insubstantial decor adorning the *real* stuff of scholarly concern—sermons, conversion narratives, and revival journals. Instead, a vast library of poetic productions served as one of the primary actors in the creation, maintenance, and adaptation of evangelical culture. Without reading what evangelicals actually wrote and consumed in such massive quantities, we cannot understand their culture as it first took shape.

The primacy of revival poetry in evangelical culture is not surprising given the status of verse in the eighteenth century. Even a cursory survey of eighteenth-century American print reveals that poetry flourished in the colonies and the early republic, and its presence in daily life extended far beyond books, newspapers, and broadsides. Poetry was not only printed but read at formal and informal occasions, cultivated in salons and coffeehouses, recited after dinner for entertainment, performed from the pulpit and the street corner, and written and shared among family, friends, and poetic coteries. Verse played an essential role in the functioning of public life—both political and religious, often without distinction—and was understood to be a powerful tool to effect change in the world. Evangelicals were both influenced by and helped to produce this pervasive verse culture.

Even so, American literary history has marginalized poetry. Over a decade ago, Max Cavitch in *American Elegy* (2007) pointed out the continued exclusion of poetry from the main narratives of early American literature—and this a decade after David Shields's groundbreaking work on the centrality of manuscript poetry to early American culture.[5] Shields convincingly argues that eighteenth-century poetry is "missing" because the primary verse form of the period—belletristic poetry in manuscript—wanted to be.[6] It was deeply occasional and eschewed the goal of permanence. William Spengemann emphasizes external pressures, such as the profound disconnect between aesthetics and history for the immediate needs of nation building.[7] Most recently, Virginia Jackson accounts for both internal and external forces in her theory of the lyricization of poetry that occurred unevenly over the course of the late eighteenth and early nineteenth centuries and effectively subsumed a whole field of verse genres into lyric poetry. Reading lyrically rather than historically, she argues, eclipses the diverse verse forms that came before.[8]

Foundational work by Katherine Clay Bassard, Rafia Zafar, and Henry Louis Gates paved the way for the important studies of early African American and Native American poetry, especially that on Phillis Wheatley by Joanna Brooks, John C. Shields, Katy Chiles, and many others. This book contributes to the long awaited shift toward the inclusion of early American verse that finally appears to be gaining momentum with important recent and forthcoming work by Colin Wells, Susan Stabile, Christopher Phillips, Patrick Erben, Joanne van der Woude, Meredith Neuman, and others, that analyze the cultural significance of early America's diverse and prolific poetries.[9] The recovery and analysis my book undertakes helps us understand one of the largest upswells in eighteenth-century American verse by attending to what poems meant to the people who formed them out of their devotion to God and how that devotion left its imprint not only on the individual's soul, but also in the formal features of eighteenth-century verse, features which today make it illegible to so many.

We can begin by asking what separates a poem from a hymn. Both were important to evangelical culture, and both engaged in the practices of revival. Yet these literary forms are not the same—and it was evangelicals like Isaac Watts, the renowned poet and hymnist, who defined their difference.[10] Watts dramatically reconfigured English Protestant worship and poetry with the 1707 publication of *Hymns and Spiritual Songs*, a book that rivals all others for infusing popular verse into the poetic discourse of eighteenth-century Protestantism and all subsequent Protestant poetics. Combining metrical psalmody and the devotional lyric, Watts essentially spurred a new communal genre of verse that inspired the production of thousands of hymns by refined and unrefined poets on both sides of the Atlantic. Watts's enduring and ubiquitous effect on popular verse rivals that of any other poet in English history.[11] Yet, he not only spurred hymnody across an expanding experiential mode of Christianity, as he is primarily remembered; he also spearheaded a revitalized enthusiastic poetry that explicitly aligned aesthetic pleasure with the purposes of God. In many ways, this is what he attempted with his hymns as well, but with a key difference: he reserved the religious sublime and its attendant poetic techniques for what he designated lyric poetry. The invention of the Watts hymn, which aimed to utilize language appropriate for the skill level of the "vulgar" or common Christian, entailed a separation from higher forms of poetry fit for the cultured and educated reader.

More than a distinction between sung and unsung verse, the difference between a hymn and a lyric poem hinged on class. A year before Watts published his transatlantic phenomenon *Hymns and Spiritual Songs* (1707), he released a book of poetry entitled *Horae Lyricae* (1706), the first section of which he culled from his hymnal project because they were not "suited to the plainest Capacity."[12] He provides an extended explanation about the difference between his lyric poems and hymns in the preface to *Hymns and Spiritual Songs*. Regarding the creation of hymns, he states:

> The Metaphors are generally sunk to the Level of vulgar Capacities. I have aimed at ease of Numbers and Smoothness of Sound, and endeavour'd to make the Sense plain and obvious; if the Verse appears so gentle and flowing as to incur the Censure of feebleness, I may honestly affirm, that sometimes it cost me labour to make it so: Some of the Beauties of Poesy are neglected, and some willfully defaced: I have thrown out the Lines that were too sonorous, and giv'n an Allay to the Verse, lest a more exalted Turn of Thought or Language should darken or disturb the Devotion of the plainest Souls. But hence it comes to pass, that I have been forc'd to lay aside many Hymns after they were finished, and utterly exclude 'em from this Volume, because of the Bolder Figures of Speech that crowded themselves into the Verse, and a more uncontain'd Variety of Number which I could not easily restrain.[13]

Instead of appearing with *Hymns and Spiritual Songs*, these "spoiled hymns" appeared in *Horae Lyricae*, a book in which he "endeavour'd to please and profit the politer part of mankind."[14] For Watts, the intended audience proved to be a crucial distinction between literary poetries and hymnal verse. Literary history's reticence to incorporate hymns into its canon of esteemed verse dates to their very invention as a derivative poetry for the masses.[15]

Of course, when Watts insisted upon this difference, the very terms for poems and hymns had not become codified as they have for today's readers. Poetry was not yet equated with lyric poetry; instead, it designated a host of poetic forms that included the lyric and the hymn. Even the eighteenth-century hymn is a much more capacious term then scholars have traditionally imagined. It encompassed a wide range of poetries and verse forms both in its classical and Christian varieties. John Knapp rightly criticizes scholars for not adequately treating the non-Congregational hymn outside the context of Christian worship.[16] This book aims to correct a similar problem, but from the opposite direction: the ubiquitous treatment of the hymn as the sole poetic interest of revivalists. Hymnody was, of course, a seminal achievement of evangelical culture, but it was not its only poetic achievement. Alongside revival hymns, evangelicals cultivated a poetics that engaged the belles lettres of their day and sought to remake it into a poetry that expressed the "language of heaven" for the common person. *Awakening Verse* adds to our understanding of the prolific production of religious poetry by addressing verse that has been lost to both histories of literary poetry and religious histories of the hymn.

The story of eighteenth-century revival verse begins not only with Watts but also with the work of John Dennis, who helped meld religion, feeling, and verse. The critical writings of Dennis, one of the century's most important British literary critics, offer the most thorough articulation of the effort to revivify Christian and enthusiastic poetry at the turn of the eighteenth century.[17] For the person unfamiliar with eighteenth-century poetry, the idea that Christian verse needed justification or reinvention seems odd at best. John Milton's *Paradise Lost* (1667) serves as the apotheosis of Protestant poetry. Yet, at the beginning of the eighteenth century the reigning sensibility retracted from the notion of writing verse inspired by biblical themes and Christian experience.[18] Though English poets and critics would soon associate the religious sublime with Milton's epic and praise the poem for it, the concept first had to be justified.[19] Much of the aversion to an infusion of religion into poetry was its associations with the religious enthusiasm of the seventeenth century, which fueled the English Civil Wars and Protestant sectarianism. Dennis was instrumental in remaking enthusiasm into a poetic virtue. His two major works, *The Advancement and Reformation of Modern Poetry* (1701) and *The Grounds of Criticism in Poetry* (1704), sought to reunite Christianity and poetry. Through his creative explication of Longinus's *Peri Hupsous*, translated into English by Boileau in 1674, Dennis recommended sacred poetry because verse was foremost an art of raising passions, thus introducing the first cogent theory of the religious sublime in English.[20]

Revivalists made good on this idea. They were essential to a hard-won struggle in the eighteenth century to secure a firm, seemingly intractable relationship between feeling and verse, which still governs poetic experience today. Indeed, scholars of eighteenth-century British enthusiasm have detailed how feeling and poetry slowly coalesced by reimagining religious enthusiasm, despised and ridiculed by the literary elite, as poetic enthusiasm. Jon Mee importantly underscores that not all enthusiasm, but only enthusiasm in the poetic sphere, became more acceptable over the course of the eighteenth century.[21] Yet this story usually highlights how the reinvention of enthusiasm as a poetic enthusiasm emptied its traditional religious content and provides no sustained account of the reinvigorated revival poetics evident in the culture at large. The options, it seems, are to elaborate a prehistory of Romanticism already invested in the disemboweling of certain types of religious poetic practice or to ignore those practices altogether.[22]

Many literary histories, in other words, have hidden a powerful tradition from view: the profound and continuing belief in poetry's redemptive power, which was *especially* true for revivalists.[23] This book demonstrates that a broad strand of early American poetry was not only connected to literary enthusiasm, but its practice, consumption, and guiding aesthetics were intimately tied to the extraordinary revivalist impulse that pervaded American culture from the "Great Awakening" of the early eighteenth century to the "Second Great Awakening" at the turn of the nineteenth. Poetry performed important religious work, from spreading revival and converting souls, to educating, consoling, and uniting believers, and provided a larger cultural framework for popular expectations about poetry's work in the world. By 1766, John Wesley's *A Plain Account of Christian Perfection* reiterated what converts knew: poetry was the language of the saint and of heaven.[24] While Dennis and others tried to empty enthusiasm of its radical religious and political associations by remaking it into a literary aesthetic, a myriad of poet-ministers refused this project and instead sought to save poetry and "real" religion from its debased state by infusing it with radical religious passion. Theirs was a successful and lasting enterprise.

It is their story that animates this book. But first, let me pause to define who I am talking about when I say "evangelical" and what the phrase "revival poetry" means. The term "evangelical" is notoriously difficult to define and has many potentially conflicting meanings. Linford Fisher provides the most recent and insightful treatment of the term's historical and scholarly meanings, which centers not on a set of doctrinal definitions, but on the way being evangelical denoted one's way of doing Christianity as more authentic than others.[25] Because evangelicalism was a movement that employed similar practices that confirmed one's authentic Christianity, it involved multiple denominations and diverse Protestant beliefs, including Calvinist, Arminianist, and Universalist doctrines.[26] I use the term, then, to designate the transatlantic revivals during the eighteenth and nineteenth centuries revolving around a certain style of preaching that prompted dramatic conversions to authentic Christianity—and, as this book suggests, a type of preaching and conversion tied to a new poetics. I will often employ labels used by revivalists, such as "experimental," "heart religion," "revivalism," or even "Whitefieldian," as suggested by the deep archival work of Doug Winiarski.[27]

Because any Christian poem expressing the good news of the gospel could be considered evangelical in the broader meaning of the term, I prefer the phrase "revival poetry" to avoid confusion and to designate poetry produced by (or taken up by) participants in the eighteenth- and nineteenth-century revivals. When I use the phrase evangelical poetry, it is as a synonym for revival poetry. Rather than a particular poetic form, such as the elegy, pastoral, or epic, or a particular poetic strain, such as the religious sublime, neoclassical, or romantic, "revival poetry" designates the wide range of verse that was written or recommended by those who participated in the revival culture arising in the eighteenth century. While I will primarily be addressing generic forms of evangelical verse other than hymns and spiritual songs, the term itself should not be taken to exclude hymns. Rather, I seek to rearrange our sense of what constitutes the poetic culture of revivalism. Hymnody has a rich and extensive history that sometimes follows, intersects, or deviates from other revival poetries. My term acknowledges this rich tradition of hymn-poetry, but follows a different trajectory.

By using the terms "poetry" and "verse" interchangeably, my intent is to mitigate reinstating "poetry" as a monolithic term that collapses various verse genres under the specific idea of the lyric. Because this book does not attempt to be exhaustive, but rather offers a window into the prolific verse world of revivalists, primarily the Calvinist strain most popular in English in British North America, it is, I hope, an invitation for other scholars to further detail these forms, their functions, and their influences.[28]

Awakening Verse argues that from the beginning, evangelicalism was deeply tied to poetry and aesthetics, which were foundational to its belief systems and practices. Foremost, revival poetry was securely anchored to aesthetic pleasure as it aligned with the purposes of God in history and, specifically, as aesthetic pleasure served as one foundation for both soteriology and anthropology. If a particular emphasis on an identifiable, affective conversion was a primary characteristic of most early evangelicalism, as has been argued, and, furthermore, marks a sea change in how religion came to be conceived in the eighteenth and nineteenth centuries—that of being primarily about feeling—then poetry is the unacknowledged mechanism by which evangelicals felt themselves to be more piously religious than others; that is, born again, awakened, or evangelical.[29] Taking up the specificities of poetic form and language, this book traces how this revivalism of the eighteenth century endowed poetry with religious power ready for minister and lay-person alike to take up in the nineteenth century.

Each chapter focuses on different revivalist poetic forms and practices to show how evangelicals engaged the verse forms of their day and transformed them into a distinct poetics—a revivalist poetics—with its own peculiar set of practices, expectations, and influences. In addition to theology, revivalist poetics was closely tied to the sermon and the new practice of itinerancy, and it valued language for the common Christian. The different chapters reveal not only how revivalists' common poetics and theology informed each other, but also how their poetics enfolded and butted against eighteenth-century ideals of taste and social standing. The chapters detail how poetic expec-tations and forms, including the rhymed couplet, harmony, personae, and poetic address or practices of wit, exchange, revision, public leadership, and coteries, were negotiated with the larger poetic culture and transformed in different settings. This is particularly true when the fusion of heavenly lan-guage and poetry enabled different forms of revival poetics in relation to var-ious constellations of gender, race, and class.

From the beginnings of the eighteenth-century transatlantic revivals, po-etry was expected to shape profoundly the quality of one's lived theology and to acclimate one to the eschatological hope of heaven and its attendant lan-guage of song and verse. Part of the expansion of non-hymnal revival poetry included the creation of what I call the poet-minister, a role borrowing its au-thority from both the pulpit and the elevated role of poetry as the true heav-enly language. Though dissenting pietist groups from which evangelicalism emerged practiced devotional verse, the upsurge of transatlantic revivalists beginning around the 1730s initiated a revitalized practice that accompanied the turn toward the affective sermon and the introduction of the religious sublime into British literary history.[30]

Uniquely equipped to allow for effecting God's grace and to circulate widely, sacred poetry could set ablaze revival. Turning the seventeenth-century poet George Herbert's line into a revival maxim, "A verse may find him who a sermon flies," revivalists viewed poetry as an extension of the evangelical sermon and of the itinerant's movement. While histories of evan-gelicalism typically focus on the charismatic ministry of such new itinerant preachers as the Rev. George Whitefield, the hymns penned by Watts, Wesley, Doddridge, and others enveloped revival language and thought and circu-lated to a degree simply unmatched by any traditional itinerant preacher's reach.[31] The revival poet magnified and expanded the meaning and impact of itinerancy, even being imagined as a print itinerant. The association of the itinerant minister with popular poetry was so strong that Edmund Burke toggled between them to make his own point regarding the superior efficaciousness of poetry as an art form for provoking the affections.[32] It is not as if ministers were not poets before eighteenth-century revivalists took center stage. Rather, my use of the terms "poet-minister" and "print itinerant" point to particular historical formations that occurred within early evangelicalism as the sermon, the itinerant minister, print, and verse forms were in flux.

We can see this constellation clearly when we fill in the starkest absence in the history of early American evangelical verse: the first American publication of the Scottish minister Ralph Erskine's *Gospel Sonnets* in 1740. His book was a transatlantic bestseller, ubiquitous throughout the eighteenth century, and yet Chapter 1 of this study provides the first literary treatment of the text. While scholars have examined various print, manuscript, and oral genres that early revivalists produced, we have no sense of how pervasive evangelical poetry was and the functions it performed. By looking closely at Ralph Erskine's seminal poem, Chapter 1 argues that we can see how poetry and homiletics enabled each other and, as they did so, fused together the minister and the poet, the itinerant and the poem, soteriology and the form of the verse.

The poem *Gospel Sonnets*, praised unanimously by revival leaders, explicitly worked out the relationship between affective religion, aesthetics, and poetic language and form. Erskine's poem affirms affective religion's commitment to holy metaphors, most importantly the language of the believer's espousal to Christ. In the poem, all of Calvinist theology is sifted through the affective experience of the believer as a divorced wife and Christ as the new spouse. The successful living out of this relationship in the Christian life, the poem argues, depends upon effectively balancing multiple paradoxes inherent to Calvinist belief.

When we understand Erskine as a poet-minister and *Gospel Sonnets* as a print itinerant, it becomes clear that revivalist soteriology became fused with rhyme, and the rhymed couplet became a particular instantiation of divine metaphor. That is, the couplet came to express in its very form the reality of heavenly espousal and the affective balances required of Calvinist belief. To this end, I argue that the poem creates "sound believers": Christians who learn to manage the theological tensions of Calvinism through a poetics of espousal that weds rhyme and metaphor to salvation. Given that this is the case, the evangelical emphasis on the divine metaphor of espousal functioned even more broadly in revival culture than has been previously recognized through its very embeddedness within evangelical prosody. To state it simply: what is considered the preeminent verse form of the eighteenth-century, the couplet, had the special meaning of betrothal exercised in one of the largest religious movements of the period. Theirs was not the Popian couplet. Instead, the Calvinist couplet expressed and encapsulated the holy language of espousal to produce a lived and affective experience of theology. The poem both theorized sound believers and created them.

This metaphor of espousal placed the figure of the woman at the center of revivalist poetics and its affective, lived theology. Yet, it did not end with the figurative imaginings of male ministers as the only visible and honored place for the evangelical woman. Revivalist women crafted poetry, too. Chapter 2 argues that women were instrumental in the development of revivalism and its verse. In fact, a primary reason why attending to early evangelical poetry is essential to understanding its history and culture is that it demonstrably shakes up the basic building blocks of most evangelical historiographies, which have relied excessively on male leadership and prose to explain the rise of white evangelicalism in British North America. It does this because the essential role of the poet-minister in this transatlantic and pan-continental pietistic movement was exercised by a growing number of evangelical women who might well be the best window into this early American religious landscape. At the very least, their poetry tells us that women exercised more public religious authority in revivalism than has been considered because of the poet-minister and print itinerant function in evangelical poetics.

Chapter 2 highlights two prolific English female poets—Elizabeth Singer Rowe and Anne Dutton—who engaged affective religion from different poetic sensibilities, social positions, and denominations. Nevertheless, this chapter argues that they both developed public (in print and in manuscript) poetic personae for the woman poet-minister. The Congregationalist Rowe, whom Watts famously named as his poetic muse, inhabited and made prolific the persona of the idealized poetess who became a particular type of evangelical muse for revivalist audiences. The Baptist theologian Anne Dutton, in contrast, crafted a public spiritual director persona that meshed seamlessly with and into the poet-minister role. Their poet-minster personae, though very different formally, were nevertheless specifically female and were imbued with public religious authority and leadership.

Their poetic ministries were highly influential in early British North American revivalism. Chapter 2 emphasizes this transatlantic legacy by examining both known and newly recovered poems by the Boston revival poet Sarah Moorhead, whose husband, the Presbyterian minister John Moorhead, is well known to evangelical historians. I argue that Moorhead drew on both the idealized poetess and spiritual director personae in order to engage male clergy in the most heated revival controversies of her day and to shape their outcomes. She became an authorizer of revival itinerants and their ministries—in fact, she became the authorizing poetess of Erskine's *Gospel Sonnets*. Women, both lay and preacher, were thus vital to early evangelicalism. Turning to revival poetry amplifies this claim because it shows how women preached sermons and advised central male figures even when they were not in a formal pulpit. If the sermon and the poet, the itinerant and the poem, and soteriology and verse were wed in evangelical culture—as Erskine's revival poem makes abundantly clear—then women influenced and shaped eighteenth-century revivalism far beyond what has been thought. If poems were sermons, or even better than sermons, then these women poets were evangelical preachers, the best and most effective sort. It is no coincidence that Joseph Bates, with whom I began this introductory chapter, was saved by a woman poet. Additionally, and perhaps most importantly to the literary scholar, eighteenth-century revival poetry lays the groundwork for a nineteenth-century American poetic and religious culture attuned to the voice of the poetess.

To be clear: it was not only women who admired Rowe. When the first "new light" itinerant minister went south to Virginia, the Rev. Samuel Davies drew inspiration from her espousal piety. For Davies she served as an evangelical muse and the authorizer of the religious sublime and espousal piety he employed. Chapter 3 shows how Davies's poetry brought together the religious sublime and its lofty language and images, which Watts had reserved for highbrow lyric poetry, with the intent to please the "plainest capacity" Watts had designated as proper to the hymn. Davies based the importance of his type of poetic ministry on evangelical harmony—a foundational concept to evangelical verse that located the image of God in humanity in the universal and innate enjoyment of poetry. This, as it turned out, did not sit well with the Virginia gentry.

This chapter begins by unpacking Davies's revival poetics and then turns to a major controversy over his poetry collection that broke out in the *Virginia Gazette* between 1752 and 1754. I argue that scholars have missed *the* crucial feature of this public debate in Virginian revivalism: its socially and politically contentious relationship to elite poetics. Elite poetry fenced class, gender, and race in a manner that revival poetry challenged. Davies's poetics influenced his slave literacy campaign, the most successful of its time, and informed his preaching to a record number of enslaved people. The *Virginia Gazette* episode underscores the ways that revival verse was barred from sociable poetry and its elite forms because of its association with the lower classes, effeminacy, and blackness. While Davies aestheticized and theologized the singing of slaves to serve as evidence of an evangelical anthropology grounded in the concept of harmony, the gentry rejected his poetry as black noise.

Evangelical harmony set the stage for a broad engagement with revival verse across class, gender, and race. The most famous person to take it up was the black woman and slave Phillis Wheatley. Wheatley, of course, wrote a poem praising the talented Boston artist and fellow slave, Scipio Moorhead, whose mistress was the poet-minister Sarah Moorhead. Perhaps because male ministers needed to sign an attestation to the authenticity of Wheatley's poems before the publication of her book and because one of these ministers, Mather Byles, was an active Boston poet with a book in print, he has seemed to be Wheatley's most influential local poetic influence and mentor. Indeed, his brand of Christian belletrism, rich with neoclassical influences and the religious sublime, did inform an important strand of Wheatley's poetics. Yet, she was a complex poet with multiple influences. In the home in which she was enslaved, she was enmeshed in revival activity, news, and culture. And she made the rounds, both in person and in manuscript, among the local women's poetic coteries. Given that Moorhead taught her own slave to paint, it is highly likely she also influenced Wheatley's work, which, I argue in Chapter 4, is confirmed by the textual evidence in the poems themselves.

But my argument is not only that Moorhead and the larger practices of women poet-minister's influenced Wheatley's work; it is also that a history of revival poetry in early America is necessary to fully understand the meaning of Wheatley's diverse poetic choices. Wheatley has for decades sat uncomfortably between evangelical culture and a commitment to a neoclassical style and a nascent romantic aesthetic. Often scholars have felt they needed to make a choice and to make clear on what side of poetic culture Wheatley resided. I do not make a choice, but show instead how a more capacious understanding of evangelical poetic culture—especially espousal poetics, poet-minister personae, and harmony—reveals Wheatley's subtle negotiations between pro- and anti-revivalists and their respective notions of aesthetic taste, soteriology, and anthropology. Put simply, when Wheatley broached the art of poetry, she managed and critiqued a range of racialized aesthetics as she moved between revivalist verse and the more dignified style of Christian belletrism. In this sense, Wheatley is the culmination of the poetics I trace in the first three chapters, as well as one of its most effective critics.

As the various controversies over revival poetry suggest, there was a strong and lasting desire to exclude revivalists from the literary and to resign them to the bathos. Yet, revivalists were highly invested in much of what defined the broader poetic culture of the eighteenth century; indeed, they were a large part of it. The seriousness of evangelicalism and of the stakes of conversion can give a dour and humorless picture of revivalists that seems in complete contrast to the eighteenth-century poet of sensibility with his refined taste and superb wit. My final chapter argues that when the centrality of poetics to revivalism comes into view, it changes the way that we describe evangelicalism in relation to the larger culture, which was saturated in poetry. From the beginning, evangelicals worked in the idiom of the day to spread their message, entering into new forms of distribution and circulation (for example, use of print, tracts, and itinerant networks). Though evangelical wit and revivalist poetic coteries sound oxymoronic within traditional American literary histories, wit and poetic networks were central to evangelical conversion, itinerancy, and verse culture. In fact, extemporaneous sermons *were* an exercise of the highly valued eighteenth-century wit, and itinerant circuits *were* large-scale poetic coteries.

My final chapter focuses on one extraordinary example, the Virginian itinerant minister James Ireland's conversion narrative, to show how this centrality of poetics and sociability in the conversion culture of the second half of the eighteenth century and early nineteenth could work in the opposite direction of Erskine's, Moorhead's, Davies's, and Wheatley's deployments. Ireland lived through the early development of revival poetry. His family were long-time friends of the Erskines, who themselves were also well acquainted with the Moorheads' ministries; traveling through many of Davies's harvested fields in Virginia, he witnessed the celebrity of Wheatley. Yet, he paints a picture that deviates from theirs in a crucial way. His poetics emphasizes an explicit and robust white masculinity in response to the feminized nature of evangelical conversion. Rather than a love affair culminating in an espousal, his controlling metaphors revolve around battles of wit. His conversion narrative, which should be read as a revivalist *ars poetica*, reveals how evangelical conversion retained practices of the larger poetic culture, such as wit and imitation, as well as exposes the limits of cultural synthesis, such as embracing a sermonic poetic address and refusing ephemerality. The criteria for transferability were not uninterested. Importantly, the forms of sociability that Ireland retained from Virginian culture were central to constructing white masculinity among male poet-ministers who felt effeminized. Though resistance to the feminine images central to experimental religion and its poetics may have risen by the turn of the nineteenth century and women's ministries severely curtailed by denominations seeking middle-class acceptance, the role of the woman poet-minister—both the idealized poetess and the spiritual guide—was already deeply embedded in the American poetic landscape, as was an abolitionist strain tied to the interventionist power of revival verse. James Ireland was one way of being a poet-minister. There would continue to be many more.

Together these chapters tell a story of an early evangelical culture steeped in poetry. The chapters move loosely chronologically, while gesturing at the dynamic nature of the forms in different contexts. Ralph Erskine's espousal poetics, which deployed the poet-minster role in a poem that took off as a popular print itinerant binding espousal to poetic form and tying feminine piety to theology, became, in the hands of Sarah Moorhead, a gateway to the pulpit. Erskine worked within a biblical, plain style, while Moorhead brought the high belletrism of Rowe together with the plain style of Dutton. Samuel Davies wrote in the tradition of the religious sublime but, through the concept of evangelical harmony, bound it to the plainest capacity. Phillis Wheatley turned back to Rowe's belletrism and neoclassicism with insistence and lopped off the plainest capacity. James Ireland embraced masculine sociability and wit to resist "effeminate" religion, and he rejected belletristic ephemerality and an emerging lyric poetic address for theological reasons. Revival poetry was anything but simple and static. It was as complex as the religious movement it helped create, and we cannot understand that movement without attending to the dynamics of this poetry.

In the eighteenth century, once understood to be the hotbed of a purely rational enlightenment, revivalists met their God and the revivalist God met his people through poetry. *Awakening Verse* does not, then, simply restore some forgotten verse to our collective literary memory in order to mourn or to celebrate a lost enchantment, but deliberately contributes to a modern history of poetry that is equally a story of the gods interacting with people as they went about their daily lives.[33] When revivalists read poetry, they expected that God would act. Oftentimes he did. Through poetry, God would bend the body, contort the soul, and redirect the purposes of everyday people. As these converts and their poetry moved out from that encounter, their God did as well. Their circulation of manuscript and print poetry was at least, but not only, a material event. To understand it in this way is to allow the gods to break open the literary tradition and trade stories with the rest of us.

1

"The Sound in Faith"

The Calvinist Couplet and the Poetics of Espousal

Poetry spurred awakenings. Sarah Pierpont Edwards's sudden recollection of two simple lines from Ralph Erskine's *Gospel Sonnets*—"I see [God] lay his vengeance by, / And smile in Jesus' face"—calmed her agitated mind and precipitated her first ecstatic experience. She writes:

> It appeared to be real and certain that [God] did so. I had not the least doubt, that he then sweetly smiled upon me, with the look of forgiveness and love, having laid aside all his displeasure towards me, for Jesus' sake; which made me feel very weak, and somewhat faint.[1]

Sarah Edwards soon became a model for future converts on both sides of the Atlantic—in large part because she was the wife of Jonathan Edwards, a minister and theologian famous for presiding over the Northampton revivals, who promoted her awakening. That she responded to Christ as a wife—the very manner the poem suggested—demonstrates poetic metaphors were tangible and authoritative in the believer's life.

According to Jonathan Edwards, such a response to Erskine's poem was not out of the ordinary. He reported to the Scottish minister James Robe, editor of the revival magazine *The Christian Monthly History* and a central leader of the Kilsyth revival, that *Gospel Sonnets* was held "in great repute among God's people here."[2] The poem that had affected Sarah and others in her community so profoundly was part of a transatlantic movement of Protestant Pietism which held poetics to be a sacred and powerful tool of revival.

Religious poetry was, of course, not new to New England or its communal worship. Eighteenth-century British North Americans were well versed, so to speak, in poetry, be it from books, newspapers, broadsides, or oral performances. Though hymnody was not originally part of Puritan communal practice, the singing of the metrical psalms had already become

Awakening Verse. Wendy Raphael Roberts, Oxford University Press (2020). © Oxford University Press.
DOI: 10.1093/oso/9780197510278.001.0001

a mainstay of Northampton worship before the revivals introduced hymns into church services. Sarah Edwards's account records some of the most revered versifiers—Isaac Watts, Elizabeth Singer Rowe, and John Mason—as "the real language of [her] heart."[3] The iconic Northampton revivals, which became central to the imagination of Christians on both sides of the Atlantic long after they had waned, were enmeshed in the evangelically focused shift in hymn and poetic culture.

Verse was a powerful actor in this movement. A large part of the success of these communities depended upon shared rubrics of hearing attuned not only to homiletics and hymn, but also to other poetries and verse forms, including the most pervasive of the century, the heroic couplet. The early eighteenth century's emphasis on the religious sublime and poetic passions situated the Bible as the source of the most powerful poetic language. As such, evangelicals, who daily meditated on scripture, hymns, and sermons and shared stories of their converting effects, were immersed in poetic language. The affective sermon, a hallmark of eighteenth-century evangelicalism, gained much of its traction through its overlap with poetic language, which also aimed at moving the affections.[4] This in turn validated the heightened role of the poet-minister in revival culture.

The poetry of the Reverend Ralph Erskine, a major figure in the Presbyterian Church in Scotland, was vital to the longevity of this shift. He engaged contemporary debates regarding poetic form to extend a long established tradition of Dissenter poetry into the revivals that helped channel what evangelicals considered to be a radically new work of God.[5] His contribution is particularly important for the study of revival poetics because it explicitly attempts to work out the relationship between affective religion, aesthetics, and poetic language and form. The powerful affective preaching of the early revivalists, long a staple of evangelical historiography, shook up British North American congregations; Erskine's poem shows how verse was bound up in the entire enterprise as poetry and homiletics enabled each other. The minister fused with the poet, the itinerant with the poem, and soteriology with verse form.

Erskine's influential poem crystallizes two elements that appear across various types of eighteenth-century revival poetries: salvific status as the premise of aesthetic judgment, and aesthetics as both an effective means of conversion and a bulwark against heresies. The first radically challenged the grounds of most British literary criticism that, in the eighteenth century, prioritized cultivated taste. The second participates in a tradition of public intervention upheld in Augustan verse. With these two principles, *Gospel Sonnets* attempted to mold a dispersed community of believers into espoused Calvinists capable of balancing the tensions of doctrine (the law and grace, works and faith, justification and sanctification) through poetic imagery and versification—what might be called "sound believers."[6] To this end, Erskine employed a Calvinist couplet that expressed in its very poetic form the believer's espousal to Christ and the affective balances required of Calvinist belief. Prosody embedded theology. One of the largest religious movements of the century utilized the couplet and imbued it with a meaning specific to affective conversion, not Augustan values or Popian intellect.

Erskine's espousal poetics was a call to examine one's heart and aesthetics. When converts awakened to a new experience of their relationship to Christ, they underwent a simultaneous aesthetic and theological shift—or, more accurately, an experience in which these were practically indistinguishable. In this environment, poetry not only served to explain theology in a pleasing manner or communicate spiritual experiences; its very form communicated meaning and acclimated the convert to the rhythms of living in an experiential knowledge of Christ. Reading or hearing the content of the verse was part of poetry's effectiveness; the repeated experience of the form and its associated meanings another. As this chapter will argue, Erskine's poem helped infuse espousal piety not only into the language of revivalism, but into the experiential meaning of the couplet itself—a form that helped wed together the tensions of Calvinism not through theological argument but through sound.

Rubrics for Sound: High and Low

On February 12, 1740, Bostonians picked up *The New England Weekly Journal* to find half of the front page covered with an excerpt from the Scottish minister Ralph Erskine's *Gospel Sonnets*. Already a sensation among revivalists in both Scotland and England, the book was in its fifth edition, and Benjamin Franklin would soon debut the first American reprint (Figure 1.1).[7] With recent revivals in New England and abroad gaining public attention and with the legendary Methodist itinerant George Whitefield already on American soil for his second visit and first colonial tour, Erskine's poem was front-page news.[8] Timed to correspond with Whitefield's visit, the American publication of *Gospel Sonnets* attests to what Franklin knew but most modern

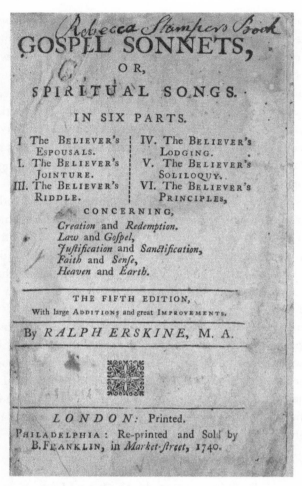

Figure 1.1. Benjamin Franklin's first American reprint of Ralph Erskine's *Gospel Sonnets* (1740).
The Library Company of Philadelphia.

scholars of American religion and literature have forgotten: poetry accompanied revival.[9]

That Franklin reprinted *Gospel Sonnets* during Whitefield's first colonial preaching tour attests to the poem's popularity with an audience already gripped by a revival whose unprecedented media coverage accompanied Whitefield's every movement.[10] Whitefield's journal drummed up potential readers, while a four-page broadside circulated part of Erskine's poem the same year. The American reprint also points to the book's involvement in the ongoing flow of revival texts that created a sense of revival community across towns, colonies, and continents. In fact, the publication history of *Gospel Sonnets*, which includes at least 26 editions in Scotland and England, correlates with spikes in religious fervor. In British North America specifically, Boston and Philadelphia reprintings in 1742, 1743, 1745, and 1749 marked the book as a bestseller among colonial revivalists.[11] This is all the more remarkable given that the book surpassed (by a substantial margin) the number of sheets most colonial printers would produce at their own financial risk. Franklin's decision to print *Gospel Sonnets* meant that its popularity far exceeded that which could be met by cheaper imports.[12]

Even after the concentrated awakenings of the 1740s, *Gospel Sonnets* continued to thrive with an additional American reprint in 1760, the first original American edition published in Philadelphia in 1793, soon followed by the second American edition by Isaiah Thomas in 1798, and reprints in Troy, New York, in 1806 and Pittsburgh in 1831. Thomas's publication prefaces the book with this assessment of its popularity: "If the number of EDITIONS of any performance, be a mark of public approbation, Mr. ERSKINE'S GOSPEL SONNETS have a claim to that distinction, and they may be ranked amongst those of general esteem and usefulness; few books have been so often printed in the same space of time."[13] Book advertisements in both the northern and the southern colonies appeared regularly throughout the century and into the nineteenth, and it became a standard in book collections and commonplace books. The poem's importance in revivalist culture appears to have been common knowledge. The longevity of *Gospel Sonnets* suggests that printed poetry, like local ministers, cultivated revival piety long after great itinerants left town.

Though the poem can appear stale and unreadable to a modern critic, it powerfully intervened in the lives of thousands of early evangelicals as well as the world at large. The best-known revival leaders, including both Whitefield and Edwards, testified to this. While on his way back to England after his first successful tour, Whitefield wrote to Erskine, "Your Sonnets and Sermons have been blessed to me and many. The former are reprinted in America. I want all your own and brother's works. . . . [T]his morning [I] have been solacing myself with your Paraphrase upon Solomon's Song."[14] That same year the London revival journal *The Weekly History* lists *Gospel Sonnets* among the books "much recommended by the Rev. Mr. Whitefield" to his transatlantic revivalist readers, a fact used in America to promote sales alongside the colonial new light leader Rev. Gilbert Tennent's endorsement.[15] Rev. John Moorhead, the ardent revivalist and pastor of the Church of the Presbyterian Strangers in Boston, also attested to both the powerful effect and the wide acceptance of Erskine's poem: "My soul has been often refreshed with the savoury performances of you and your dear brother's. They are much admired here. The Gospel Sonnets have been lately reprinted with great acceptance here."[16] And, as already noted, Edwards proclaimed the book's pious effects in Northampton. According to Edwards and Whitefield, the desire to read the sonnets not only resulted from a changed heart, it also changed hearts.

Part of the attraction of revivalist ministers to Erskine's work was its combination of robust Calvinist theology with a piety-focused evangelism. Contrary to the title's implications, *Gospel Sonnets* is not composed of short poems; it is a hefty six-part book approaching 300 pages, primarily composed of heroic couplets, long meter, and common meter. Interspersed with opportunities for devotional response, the narrative poem details the tumultuous and emotionally drawn-out divorce of the believer from her first love, the law, and her subsequent marriage to her new lover, Christ. This paraphrase of *Song of Songs* meditates on the nuances of Calvinist theology and its implications for the personal relationship between Christ and the believer.

From its inception, Erskine's poem was invested in the relationship between correct theology and prosody. It was published during a tumultuous moment in the Church of Scotland, then in the process of fragmenting into a Succession Church, led by the Erskines. The poem first saw publication in Edinburgh in 1720 under the title *Gospel Canticles*, the same year in which the General Assembly of the Church of Scotland officially condemned *The Marrow of Modern Divinity*, an older Calvinist work by Edward Fisher that had recently been reprinted.[17] In so doing, the Church of Scotland officially identified church doctrine with Neonomianism, or the new law of the gospel, a doctrine that Calvinists ardently believed altered the gospel message of grace into salvation through works.[18] Ralph Erskine and his brother Ebeneezer were two of 12 ministers who objected to the creed adopted by the Church, considering it a dangerous departure from the gospel of grace, and began a lengthy battle that culminated in succession and the formation of the Associate Presbytery. It is not mere coincidence that Erskine would take up the issue of prosody and the role of poetry at the same time he challenged the Church of Scotland—the role and writing of Christian poetry was a pressing question at the beginning of the eighteenth century that had everything to do with politics, religion, and order.

The poem, written and revised amidst this turmoil known as the Marrow controversy, amounted to a public statement and bulwark against new doctrines infiltrating and corrupting the church. *Gospel Sonnets* clearly reflects the theological concerns at stake in the Marrow controversy; it explicates at length the nuances of a covenantal relationship with Christ based on grace as opposed to works, and it does so through the metaphor of espousal used in Richard Baxter's arguments for Neonomianism. The preface to the second edition, published in Edinburgh in 1726, explicitly positions the book against the Arminianism taking root in the Church of Scotland and attributes this error to the introduction of alternative theological language in the catechism. In contrast, Erskine assures his readers that apart from "*Poetical Licence*" he has "endeavored, in [his] Manner of Expression, to keep close by the Form of sound Words" taken from the Scriptures, the Church's traditional standards, and the most renowned orthodox ministers.[19] By implication, his poem instructs the faithful better than the Church's own catechism.

That Erskine challenged the Church of Scotland in meter integrates his critique of Neonomianism with the form of his writing. Erskine's explanation for preferring traditional words versus contemporary phrases hinges in part on their aural reception:

> I am not fond of Novelties, *New Schemes* of Doctrine, nor new Ways of speaking, which I find some late Writers have run into. . . . In Opposition to which, I prefer the Truths, and Ways of expressing the same, which are laid down in our excellent Confession of Faih [*sic*] and Catechisms, plainly founded on the Scriptures of Truth, and which we in this Church are strictly and solemnly bound to maintain. The Language whereof, on these Points, seems to have another Sort of a Sound. . . . These are a Part of our Form of sound Words, worthy to be considered and compared with the former different Sound above mentioned, in order to try if they can make a Consort. But it is not my Work to inlarge [*sic*] on these Things at present; only, 'tis upon these, and the Like Positions in our Standards, that the Foundation of the most of the following Sonnets is laid, not upon any *new* Notions.[20]

Erskine alternates between using "sound" as an adjective, describing the rightness of orthodox beliefs, and as a noun, designating not only the significance but also the auditory effect of the words. This second meaning becomes more apparent as Erskine goes on to argue that even though the words and phrases may not differ in meaning, the newer articulations can still easily mislead the listener into error.[21] The passage implies that hearers can register an affective difference between the words. For instance, the first of many phrases Erskine juxtaposes in the passage (elided in the preceding for brevity) are "*That the Sins of Believers, tho' in a justified State, bring on them a Liableness to the threatned and deserved Punishment, from the penal Sanction of the Law*" compared to "*these, that are justified, can never fall from the State of Justification; yet they may by their Sins fall under God's* fatherly Displeasure."[22] Erskine's explanation of the difference between the two theological statements does not hinge on the denotative meaning, as he says they "express . . . the same [thing]," but rather the connotative, which "have another Sort of a Sound"—a contrast that makes stark the primacy he attributes to the power of auditory impressions and their collective associations, especially as they relate to salvation in contractual versus covenantal terms.

The poem itself continually underscores the association of the covenant of grace and desirable sounds. The most explicit example comes through an authorial change from the 1726 edition that appears in the 1740 text. Originally reading "The Gospel Grace no change of Terms allows," the line becomes by the 1740 version "The joyful Sound no Change of Terms allows."[23] Playing on two meanings—changes in the aural articulation and changes inherent in contractual language—the poem as a whole equates "Gospel Grace" with "The Joyful Sound" by always associating the aural pleasures of heaven (exemplified by the community of saints and the heavenly choir) with covenantal grace as opposed to contractual works. For Erskine, poetry can register the crucial difference that sound and words make in orthodox Calvinist theology and the reception of grace. Poetry and theology thus make for harmonious bedfellows.

Erskine's specific stakes in the Church of Scotland were not, however, what sustained the poem's transatlantic popularity. For the poem's subsequent publications in London and British North America, Erskine revised the preface to be less specific to the Marrow controversy and more relevant to a transatlantic community invested to various degrees in a revivified experimental religion of the passions in which salvation and sound had become heightened issues.[24] Sound played an indispensable role in drawing people to or repelling people from revival activity. From outdoor preaching to hymn singing, from women and slave exhorters to wailing converts, evangelical itinerant preachers stirred up a host of controversies that opponents often framed in terms of sound.[25] One of many ministers to speak against

Whitefield, the South Carolinian Reverend Alexander Garden, warned in 1740 that the primary reason people were introduced to enthusiasm was "*the Itching of the Ears*" for which "Men run *to and fro*." The people run after a preacher, he continues, as they would to "*a very lovely Song of one that hath a pleasant Voice* . . . accounting when their *Ears* and Fancies are most *pleased*, their *Minds* are best *instructed*." Garden's comparison of the revival sermon with a beautiful song points to the way that the pleasures of versified sound had converged with homiletics for revival participants and produced hearers who prized affective aesthetics. But rather than celebrating their spiritual awakening, Garden stresses how revivalists incorrectly substitute the pleasures of sound for meaningful content. He likens such people to the Hebrews that "came only for *Sound*, and *Sound* they had, and *Sound* they carried with them, and no more."[26] Rather than the fullness of the grace of God, this sound rings empty.

In this way, how someone heard the gospel could be a matter of life and death. Whitefield himself warned crowds against flocking to hear him for the sake of spectacle alone. In "Directions How to Hear Sermons," Whitefield preached that "a notorious Sinner . . . forcibly worked upon by a publick Sermon, and plucked as a Fire-brand out of the Fire" was "not God's ordinary Way of acting." Instead, most of the time God gives "the Power of his Word" to those "who humbly wait to know what he would have them to do." Those who would come to hear sermons for entertainment Whitefield calls "unqualified Hearers" who will find themselves sent "not only empty, but hardened, away." He solemnly warns them, "Take heed, therefore, ye careless, curious Professors, if any such are here present, how you hear."[27] That at least half of the population of the colonies had heard him preach by the end of his first of seven tours to the colonies could indeed be dangerous.[28] For Whitefield, the tragedy would be that hearers would be worse off than before they listened. How they heard would have radical implications for their salvation.

At its core, the basic exhortation to examine one's hearing—the motivations of one's heart—was also a call to examine one's aesthetics before God. Though Erskine's poem can rightly be called conservative in that its polemic was to preserve Calvinist theology against modern heresies, it was also at the forefront of a push to value poetry for the common person and to critique elite aesthetic taste. By the 1740 American reprinting of *Gospel Sonnets*, Erskine had refined his preface so as to succinctly introduce a Christian poetics that accounted for the tastes and capacities of the general public whom revivalists sought to awaken. Like Watts, Erskine acknowledged a place for high literature and its accoutrements in polite society, but demanded that Christians refine their aesthetic principles according to those of the gospel. Erskine's 1740 preface declares, "*I do not intend, by any Corrections I have made upon this Book, to act the part of the lofty Poet, nor to affect what is call'd the Sublime.*"[29] Admitting that he could never please "the critical Palate of a learned Age" nor " gratify . . . those of a polite Education," he instead "framed" the lines "merely for the Benefit of vulgar Capacities, and of the common sort of People, that make up the Generality of Christian Congregations."[30] Though Erskine revised his poem in an effort to "render [it] still obvious to the Vulgar, and not altogether nauseous to the Learned,"[31] he encouraged "those Readers, who chiefly affect Politeness of Language and lofty Strains" to improve the lines as it would benefit their souls, which would in turn cause them to "dispense" with their pretensions to high literature.[32] Experiencing the soul-changing message of the gospel, then, effectively regenerated one's poetics because it humbled aspirations and initiated one into a community that embraced the common person.

This meant that rhyme should be valued. Erskine spends little time in the 1740 preface discussing prosody and rhyme directly; instead, he refers to the taste level of his readers. Rather than entertain the elite, presumably those who preferred their long poems in blank verse, Erskine explains that the poems in the 1740 printing would be useful for "the Instruction of the Ignorant and Illiterate, to whom the Gospel is much hid; or to the Edification of the Serious and Exercised, to whom the Gospel, even in its most simple Dress, is a joyful Sound."[33] Like the 1726 preface and the line change from the 1726 to the 1740 version discussed earlier, here Erskine equates the gospel with sound. This conjunction hinges on the acceptability of the acoustics emanating from its affect, not its quality. If the reader considers himself a mature Christian, his heart will respond with joy to the gospel dressed in simple rhyme, just as the reader ignorant of both poetry and Christ's message will be pierced to the heart.

Erskine's earlier editions reveal a fuller picture of the specific prosodic theory behind his general statements. In the 1726 edition, Erskine provided a brief defense of religious poetry by appealing to its precedents in scripture, an argument John Dennis and Watts had made at the beginning of the century.[34] Because "the great God, by his holy Spirit, pleased to speak to us (as it were) in Meeter [*sic*]," Erskine hoped that any work that "set forth some of the most necessary, Scriptural and Gospel Truths, shall not be the less regarded, that it is framed into the Mould of common Meeter and homely Ryme [sic]."[35] The three meters of *Gospel Sonnets* all rhymed and, according to Erskine, came to him naturally, which formed his belief that they were "most adapted for gratifying only [those] of the most common Taste."[36]

Though he would not "pretend to lofty Poesy," instead aiming his work "to those of a meaner Capacity, and to the common Sort of People," Erskine explains that he could take satisfaction in the fact that the "*Matter*" of the poem as opposed to its "*Manner*" "is not below the Consideration of the most learned and knowing Persons." While taking comfort in the idea that his theological knowledge would satisfy his cultivated readers, he also urged them to follow his own example and the example of the gospel in being "merciful to the rest of the rude and illiterate World, as to be well pleased and content that some Essays of this Nature are sunk to the Level of vulgar Capacities, considering that to the Poor the Gospel is preached."[37]

These lines become his major argument developed at length in the 1726 edition and succinctly refined by the 1740 printing. He maintained that the very form of his poem—the lowest manner of poetry fused with the highest matter of theology—reproduced the central paradox of the gospel message preached "to the least of these." The 1740 preface encapsulated the longer 1726 second edition preface through an explanation of the title of the book: the matter—*Gospel*—pertains to "Evangelical Mysteries . . . not below the Study of elect Angels in Heaven," while the manner—*Sonnets*—is far below the quality of "true Poesy." Choosing the term "sonnets" aligned the book with the small and humble as opposed to a "lofty Title," which, in the eighteenth century, would have normally graced a poem of such length.[38] In simple terms, *Gospel Sonnets* announced Christian aesthetics as an embodiment of the paradox of Christ's incarnation.

Erskine's continued investment in rhyme as an expression of gospel truth and a tool for evangelism can be seen in his later work as well. At the end of his life, Erskine prepared a preface to his book of songs, *Job's Hymns* (1753), which explicitly addressed literary debates regarding the status of rhyme in English.[39] His "Preface in Defence of Rhyme and Musical Metre" displays his extensive reading in English poetic criticism and succinctly pinpoints the reasons behind his investment in rhyme, which include its aid in memorization, its powerful affect, and its kinship with the divine. Combining both the sentiments of Edward Bysshe in *The Art of English Poetry* and Alexander Pope in *Essay on Man*, Erskine replaces literary fame with religious aims as the primary goal of employing rhyme:

> that the divine truths may be delivered in a strain tending both to please the ear, and by that to strike the heart of the reader, and facilitate the retention or remembrance of the songs, which, in that form . . . are more easily committed to the memory, especially if the truths delivered therein be duly apprehended by the mind, and embraced in the heart.[40]

For Erskine, rhyming engaged both the heart and the mind for the benefit of instilling religious truth in the singer and reader. Drawing again upon Pope, Erskine concluded his defense of rhyme by linking it to the essential musicality of heaven: "And hence it may be said, especially of sacred and spiritual songs, the more musical, the more celestial."[41] Erskine's commitment to the gospel as a "joyful Sound" continued through to his last poetic publication, which specifically tied the use of rhyme to the efficacious spread of the gospel.

While acknowledging that one could delineate classes by their receptivity to certain prosodies and their corresponding markers of elevated or debased tastes, Erskine nonetheless recognized the lower classes by making them privy to discussions of prosody. He also merged aesthetic choices with theology, demanding that cultivated audiences apply gospel principles to their reading of Christian poetry and acknowledge the needs of common believers over their own exclusive communities of taste. The audience that Erskine worked to form, then, would be highly invested in communal reading practices and delight in an aesthetics accessible (at least in theory) to everyone.

This is what *The New England Weekly Journal* highlighted when they featured an excerpt from Franklin's reprinting of *Gospel Sonnets*. One stanza in particular dramatizes the importance of sound in Christian community for its ability to alleviate the stratifying function of taste. The poet poses the question: who among the heavenly choir (the saints) owes the highest praise to grace? Erskine describes an array of people from infants to the elderly all vying for the highest position until "[t]he list'ning Millions round about" object to the hierarchy with a loud "shout":

> We can't allow of such a Sound,
> That you alone have highest Ground
> To sing the Royalties of Grace,
> We claim the same adoring Place.[42]

The "list'ning Millions" explain in unison that since "no Rival Singer" will "yield" to any other the "highest" place, all should come together and "agree / To praise upon the highest Key."[43] Erskine's theology of grace and aesthetics hinges on the crowds who redefine taste as a heavenly project where low and high combine into one elevated note.

The concept of the "heavenly choir" required that both writer and reader imagine they were part of a larger community that could mutually encourage and sharpen each other as they matured in the gospel life; in this case, one's poetic enjoyment could not be isolated from, but needed to be defined in relation to, the capacities and pleasures of other potential readers. The communal experiences of worship in church and in the home, hearing and reading the word, singing and reciting verse, speaking and silently praying, carried over into the relationship between writer and reader. The Christian's final hope of joining the choir in heaven underscores how expectations surrounding sound, here specifically the joyful sound of the gospel, crossed genres and religious practices, to mold believers into communities engaged in lively, or heartfelt, religion.

The Poet-Minister and the Poetics of Espousal

Defending his sermonic verse, Erskine emphatically proclaimed, "If this don't please, yet hence it is no Crime / To versify the Word, and preach in Rhime." Additionally, he advised, "Slight not the Call, as running by in Rhime" especially "Since the prime Fountains of the sacred Writ, / Much heav'nly Truth in holy Rhimes transmit."[44] Elsewhere, Erskine viewed his preaching rhyme as an evangelist and hoped for the efficaciousness of a great itinerant. As he wrote to Whitefield:

> It refreshes me to hear that any of my poor writings in verse or prose have been and are blessed, in this or any other part of the earth. If I travel by pen as far as you do in person, and contribute my mite for spreading the gospel light, I rejoice in it, and bless his name for it, who has ordered this beyond my view and expectation.[45]

While making revisions to the book for editor John Oswald, Erskine imagined that the poem might even go beyond the reach of a traveling evangelist by spreading the gospel after his own death. "This evening, after family worship," he wrote, "I was strengthened mightily in secret prayer.—I was made to look to the Lord, that the Sonnets might be made useful even when I was in the dust, and was led to seek I might be made to glorify the Lord Jesus."[46] He described his desire for the wide circulation of his book in terms of a print itinerant minister.

At the same time that Erskine's poem made its rounds as a print itinerant, Jonathan Edwards preached his most effective itinerant sermon, "Sinners in the Hands of an Angry God," which abounded in poetic imagery. For Edwards, and other ministers of revival, rhetorical devices common to the Puritan sermon—such as the repetition inherent in a homily devoted to a small phrase, the weight of key words and phrases as they accumulated meanings, and the intertextual nature of systematic exegetical work—could be activated to elicit the congregation's affections. Part of Edwards's revision of Puritan conversion morphology had to do with what Patricia Roberts-Miller has called the paradox of Puritan rhetoric, the "Puritan tendency to see language as simultaneously dangerously powerful and utterly ineffectual."[47] As such, it participated not only in the eighteenth century's renewed focus on affective homiletics, but also in a renewal of Christian poetics.

Charles Chauncy, the figure commonly juxtaposed to Edwards as a result of his adamant and systematized attack on the revivals in *Seasonable Thoughts on the State of Religion in New England* (1743), was particularly concerned with the threat to order that was posed by the rampant emotion of revivalism. The intent to flatten or to activate the affections can be discerned in Chauncy's and Edwards's differing treatments of metaphor in their sermons—their engagement with, or refusal of, poetic language. Chauncy's sermon "Man's Life Considered under the Similitude of a Vapour" (1731) takes up the issue of imminent death after the passing of an honorable congregant. Rather than employ his own metaphors as he speaks of the frailty of man's life, he explains the metaphor in his chosen scripture: James 4:14: "For what is your Life? It is even a Vapour, that appeareth for a little time, and then vanisheth away."[48] Chauncy spends the entire sermon interpreting the several nuances of James's metaphor and repeating at each new point an aspect of what "the *Metaphor* in the *Text* represents to us."[49] Introducing no innovative language, the sermon meticulously explains the vaporous quality of life, and calmly reasons with the congregation that the rational response to such a state is to live a thoughtful life. In the single instance in the sermon in which Chauncy ventures upon his own metaphor, he compares the vapor to an "*inconstant variable* Meteor" that "*while* it extends it self far & wide, *anon* it dwindles away into Nothing."[50] The effect of his chosen metaphor moves

James's figure of vapor as far from his listeners as possible—from the earth into the cosmos.

The explication of metaphor in Chauncy's sermon comes into high relief when compared to Edwards's "Sinners in the Hands of an Angry God," which employs four different metaphors just to make the first point. Starting from the small biblical verse Deuteronomy 32:35, "Their foot shall slide in due time," Edwards creates a visual masterpiece where "heaps of light chaff before the whirlwind" and "large quantities of dry stubble" collide with "devouring flames," and as easily as worms are crushed or "a slender thread" is cut, confirm that "God when he pleases" may "cast his enemies down to hell."[51] In George Marsden's words, "What is extraordinary in this sermon is not such doctrines but the sustained imagery."[52]

Chauncy and Edwards provide succinct examples of two opposing treatments of metaphor in the sermon: the explication of the scriptural metaphor's meaning versus the amplification of scriptural metaphor and the creation of new figures. Both ministers, of course, treat specific words with increased focus and organize their presentation around a word or phrase in typical Puritan fashion. The difference lies in Edwards's belief that images can and should provoke the affections, which results in the multiplication and layering of poetic language, while Chauncy refuses to encourage the spread of metaphor for fear of its irrational and social consequences. While Chauncy aims for rational nuance in his explication of a Scriptural metaphor, the explosion of metaphors in Edwards's sermon aims for affective precision; that is, though the figures might grow larger and more diverse, their intent is to focus emotion tightly and to produce affect capable of spurring belief and piety.

Given Edwards's multiplication of poetic language, it should not be surprising to discover that the most repeated, and most memorable, image in his sermon—God dangling the listener "over the pit of hell much as one holds a spider . . . over the fire" or as one being held "by a slender thread, with the flames of divine wrath flashing about it"—was also a Wigglesworthian image, which many in his audience would have recognized from the long poem *The Day of Doom* (1666):[53]

> Consider well the greatness of thy danger,
> O Child of wrath, and object of Gods anger.
> Thou hangest over the Infernal Pit
> By one small threed, and car'st thou not a whit?

> There's but a step between thy Soul and Death,
> Nothing remains but stopping of thy breath,
> (Which may be done to morrow, or before)
> And then thou art undone for evermore.[54]

That Edwards's image engages the New England poet Michael Wigglesworth's bestselling poem attests to the poetic spirit of the affective sermon and the power it could draw from the language of poetry.[55] Edwards's sermon materializes the poetic impulse in the pulpit that would forever alter American homiletics, and would go hand in hand not only with encouraging communal and individual piety through song and hymn, but also with poetry as an evangelical and ministerial tool.[56]

Edmund Burke acknowledged this coalescing of the itinerant minister and verse. Part of the turn toward the sublime included the ascendant place of words—particularly poetry—for inducing the passions while also carefully distinguishing its highest forms from low enthusiasm. In Burke's *A Philosophic Enquiry into the Origins of Our Ideas of the Sublime and the Beautiful* (1757), the itinerant minister serves as a trope for low poetic passions and a foil for the high aesthetic sublime. While arguing for poetry's superior and "powerful dominion over the passions," Burke writes, "But it is most certain that [the common sort] are very strongly roused by a fanatic preacher, or by the ballads of Chevy-chase, or the children in the wood, and by other little popular poems and tales that are current in that rank of life."[57] Here Burke slides easily between the trope of the fanatic itinerant minister and common verse because for him and his readers, both seem to trade in the same language and affect of the same social class. Burke's argument attests to the degree to which early evangelicalism rooted itself in the power of poetic language to induce sensation and religious experience.

That *The Day of Doom* rivaled the *Bay Psalm Book* in the second half of the seventeenth century points to a New England readership and private religious practice increasingly invested in sermonic poetry, a fact that at least partially explains why Watts's hymns—themselves homiletic rather than liturgical—were so appealing at the turn of the century.[58] Though seventeenth-century New England churches did not use the liturgy or introduce non-biblical texts like religious poetry in their services, Wigglesworth helped wed the pulpit and the extra-Psalmic poet in the British North American imagination.[59] His preface declares with George Herbert: "A Verse may find him who a

Sermon flies, / Saith *Herbert* well. Great Truth to dress in Meeter; / Becomes a Preacher, who mens Souls do prize."[60] Poetry as a preacher would become increasingly important in the evangelization of souls as heart religion expanded in the eighteenth-century transatlantic revivals, an idea that the prolific *Gospel Sonnets* helped to popularize.

A central aspect of Erskine's revival poetics that fueled the spread of the gospel was his theory of the couplet. When he turned to meter and rhyme to defend Calvinism, he did so because they expressed sound faith in their very form. To see the depth of their significance to covenantal grace and the education of the laity, we first need to return to the concept of the believer's espousal to Christ and its centrality to early evangelicalism.[61]

In 1708 Erskine published a small 24-page poem, *The Believer's Dowry*, which would bloom into his masterpiece, *Gospel Sonnets*. This poem, based upon Isaiah 54:5, "Thy maker is thy husband," and later to become "Part II, The Believer's Jointure" of *Gospel Sonnets*, elevates the union of Christ and the believer into the central religious experience for the Christian and the primary metaphor through which to address soteriology. Not surprisingly, Erskine's own religious experiences centered on the marriage metaphor. On August 19, 1721, he wrote in his diary that the "sensible presence" of God was made known to him at the Lord's Supper in Dunfermline through the sermon text "My beloved is mine, and I am his: I am my beloved's, and my beloved is mine." Erskine recorded that though he expected, as usual, to forget the sermon, he would forever remember the verse because it had made such a remarkable impression.[62] The versified introduction to *The Believer's Dowry* situates the poem in the context of Holy Communion, a fact that reveals Erskine's long association of the central sacrament of the Lord's Table with the believer's espousal to Christ. The influence of the Scottish sacramental season on revivals both in Scotland and America has been well documented, and *Gospel Sonnets* is one more avenue through which the religious experiences during such "holy fairs" traveled to the colonies.[63]

The marriage metaphor was central to eighteenth-century revivalism; in fact, it formed the crux of one of Whitefield's most preached sermons.[64] *Gospel Sonnets* shares many affinities with Edwards's vision of genuine religion, including its emphasis on affective experience tempered by deep theological understanding and a central feminine image as the pattern for the pietistic life. In *A Faithful Narrative* (1737) Edwards's own primary examples of the heart changed by Christ's grace were female. In the pulpit, he utilized various techniques to "symbolically identify . . . himself with the feminine soul, Christ's bride."[65] The bride of Christ's heightened and prolonged spiritual struggle in *Gospel Sonnets* details the emotional outbursts, both high and low, that Edwards reported his awakening parishioners experienced, and listeners of Edwards's sermons would have found similar spiritual direction and comfort in Erskine's poetic text.

Andrew Fuller, an important Baptist minister in England, lists *Gospel Sonnets* as central to his awakening in 1769. In his conversion narrative he details how God would not leave him alone to enjoy "vain songs."[66] Such statements were characteristic of many evangelicals, including Edwards, who considered a change from profane to sacred singing evidence of true conversion. As Fuller began to be stirred by the Christian message, he turned to Erskine's poem. He writes:

> One day, in particular, I took up Ralph Erskine's *Gospel Sonnets*, and opening upon what he entitled *A Gospel Catechism for Young Christians, or Christ All in All in our Complete Redemption*, I read, and as I read I wept. Indeed I was almost overcome with weeping, so interesting did the doctrine of eternal salvation appear to me; yet, there being no radical change in my heart, these thoughts passed away, and I was equally intent on the pursuit of folly as heretofore.[67]

Following the typical trajectory of evangelical conversion narratives, Fuller attempts multiple times to turn to Christ. Though the poem might appear to fail in this instance—producing only a temporary affect that does not produce salvation—the inclusion of *Gospel Sonnets* at this particular moment actually points to its success as a tool that can usher one through the various stages of conversion. By enacting the very failings of the protagonist of Erskine's poem, Fuller demonstrates the book's efficaciousness. He records his moment of conversion in this way:

> I never before knew what it was to feel myself an odious lost sinner, standing in need of both pardon and purification. . . . I was absolutely helpless. . . . Indeed I knew not what to do! . . . So I had no refuge. At one moment I thought of giving myself up to despair. "I may (said I within myself) even return and take my fill of sin; I can be but lost." This thought made me shudder at myself! My heart revolted. What, thought I, give up

Christ, and hope, and heaven! Those line of Ralph Erskine's then occurred to my mind—

> "But say, if all the gusts
>   And grains of love be spent,
> Say, farewell Christ, and welcome lusts
>   Stop, stop; I melt, I faint."

I could not bear the thought of plunging myself into endless ruin. . . . Yet it was not altogether from a dread of wrath that I fled to this refuge; for I well remember that I felt something attracting in the Saviour. I must—I will—yes, I will trust my soul—my sinful lost soul in his hands.[68]

Like the Christian speaker in "The Believer's Soliloquy," the section of the poem from which he quotes, Fuller quickly concludes that he cannot depart from God who once "didst with Grace perfume."[69] Like a sentimental heroine fainting from a confrontation with a lusty suitor, Fuller forestalls both his endless ruin and his own will, trusting himself entirely to the attracting power of his new lover, Christ.

Fuller was representative in his response to *Gospel Sonnets*, which followed the model provided by "A POEM, Dedicated to the Rev. Mr. RALPH ERSKINE, by a LADY in NEW ENGLAND, upon reading his *GOSPEL SONNETS*." In this poem, which begins to appear in the introductory material in editions of *Gospel Sonnets* after 1760, the female poet presents herself as one who shares in the vision of Erskine's sonnets, herself having been "charm'd" and "won" by Christ. Addressing the poet Erskine as a "Seraphic preacher," she proclaims:

> Mere moral preachers have no pow'r to charm,
> Thy lines are such, my nobler passions warm;
> These glorious truths have set my soul on fire,
> And while I read, I'm love and pure desire.[70]

Such sensually charged responses pervaded evangelical writing. The spiritual account of Sarah Prince Gill, daughter of Thomas Prince, minister and editor of *The Christian History*, and her correspondence with Esther Edwards Burr, daughter of Jonathan and Sarah Edwards, reveal how fluid sermons, poetry, and sentimental fiction could be.[71]

Gospel Sonnets was one of the most popular revival poems that instructed believers through a sensuous sentimental narrative. Organizing theology and biblical exegesis around the emotional highs and lows common to the eighteenth-century novel, *Gospel Sonnets* encourages believers to conceptualize their Christian experience and salvation in terms of a redeemed (and remarried) fallen woman, validating the emotional journey people make through a series of relationships that begin with love for the law (a bad lover) and end with love for Christ (the perfect lover).[72] Watts conceptualized the power of poetry as a form of seduction with life and death consequences; Erskine grounded the entire poetic experience for his reader in the attraction and fall of a woman to the law and then her subsequent seduction by Christ. This titillating aspect of the poem was well known and ridiculed; for example, the elegy for the late Connecticut governor Jonathan Law (1751), which features attacks on enthusiastic evangelicals, describes the book as an erotic script: "But if the softer rites of *Venus* move, / Address the tempting dame with holy love: / Sigh *Jesus* to her in the fond embrace, / And prattle *gospel sonnets* on free grace."[73] *Gospel Sonnets* was an easy reference with which to ridicule revival gatherings as promiscuous sensuality.

Such disparagement of revivalist passion was commonplace among outsiders, even though the larger culture was also enmeshed in romantic narratives to direct one's moral sense and purpose. Ruth Bloch succinctly summarizes the interrelationship between evangelicalism, Scottish moral sense philosophy, and domestic fiction in the eighteenth century through their mutual idealization of erotic heterosexual love. She observes that "the dramatic rise of religious revivalism in eighteenth-century America shares characteristics with the popularity of sentimental fiction," most importantly in their "similar conceptions of the role of the emotions in moral life."[74] Most importantly, in evangelicalism, moral sense philosophy, and fiction, romantic love "mediated the longstanding conflicts between the physical and the spiritual, the individual and the social."[75] Bloch's argument stresses the larger cultural stakes involved in the investment in romantic love and emotion across a large swath of society. *Gospel Sonnets* in particular emphasizes how the espousal metaphor wed to poetic form could mediate the central paradoxes of Calvinist theology and affective religious experience.

When progressive theologians who were invested in a more rational approach to exegesis and religion countered affective religion, they did so by refusing the espousal metaphor. The prominent liberal English minister and author John Tillotson explained the meaning of the believer's marriage to Christ in a manner that evacuated the ecstasy from which the metaphor had traditionally drawn its energy: "We believe in him, and heartily embrace his doctrine. . . . There is no other mystery in this union."[76] Michael Winship details provocative evidence of the Anglican mistrust of traditional descriptions of the believer's union with Christ:

> For the Anglicans, older theological conceptions of faith that allowed for activities like the soul going out to meet Christ were based simply on "a conspiracy of metaphors" (Tillotson 2:340). And, as Samuel Parker put it, doctrines which can be "expressed only in metaphorical terms, are not real Truths, but the meer Products of Imagination, dress'd up (like Children's *babies*) in a few spangled empty words" (*Impartial Censure* 75). Grace, that mysterious element at the heart of the encounter of the Bridegroom and the Bride, stripped of its "Metaphors and Allegories . . . plainly signifie(s) nothing but a virtuous temper of Mind" (Parker, *Ecclesiastical Politie* 72).[77]

Phrases like "a conspiracy of metaphors" and "empty words" attempt to demystify theological language to cleanse it of its indulgence in supposedly primitive, pre-modern imaginative thought. For practitioners of heart religion, however, these metaphors were not mere words that could be stripped away to reveal something else at the core, but rather were essential tools that relayed special information via the image: that is, God gave specific metaphors because they uniquely imparted something to the believer that other language could not. These metaphors indicated presence, not absence, for many evangelicals.[78] Erskine's attempt to embed the image within Calvinism by structuring theological arguments through the controversial metaphor acted as a bulwark to dangerous heterodoxies that reduced the gospel to matters of morality. And it was within the structure of the rhymed couplet—the most useful place for training believers in the sound faith of Calvinism—that he embedded the metaphor of espousal.

From the first lines of *Gospel Sonnets*, the poet highlights the tensions between body and spirit, poetic form and gospel content, and human language and scripture. The first line of Part I's preface, "*HARK*, dying Mortal! *if the Sonnet prove*," forcefully addresses the reader as both a listener and decaying flesh: the meter stresses the first word, followed by a minor pause and the following stressed syllable, while the standard typeface calls attention to the label "dying Mortal!" punctuated to indicate a strong caesura.[79] The poem continues to inform its hearer that "*if the Sonnet prove / A Song of living and immortal Love*," then it is of the utmost concern that the reader know its theme.[80]

Having set into play the stark contrast between the dying body and the immortal song of love, the poet then emphasizes the chasm between their attendant aesthetics:

> *Are Eyes to read, or Ears to hear, a Trust?*
> *Shall both in Death be cramm'd anon with Dust?*
> *Then trifle not to please thine Ear and Eye,*
> *But read thou, hear thou, for Eternity.*[81]

Emphasizing both the eyes and the ears as primary senses engaged in the process of poetic reception, the poet draws his distinction not between the usefulness of the different senses but between their temporal and eternal attunement. The last line slightly disrupts the pleasing iambic rhythm of the previous three lines to present the reader with a choice: embrace the trifling delights of prosody or the enduring sounds of eternity. Unlike elite verse, the poet claims he does not desire "*To please the Fancy or allure thy Sense*" but instead "*To clear thy Mind, and warm thy Heart through Grace.*"[82]

It is after the poet introduces the discordance between the dying body and the immortal song and the temporal and spiritual ears that he then frames them by the controlling image of the poem, the mystery of marriage:

> *A Marriage so mysterious I proclaim,*
> *Betwixt two Parties of such different Fame,*
> *That human Tongues may blush their Names to tell,*
> *To wit, the* PRINCE *of* HEAV'N, *the* Heir *of* Hell!
> But, on so vast a Subject, who can find
> *Words suiting the Conceptions of his Mind?*
> *Or if our Language with our Thoughts could vie,*
> *What mortal Thought can raise itself so high?*
> *When Words and Thoughts both fail, may Faith and Pray'r*
> *Ascend by climbing up the Scripture-Stair:*
> *From Sacred Writ these strange Espousals may*
> *Be explicated in the following Way.*[83]

The mystery of marriage unites opposites—the eternal prince of heaven, Christ, and the temporally bound heir of hell, man. But this mystery itself produces another enigma: the method through which the eternal message of the gospel can be relayed to the heir of hell, limited as he is by his faculties of thought and language. The mystery of the marriage between Christ and mankind acts as an umbrella figure, embracing other oppositions and imparting the mystery of union to them as well. The poet claims that through faith and prayer one can ascend to the truths of the gospel *"by climbing up the Scripture-Stair."* Poetry, once it is properly focused on the eternal, becomes the avenue through which *"these strange Espousals"* may be understood. By the end of the preface the earlier de-emphasis on poetry has been undone by undermining *all* of language's and thought's ability to vie with the eternal; at the same time, the poem affirms poetic language through employing the metaphor *"Scripture-Stair."* Ultimately, then, poetic form does not fail, but rather acts to save the inadequacies of language and thought through its authorization of metaphor and its embrace of paradox. The *"Marriage so mysterious"*—the gospel message—functions not only as the mechanism through which the good news is accomplished and understood; it specifically undergirds the efficacy of poetic form as a viable tool for explicating scripture.

The paradox of the marriage metaphor is the access point through which poetic form and scripture can be understood, effectively creating a specialized public for the poem's generative reading. As Erskine explains in the preface, reiterates in a prefatory note to Part II, and continues to emphasize in Part III, "The Believer's Riddle: Or, the Mystery of Faith": only Christians can access the meaning of his poem. And like the exercised believers of Part II for whom repetition provides a special pleasure, the saints of Part III differ from worldly aesthetes through their ability to *"read this Riddle truly in their Heart."*[84] The preface to Part III plays with the learned but earthly reader:

> READER, *the following Enigmatick Song*
> *Does not to wisest Naturalists belong:*
> *Their Wisdom is but Folly on this Head,*
> *They here may ruminate, but cannot read.*
> *For tho' they glance the Words, the Meaning chokes;*
> *They read the Lines, but not the Paradox.*[85]

Drawing upon Paul's formulation of the foolish confounding the wise, the poet patterns his *"Enigmatick Song"* on disorienting the discriminating reader. Though the wise may ruminate on his verse (and most likely criticize it), they *"cannot read."* This is subtly supported by the use of eye rhyme. The eye rhyme of *"Head"* with *"read"* meets the wise on their own terms, yet plays with their ability to scale the heavenly logic of this poem by toggling between correct poetic form (a full rhyme) in which case the wise cannot read correctly, and correct pronunciation (an eye rhyme) in which case the poem denies wise readers the pleasure of a fully rhymed couplet. Already, the poet has his potential wise readers "*glanc[ing at] the Words*" in order to determine pronunciation, when the next rhyme again comes at a slant, confirming for them that they are merely ingesting lines without understanding the paradox. The subject of the poem, however "*blunt*" the phrasing, will "*surmount*" the "*most acute Intelligence*" that approaches the poem with the "*natural and acquired Sight*" to the exclusion of the "*divine evangelick Light.*"[86]

The poet frames the efforts of the skilled literary reader of his poem as un-regenerative work in contrast to the efficacy of espousal poetics. He writes, "*Great Wits may rouse their Fancies, rack their Brains / And after all the Labour lose their Pains.*"[87] Playing on the phrase "for their Pains," the poet emphasizes that "*Great Wits*" will receive neither aesthetic pleasure nor eternal reward for their reading labor. The humor and poignancy of the lines hinge on the word "*Pains,*" which refers both to a type of side-dish as well as the suffering endured by souls in hell. The ill-rewards for the learned reader's efforts, which are both physical and spiritual, are a mockery of incarnation: the reader will vomit and gain nothing theologically to benefit her eternal soul. The aesthetic and theological principles of the poem merge in this moment: human effort will not suffice to attain the pleasures or knowledge of the poem and the gospel. Underscoring the point again with slant rhymes, the poet declares, "*No unregenerate Mortal's best Engines, / Can right unriddle these few rugged Lines; / Nor any proper Notions thereof reach, / Tho' sublimated to the highest Stretch.*"[88] The poet ardently disentangles elite taste and human works from Christian aesthetics and grace. The revival public to whom he writes must understand that their theology of grace will necessarily change their aesthetics, while the unbelieving public of educated readers must be convinced that they are excluded from its highest pleasures and knowledge without an experience of Christ's grace.

This continues when he opposes "*Great Wits*" and "*Masters of Reason,*" who cannot plumb the "*mysterious Deep*" of the poem, to "*Sinners*" and "*weakest Saints,*" who "*sound the divine Depth of sacred Writ, / [. . .] by the golden Line of Heav'n-spun Faith.*"[89] While describing these believers, the poet speaks in full rhymes, returning the pleasures of poetry along with the accessibility of gospel knowledge:

> *These Sinners that are sanctify'd in part,*
> *May read this Riddle truly in their Heart.*
> *Yea, weakest Saints may feel its truest Sense,*
> *Both in their sad and sweet Experience.*[90]

Experience with the gospel opens up the riddle of the poem to be read by the heart.

Fully accessing the poem requires readers to participate in the riddle: that of being both sinners and saints simultaneously. The poet explains:

> *High Strains would spoil the Riddle's grand Intent,*
> *To teach the weakest, most illiterate Saint,*
> *That Mahanaim is his proper Name;*
> *In whom two struggling Hosts make bloody Game.*[91]

Here again the tension between the form and content of the poem directly participates in, and points to, the central theological principle taught in the poem: the union of opposites. Writing in "*High Strains*" would contradict the expressed purpose of the poem to teach the poetically uncultured Christian, yet the riddle evades even the wisest non-Christian reader.

"Mahanaim," meaning two camps or companies, was a place-name Jacob imparted after an angelic visitation awakened him to the fact that his encampment was sharing the site with God's angels. The place-name Mahanaim expresses the doubleness of the Christian experience—already a saint yet still warring with the flesh—that the poet declares is a "*Paradox [. . .] fitted to disclose / The Skill of Zion's Friends above her Foes.*"[92] The experiential knowledge of doubleness that the believer possesses endows the Christian reader with the exegetical dexterity necessary to avoid "*All fatal Errors in the World*" which "*proceed / From Want of Skill such Mysteries to read.*"[93] Discerning the truth of the gospel resides in a readiness to embrace paradox, an ability that flowers naturally out of the Christian's own experience of salvation. As the poet concludes his preface, '*Tis all a Contradiction, yet all true, / A happy*

Truth, is verify'd in you. / Go forward then to read the Lines, but stay / To read the Riddle also by the Way."[94] This last exhortation returns the audience to the process of reading lines of poetry, which the poet endorses if one inhabits the riddles of Scripture, Christian life, and, by implication, aesthetic pleasure. Riddle and paradox function for Erskine much like parables for Christ—to teach those who have ears to hear and to keep truth hidden from those who do not.

Though Erskine warns against the pitfalls of high art in his preface, and the poem continues to make distinctions between *"towr'ing Literature"* and *"the plainest Diction fetch'd from sacred Writ,"* the verse in which he writes nevertheless carves out a space for a Christian poetics that is aesthetically so-phisticated on its own terms.[95] What the poet calls the *"Majestical Simplicity / of Scripture Orat'ry,"* stands against the *"soaring Orators"* who *"under-rate a Jewel rare and prime"* because it is *"wrapt up in the Rags of homely Rhime."*[96] The riddle, Erskine knows, is a low literature, yet it is a form that can hold the highest paradoxes of heaven. The poet himself declares that he would de-mure from writing lofty verse even if he could:

> *Slight not the Riddle then like Jargon vile,*
> *Because not garnish'd with a pompous Stile.*
> *Could th' Author act the lofty Poet's Part,*
> *Who make their Sonnets soar on Wings of Art,*
> *He on this Theme had blush'd to use his Skill,*
> *And either clipt his Wings, or broke his Quill.*[97]

The purpose, or use, of the riddle and its power is that it causes fools to see *"their Wit, and Wits their Folly see."*[98] It is for this reason that one should not slight the riddle as if it were like jargon—a term encapsulating both the sense of poetry as jingle, or excessive rhyme without content, as well as acknowl-edging the overtones of elitism and religious intolerance bound up in the judgment of riddle as incoherent babel.[99]

The poet turns to the errors of *"Vain Men,"* which includes Arminians, Papists, Legalists, Antinomists, Socinians, and Arians, all of whom cannot reconcile seeming contradictions: whether they be reconciling the freedom of grace with the freedom of the will, the goodness of works with their in-ability to justify, God's righteousness with personal righteousness, the cost of heaven versus the free gift of salvation, or the nature of God as both truly

God and truly Man.[100] Regarding these costly heretical mistakes, the poet concludes:

> The Sound in Faith no part of Truth controul,
> Hereticks own the half, but not the whole.
>   Keep then the sacred Myst'ry still entire,
> To both the Sides of Truth due Favour bear,
> Not quitting one, to hold the other Branch;
> But passing Judgment on an equal Bench.
> The Riddle has two Feet, and were but one
> Cut off, Truth falling to the Ground were gone.[101]

Because of the nature of true theology, which requires one to balance two parts to keep "*the sacred Myster'ry still entire*," the riddle's form provides the anecdote to heresy.

In Erskine's writing, the riddle takes the poetic form of the couplet—a form invested in the primacy of rhyme, which we have already seen was central to Erskine's vision of prosody.[102] The ability of the couplet to hold elegantly and precisely two lines in harmony through rhyme matches the task of a balanced Calvinist theology, both modeling and producing sound faith. For over half the book, the poet exhorts, teaches, and edifies "*the Sound in Faith*" through the repetition of the couplet's rhyme, training potential lay readers in the art of theology and successful Christian living figured through the harmonizing (as opposed to the absolving) of tensions.

Eighteenth-century poets galvanized the potential of the couplet for various purposes, from serving as a vehicle of reason to enabling the play of appetite.[103] Erskine's specific use of the couplet, what we might call his Calvinist couplet, provides the structural integrity for balancing art and Christian truth. It is espousal in poetic form: the marriage of "*the* PRINCE *of* HEAV'N" and "*the* Heir *of* Hell."[104] The metaphor of coupling, so central to Erskine's poetic project, has been considered a hallmark of affective religion and ecstatic experience. The poetic theory of *Gospel Sonnets* enlarges the domain of the espousal metaphor by recognizing it as a type of shorthand for melding theology and poetics and the minister and the poet in a revivalist community that believed, in the words of Charles Wesley, that poetry was the language of the saint and of heaven.[105] And a community that hoped for, in the words of the Presbyterian minister Samuel Davies, a poetry that would "diffuse celestial Fervor through the World."[106]

The Versified Convert and the Breaking of Form

Drawing on a long tradition of didactic poetic catechism, Erskine's text became a theological standard for the layperson enmeshed in an experiential and versified Christianity. Watts had argued that versified Psalms were not sufficient for worship because they did not fully translate into the historical and cultural moment of the eighteenth-century Christian. Watts's turn to immanent rhyme—by which I mean rhyme with content directly pertinent to the contemporary Christian and his own salvation—as a consistent feature of early British North American evangelicalism meant that many believers internalized this particular poetic element with conversion. Examples of this are prolific enough to appear prosaic and unremarkable: conversion narratives, journal entries, prayers, sermons, newspaper articles, and even poems themselves use rhymed verse to indicate God's salvific intervention. Sarah Prince Gill in an exemplary passage of her conversion narrative attributes Watts's verse that she "breathes out" to the language of the Holy Spirit praying through her.[107]

Perhaps most emblematic of the versified convert is *A Brief Account of God's Dealings with Edward Godwin* (1744) in which Godwin proclaims his conversion story in quatrains of iambic pentameter. The well-known itinerate preacher and hymn writer John Cennick explains in the introduction: "One Reason why I wrote so much by way of Preface as, with this Hope, that peradventure somewhat I have written may be a Means of plucking some out of the Fire, and if he who reads escapes the Prose, I trust, will be caught in the Poetry."[108] Like many other revivalists, Cennick exhorts those with exquisite taste to overlook rhyme, defends its use through the logic of George Herbert, and encourages the unawakened to surrender to it.

But verse forms, like theologies, were not static. By the early nineteenth-century revivals, or what many have called the Second Great Awakening, the burned-over district of upstate New York was awash in revival poetry. Among the famous names of Isaac Watts, Elizabeth Rowe, Ralph Erskine, Edward Young, and Felicia Hemans, one of the lesser known poets, a man named John Allen, published the versified sermon *Thoughts on Man's Redemption* (1805). Its invitation to accept the gospel follows in the well-worn tradition of Erskine's poem: rhyme, gospel sound, and espousal:

> Th' inviting sounds of gospel grace,
> Enchants the soul with joy and peace,

And for the Saviour's lovely charms,
Eager she flies into his arms.[109]

Yet, the poem deviates from Erskine in at least one crucial way: it advocates universal salvation rather than the limited election of Calvinism. Because *Gospel Sonnets* was published throughout a century of revivals, its success meant that it circulated in a wide nexus of expanding revivalist forms and contexts.

This fact is made quite stark with the sudden appearance of a new *Gospel Sonnets* in 1830—one written not by the staunch Calvinist Erskine but by an Arminian Methodist (Figure 1.2). Using Erskine's original invocation as the book's epitaph to make his project clear, Jonathan Lamb reinvented the theologically focused writing of an old school Calvinist minister by turning it into a Methodist camp meeting primer written by a layman.[110] The title page's emphasis on the poet's status as a layman extends Erskine's common aesthetic into a new century's revival milieu in which the coupling of aesthetics and soteriology continued in full force—though often by poet-ministers with very different views of Calvinism. Like Erskine's poem, *The Christian Journal* of Utica, New York, a hotbed of revivalism, rested the evidence for a true revival of religion on a change in aesthetic attachments that favored illiterate rather than refined poetic language.[111] The common reader and rhyme were still crucial, but the meaning of the verse form in relation to a specific account of soteriology in new contexts was dynamic.[112]

One thing remained the same; genteel readers still did not recommend Erskine's poem. An article written by "The Lay Preacher" in 1797 prescribes the activities that a gentleman should enjoy on a Sunday, which include resting from work, enjoying nature, and reading serious poetry. For this, he writes, "The gospel sonnets of Erskine are not recommended, but the moral Young, and the enthusiastic Gray."[113] This dismissal of Erskine appeals to the polite reader who eschews certain types of religious zeal and instead prefers the refined sentiments of Young and Gray.[114] Erskine's combination of rhyme, biblical imagery, and theology placed him alongside Wigglesworth, which one article slighted by categorizing both as works that "Genius is too impatient for."[115] However, the contrast the writer sets up between these poets is misleading because it seems to indict Erskine for being a revival poet while rescuing Young and Gray from such lowbrow enthusiasm. For many readers, especially Wesleyan Methodists, Young was a highly celebrated revival poet who directly inspired their hymns. Charles Wesley extensively

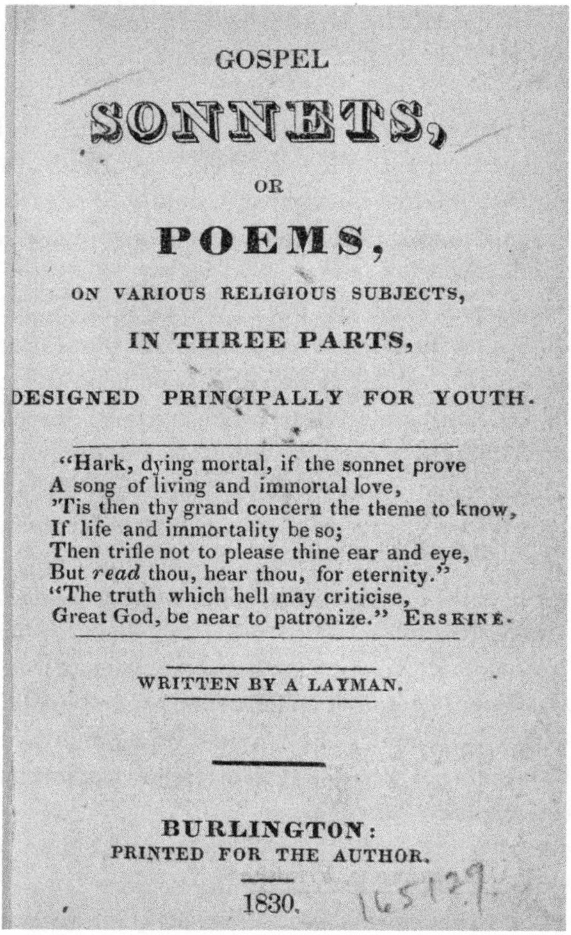

GOSPEL

SONNETS,

OR

POEMS,

ON VARIOUS RELIGIOUS SUBJECTS,

IN THREE PARTS,

DESIGNED PRINCIPALLY FOR YOUTH.

"Hark, dying mortal, if the sonnet prove
A song of living and immortal love,
'Tis then thy grand concern the theme to know,
If life and immortality be so;
Then trifle not to please thine ear and eye,
But *read* thou, hear thou, for eternity."
"The truth which hell may criticise,
Great God, be near to patronize." ERSKINE.

WRITTEN BY A LAYMAN.

BURLINGTON:
PRINTED FOR THE AUTHOR.

1830.

Figure 1.2. A new *Gospel Sonnets* (1830) written by early nineteenth-century poet-minister Jonathan Lamb.
The Newberry Library.

annotated his copy of Young's *Night Thoughts*, and one of the best-known converts in London hinged his conversion narrative on an encounter with the revered poem.[116] One English Baptist was said to have memorized the entire book, which was, of course, in blank verse. The comment by "The Lay Preacher," then, takes aim at several specific targets at once: not only backward Calvinists, but also enthusiastic Methodists, and low verse form. The gentleman writer tries to claim Young and Gray for his ilk, and wrestle them away from what he considers lowbrow sorts.

Though Milton, Young, and Thomson were revered as exemplary revival poets, few British North American revivalists followed their use of blank verse. The Calvinist couplet remained a tool for inculcating a certain type of sound believer—Timothy Dwight's *Conquest of Canaan* (1785) serves as one epic example.[117] Sectarian arguments over Calvinism, Arminianism, and Universalism abounded in couplet form. We might then pause over those few who chose to write in blank verse. The first American poem to title itself an epic was the Reverend Thomas Brockway's *The Gospel Tragedy* (1795), which was composed in blank verse. Brockway, an active revivalist minister who was part of the Eleazar Wheelock circle and married into the Lathrop family,[118] found his epic inspiration primarily in Thomas Ellwood's *Davideis* (1712), the life of David versified in heroic couplets, and Milton's *Paradise Lost*, the revered exemplum of the religious sublime metered in blank verse. He seems to have taken Ellwood's championing of the common aesthetic and applied it to elite blank verse.[119] Brockway's blank verse, then, sacrificed rhyme not to undermine Calvinism, but to spread it by leveling another elite verse form for the masses.

This is not the same for Elhanan Winchester. Winchester began his successful career as a minister, hymn writer, and Baptist Calvinist. Yet, when he wrote and published his 12-book epic poem *The Process and Empire of Christ* (1805), one of the few British North American revival poems in blank verse, he was a committed Universalist. Universalists still revered portions of *Gospel Sonnets* in their own hymnbooks and sermons, and Winchester knew Erskine's verse well—a fact that makes his choice of blank verse to proclaim a new soteriology all the more important. While the epic genre itself could have influenced the choice of verse form, it was not a given. In fact, most early national American epics, such as Timothy Dwight's *Conquest of Canaan* (1785), Thomas Branagan's *Avenia* (1805), and Joel Barlow's *Columbiad* (1807), were in heroic couplets. Instead, Winchester's choice of blank verse enacts that which the explicit subject of his poem celebrates—the break from the history of Calvinist election to a future defined by a theology of universal salvation.

In light of Erskine's Calvinist couplets and Winchester's meaningful deviation from them as a Universalist, a single manuscript poem in the revered Baptist leader Isaac Backus's library appears even more provocative. When the Calvinist Backus, or someone close to him, wrote or copied the Baptist epic "Nebuchandezzar: A Poem," he or she did so in blank verse.[120] By the early nineteenth century one of his descendants, Sarah Backus, also wrote revival verse in multiple forms, including blank verse. Attention to Ralph Erskine's *Gospel Sonnets* and his accompanying poetics underscores the weight of these aesthetic choices for revival poets across variegated communities in which soteriology expressed through espousal was so often wed to sound.

Erskine's *Gospel Sonnets* was central to a growing revivalism grounded in affective experiences with Christ. It helped popularize espousal piety not only as a devotional metaphor, but also as a tool distributed through verse form to bind theology and poetics and the poet and the minister together. The next chapter turns to how gender affected the deployment of this tool by highlighting the relationship of espousal piety not to the Calvinist couplet, but to new forms of poetic personae created by women revivalists. When Sarah Edwards, with whom this chapter began, fainted in the arms of Christ, she performed the actions of the idealized revival convert—the spouse of Christ. Erskine's influential dramatization of *The Song of Songs* was a blueprint for the devotional life of the Christian. Its lengthy focus on the emotional responses of a woman, the spouse of Christ, not only helped form the devotional imaginaries of converts, but also served as the material from which evangelical women built up and sustained influential verse ministries.

2

"A Lady in New England"

Forms of the Poet-Minister

Reprints of Ralph Erskine's *Gospel Sonnets* appeared at least every six years throughout the eighteenth century. In 1762, presses in London, Glasgow, and Edinburgh all printed *Gospel Sonnets*, which is not surprising given this was the year of the great Wales revival, a stirring often attributed to the songs, hymns, and poetry of the Welsh itinerant William Williams, and a major boon for Calvinists. What is remarkable is that the Edinburgh edition featured the first dedicatory verse to ever appear in the *Gospel Sonnets*, and that the poem, which would remain in almost all subsequent editions, was penned by a New England woman.[1] This change to *Gospel Sonnets* summons the special significance of the New England awakenings in the transatlantic evangelical imagination in order to highlight Erskine's poem as an enduring tool of revivalism. Most importantly, it does so through the endorsement of a woman poet-minister. The honorific placement of the poem exemplifies the continuous feedback between the idealized female convert, such as the featured character in Erskine's poem, and the evangelical woman poet in the culture of revivalism.

Much has been written about the way women and feminized men became idealized converts in the evangelical imagination; less has been said about the role poetry played in this process.[2] The previous chapter located a profound relationship between Calvinist theology and the couplet in *Gospel Sonnets* that embedded espousal within soteriology and prosody. One of the results, this chapter argues, was that Erskine's prolific poem helped open a space for evangelical women's poetry.

As the additional poem in the 1762 Edinburgh printing of *Gospel Sonnets* itself suggests, it is not enough to acknowledge the abstraction of the female convert within *Gospel Sonnets* and by other leading male revivalists. The prefatory poem points toward a productive convergence of feminine-inflected soteriology with the role of the poet-minister, which transformed the value accorded to women's verse ministry. The poem opens up historical questions

Awakening Verse. Wendy Raphael Roberts, Oxford University Press (2020). © Oxford University Press.
DOI: 10.1093/oso/9780197510278.001.0001

about early evangelical women's ministries that need further attention. In particular, who was this actual woman from the colonies who, by introducing the well-traveled Erskine poem, authorized its efficacy? How did she nego- tiate such a distinguished role in the evangelical revivals and its attendant poetics? And what does her legacy reveal about the function of evangelical women poets in colonial revival culture? By answering these questions, this chapter adds to recent scholarship that has begun to attend to influential evangelical women leaders across the Atlantic world, such as Sarah Osborn and Rebecca Protten, as part of a complex religious phenomenon that arose across nationalities through a number of media and mediators.[3] One of these central media was verse.

While Jonathan Edwards promoted a silent woman as the idealized con- vert in *Some Thoughts concerning the Revival* (1743), evangelical women poets pursued a different vision of ministry for themselves and their fellow sisters in Christ. Women were active participants who occupied a con- tinuum from anonymity to recognized transatlantic leadership. Some colo- nial women became well known when they joined the new print evangelism and revival leadership—Sarah Parsons Moorhead, Martha Brewster, Phillis Wheatley, Jane Dunlap—while countless others worked tirelessly in their local communities and networks with no further recognition. Like the hun- dreds of pastors who nurtured evangelical spirituality after grand itinerants moved on, women took up various calls in their newfound piety and freedom from the law, many of which entailed verse. Though Watts, Wesley, and Erskine were religious celebrities then and now, evangelical women were no less primary actors in the creation and spread of eighteenth-century revival poetry and culture. Given the centrality of white female piety to Puritanism (both as a historical reality and as a concept constructed by historians) as well as to the formation of the liberal pubic sphere, evangelical women's verse might well provide one of the best windows into this early American reli- gious landscape.[4]

This chapter works toward two complementary ends. The first is elemental yet necessary: it establishes the significant presence of British and colonial female poet-ministers in the colonies. Second, it unfolds how revival poetry and the heightened role of the poet-minister enabled evangelical women to embrace and to utilize two significant aspects of transatlantic culture discussed in the previous chapter—the template of espousal piety for the convert and the role of the print itinerant. As elaborated by many scholars, evangelicals elevated feminine piety as a spiritual ideal and by the end of the century located religion in the private space of the feminine. At the same time, evangelicals initiated and then accelerated the growth of mass media. From the earliest outpourings, revivalists conceived of their printed works as an extension of the itinerating minister, a concept I term a "print itinerant." This chapter shows how revivalist women adapted and navigated the role of the poet-minister through crafting poetic personae that brought the idealized female convert and the print itinerant together.

It does so by first turning to two of the eighteenth century's most prolific English women writers who carved out successful verse ministries. Nonconformity was the most conducive space in British society for women's political engagement through both coteries and print, so it should be unremarkable that the Congregationalist Elizabeth Singer Rowe and Baptist Anne Dutton, both English poets, became transatlantic figures who influenced the culture and direction of revivalism. Their divergent poetics of Christian belletrism and Puritan plain style exemplify two very different ways of inhabiting the role of the revival poet-minister. Though all but ignored in scholarly accounts of British American colonial verse, Rowe and Dutton energized colonial revival verse through two different poetic personae, that of the idealized espousal convert and that of the spiritual director, either of which could appear separately or inflect each other as they were taken up by other poets and traveled across various verse genres. This chapter argues that Rowe and Dutton proved to be important precursors to one of the preeminent colonial woman poet-ministers, Sarah Parsons Moorhead, who took up both poetic personae utilized by Rowe and Dutton to create a successful verse ministry as Boston's spiritual director and well-traveled print itinerant.

Verse Ministries of Early Evangelical Women

The Idealized Convert and Muse

Even before Whitefield's sermons and Erskine's verse had helped embed espousal in conversion and prosody, making affective religion feel right on the level of sound, women's enthusiastic responses to Christ had begun to be universalized. This was aided by the posthumous publications and reprintings of works by the primary architect of devotional feeling in British early eighteenth-century writing, Elizabeth Singer Rowe.[5] Seeming to hover within and above sacred poetics and the inspired poet-minister, Rowe's voice came to embody devotion itself. Put differently, true devotion included the aspiration to inhabit her divinely enraptured persona. Rowe was the prototype for the nineteenth-century poetess of feeling, and she presided over not only a belletristic and upper-class enthusiastic religious verse, but also a revivalist imaginary that superimposed the ideal of espousal piety onto verse itself.

Elizabeth Singer Rowe exerted nearly as much lasting influence on revival culture as Isaac Watts, gaining a significant audience after her death. Her works circulated in manuscript and in print early in the eighteenth century, and after her death in 1737 print editions proliferated further. In fact, one year before *Gospel Sonnets* (1740) debuted in British North America, Benjamin Franklin published Rowe's narrative poem *The History of Joseph* (1739)—the first of more than 50 British North American printings of her various works that would appear between 1739 and 1816. Boston saw the first American printings of the two most popular of Rowe's works—*Devout Exercises of the Heart in Meditation and Soliloquy, Prayer and Praise* and *Friendship in Death*—in 1742 and 1747, respectively. The London edition of *The Life of Mrs. Elizabeth Rowe* was also reprinted in Boston in 1747. Her books were standard fare for any eighteenth-century bookseller, especially those who specialized in religious works, and her writings were regularly copied and emulated in commonplace books on both sides of the Atlantic.

Yet Rowe's publications encompass only part of her presence. Admired by radical, moderate, and non-evangelical Christians alike, Rowe came to be among the most widely known devotional poets of the eighteenth century in British North America. As verse in the "Age of Sensibility" became associated with displaying and producing morality, multiple audiences came to admire Rowe's works. Rowe had an extensive influence on the development of British religious poetry, including the poet's narration of biblical tales and her invention of the genre "devout soliloquies" that influenced British literary women of the period, as documented by Paula Backscheider. In passing, Backscheider surmises that Rowe surely influenced poets involved in the evangelical revivals as well.[6] Indeed, her works paved the way for the most noted British evangelical women poets of taste and spiritual authority in the second half of the century and early nineteenth century, including Hannah More and Felicia Hemans, as well as refined American poetesses, such as Phillis Wheatley and Lydia Huntley Sigourney. Even when Rowe was not explicitly named, evangelical practitioners strove to follow her example. Because she served as Watts's spiritual (and at one time romantic) muse, when Watts's lines rose from worshiping lips, "The Heavenly Singer," as she was called, practically seemed to hover in the air.

Watts said as much. When he edited and provided the forward for "the late pious and ingenious Mrs. Rowe's" *Devout Exercises of the Heart*, he offered his own experience of Rowe's poems in which he "*attempted to assume her Language as [his] own*" as a paradigm for all her readers to follow:

> LET *me persuade all that peruse this Book, to make the same Experiment that I have done; and when they have shut out the World, and are reading in their Retirements, let them try how far they can speak this Language, and assume these Sentiments as their own: And by aspiring to follow them, may they find the same Satisfaction and Delight, or at least learn the profitable Lessons of Self-Abasement and holy Shame. And may a noble and glorious Ambition excite in their Breasts a sacred Zeal to emulate so illustrious an Example.*[7]

Rowe's words were meant not only to inspire praise but also to stand in for all Christian devotion. Put another way, Rowe's words were the embodiment of an idealized heavenly language of piety. As such, her otherworldly persona can often be overlooked because it appears everywhere. She and her words became synonymous with piety itself.

In formal terms, this idealized heavenly language veered in different directions for the elite and common reader, as well as the non-revivalist and revivalist audience. When Watts declared Rowe a heavenly muse, it was in a poem he wrote in 1706 and included in his second edition of *Horae Lyricae* (1709), a collection he explicitly created for those with elevated taste, as opposed to his hymns aimed at the common person. As such, he employed belletristic conventions, including neoclassical imagery and cognomens for those in his coterie:

> On the fair Banks of gentle *Thames*
> I tun'd my Harp; nor did celestial Themes
>   Refuse to dance upon my Strings:
>   There beneath the Evening Sky
> I sung my Cares asleep, and rais'd my Wishes high
>   To everlasting Things.
> Sudden from *Albion's* Western Coast

Harmonious Notes come gliding by,
The neighbouring Shepherds knew the Silver Sound;
   " 'Tis PHILOMELA's Voice . . .
I was all Ear, and PHILOMELA's Song
   Was all divine Delight.[8]

In this poem, Watts positions himself as the Psalmist David who sits beside the river to play sacred music. Yet, another poet's divine notes dwarf
his celestial song, and he becomes "all Ear"—completely subsumed into
the most divine music, "PHILOMELA's Song." Ovid's Philomela had been
transformed by the gods into a nightingale after she was violently silenced by
her rapist, who cut out her tongue. Here, the modern David, Watts, redeems
the power of poetry for its true sacred purpose and declares the Christian
muse to be Philomela, the keeper of divine song. It is she—that is, Rowe,
who used the cognomen Philomela—who presides over the highest poetic
expressions. Rowe's cognomen captured the essence of her poetic persona
that depended upon the abstraction of the power of the woman's tongue into
song itself. Even as Watts metonymizes himself into "all Ear" and hence an
empty vessel waiting to be divinely filled, Philomela is already ether: she is
not "all Tongue"; she is song and "all divine Delight."

Rowe exemplified the ideal poet John Dennis desired when he called
for a truly sacred highbrow poetry in *The Grounds of Criticism in Poetry*
(1704). Dennis specified the type of person that would make "Enthusiasm
in Poetry . . . Wonderful and Divine": "now all the Ideas of God are such, that
the more large and comprehensive the Soul of a Poet is; and the more it is capable of Receiving those Idea's [sic] the more is it sure to be raised and fill'd
and lifted to the Skies with wonder."[9] Watts, in no uncertain terms, declares
Rowe to be this revivified poet who can see into the great "Evangelical day":

*THE Reader will here find a Spirit dwelling in Flesh, elevated into di-
vine Transports, congenial to those of Angels and unbodied Minds. Her intense Love to her God kindles at every Hint, and transcends the Limits of
Mortality: I scarce ever met with any devotional Writings which gives us an
Example of a Soul, at special Seasons, so far raised above every thing that is
not immortal and divine.*[10]

It is not unremarkable that Rowe's poem "The Vision" first appeared in
the same year that Dennis called for the re-establishment of the sacred art

of poetry, and that she places this poem first in her arrangement of her post-humous *Miscellaneous Works* (1739), for through it she clearly stakes out the territory of the revivified sacred poet for herself.[11] In it, she experiences a "shining vision" in which a celestial youth in the garb of the muses commands her in "his tuneful voice" to devote her lyre entirely to God's "unbounded glory" because, echoing Dennis and Watts, "To heav'n the muse's sacred art belongs."[12] If she takes up this heavenly call, she will resurrect an immortal poet:

> And when death's fatal sleep shall close thine eyes,
> In triumph we'll attend thee to the skies;
> We'll crown thee there with everlasting bays,
> And teach thee all our celebrated lays.[13]

Rowe describes the Christian believer's crown of salvation as the poet's laurel, suggesting that the culmination of Christian life is induction into the full knowledge of the canon of heavenly verse. This should not be glossed over as simply decorative poetic metaphor. For revivalists, it was an apt description of a real, embodied eschaton infused with poetry. If Erskine helped define a prosody that embedded Calvinist espousal and its attendant theological paradoxes, Rowe's enthusiastic devotion—which so often engaged the theology of espousal—helped extend and recreate a universalized woman's voice that embedded espousal and feeling in the nature of evangelical verse. Her persona was evocative of a perfected attunement to heavenly sound. As repeated by Erskine and others, the heavenly choir represented the fulfillment of revival soteriology and eschatology; Rowe, the Heavenly Singer, was the abstraction of its very sound.

In this role of the sacred poet and idealized heavenly muse, Rowe inspired a generation of male and female Protestant poets who embraced both Dennis's and Watts's projects of reclaiming the highest exercises of poetry for Christ primarily through rehabilitating enthusiasm, which had been tainted by the English Civil Wars, by embracing the religious sublime and Christian belletrism. The religious sublime, first described in detail by literary historian David Morris, was a formal mode of writing marked by flights of the imagination through bold and numerous sensorial descriptions inspired by new readings of Longinus, Milton, and the Bible.[14] A large part of this renewal of Christian poetry through the religious sublime also engaged the new wit and politeness that undergirded the eighteenth-century ideal of *sensus communis* proposed by moral sense philosophers the Earl of Shaftsbury and Francis Hutcheson. The result was Christian belletrism, a literary project that asserted both the supernatural and the virtues of polite society.

For anti-revivalists and conservative revivalists, Rowe was revered as a muse of Christian belletrism. As David Shields eloquently narrates, the Rev. Benjamin Colman, who was a conservative revival supporter, brought the belletristic sublime to Boston, complete with a preference for manuscript, coteries, cognomens, wit, conversation, and sublime language, after spending time with Rowe and others in England.[15] It quickly became the fashionable poetic mode of the colonies, with its emphasis on an elevated, neoclassical language and intense and prolific sensorial descriptions, which marked a radical departure from the sparse adjectives and biblical metaphors of earlier colonial Puritan poets.

Turning just one page of Rowe's poem *The History of Joseph* (1736) quickly reveals the difference in style. Rowe addresses God as a poet—"Thus sung in lofty strains the noble bard; / The heav'ns and earth their own formation heard"—as she concludes her epic invocation: "Let others tell, of ancient conquests won, / And mighty deeds, by favour'd heroes done; (Heroes enslav'd to pride, and wild desires,) / A virgin Muse, a virgin theme requires; / Where vice, and wanton beauty quit the field, / And guilty loves to steadfast virtue yield."[16] Under the cognomen Philomela, the idealized lover of song, Rowe held court in her belletristic coterie, which included those with a staid Old Light sensibility as well as socially conservative ministers who supported the revivals, such as Reverends Colman and Thomas Prince.

Rowe's presence induced varying responses in divergent religious circles. According to Shields, New Light revivalists rejected Christian belletrism and its practitioners as Old Light.[17] While generally true, revivalists existed along a broad continuum from socially radical to conservative. For instance, Prince, the editor of the revival journal *Christian History*, tried to harness the excitement of revivalism to support the values of British polite society.[18] Refracted through the Old Lights and conservative revivalists, Rowe was a Christian belletrist who often functioned as an idealized muse within the scripted play of polite society; refracted through a diverse spectrum of New Lights, she appeared as an idealized convert voicing and inspiring the language of revival poetry. Unlike proper Christian belles lettres, revival poetry did not seek so much to rehabilitate enthusiasm into a polite aesthetic as it did to loose verse and its effects upon the world. Poetry's job was not to help one feel proper, but to help one feel radically transformed by God. Because it did so by acting upon the reader in order to convert the affections to God, the figure of the idealized poetic muse revered by Christian belletrists shifted valences within revivalism and instead appeared as the idealized convert of experiential religion.

As such, Rowe not only spearheaded a particular strain of eighteenth-century Protestant belletristic poetics exemplified by middle-class female piety, she also helped instantiate a lasting persona for poets invested in religious awakenings. While most revival poets eschewed the pagan muses, she became the de facto muse of early evangelical poetry as she was abstracted into not only the inspiration for, but also the presence of, feeling entangled with verse. Samuel Davies, whom will be the focus of the next chapter, invoked her as such. Following Watts's example, revival poet-ministers worked from a foundational prototype of heavenly song embodied in Rowe who could "excite in their Breasts a sacred Zeal" to help them "speak her language." The ease with which Rowe's persona of the idealized muse and convert could travel and morph between poetic genres and reading communities should give pause. If one were to trace the seeds of the nineteenth-century poetess to the eighteenth century, she would find the ever-present, ethereal Rowe. Yopie Prins and Virginia Jackson have resuscitated the term "poetess" in the study of nineteenth-century women's poetry as a generic marker for what would become the modernist's conception of lyric poetry.[19] For them, the poetess is a negation of a specific self and a generic expression of women's emotion as verse itself. In the revivalist uses of Rowe, heavenly language, which is verse itself, arises in affective response to one's espousal to Christ. This generic language of the believer expressed through poetic feeling was bound to an idealized feminine muse and convert in early evangelicalism. The way that revival poetry took up the idealized muse Rowe as the expression of heavenly music, the real language of religion, was foundational to the proliferation of pious women poets in the late eighteenth and nineteenth centuries and what would become the modern lyric.

In evangelical poetics, women often function as heralds of true outpourings of God's spirit and testify to the presence of genuine "heart religion." As was evident in *Gospel Sonnets*, the Bride of Christ served as a vehicle through which men and women understood and internalized central elements of theology, as well as inhabited pietistic practice. While Erskine does not entertain even the slightest humor toward the pagan muses, his poem nonetheless focalizes the prototypical Christian journey through the experience and words of a bride who would one day join the heavenly choir.

As such, an evangelical enjoying Erskine's plain, theologically directed poem could (and did) easily respond affectively through Rowe's devotional persona regardless of her belletristic aesthetics. For instance, Sarah Pierpont Edwards had no qualms with expressing her own awakening through the verse of both poets even though one was plain style and one was belletristic.[20] For such readers, the idealized Christian muse was the idealized revival convert who fully responded to, and then spoke, the language of heaven. In evangelical circles, Rowe became shorthand for both this affective religion and heavenly poetics. Though even Watts considered Rowe's emphasis on the espousal of the believer and Christ to be overly enthusiastic as well as an outdated trend, this was not the assessment of evangelical audiences for whom rapturous language was the heart of pietistic experience. As such, the Christian belletrist Rowe inspired revival poet-ministers who consistently modeled the ideal convert as a woman even as they aspired to write, in Watts's words, for the "plainest capacity."

Rowe was not only an evangelical muse for clergy, she was also at the head of a dissenting poetry written by women, many of whom named her as their muse, and some of whom were revivalists.[21] Given that the conservative, pro-revival minister Colman helped bring Rowe's poetry to Boston, it is not surprising that his daughter, Jane Turell, also claimed Rowe as her own muse in "To My Muse" (1735):[22] In the poem, Turell nods to both Katherine Philips (Orinda) and Rowe (Philomela) and aspires to their greatness. She specifically calls on Rowe, known as the "chaser Sappho" to lead her as she meditates on heavenly ideas that are only available to poets.[23] The poem echoes Rowe's "The Vision," in which Rowe retreats to "a shade for sacred contemplation made" and "strive[s] [her] faint, unskillful voice to raise" before receiving her dream vision. Turell asks to see the "fragrant soft retreats" to which Rowe retired, and then she will, like Rowe, devote herself to the all-consuming call of sacred poetry.[24]

Though Turell's death at a young age precluded a lengthy poetic career, other colonial women regularly took up the art of verse as both a participant in polite society and as a devotional exercise in the vein of Rowe. Because of this, it is often quite hard to tell where Christian belletrism ends and revival poetry begins, especially since a writer's or reader's relationship to revivalism often changed over time. For instance, Turell's poem "On reading the Warning by Mrs. Singer" speaks equally to Christian belletrists and revivalists:

Dauntless you undertake th' unequal strife,
And raise dead Virtue by your Verse to life.
A *Woman's* Pen strikes the curs'd *Serpents* Head,
And lays the Monster gasping, if not dead.[25]

Alluding to the Genesis story of Eve's sin in which Christ crushes the head of Satan, Turell stunningly positions women's poetry as the definitive weapon in the cosmic battle between Christ and Satan. Yet, the reader's investment in belletristic language versus an accurate description of spiritual warfare based upon biblical precedence casts the poem's meaning in slightly different shades. For the belletrist, the primary aim of this poetic power is entrance into the sociable world of belles lettres. For the revivalist, the idealized convert primarily activated verse as a ministry for women that, like other forms of the advancement of the gospel, crushed the work of Satan. Just as Rowe's pen broke open opportunities for women in letters, the idealized convert was anything but a passive persona in the hands of the colonial women poet-ministers she inspired.

In fact, Sarah Edwards's conversion narrative, which opens the first chapter of this book, uses Rowe's poetry to confirm and to undermine a minister's closing words after a moving religious meeting. After the Reverend Pomeroy spoke for nearly an hour, he concluded, "I would say more, if I could; but words were not made to express these things." Recalling Rowe's lines, Sarah swoons under her "impressions of heavenly and divine things":

More I would speak, but all my words are faint:
Celestial Love, what eloquence can paint?
No more, by mortal words, can be expressed;
But vast Eternity shall tell the rest;[26]

Rowe's lines both substantiate and undermine the minister's speech. Human words do fail for the expression of divine mysteries, as Rowe's authoritative lines affirm. Yet, poetic words partake of what Rowe called elsewhere "the mystick sound" in which God dwells, a force that continually points the listener toward the divine and eventually subsumes the believer in an eternity characterized by harmony.[27] Much like Erskine, Rowe believed that poetic words were uniquely suited to express divine things because of their heightened attention to the auditory, and Sarah's narrative corroborated that they could have a palpable effect in the world, often more than other forms of religious speech, including that of the minister.

The Spiritual Director and Woman Print Itinerant

The persona of the early poetess was not the only one crafted and utilized by revivalist women poets. A more earthly and less genteel woman poet-minister persona also became part of a Whitefieldian experience of new birth and the space opened up by Erskine's espousal poetry. Though the increased association between feeling, conversion, and verse meant that reified versions of the feminine constructed many of the contours of early evangelical theology and experience, there were also actual women, Rowe among them, who wrote with and against these abstractions.

Many nonconformist British women saw themselves as writing in the tradition of Rowe—the English Baptist Anne Steele being one of the leaders in her coterie.[28] Steele engaged the Christian belletrism of Rowe and its manuscript culture of piety and sociability and, like Rowe, published a collection of writing posthumously. A generation between Rowe and Steele, another English Baptist poet successfully pursued a very different combination of piety, style, manuscript, and print. If Rowe was the epitome of both Christian belletrism and idealized pietistic devotion, Anne Dutton was the champion of plain style biblical poetics and the ministry of spiritual direction bound to the evangelical conception of print itinerancy.[29]

An emerging conception of evangelical print grounded its ontology in the supernatural work of Christ and his ministry as an itinerant preacher to the crowds. As such, print did not conflict with enthusiastic experience and orality, but multiplied it through preaching to a larger gathering. Michael Warner argues that evangelicals normalized anonymous publics that came to define modern print through what he identifies as the unique feature of evangelicalism, their "conversionistic address to the stranger."[30] Dutton distilled this evangelical conception of print in the form of a hymn in which she eloquently equates evangelical print with the miracle of Jesus feeding the five thousand who had gathered to hear him preach.[31] Because "[m]an shall not live by bread alone, but by every word that proceedeth from the mouth of the Lord," God's message, the true sustenance of life, could go forth through the miracle of evangelical print itinerancy.

It was fitting, then, that Lewis printed the hymn in his flagship revival journal, *The Weekly History*, which was an arm of Whitefield's ministry and central to the creation of a transatlantic evangelical imaginary.[32] *The Weekly History* advertised Whitefield's travels, his favorite publications, and accounts of revivals situated as part of a monumental turning point in the course of Christian history. Evangelical journals like *The Weekly History* thus promoted awakenings and a sense of continuity between them.[33] By the spring of 1741, Lewis primarily printed epistles that were read in the London Tabernacle on designated "Letter Days," sometimes accompanied by an original hymn to punctuate the occasion.[34] Though men wrote the majority of the journal's material, two issues in the summer of 1742, which included Dutton's hymn for the press, stand out because they were almost entirely devoted to her writing.

Like many of the leading ministers, Dutton's letters and hymn were printed in the journal to extend her influence and authority in the revivals—which, for Dutton, had already extended to male ministers. In fact, at the time of the hymn's printing, Dutton (alongside Whitefield) had served a leading role in Lewis's editorial decision-making for at least a year. The first, and as of yet only, book-length study of Anne Dutton convincingly identifies her as a "transatlantic spiritual director" to the most well-known male leaders of the evangelical movement.[35] Dutton was accepted within the inner circle of a transatlantic evangelical letter-writing network, through which she instructed major and minor leaders, including John Wesley, the Countess of Huntingdon, William Seward, George Whitefield, Howell Harris, James Robe, and Phillip Doddridge.[36] This role of spiritual director or guide was not new; it appears in all branches of Christianity with various emphases according to time and place, and, as one would expect, was often exercised through letters in the eighteenth century. The most well-known woman spiritual director in early evangelicalism was Selina Hastings, the Countess of Huntingdon, who provided one-on-one counseling to Whitefield. Dutton was not far behind. Her published writings show that the advent of the print itinerant minister in early evangelicalism also fueled the spiritual director. And where formal qualifications for preachers waned, the inability to decipher between the print itinerant minister and the print itinerant spiritual director waxed.

A closer look at *The Weekly History*'s July 31, 1742, issue demonstrates this. It features two of Dutton's letters and then concludes with "An HYMN Compos'd upon copying something for the Press." Rather than report on her own spiritual state, as many laypeople did, or on revival activities, like many ministers did, Dutton offers moral and theological instruction. Doing so underscores Dutton's ministry of spiritual direction. At the same time, many Baptist preachers paired hymns with their sermons, a form that Lewis follows with Dutton's material. Whichever way readers parsed her ministry—as a separate ministry of spiritual direction or one even more closely aligned with the revival itinerant minister, verse buttressed it. That Dutton expressed the logic of evangelical print through a hymn gestures toward the ways that verse could announce and authorize the print itinerant. In fact, this partic- ular hymn later appeared on the first page of Dutton's own book to figure it as a print itinerant.[37]

The role that Dutton occupied through verse and letters was foundational for British North American revival poets, women in particular, and for trans- atlantic evangelicalism in general. She not only provided justifications for en- tering print, she also consistently published.[38] She used Christ's message of an upside-down Kingdom in which the low would come before the high to her advantage. By recognizing herself as the poor widow who, in Jesus's par- able, gives the greatest gift, she placed women's writing and print at the center of Christian worship. Whereas women's testimonies were often controlled by editors in narratives of revival, Dutton inserted herself as a theologian, poet, religious guide, and eventually an editor of her own revival journal.

The hymn she sent to *The Weekly History* encapsulates a central vision of Dutton's Christian life, which treats print as a divine calling coextensive with conversion. Men's evangelical conversion narratives often proceed in two parts: the first leads up to conversion, the second details a call to, and successful start at, ministry. Dutton's conversion narrative relates her con- version and then chronicles her call to, and fulfillment of, print itinerancy. Conflating birth, salvation from sin, and print, Dutton weaves her spiritual narrative into what might be said to be the *sine qua non* of evangelical itin- erant conversion narratives: the integration of the process of print into the stages of conversion. In a world that questioned the propriety of publishing women, Dutton constructed it as essential to the evangelical life of women ministers.

It is part three of her autobiography, which is included in the 1750 edition, that most strongly resembles male itinerant minister narratives. Like them, she details her spiritual and material struggles, both with herself and with those that persecute her, as she pursues her call to itinerancy—in her case, print itinerancy. Dutton explicitly frames the story of her spiritual journey and ministry as a grand biblicalization of her own print history that reaches from the Abrahamic covenant to the culmination of Christ's Kingdom. God confirms to her that his promise to make Abraham a father of many nations applies to her print calling as well. He assures Dutton that he will make a great nation of her, not through the miraculous healing of her barren womb as he did for Sarah, but through print.[39] Through the parables of Jesus, God reveals to her that Christ will use her books to feed thousands.[40] And, through the Book of Revelation, God reveals to her that he is in the book distribution business by equating the prophetic book and seven seals with the sending out of her books into the world.[41] By the time Dutton completed her account in 1750, it had become the story of her print ministry, which, like the apostle Paul, had been laid on her "as a necessity."[42]

Dutton did not take lightly this call from God to offer her "mite" for Christ in order that he might multiply it. Like Rowe, she was a prolific writer. Her letters, hymns, and poems were printed alone and as collections, as were her theological expositions. In all, she published around 50 distinct works.[43] Even on her deathbed, she was in the process of preparing eight more works for publication and left more than 25 volumes of manuscripts, many of which were burned upon her death.[44] She consistently preferred print to conduct her ministry. For instance, when publishing a letter in Philadelphia she declined to send it in manuscript because she thought it would be more "useful" if she sent it in print.[45] In her autobiography, she explains that her spiritual conversation with parishioners was not a useful enough ministry; instead, she receives a wider call to print ministry:

And *here* has the Lord employ'd me to write many Letters to his dear Children in divers Parts; which thro' his Blessing upon them, have refresh'd their Souls. Yea, *here* has the Lord given me a Heart, and Opportunity, an outward Call, and inward Inclination, to write and publish many little Tracts: Which thro' his gracious Assistance, and kind Providence, have been brought out, and dispersed abroad in divers Places and Nations. And blessed be his Name, HE has given me to hear, that he has us'd most of them for the Good of his People.[46]

She then immediately enacted this ministry by writing the conclusion to her narrative as a letter to Christians "for their improvement."

While scholars have begun to address the many writings that make up her successful print ministry, poetry was especially crucial to the stature she attained within revivalism. Dutton's public career as a friend, confidant, and guide to revivalist leaders, as well as an avid writer, and eventual editor of a revival magazine, all began with poetry—a theological treatise in verse with appended hymns entitled *A Narration of the Wonders of Grace* (1734).[47] For Dutton, hymns and poetry became an avenue into the male-dominated world of pastoral ministry and theological exposition.

She justified her Spirit-led endeavor as a natural progression of spiritual and physical birth. Characterizing one's poetic production in terms of motherhood was not unusual for her, or for other female poets, including the seventeenth-century colonial Puritan poet Anne Bradstreet. Elsewhere, Dutton emphasizes God as the midwife that delivers her much labored books: "Long have I look'd upon my poor *Books* as my *Children*, by which I hop'd to serve and glorify GOD. And having conceiv'd Hopes that the Lord would bring them out, and use them; when the Time drew nigh, I have *cried, travailing in Birth, and pained to be deliver'd*."[48] But while Bradstreet appealed to birth to explain the attention she dedicated to her work, Dutton makes a specific argument about genre to justify the publication of a theological treatise:

> *The Lord having (as was said) fill'd my Heart with Joy unspeakable, I sought to express my Thankfulness in some Hymn of Praise (in which I had many precious Seasons) but not finding one that did fully express the comprehensive Views I then had, I set about making one, which I chiefly designed for my own private Use. But when my Beloved had took me by the Hand, and led me to take some Turns with himself in the vast Field of boundless Grace, he there shew'd me a Variety of Wonders, which so multiplied upon me, that I soon saw I could not contract 'em into the narrow Bounds of an Hymn, and therefore gave my self further Scope.*[49]

Unlike Watts, who delineated hymns from other poetry according to their elevated language, Dutton characterizes a key difference between her hymns and poetry as a matter of length. While her long narration "in verse" retains hymnal meter (as did large portions of *Gospel Sonnets*), a second poem that immediately follows *A Narration*, entitled "A Poem on the Special Work of the Spirit in the Hearts of the Elect," employs heroic couplets. Her large collection of hymns that completes the volume employs the expected hymnal forms. All three sections display verse written in plain rather than sublime style, with a high level of biblical explication, marked by margins filled with

biblical citations. If Watts seemed keen to elevate belletristic poetry while producing hymns for the "plainest capacity," Dutton pursued the common reader
in all of her writing. Her struggle was not primarily with aesthetics at all, nor
with projecting her spiritual exercises for others to imitate, but to fulfill her
calling as a spiritual director and print itinerant. To do so, she strategically
intertwined poetry with the female body to open up a public space for female
theological and pastoral service. As already mentioned, in her autobiography
she projected the proliferation of books, not the reproduction of children, to
be the modern fulfillment of the Abrahamic covenant applied to her own life.

In her introduction quoted earlier, Dutton shows herself moving from
hymn singer to hymn writer to author of a long poem, in order to present
her work as following the natural progression of a heavenly erotic love: her
beloved takes her by the hand and leads her to the "vast Field," which results
in her experiencing multiple, uncontainable wonders. Here, Dutton toys with
the conjugal union of the Bride and Christ through an image of either orgasm
or gestational expansion to justify her book. Her union with Christ expands
the bounds of a hymn (that is, both the length of the individual verse and the
actual book binding) and demands more room to elucidate her now "comprehensive Views." The final product becomes essentially a theological exposition, much like a sermon, followed by a response in worship through hymn.

Dutton begins *A Narration* as a minister's invocation:

> The Wonders of God's ancient Love,
> Which Being had in Heaven above,
> To us they are amazing Great,
> And bear their everlasting Date.
> May we be led in th' Spirit's Light,
> To see by Faith, Love's Mystery bright,
> As in Christ's Face it radiant shines,
> In all Jehovah's vast Designs![50]

After this prayer for God's Spirit to lead the reader to see the mystery of
God's love, she turns to the language of the Song of Songs, Psalms 1, and the
English pastoral:

> Come, my Beloved, let's go forth,
> Let's take a Turn beyond the Earth,
> Into the Field of boundless Grace;

> For that's our pleasant feeding Place.
> Our Pastures are exceeding wide,
> There let us still by Faith reside;
> Whilst with their Fatness we solace
> And rest in Settlements of Grace.[51]

The invitation to come "take a Turn beyond the Earth" repeats Dutton's narrative of her inspiration for the book's composition detailed in the preface. As such, it first appears to narrativize Christ beckoning to her to come with him into the "Field *of boundless Grace.*" However, with the next lines, the speaker shifts into the voice of a fellow Bride and poet:

> There let us, as it were, entranc'd,
> Behold our glorious Lord advanc'd,
> To all those Heights of Glory, He
> With God had from Eternity.[52]

As one "entranc'd" with a vision of God's glory, the poet proceeds in six books to provide a biblical theology of each of the major branches of theology: the nature of God, Christ, the Spirit, Sin, the Church, and the return of Christ. Every page is laden with biblical citations. And though it is in verse, Dutton's title, *A Narration of the Wonders of Grace. In Verse* (1734), is a clear nod toward theological discourse that harmonized the Bible and Christianity with history. The interest in verse, following very much in the footsteps of Erskine, made her theological writing palatable. Given the direction that Dutton's writing takes in the rest of her publications—primarily spiritual direction epistles and theological expositions—her justification for taking up the form of a long poem naturally extended into prose.

Dutton became known for her censure of leading revival ministers. In his revival journal, *Christian History*, Prince published Dutton's correction to the well-known revival minister James Robe, and she entered into multiple disputes in print, one of which was with Wesley over his Arminianist doctrine, in which she engaged his hymns as part of his formal doctrine. Dutton's theological legacy as a spiritual director and print itinerant appears in a curious and poignant fashion after her death. In 1778, Dutton's *A Treatise on Justification* was reprinted in Glasgow with a large list of subscribers and plans for more posthumous works. While the prefatory materials praise early works of the writer by their titles—all of which were known to be by Anne

Dutton and some of which were designated in print as by A. Dutton—this reprinting is the first known of her works published under a male pseudonym: "the Reverend Mr. Thomas Dutton, Late Minister in London." Though little is known about the circumstances and reasons for this edition, given what is known about Dutton's ministry, at least one point should be clear: all but the name "Mr. Thomas" are true.[53]

Though only a few of Anne Dutton's works were printed in America, most of her works circulated in the colonies. Interestingly, she held America up as a land of promise for the woman print itinerant: "When some in *England* slighted my Books, and would *None of me*: God sent 'em *beyond the Seas*: Wrought Marvels by his mighty Hand, for their Disposal, and *there* he would bless them!"[54] She even characterized her husband's preaching tour of America as primarily a bookselling errand to fulfill God's promise to extend her own ministry: "So, when the *Time of the Promise drew nigh;* my dear *Husband*, having Thoughts of going into *America* on another Account, which he judg'd to be a Call of Providence, He resolv'd to print and take many of *my Books with him*. Did ever any *seek the* Lord in *vain*?[55] And, in typical Dutton fashion, the Bible contained a type for her specific spiritual struggle. She, like the woman in Revelation, flees to the American wilderness, to escape danger (Rev. xii 6.14): "*Where* my poor Books were to be *us'd*, even in the *American* Wilderness; that there I had a *Place* prepared of God, *Father, Son* and *Spirit*; that there were *Two Wings*, a Fulness of *Power*, given me to fly into *that* my Place, and that there I should be *Nourish'd* from the Face of the Serpent; who by his Rage forc'd me out of *England*."[56] Ultimately, the woman, who is the Church, will not be destroyed. And for Dutton, neither will the woman print itinerant.

After the publication of Dutton's account, more evangelical women in the colonies were moved to work for the good of souls not only in manuscript but also through print ministry. For a number of female evangelical ministers, poetry was a gateway to, or a confirmation of, authority. This can be detected in recurring motifs, for instance, women whose verse could be mistaken for Watts's poetry, such as such Jemima Wilkinson and Martha Brewster. Additionally, poetry, often appended to the end of a woman's life story, could attest to her true piety and blessed ministry. And perhaps most notable, the colonial evangelical lay theologian and revival leader Sarah Osborn, whose pseudonym "a gentlewoman in Rhode-Island" echoed Dutton's "a gentlewoman in the country," was memorialized as a prolific devotional poet in her later years by her minister, who included one of her poems at the end of her *Memoirs*. Even earlier, in the 1740s a local Boston woman took on the roles that Anne Dutton and Elizabeth Rowe had carved out in the culture of revivalism.

"A New England Lady" as the Idealized Convert and Itinerant's Guide

At the same time that the Scottish *Gospel Sonnets* (1740) debuted in the British North American colonies in tandem with a momentous Whitefield tour, Rowe's writings circulated prolifically, and Dutton aggressively set her sights on America, Boston poets took up their pens in response to transatlantic and local itinerant preachers. Publishing in newspapers, broadsides, books, and revival magazines, and circulating in manuscript, poets in the colonies and abroad promoted revival leaders, invited crowds to gather, encouraged acts of charity and piety, and engaged in apologetics. Boston attracted the leading itinerant ministers during the 1740s, including George Whitefield, Gilbert Tennent, and James Davenport, all of whom inspired poetic productions. Transatlantic revival poetry blossomed with intensity in the 1740s; the "American Wilderness" to which Dutton's books and letters traveled was flush with verse. One of the most well-known of these colonial evangelical poets was Sarah Parsons Moorhead of Boston, who became a public voice for promoting and spiritually directing the burgeoning revivals.[57]

Sarah Moorhead was respected in her own right as a poet and artist, though today she is usually remembered as the wife of Boston's Scots-Irish Presbyterian minister John Moorhead. Among contemporary scholars, she is most often mentioned in relation to the poetry of Phillis Wheatley, who likely wrote a poem dedicated to the artist Scipio Moorhead, Sarah's slave and art student, and dedicated an elegy to Mary Moorhead, Sarah and John's daughter, upon John's death. The English lady, as her biographers call her, married John soon after he immigrated to Boston and established the Church of the Presbyterian Strangers.[58] She and her husband praised Whitefield and the awakenings that followed and firmly promoted orthodox Calvinism along with sucession from the Church of Scotland. Though often overlooked in histories of revivalism in New England, Sarah and John were central to its cultivation both at home and abroad.[59]

Reverend John Moorhead exchanged letters with several key figures in the new evangelical movement, including the primary facilitator of revivalist news via manuscript in New England, Reverend Eleazar Wheelock, as well as the engine of transatlantic revivalist book circulation, the Scottish Reverend John Erskine.[60] In one of John Moorhead's letters published in *The Weekly History* (1742), he boasts to "his Friend near Glasgow," Ralph Erskine, that his own ecstatic congregation is the most "remarkably favour'd of God" in New England and that Whitefield never "saw God so victorious by his Grace as he has been since [Whitefield] left this Land." He highlights the ecstatic experiences of "Divine Love" full of "flowing Tears" and "heaven-born Language" that come from "*Baptists, Episcopalians, Papists, Independents, Pagans, Negroes, Quakers,* &c old Sinners of sixty Year and upwards" and drown out his own preaching. Refusing to tone down his descriptions of what nervous Boston ministers considered "unruly" behavior, Moorhead predicts that Whitefield's spectacular visit is only the beginning of God's work.[61] Even in the face of intense backlash by religious leaders and the public, John Moorhead remained an adamant supporter of pietistic awakening in its various expressions of "Divine Raptures," as well as a minister known for his unwavering polemics.[62]

But it was another Scots-Irish minister who most famously and controversially tended the blaze of revival immediately after Whitefield returned to England in early 1741. The itinerant minister Gilbert Tennent, who had already traveled throughout the Middle Colonies, first with the Dutch Reformed minister Theodorus Frelinghusen and then with George Whitefield during his dramatic American tour, drew large crowds to his fiery sermons that earned him the nickname "Son of Thunder." One sermon that Tennent preached and then published resulted in his eventual expulsion from, and the split of, the first (and as of then only) Presbyterian Synod in the colonies. In *The Danger of an Unconverted Ministry* (1740), Tennent argued that conversion was a necessary requirement for a legitimate Christian minister and that church members should only hire converted ministers and even leave congregations led by unconverted ministers.[63] This, of course, entailed that laypeople judge whether or not their minister exhibited sufficient signs of a pietistic conversion. Not surprisingly, a torrent of polemical print ensued.

While Sarah Moorhead's bellicose husband instigated a vicious newspaper war in Boston over ministerial qualifications, she published at least three poems between 1741 and 1745, each dedicated to a famous itinerant— Gilbert Tennent, James Davenport, and George Whitefield—all of whom share the title for the most appearances in colonial newspapers.[64] Her skilled verse placed her in stark contrast to her husband, whom critics routinely lambasted as illiterate. Crafting a sophisticated poetic persona that drew on elements found in both Rowe's and Dutton's verse, Sarah Moorhead attempted to persuade the community to acknowledge and to enable the wonderful work of God among them. Sarah Moorhead's public encouragement of, and instruction to, popular itinerants should be understood as part of a significant, transatlantic practice within revivalism whereupon certain women not only embodied the ideal of affective conversion, they also acted as authoritative poet-ministers.

Sarah Moorhead's first known appearance in print amounted to a decisive step into the fray. The issue of itinerancy—whose right it was to preach to which congregants—was already a contentious issue. Her poem, "To the Rev. Mr. GILBERT TENNENT, upon Hearing him display both the Terrors of the Law and blessed Invitations of the Gospel, to awaken Sinners, and comfort Saints" (1741), attempts to steer opinion on both sides of the hotly contested issues of itinerancy and unconverted ministers that had become focalized through Tennent.[65]

With the same striking fervor as the itinerant Tennent, Moorhead slides between several addressees—a revival crowd, Tennent, herself, God, scoffers, and saints—accompanied by specific spiritual directives for each. With the first lines, Moorhead assembles a revival crowd by directing their sight and hearing toward Tennent's awesome performance:

> S E E Heaven-born TENNENT from Mount *Sinai* flies,
> With flaming Targets, light'ning in his Eyes!
> Hear him, with bless'd Experience, tell,
> The Law can do no more than doom to Hell!
> He rends the Cov'ring off th' infernal Pit,
> Lest tho'tless Souls, securely, drop in it.[66]

Speaking for and in front of the crowd, Moorhead then officially welcomes Tennent, "Welcome, dear thund'ring Herald of the Lord," blesses his ministry, "GOD prosper in thy Hand the flaming Sword," and counsels him, "O dear sacred *Tennent*, pray beware, / Lest too much Terror prove to some a Snare." She charges him with a specific duty in the performance of his ministry: he must understand the distinction between hardened sinners and frightened sheep in order to utilize the appropriate rhetoric for each. Though this moment has sometimes been offered as evidence for Moorhead's general criticism of the revivals, she clearly positions herself as a friend and spiritual guide of the awakening and its itinerants. In fact, her specific admonishment for Tennent to consider his rhetoric's effect on frightened lambs is the same that Anne Dutton had given to Howell Harris, the leader of awakenings in Wales.

After addressing the crowd she has called forth, Moorhead turns to address herself and then God. She exclaims:

> O! that I could his Vertues live and speak;
> For GOD couragious, to his Foes is meek.
> Tho' Demons rage, when ere he comes in Sight,
> CHRIST's Lambs surround his Feet, with bless'd Delight;
> Repeat the awful Musick of his Tongue,
> And strike with Pleasure all the list'ning Throng.
> Let cursed Scoffers now with Anguish mourn,
> Alas! from us he goes; but ah! from you he's torn.[67]

Rather than "write or speak" the unwelcomed news, she will "live and speak" his virtues. She moves from a moment that calls attention to her status as the writer of the poem to her status as the performer of its actions. Here, at the center of the poem, Moorhead pivots from instructing Tennent about his rhetoric directed at the crowds to taking up the thundering itinerant's voice by warning scoffers herself. Like the prophet Moses (to whom she compares Tennent in the first lines of the poem), she declares the dire consequences of turning away from God's messenger, as well as the pleasure of hearing the prophetic words, which now include her poem. By turning to an address between herself and God that displays her heartfelt piety induced by the itinerant, she becomes the ideal convert afforded with authority to speak to the crowds.

While the poem begins by counseling Tennent on gentler methods of conversion, a correction that conservative ministers could applaud, it ends with Moorhead repeating "the awful Musick of his Tongue" and calling down curses on those who would scoff at God and Tennent. In Moorhead's poetic enactment of Tennent's ministry, the scoffers suffer anguish because Tennent, an agent of God's grace, is "torn" from them and, rather than salvation, they are struck "with Blindness, or with Fear." Moorhead is able to gather the crowd together with the first word of the poem that demands they "S E E" Tennent and then to disperse it when she ends the poem by calling down blindness on his enemies. The poem gathers to a crescendo as the poet, now surely poet-minister, summons the angels and sends Tennent forth with a thundering benediction: "O now, bless'd Champion! let thy Courage raise, / Thou'rt safe in CHRIST, tho' many Hells should blaze." At the same time, Moorhead declares Tennent's departure a "Resurrection Day," "a glorious Spring of blooming Joy, / When Birds of Paradice their Tongues imploy."[68] Saints rejoice at the itinerant's departure because it signals the commencement of their own ministries, which, in the hands of Moorhead, is the day of the poet to sing the praises of God. Moorhead's poem on Tennent demonstrates her assertive use of the spiritual director persona, a role that is predicated, as the title indicates, on her representation of herself as a convert affected by hearing the itinerant preach. It is this representation of herself as an idealized female convert that launches her into the practice of a woman poet-minister.

Moorhead's next known published poem came at another crucial moment for the development of evangelicalism in the colonies and successfully extended her role as a spiritual director to itinerants. Religious historians regularly point to the Long Island minister James Davenport for bringing to a crescendo the brooding crisis within revivalism over unconverted ministers and disorderly worship.[69] Taking his cue from Tennent, Davenport established his authority to itinerate in other ministers' parishes according to their salvific status. He became controversial for publicly proclaiming specific ministers unconverted and for leading enthusiastic gatherings in which he paraded with believers through the streets, ecstatically singing original hymns and burning religious books along with his clothes.

Davenport provoked a flurry of pro- and anti-revivalist writings in 1741 and 1742. Public letters flew back and forth between Davenport's defenders, various skeptics, and moderate revivalists. Already expelled from his birth state of Connecticut, Davenport soon found himself summoned before Boston's ministerial association in 1742, banned from the city's pulpits, and declared insane. Fourteen Boston-area clergy, including moderate revivalists like Prince, signed the public declaration against him. The next year would see the now famous "press war" between the Reverends Jonathan Edwards and Charles Chauncy and an influx of anti-revivalist print, which exceeded the number of pro-revivalist publications for the first time.[70] The future of revivalism suddenly became ambiguous. Amid the slew of clergy-authored sermons, letters, declarations, and treatises that attacked and defended revival practices and leaders, Sarah Moorhead again intervened with verse.

But this time her persona and poetic style changed to address the shift in the tempo and tenor of the revivals.

Moorhead's poem "To the Reverend Mr. *James Davenport* on his Departure from *Boston*, By Way of a Dream" (1742) employs both the persona of the spiritual director and the persona of the idealized muse of Christian belletrism to navigate effectively the turbulent and growing split in New England evangelicalism. While the poem expresses criticisms of Davenport, they are offered, as in her Tennent poem, in the spirit of spiritual direction in order to keep the momentum of revival alive. Moorhead's eight-page broadside, which also includes a poem correcting the controversial Rev. Andrew Crosswell, extended an olive branch to the ministerial community of Boston who had shut their pulpits to Davenport by the wife of a minister whose pulpit remained stubbornly open to him.[71]

Epistles to ministers served as the bulk of printed matter in Boston surrounding the controversies, and few (if any) women claimed to author them. Moorhead perceived that the elevated status of the epistle in transatlantic revival culture presented an opportunity for women because of its natural association with personal, domestic space, and she entered the clergy-dominated conversation by couching her poem as a personal letter from "a Female Friend," while simultaneously titling the poem like the other public attacks and defenses. The Moorheads were strong supporters of the Reverend Eleazar Wheelock's Indian School (later Dartmouth), and Wheelock's sister was Davenport's wife. Sarah Moorhead's authorial identification as "a female friend" was, in fact, pointedly true. This relational identification was a common strategy for women in eighteenth-century print, including Rowe and Dutton. Moorhead's use of both poetry and the public epistle to guide revival ministers resembles the practice of Dutton, whose public ministerial voice combined both forms. At the same time, Moorhead's subtitle—"by Way of a DREAM"—combined with the first line of the poem—"ASSIST celestial Powers my grieved Heart"—clearly situates her broadside within the tradition of Rowe's sacred soliloquies, which were often written in the form of a letter to a friend, and employed similar belletristic conventions, such as invocations to heavenly beings. These familial, ecclesiastical, and poetic kinships confirmed Sarah Moorhead's authority to intervene on behalf of Davenport to calm the Boston clergy who had turned against him.

Moorhead's Davenport poem, which sought to mitigate the rift in the revival community, was a fitting antidote to the strife-inducing poetry printed by Rogers and Fowle. Knowing that Davenport's street singing had come to epitomize his unruly enthusiasm, Rogers and Fowle issued the broadside "Rev'd Mr. *Davenport's* Song" (1742) to advertise publications on both sides of the controversy. In contrast, Charles Harrison, who specialized in works that cultivated revival piety and steadfastly avoided controversial apologetics, printed Moorhead's poem. Her work, though appearing less polemical, positioned itself as a kinder alternative to the anonymous Rogers and Fowle broadside, "A Poem Occasioned by the spreading in this Province the Result of a *Consociation* in a Neighborhood Government" (1742), which defended Davenport's right to preach in Boston with warring rhetoric. Echoing some of the same sentiments as this anonymous poet, such as responding with wonder rather than criticism to the unusual bodily signs that accompanied the revival, Moorhead nevertheless spends more energy diffusing the specter of Davenport and the controversy he represents than magnifying it.

She does this by resting strategically above the fray—offering a repentant Davenport to conservative revivalists in exchange for a renewed ecumenical charity that will ensure that "GOD's glorious Work, which sweetly did arise, / By this unguarded sad Imprudence [will not die]."[72] She carves out a space for herself to directly counsel the Boston ministers and community through a poetic dream in which she stages Davenport's public recantation of his excesses and his subsequent restoration to the fellowship of saints. Dreams in Christian pietistic literature have a long history, and both Rowe and Dutton used them. But dreams and visions could also invoke revivalist excess, something that many ministers tried to tame in their public presentation of special outpourings in order to eliminate criticism. Dreams and visions by female converts were especially subject to intense scrutiny and were often excised from testimonies.[73] Sarah Moorhead's specific employment of a dream performs the same rhetorical work as these types of ministerial excisions because her dream contains, rather than encourages, Davenport's feminized visions and excesses. That her vision eventually came true when Davenport finally recanted his words and actions surely helped to solidify her authority as a respected poet-minister.

The poem proceeds quickly from an invocation to God to an evenhanded response to the controversy embroiling Boston:

> ASSIST celestial Powers my grieved Heart,
> For Love and Sorrow bear an equal Part;
> I love the Zeal that fires good DAVENPORT's Breast,
> But his harsh Censures give my Soul no rest;[74]

Moorhead performs equally her love for Davenport and her respect for the ministers he has accused of being unconverted. Rather than situate herself as the fully entranced listener of Davenport's sermons, she presents her heart as restlessly troubled by his words.

To escape the undue stress the controversy has placed on her mind, the poet seeks to fall asleep:

> But as these Thoughts my troubled Mind opprest,
> *Sleep* sweet Cessation instantly refresh'd,
> My Tumults calm, and new-born Pleasure rise,
> A charming VISION swims before my Eyes.[75]

It is then that Moorhead sees a vision—avoiding the form of an ecstatic vision, in which people would testify that they were not sure if they were awake or asleep. Instead of an ecstatic vision, Moorhead portrays the dream in the elevated language of the Christian belletrists, reminiscent of Rowe's description of the bower in her poem "The Vision." "The sacred Man is to his Shade convey'd" under "beauteous Arches" filled with "pretty Birds," calming spices, and "gilded Clouds" that "*Ambrosia* Drops distill." Within this classical bowers scene, the Angels guard Davenport's bed and "*gentle Checks . . . whisper in his Head*."[76]

After offering the "Favorite of Heaven" gentle corrections, Moorhead then records the scene of Davenport's repentance and his integration back into the Christian community. Importantly, she emphasizes his return to song, and his ordained role. He "weeping sweetly sings," speaks in "lovely Language," and even angels "bear his mournful Song."[77] When the Revs. Colman and Sewell, two ministers he accused of being unconverted, welcome him back into communion, they do so by "twist[ing] up a Lawrel for his sacred Head." With the forgiveness of God and community, Davenport becomes once again "fill[ed] with Raptures," this time crowned as a poet.[78]

Moorhead directs Davenport's apologies to Colman and Sewell not only to counteract the specificity of the charges he laid on the Boston clergy, but also to reaffirm the religious and poetic expectations of genteel society. These more cosmopolitan ministers rejected visions and prophesies as enthusiasm; yet, their cultivated connections to the genteel society of London meant that they admired the religious sublime that transformed ecstasy into a poetic device.[79] Moorhead's verse, then, can totter successfully between poetic enthusiasm and the enthusiast's poetry. By drawing on Rowe's Christian belletrism,

Moorhead attempts to pacify conservative revival supporters like Revs. Mather Byles and Colman, who were invested in what Shields describes as "polite Christianity." Davenport's freakish and uncivilized oral performances can be remedied through printed verse—a form that Shields argues can effectively mediate religious enthusiasm and polite society.[80] However, unlike advocates of polite Christianity, which included the editor of Boston's revival magazine, Moorhead uses print, like Whitefield, Dutton, and other radical revivalists, as a tool to produce more enthusiastic religion.

Moorhead establishes a voice of reasonable authority and promotes a moderate response to revivalism through verse. Her prosodic skill, vocabulary, and fecund dream vision answer any scoffer who would cast her aside as an unlearned revivalist, as they did her husband.[81] John Moorhead was openly mocked in the local paper for his illiterate, nonsensical writing and enshrined in a much circulated manuscript poem as a man that will never "preach common Sense."[82] Aware that the "genius of tavern wit," the distiller Joseph Green, mercilessly caricatured revivalists, Sarah Moorhead targets him when she laments that Davenport's censure of Boston ministers has turned "conversion" into "the Drunkard's Song."[83] Green had recently published "Hail! D----p--t of wondrous fame" in the *Boston Weekly Post-Boy*, in which he ridicules Davenport's public singing by turning it into a sexually explicit tavern song, and Green's manuscript poetry was no different.[84] Of particular concern to a female revival poet, Green singled out the unruly mouths that revival song loosed: "Sisters, no longer mind old *Paul*, / To teach, we know you have a Call."[85] In the face of such criticisms, Moorhead's elevated poetics worked to prop up a reasonable dream vision—one that established a strong persona for correcting, teaching, and directing the larger ecumenical community of revivalists.

Because Moorhead positions herself as inspired by the sermons the controversial Davenport and Croswell preached, as well as by the established ministers whom they questioned, she is able to orient herself as a spiritual director and prophetic peacemaker. Like the signed declaration by 13 Boston area clergy condemning Davenport, Moorhead corrects him in the name of protecting and continuing the special work of God. Yet, though she rhetorically disperses the heated emotion surrounding Davenport, she also resuscitates him as a feminized ideal convert who has heeded her correction. At the same time that she describes Davenport as a feminine "fainting Hero" blushing with sorrow, the poet chides those that persecuted him for "dar[ing to]. . . appear . . . in . . . Cob-webb Garment[s]" of their own morality and urges them to "repent" and "reform."[86] Taking up Davenport's own rhetoric, Moorhead, the poet-minister, disarms Davenport in order to move him to repentance and restore him again to the power of his ministry through her verse exhortation.

The poem affords emotional satisfaction and spiritual redirection that comes through imagining his repentance and reintegration into community rather than simply calling for it. Much like the visually rich revivalist sermons that heated the affections, Moorhead employs a poetic vision to move her readers into the act of reconciliation. Like other revival poets, she believed that poetry could change people and rekindle the flames of the Spirit. Or, in Jane Turell's words, a woman's pen could definitively crush Satan's work. Most importantly, the poem can speak with two tongues. Moorhead's belletristic style has the potential to neutralize embodied religious enthusiasm for those readers invested in polite Christianity, while at the same time the healing words of the poet-minister can restore and spread affective religion for those readers invested in a radical piety.[87] In fact, Rev. Prince would attempt to do something quite similar with his revival magazine, *The Christian History*, though working toward conservative ends.

In Moorhead, we see how poetry enabled colonial women to enter crucial religious controversies, negotiating moderate and conservative positions to gain a ministerial voice of their own. Moorhead entered print with the appropriate moderate garb to correct a radical evangelical who upset the social order, while at the same time she exercised a religious authority supported by the radical wing she seemed to rebuke. Fixing herself as the local minister who traditionally exhorted his flock and continued the revival upon the itinerant's exit, Moorhead reveals how revival poetry could be a means to a ministerial voice within evangelical print culture. Actively using poetry to create a vibrant and unified religious community, Moorhead intercedes to mend the painful rifts created by ministers, including her controversial husband. Her interventions in the revival controversies of Boston provide an early example of a colonial woman authoritatively addressing key revival leaders and the community through poetry.

When her next known published poem appeared, she boldly exercised her well-worn role as an idealized convert and a spiritual director. The subtitle of the poem positions her as a "Gentlewoman" in Boston who "composed upon hearing [Whitefield] preach with so much Flame the Truths of the blessed Gospel of the Son of God" (Figure 2.1). Moorhead commences the poem with the authority of a minister who can open the region to the famous itinerant at the very moment in which his presence in New England pulpits became highly contested: "Welcome dear *Whitefield* to these joyful Coasts; / Couragious Soldier of the GOD OF HOSTS, / The Gospel Trump, seraphick Herald, sound: / The *Heavens* applaud; the *Earth* with Joy resounds."[88] She goes on to commission Whitefield's work and send him forth, to

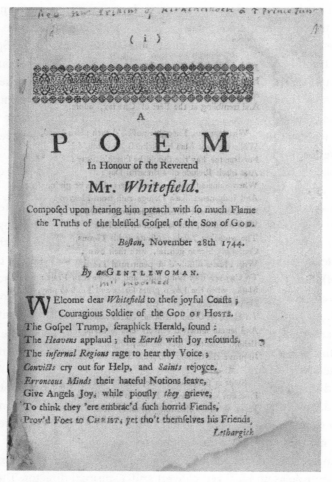

Figure 2.1. Sarah Moorhead's poem welcoming George Whitefield to Boston. Ascribed to the hand of Thomas Prince, Sr., to Sarah Moorhead and inscribed: "Rev Mr [John] Erskine of Kirkintilloch [Scotland] à T[homas] Prince Junr."

invite sinners to repent, to pray for Whitefield's bodily healing, to counsel minister's on their spiritual zeal and rhetoric, and to ask God to bless her own ministry. She then ends the poem with the same desire she expressed in her Tennent, Davenport, and Croswell poems—the expansion and triumph of revival: "Then shall the Doves unto their Windows flock, / And scoffing Rebels be asham'd to mock."[89]

Moorhead's Whitefield poem, noted by archivists to have once been part of a larger work, was likely produced for a community that respected Moorhead's role as an ideal convert and a spiritual director. Because Thomas Prince, Jr., and John Erskine exchanged "Mrs. Moorhed's" poem, it has been suggested that the poem may have been part of a work published in Scotland.[90] However, the content of the poem, the material features of the extant copies, and the advertisement for the work itself all point in a different direction. According to an advertisement for the poem in the *Boston Weekly News-Letter*, the poem was printed as a stand-alone broadside and for sale by Kneeland and Green in Boston. The material condition and markings on the extant copies of the poem reveal that they were bound with other titles sometime after publication.[91] While it cannot be definitively determined when and from what the poem was disbanded, the context of its publication points toward the distinct possibility that it was expected to be collected with other revival pamphlets, especially since Kneeland and Green printed the poem paginated by roman numerals, which would be standard for a preface rather than a stand-alone pamphlet.[92] Provocatively, the particular advertisement for Moorhead's poem in the *Boston Weekly News-Letter* was listed alongside two advertisements for anti-Whitefield pamphlets. These two pamphlets addressed the same controversy that Moorhead did, but from the opposite side.

There was another pamphlet published at the same time by the same publisher in relation to the same controversy that was on the same side as Moorhead. Though they were not bound together by the printer, they nonetheless traveled together. Moorhead's position as a poet-minister who directed itinerants and mediated controversies placed her poem as a kind of prologue to *Invitations to the Reverend Mr. Whitefield, from the Eastern Consociation of the County of Fairfield* (1745). The pamphlet was one of many printed that year in defense of closing or opening pulpits to Whitefield. Endorsed by a coalition of Connecticut ministers in support of Whitefield's ministry, it features two letters—a letter written to Whitefield during his 1740 visit to invite him to several Connecticut churches, and a letter from

Samuel Cooke of Connecticut to "a Minister in Boston" "concerning the former Success of Mr. Whitefield's Ministry there." Though the Boston minister is not named, the letter describes him as a "Brother and Companion in Tribulation" of whom Cooke is "heartily glad to hear from Time to Time the Encouragement [he] give[s] to the Labours of that eminent Man of God, the dear Mr. *Whitefield*; notwithstanding the united Attempts of Multitudes in the Country to stop his Mouth."[93] The letter clearly aligns with the pro-revivalists in Boston and uses Whitefield's recent profitable visit there as an argument for opening their Connecticut pulpits to him. As Cooke laments:

> What affects me (I think) with the most pinching Sorrow, is the awful Declension of Religion among us. I have no sufficient Grounds to think there has been more than one Instance of saving Conversion in my Congregation within the Space of a Year last past; and I know of none lately brought under deep Conviction. As for those hopefully converted in the late BLESSED Day never to be forgotten, the greater Part by far do appear to this Day to be, what I hoped they were, *Israelites indeed.*[94]

While mourning the lack of recent conversions, Cooke holds up the past revival and confirms the validity of its lasting effect on the people. They are exemplary converts, indeed.

As the verse counterpart to this pamphlet, Moorhead's poem testifies to Whitefield's recent efficacious ministry in Boston during which he awakened her "lethargick" soul. Because the poem also functions as a formal invitation to Whitefield, it participates in the specific ministerial discourse of the pamphlet—as did her Davenport poem among the slew of ministers publishing epistles. While the poem on Whitefield may at first appear less polemical than her previous poems, in the context of a statement by *The Eastern Consociation of the County of Fairfield*, Moorhead has clearly been recognized and endorsed as a spokesperson for the more radical leaning pro-revivalists in the continuing controversy over itinerancy and unconverted ministers. That Prince and John Erskine exchanged Moorhead's Whitefield poem during a period in which Prince was actively trying to manage the revivals and purge them of enthusiasm and social disorder is extraordinary. Prince supported the freedom to itinerate based on his cosmopolitan ideas of the value of various opinions. Perhaps Prince hoped Erskine would have it published; perhaps it was also published in the Scottish revival journal whose extant copies show an active engagement with a shared interest of the

Moorheads, Indian missions. Whatever the exact circumstances, the poem clearly held the attention not only of the Boston pamphlet readers, but also of two of the leading facilitators of evangelical print culture on both sides of the Atlantic.

This would not be the only time—or most likely even the first time—a Moorhead poem served as the honorary introduction to a minister's work and was recognized by transatlantic revival leaders. Sarah Moorhead did more to heal Boston's revival-torn community and promote awakenings at home and abroad than has been recognized. Just as she did not shy away from her role as promoter and guide in New England, Moorhead did not deflect recognition from the most revered transatlantic ministers. By 1762, at the very latest, she was known in print among evangelicals abroad because her verse itinerated alongside Ralph Erskine's throughout the evangelical world. Sarah Moorhead was "a Lady in New England"[95] (Figure 2.2). Her dedicatory poem that graced the front of *Gospel Sonnets* easily makes it one of the most extensively printed poems by a British North American evangelical woman in the eighteenth century. The attribution of the poem to Sarah Moorhead not only reveals the reach of her verse ministry through the personae of the ideal convert and spiritual director, it also provides a glimpse into Moorhead's conception of the poet-minister.

The poem's status as the dedicatory verse for the immensely influential revival poem marks an important shift in pietistic poetry in the colonies and the concept of a poet-minister. Michael Wigglesworth's bestselling poem *The Day of Doom* (1666) remained a staple of British North American Christian catechism and piety throughout the eighteenth century. It is quite easy to see how it participated in an evangelical poetic milieu that depended on an affect induced by imagery, rhyme, and the repeated urgency of true salvation. *The Day of Doom* and *Gospel Sonnets* were supporting counterparts: one the fiery sermon; the other the conversionistic response. But the manner in which the two texts were introduced by poets separated by approximately a century reveals a stark contrast in the reception of the idea of the poet-minister.

The prefatory poem to *The Day of Doom*, "On the following Work, and Its Author," by John Mitchell, is primarily an apology for a sermonic poem, while "a Lady's" verse, "A POEM, dedicated to the Reverend Mr RALPH ERSKINE," is essentially an exemplum for effective verse ministry. Mitchell attests to the value of Wigglesworth's "costly Verse" and "laborious Rymes" that are Christian because they offer up truths rather than fables. Importantly,

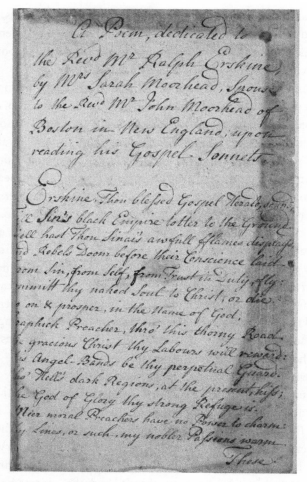

Figure 2.2. Henry Erskine, Ralph Erskine's eldest son, copied the dedicatory poem into the front of his volume of *Gospel Sonnets* and identified its author: "A Poem, dedicated to the Revd Mr Ralph Erskine, by Mrs Sarah Moorhead, Spouse to the Revd Mr John Moorhead of Boston in New England, upon reading his Gospel Sonnets."

Department of Rare Books and Special Collections, Princeton University Library.

the poem begins with a justification for sermonic poetry by paraphrasing George Herbert, a favorite of later revival poets:

> A Verse may find him who a Sermon flies,
> Saith *Herbert* well. Great Truths to dress in Meeter;
> Becomes a Preacher, who Mens Souls do prize,
> That Truth in Sugar roll'd may taste the sweeter,
>   No Cost too great, no Care too curious is
>   To set forth Truth, and win mens Souls to bliss.[96]

Mitchell's poem is defensive in large part because of Wigglesworth's seventeenth-century parishioners' criticism of their ailing minister for his absence from the physical pulpit. But this personal context is not the only reason. There is also an element of novelty to the idea of a bona fide minister absent from the local pulpit and instead acting primarily through verse. By the time that Moorhead introduced *Gospel Sonnets*, evangelicals promoted the practice of itinerant ministry, revered the print itinerant as part of the new dispensation of God's work, and associated the preaching of God's word and its fruitful reception with the God-given language of poetry. Thus, her poem begins by forcefully invoking the poet, or "seraphic preacher" to do his heavenly work, "E R S K I N E, thou blessed herald sound," and then enacting the effects of his poem through an enthusiastic awakening.

Yet, even as "a Lady" performs the beloved's part, crying out, "'Tis he hath charm'd my soul and won my heart," she also passes judgment on unawakened ministers and on the value of the poem:

> Mere moral preachers have no power to charm,
> Thy lines are such my nobler passions warm;
> These glorious truths have set my soul on fire,
> And while I read, I'm love and pure desire.[97]

Her experience testifies to the salvific status of the minister—one who is truly saved and can spread this affective salvation, rather than one who merely preaches morality. Additionally, she summons forth more revival poets: "May more like you be rais'd." This line must be read in the context of a heightened emphasis on conversion. To be a legitimate evangelical minister, one must be truly converted. This display of affect is one of the most important aspects of the evangelical movement for women because it prioritizes conversion over other qualifications for ministry. "A Lady's" performance, which embodies the ideal evangelical conversion, qualifies her to "be rais'd" into a verse ministry. The poem seamlessly performs both at once.

The tone of this poem and its emphasis between "mere moral preachers" and true ministers of affective religion depart from Moorhead's more subtle critique in her Davenport poem. If one doubted her strategic rhetorical performance in the Davenport broadside, this verse confirms it. It might have been written before the controversy over converted ministers blew up in Boston, but the fact that her passionate rebuke to "mere moral preachers" appears while writing so affectionately about reading Erskine points to a more fruitful possibility: the difference that she presses in the Erskine poem is not primarily between converted and unconverted ministers per se but a direct judgment on their chosen medium.[98] Moorhead is quite literally claiming that the best preacher of true heart religion is none other than the poet. Or, as she wrote in her Tennent poem, the one who speaks the "awful Musick of his Tongue."[99]

Moorhead's sense that verse was essential to evangelism and the profitable movement of God's spirit coalesced much earlier than the 1762 publication of her poem in *Gospel Sonnets*. Moorhead's poem circulated in manuscript under her own name decades before it appeared in print. It might well be her earliest extant poem—one that established her persona as the ideal convert and propelled her ministry of spiritual direction. Though Ralph Erskine's eldest son Henry Erskine did not date Moorhead's poem, he copied it into the front of a 1734 edition of *Gospel Sonnet* that he inscribed as "his book" on "July 19, 1740." At this point in his life he had already become a member of a literary society at the University of Edinburgh, was in the midst of his theological studies, and, in two years, would be ordained to preach. Given his interest in the Whitefieldian revivals, and the importance of his father's poetry in the colonial awakenings, he may well have transcribed Moorhead's poem in 1740. If this was the case, Moorhead's poem circulated in manuscript with her name attached to it more than two decades before it appeared in print. Given the syncing of many of her other poems with the movement of famous itinerants, it would make sense that she penned it in response to Franklin's 1740 edition of *Gospel Sonnets*, which hailed Whitefield's groundbreaking tour of the colonies. The manuscript poem could have easily reached Ralph and Henry Erskine directly through the Moorheads or indirectly through John Erskine.[100] In this case, *Gospel Sonnets* would have announced Whitefield's arrival to the colonies, but Moorhead's poem would have officially welcomed him.

Though the year in which Sarah Moorhead's poem on Ralph Erskine began circulating cannot be certain, it was definitely well known 11 years before its Edinburgh publication. In July 1751, during Whitefield's fourth colonial visit, the poem "*The* Spouse of CHRIST *returning to her first Love. An Hymn compos'd* (as 'tis tho't) by a LADY in *New-England*" appeared in *The Boston Gazette*. The title (Spouse of Christ) and pseudonym (Lady in New England) clearly reference Moorhead's persona as the idealized convert of Ralph Erskine's *Gospel Sonnets*. The content of the poem also references her poem on *Gospel Sonnets* as representative of "the golden Days, / When JESUS tun'd [her] cheerful Lays" and she experienced a "glowing . . . Heart" that neither "Art nor Language could impart." The poem narrates Moorhead's fall from sacred poetry to "trifling Toys" and "empty Sounds." She expresses her deep desire for reunion with Christ's grace and to "resume the cheerful *Lyre*" with "all [her] Soul." The poem does not specify the exact diversion from sacred poetry—perhaps too much social bantering and pleasure, perhaps something more serious—but stakes a public return to her sacred post. As the embodiment of the revival convert, the poem also functions as a call for her community to again attune their ears to heavenly sounds and, as Erskine's poem encouraged, "imitate the heavenly Choir."[101]

Moorhead's desire to "resume the cheerful *Lyre*" in the 1750s attracted the attention of college bards who extended the poetic banter of Joseph Green and Mather Byles to a younger generation of wits. Nathan Fiske, who kept a collection of his Harvard classmates's poetry, copied the poem "Verses made by a Woman in Bedlam" in the early 1750s.[102] This, it turns out, was a reference to Sarah Moorhead. The poem is part of a three-part series with the second verse entitled "J—M—'s Soliloquy" in which the satirist declares John Moorhead's behavior to be that of a "Bedlamite" and thereby confirms that the actual "Woman in Bedlam" of the first poem is Moorhead's wife—"A Lady in New-England." "J—M—'s Soliloquy" and the final poem in the series, "Muse," also appear in another fellow student's commonplace book, but as a satire of their college tutor, not Moorhead (Figures 2.3, 2.4). It appears that the final two parts were interchangeable with whomever became the target of their pranks and antics. The up and coming reigning wit of Boston, Benjamin Church, attributes the poem series to Samuel Quincy in his journal, but it may have been another poet who adapted it to John Moorhead in order to display his skill and style as a budding member of Boston's belletristic

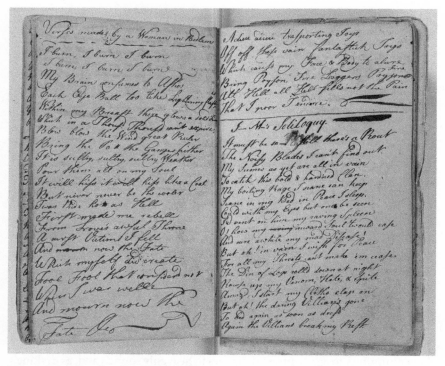

Figure 2.3. Parody of Sarah Moorhead copied in a notebook of Nathan Fiske. American Antiquarian Society.

societies.[103] Lambasting Sarah Moorhead was a sure way for the young poet to assert his poetic chops in what was a long-running feud between old light belletristic bards and the leading lady of Boston's revival verse.

Sarah Moorhead's inclusion in this poetic series suggests that her revival verse was prolific in Boston and traveled alongside Erskine's *Gospel Sonnets* long before it saw print. Even a college satirist knew her revival position as the itinerant's guide, as evidenced by her placement as the introduction to her husband's soliloquy. The parody shows a keen awareness of her revival poems and her affective poetic style, complete with apostrophes and declarations of her burning passion for God. The verse in fact begins, "I burn, I burn, I burn / I burn, I burn, I burn," clearly exaggerating the language of ecstatic devotion that Moorhead uses in both of her poems pertaining to *Gospel Sonnets*—the second of which, "The Spouse of Christ," inspired the writing of the satire in the first place.[104] The poet parodies Moorhead's use

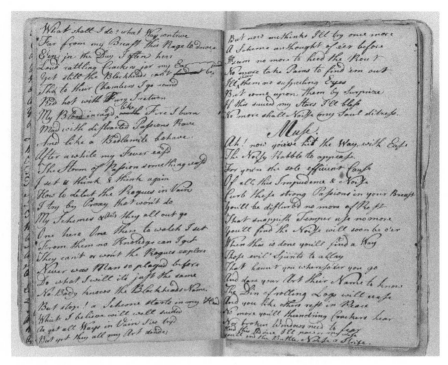

Figure 2.4. Continued parody of Sarah and John Moorhead copied in a notebook of Nathan Fiske.

American Antiquarian Society.

of exclamatory phrases, exaggerated images, and personifications. The final lines of the poem directly lift the phrases "transporting Joys" and "fantastic Toys" from Moorhead's "Spouse of CHRIST" poem, as well as mock her self-important performance of repentance, which includes a willful indifference to her husband's trials at the hands of the pranksters. The satirist mocks not only Sarah Moorhead's affective religious experience but her personal life as well. The title alone invents a new pseudonym for her that draws both on the common perception of New Lights as mentally deranged and her specific mental health struggles that had become public knowledge.

Knowing that in 1753 Sarah Moorhead sent an actual bridle along with a firm poetic rebuke to Byles in order to "curb his tongue," a copy of which Fiske also kept in his papers, she surely crafted some characteristically witty lines in response to the young pups.[105] These brief glimpses of Moorhead's manuscript verse reveal that she had mastered not only the poetic banter of Boston society and the Christian belletrism of the day, but that she did so in the role of a recognized revival poet-minister, who combined the personae of the idealized convert and the spiritual director, to perform her ministry for at least two decades. Her publication with Erskine meant that her poetic itinerancy traveled far beyond Boston. The little extant verse by Moorhead that remains shows that she publicly embodied the ideal of affective conversion, which affirmed not only the successful ministry of male revival preachers, but also poet-ministers like Erskine. The persona of the spouse of Christ or ideal female convert was not a passive acknowledgment of the efficaciousness of male leaders, it also manifested the authority of true conversion—what was becoming the single most important requirement for evangelical ministry. Through inhabiting this persona of affective conversion, Moorhead acted as an authoritative woman poet-minister who intervened in religious controversies by authorizing, welcoming, directing, and correcting well-known revival ministers.

"O that an equal zeal": The Legacy of Sarah Parsons Moorhead

Hannah Mather Crocker's history of Boston, which she wrote in the 1820s, identifies Moorhead as one of the primary poetic wits of New England and indicates that Moorhead's granddaughter, a Mrs. Jarvis, who was quite a wit herself, was in possession of her manuscripts—these have since been lost. Though correspondence is often missing to track women's promotion of each other, it would be highly irregular for an eighteenth-century poet to write in isolation. Given Moorhead's status as a versifier in Boston and a poet-minister in the larger transatlantic evangelical community, Moorhead's manuscripts would surely confirm her extensive leadership in an evangelical coterie of verse ministers. Even without further evidence, Moorhead fits the typical profile of an arch-poet: she had extensive manuscripts, she was known for her wit and versified banter, she published poetry in direct conversation with other leading poets as well as current political events, and high-profile men took an interest in circulating her verse. Crocker herself modeled her own political critiques of Boston's elites on Moorhead's authoritative and public censure of area ministers.[106]

Women's coteries circulated each other's poems quite broadly, and even without Moorhead's manuscripts, she left some traces of her influence on a diffuse network of poet-ministers.[107] In general, she was part of an initial surge in colonial women's evangelical versification, which would only expand in the early Republic. At the same time that nonconformist British women pursued verse in their coteries and, when supported, in ecclesiastical settings, colonial women also took up various evangelical verse ministries.[108] Soon after Sarah Moorhead, several others, such as Martha Griswold, Martha Brewster, and anonymous poets like "A Connecticut Lady," published revival poetry, followed by Jane Dunlap, Jenny Fenno, and Phillis Wheatley in Boston. A diverse field of women poet-ministers abounded by the end of the century, including Baptist Lucy Allen, Mary Palmer, Peggy Dow, Nancy Towle, Harriet Livermore, and the "Felicia Hemans of the United States," the Methodist teacher, poet, and editor Harriet Muzzy, and the new "Heavenly Singer," Lydia Huntley Sigourney.[109] Scores of women's commonplace books by known and unknown women recorded revival verse, and some included verse that praised women missionaries and poets, such as Mary Man, "missionary to the Indians."[110] Others, like Bethiah Parker between 1740 and 1780, included verse as part of their spiritual and social trials and in response to visions and prophecies.[111] And for those who did not leave record of their own verse, poetry often still played a remarkable role in their spiritual journeys. For instance, missionary and teacher Lucinda Read gathered inspiration from Methodist itinerant and poet-minister Joshua Marsden and records in her journal the victorious pinnacle of her own spiritual struggle in which she recites a poem to an angel.[112]

At least two well-known colonial women poets knew Moorhead directly and appear to be inspired by her ministry. Just five years before Moorhead became enshrined in the introduction to *Gospel Sonnets,* Martha Brewster became a published poet-minister. Brewster's poetry book, *Poems of Divers Subjects,* appeared in 1757—making it the first book by a colonial woman to bear her own name in print. Scholars have noted that Brewster's published volume signals her earlier participation in the verse culture of the revivals. For instance, the volume includes a provocative poem written in August 1741 entitled "To the Subjects of the special Grace of *God* and its Opposers" in which she defends the ecstatic behavior of those who had been awakened in the revivals and forcefully condemns the ministers that opposed the work:

> But you Blind, Leaders of the Blind,
>   Dumb Dogs that cannot Bark;
> Are still A-sleep, still Slumbers Love,
>   And Stumble in the Dark.[113]

Brewster's employment of various verse forms point toward an extensive circulation among evangelicals (whom she designates in her introduction as her "nearest Friends") and the likelihood that she authored some of the early revival poems that were published anonymously. She gestures toward an intense interest in her verse with an account of her extemporaneous versification of Scripture for an audience in order to counter rumors that she plagiarized Watts and other poets.[114]

Most importantly, Brewster's verse ministry came from the seat of revival country and intersected with Eleazar Wheelock's work in Lebanon, Connecticut. Because of Wheelock's strong social ties to the Moorheads, including Wheelock's pupil David McClure, whose grandfather was the first deacon of John Moorhead's church, Sarah Moorhead's poem on Wheelock's brother-in-law, James Davenport, and her Whitefield poem's publication alongside letters penned by Connecticut ministers, Brewster would have known Sarah Moorhead's verse ministry and, most likely, corresponded with her.

Brewster's extant manuscript poetry confirms that she performed her evangelical verse ministry at least from 1741 to 1769, and that she may have functioned as a spiritual director to Wheelock. Her earliest extant manuscript verse is a poem in honor of Wheelock's second marriage in 1747 that praises the revival leader's successful itinerant ministry and school.[115] A poem in 1769 continues to express a deep investment in Wheelock's ministry, with whom Brewster had entrusted her own son, while at the same time it describes a vision of her own active call to ministry:

> That hand that Spread the Earth And Arch't the skie
> That Guides the worlds below and worlds on high
> That thought of me before Creation Rose
> Doth this Last period of my Life dispose
> He Call'd me forth to A new Settlement
> Which I obey'd not knowing where I went
> Some most endearing Comforts Left behind
> My Reverend. pastor. friends. my Children kind
> So was the Ark brought [home] unto its place
> By willing [hands] yet mourning all their race
> But may not I some blessed news Impart
> The Lords been here he whispers to my heart
> His visits more than fill each vacance[116]

That these two extant manuscript poems are both addressed to Wheelock indicate Brewster's investment in her role as a poet-minister and spiritual guide—a role in which another female poet-minister declared in her manuscript verse, "I can speak for God."[117]

It was not unusual for Wheelock to receive poetry via letter. Just a month after Brewster sent the preceding poem in 1769, he received a passionate correction written in verse by Hannah Dunham.[118] A year earlier, Levi Frisbie, the missionary partner of David McClure, one of John Moorhead's parishioners, wrote a poem in praise of Wheelock's ministry.[119] The Mohegan minister Samson Occom, who became the first published Native American hymn writer, was educated by Wheelock and his social network.[120] As one would expect, this early tradition of poetry continued in the early nineteenth century, including women connected to the leadership of Wheelock's school who exchanged pietistic verse.[121] The frequency of poetic writing to Wheelock, specifically, is important because he was not just any minister. Wheelock was the representative of the more radical and advancing arm of revivalism, who remained the hub of revival news exchange long after published journals went out of print.[122] Those who sent poetry to Wheelock expected it would travel. In such as role, Wheelock likely passed on Brewster's poems. And while it is speculation, it is almost certain that Sarah Moorhead, whose family supported Wheelock's ministry and school, was actively engaged with this same revivalist poetic network.[123] Even David Avery, a young man in Moorhead's church whom John sent to study with Wheelock, had a copy of *Gospel Sonnets* given to him by his mother.[124] Given Sarah Moorhead's early transatlantic status as an ideal convert and spiritual guide, she likely presided over this revival coterie during her early years. Even late in her life when she was burdened with physical and mental infirmities, Sarah Moorhead's influence starkly appears in the work of Phillis Wheatley, which I turn to at length in Chapter 4.

The influence of "A Lady in New England" appeared even when Jonathan Lamb remade *Gospel Sonnets* in 1830 for a new camp-meeting audience. He wrote in his brief introduction that the first poem in the collection, "The Invocation to Religion [,] was transcribed from a volume of MS. Poems, written by Mrs. L***, which [he took] the liberty to correct and enlarge, and herewith present to the public." Mrs. L, presumably Mrs. Lamb, declares at the opening of the work, "Come, blest religion, fair celestial guest, / Inspire my soul and sooth my pensive breast; . . . .With joy I hail thee to my ravish'd breast; Thou art my all while I sojourn below."[125] Though most revival poets invoked God, the invocation to "fair celestial guest" also reverberates with the tradition since Rowe of gleaning inspiration from idealized female converts. Other lines in the poem echo words penned by Sarah Moorhead, including, "O tune my heart thy heav'nly charms to sing!" and "Nor shall the world with its fallacious toys / Divert my trust—or mingle with my joys."[126] While these similarities may be mere happenstance in a community that shared much of its poetic language, it is striking that Lamb began his collection with a poem from an evangelical woman's circulating manuscript collection. Though the style and theology of Lamb's *Gospel Sonnets* had changed, the importance of "a Lady" did not. In *Gospel Sonnets* newest iteration, it recognized the role of the woman poet-minister to authorize revival ministry and verse.

As this chapter has shown, in revivalism women's espousal piety became tightly woven with verse itself. The authority that women derived from that piety can be seen in the ways that they used verse to authorize male ministries, to publicly correct and to teach revered male preachers, and to intervene in the most salient issues of revivalism. This chapter has focused on the ways that white transatlantic women poet-ministers crafted particular personae in relation to the feminized position of the idealized muse or convert, and how this position conferred authority to act as spiritual directors in revival verse culture. *Gospel Sonnets* helped infuse espousal piety in revival culture and normalize the importance of women's affective response to authenticate the presence of revival. It helped open a space in early evangelicalism for women to create poetic personae and to perform verse ministries. The next chapter turns to another pervasive aspect of revivalism that was also central to *Gospel Sonnets*: writing verse for the common person. As discussed in Chapter 1, shared rubrics for hearing the sound of the gospel brought the highest form of the deity into the lowest form of verse. This formulation was not only a poetics that exemplified the incarnation of Christ, but also, as the next chapter will argue, an aesthetics tied to a particular theological anthropology.

3

Evangelical Harmony and
the Discord of Taste

Controversy followed revivals. It also followed revival poetry, not only in New England and the Middle Colonies, but also in the South. At the same time that Moorhead published verse enacting her poetic identity as the idealized spouse of Christ and the itinerant's spiritual guide, and while satire of Moorhead's poet-minister role circulated in Boston, the legitimacy of revival poetry in Virginia had also become a matter of public concern. On March 20, 1752, the *Virginia Gazette* issued a stand-alone supplement to discuss the Presbyterian minister Samuel Davies's poetry collection, *Miscellaneous Poems, Chiefly on Divine Subjects* (1752). The one-page edition featured the bombastic critique "Remarks on the Virginia Pindar" by "Walter Dymocke Anonymous," a reviewer enraged by the intrusion of Davies's collection on the refined literary tastes of his fellow Southerners.[1] The provocative essay elicited consistent press coverage for six months and sporadic attention for more than two years, including two poems and a defense from Davies himself.[2] Dymocke's ruthless mockery of Davies and his poetry sparked conversation about the merits of the collection and revival poetry more generally, and garnered enough interest that the *Gazette* editor, William Hunter, thought the debate could successfully sustain itself in pamphlet form.[3] The publication of *Miscellaneous Poems* in Virginia, like that of *Gospel Sonnets* in New England, unabashedly announced that revival had taken hold in the region. Yet, the uproar over Davies's revival poems was not only a reaction to his propagation of evangelicalism in the Anglican colony; the form of the religious propaganda—poetry—mattered. The criticism of Davies's poems shows that the stakes of the burgeoning evangelical presence were high because the maintenance of Virginian social order in part hinged on preserving the literary order.

From its inception, evangelicalism was tied to questions of aesthetics. As Jonathan Edwards argued, conversion altered aesthetic experience by

Awakening Verse. Wendy Raphael Roberts, Oxford University Press (2020). © Oxford University Press.
DOI: 10.1093/oso/9780197510278.001.0001

increasing one's sense of delight and pleasure.[4] It was not so much about one's creed, but rather how one came to know God had saved the soul. The experience of being saved and the feeling that one was more pious or more correctly religious came through affective experiences of the goodness and beauty of God. How soteriology worked depended upon a certain understanding of humankind partaking in the image of God. One's intellect did not make one more attuned to saving grace; one's innate, universal, and God-given ability to respond aesthetically made one a candidate for the wedding banquet of Christ. Yet, this aesthetics deviated substantially from that espoused by esteemed British writers who cultivated a selective and exclusive taste.[5] If taste was the hallmark of eighteenth-century sensibility, sacred harmony was the stamp of eighteenth-century affective salvation.

This chapter explores the specific function of evangelical harmony in Samuel Davies's poetics. Harmony, a ubiquitous term in the eighteenth century bound up with issues of taste and aesthetics, performed important work for Davies's practice of poetry and religion. First, it was able to bring disparate poetics together and embed that poetics in the salvific process. Davies's collection of revival verse brought the lofty aspirations of the religious sublime together with Watts's call for a poetry for "the plainest capacity" through the concept and practice of evangelical harmony. Understanding how Davies's anthropology, theology, and soteriology depended upon evangelical harmony brings Dymocke's highly charged critique of Davies and his verse into sharper focus. Davies's revival practice was dangerous to traditional social structures not only because it was a challenge to the colony's Anglican Church, but also because at its foundation it was a poetic practice for the masses that overturned the stratifying function of taste.

Evangelical Harmony and the Subtle Sublime

Samuel Davies, successor to Jonathan Edwards to the presidency of the College of New Jersey (later Princeton), is well-known in evangelical historiography. His short life has often been praised as an example of evangelical piety, passionate elocution, and compassionate slavery. Trained at the New Light Presbyterian seminary "Log College" at Fagg's Manor in Chester County, Pennsylvania, Davies became the first non-Anglican minister licensed to preach in Virginia after he moved south in 1747 to serve and organize several Presbyterian congregations in Hanover and the surrounding counties. Because his movement between at least seven growing church communities violated Virginian law prohibiting itinerancy, he quickly became known among the political elite for his multiple petitions for licenses to preach and his relentless push for religious toleration.[6]

This notoriety also accompanied his reputation as a powerful preacher, advocate for slave literacy, and sacred poet. His oratorical prowess and ability to draw crowds of sizes that often required preaching outdoors drew both admiration and ire. Likewise, his work to educate slaves with the support of the Society for Promoting Religious Knowledge Among the Poor and the Society in Scotland for Propagating Christian Knowledge was hailed by evangelicals and decried by the Virginian ruling class. And Davies's participation in a larger community of transatlantic revivalist ministers who practiced poetry for sacred ends garnered supporters who enthusiastically circulated his verse and provoked outrage by aristocracy invested in belles lettres. Religion, literacy, belles lettres—these were not separate practices, but were mutually constitutive of Virginian social order that depended upon gentry control.

Belles lettres and its relationship to evangelical poetry was not peripheral, but central to Virginian culture at the time. When William Parks introduced Virginia's first press in 1726 and established the *Virginia Gazette* (1736), he inspired the production of belles lettres.[7] The poem *Typographia: An Ode, on Printing* (1730), which specifically hailed the introduction of the press to Williamsburg, celebrated the possibility that Virginia might become the new center of literary inspiration:

> Hence *ADDISON*, the *British Maro*, rose,
> Thence *DRYDEN* soar'd the highest Pitch of Fame:
>   Leave, leave awhile those blest Abodes,
>   To view a new-arising *Land*,
>   A *Land*, whose fertile Plains,
>   And peaceful shady Woods,
>   May well demand
>   Your sweetest Notes, and loftiest Strains,
> Where, with supreme Command, your own *AUGUSTUS* reigns.[8]

Beckoning the muses to Virginia, the poet anticipates the literary prestige the new press made possible. The poem, dedicated to the governor by the poet J. Markland, bases the resurrection of the arts in the goodness of the governor, who, along with the King, serves his people beneficently by introducing print and guaranteeing order to the "*speechless* Letters, *unform'd* Words, / *Unjointed* Questions, and *unmeaning* Breaks."[9] Both the law and the arts arise together in print, joined in their mission to bring order and prestige to Virginia. Part of Markland's praise includes the maintenance of distinct classes of readers even within the print trade—the genteel associated with manuscript, law, and religion, and the vulgar connected to news reading.

The early history of printed poetry in the state continues this project. The first collection of local poems printed in Virginia, *Poems on Several Occasions by a Gentleman of Virginia*, came off Parks's press in 1736 with the express purpose of enforcing the gentry's literary culture that was lively and active in manuscript. The poems, composed by the Anglican Reverend William Dawson most likely while he was a student at Oxford, appear to have been well received, and by 1742 he was respected enough to become the second president of William and Mary College. Like Markland, Dawson participated in a high poetic culture invested in both classical and English tradition, as well as Virginian genteel society. The book demonstrated the poet's elite aims through the use of multiple poetic forms, including blank verse, invocations of the classical muses, employment of a refined religious sublime and Christian belletrism (including references to Elizabeth Rowe), and prefatory remarks that emphasized the inappropriateness of publishing bad verse.

Dawson's literary aims were not isolated. The Southern colonies of the eighteenth century cultivated literacy and belles lettres, and many Southern bookshelves included Francis Hutcheson's *An Inquiry into the Original of Our Ideas of Beauty and Virtue* (1725), Lord Kames's *Elements of Criticism* (1762), and Hugh Blair's *Lectures on Rhetoric and Belles Lettres* (1783). These books, along with reprinted and original essays in Southern newspapers throughout the century, point to an active interest in aesthetic theory among Southern readers and writers.[10]

Davies's *Miscellaneous Poems* participated in this local interest and attempted to redirect it toward evangelical aesthetic sensibilities. The next volume of poetry to be printed in Virginia after Dawson's collection, appearing just months before Dawson's death, Davies's book espoused a poetic theory in stark contrast to Dawson's genteel ambitions. Davies takes up issues of literary taste, poetic passions, the sublime, and harmony—all important concepts to the evolving transatlantic conversation regarding aesthetics and society—to argue that the most basic tenets and practices of true religion rely on a proper understanding of the purpose of aesthetics in affecting salvation.

In the introduction to his book, Davies argues that aesthetic experience is essential to both true religion and poetry. This idea was not new; it was first espoused by the British literary critic John Dennis at the beginning of the century. Dennis's two foundational works, *The Advancement and Reformation of Modern Poetry* (1701) and *The Grounds of Criticism in Poetry* (1704), together made a sweeping case for the centrality of the passions: they were the very essence of both religion and poetry, whose ends were "moving the affections." Dennis, who was the first British critic to make this claim, is foundational to eighteenth-century aesthetics. The simultaneous rise of affective religion and literary passions has been taken up by a number of scholars who have charted the shift toward enthusiasm, sensibility, and sentimentalism over the eighteenth century. It can be seen across a broad swath of thinkers from Shaftsbury to Hutcheson to Hume. The eighteenth century reworked the relationship between experience, the mind, and the heart, and in the process, religion and poetry came closer together. Dennis played a large part in this dynamic, as his writings were intended "to shew that the intention of Poetry and the Christian Religion being alike to move the affections, they may very well be made instrumental to the advancing each other."[11]

In the process of elevating passion as the supreme end of poetry, Dennis attempted to renew and remake the idea of enthusiasm as essential bedrock for society. One of Dennis's key arguments held that religious poetry is superior to profane or secular poetry because religion is better at inducing passion. There are, he says, two kinds of passion: "ordinary Passion" and enthusiasm. Profane poetry can only induce ordinary passions, while sacred poetry can elicit the strongest enthusiasm—a superior type of passion for which the "cause is not clearly comprehended by him who feels [it]."[12] Religion and poetry are important because together they become the most powerful tool for the creation of civil society. Dennis writes,

> For since Poetry has been thought not only by Heathens, but by the Writers of the Old Testament, and consequently by God Himself who inspir'd them, to be the fittest method for the inforcing Religion upon the Minds of Men, and since Religion is the only solid Foundation of all Civil Society, it follows, that whoever Endeavors to Re-establish Poetry, makes a generous attempt to restore an Art, that may be highly Advantageous to the Publick, and Beneficial to Mankind.[13]

Dennis's account of enthusiasm sought to redeem a much-disparaged term.[14] The English Revolution and beheading of the king gave a vivid political tenor to the term "enthusiasm" that lasted well into the eighteenth century. As J. G. A. Pocock has argued, "enthusiasm endowed plebian men and women with an articulate capacity for criticism and rejection of successive features of the social structure" becoming "the nearest thing to a revolutionary consciousness . . . to be found in English history; and this had by no means been forgotten a century and a half after 1649."[15] In the context of the American Revolution and the early United States specifically, enthusiasm was a catalyst for political and revolutionary critique and action.[16] This enduring history of enthusiasm as emancipatory made it suspect, especially when tied to religion.

Dennis's argument for a renewed emphasis on poetic enthusiasm was actually a conservative political project. His ultimate goal—to make the British as good in poetry as they were in empire—impels him to confine the enjoyment of enthusiastic poetry to the highest classes. Though enthusiasm was a personal experience available to anyone—hence its democratic potential and danger—Dennis subjects it to social stratification. He declares, "the Delight which Poetry gives, is neither perpetual, nor are all men capable of it. Religion alone can provide man a pleasure that is lasting, as it may be universal."[17] In this moment, Dennis not only excludes those without the proper training and taste from the benefits of poetry; he also unhinges religion from poetry in the process and risks undermining his entire project. If the ends of both religion and poetry are to move the affections, it is the proper job of poetry to do it discriminately.[18] As Dennis writes elsewhere, enthusiastic passions "are more subtle, and Thousands have no feeling and no notion of them; but where the Vulgar cannot be moved in a great degree, there the Enthusiastick are to be rais'd."[19]

Davies's poetry partakes of the religious sublime Dennis encouraged. The degree to which Davies demonstrates religious enthusiasm in his verse, and encourages it in others, is quite intense. Like Dennis, Davies underscores that poetry has a unique ability to inspire religious emotions in people and to draw them to Christianity. Davies prays that the day will come when modern poetry is redeemed from its fall from grace and powerfully disseminates religion. And, also like Dennis, Davies defends enthusiasm in poetry primarily through its use in scripture, which had become commonplace. In this general sense, then, Davies's poetry is indebted to Dennis's promotion of the religious sublime and the poetic enthusiasm that became popular in New England in the 1720s.

Yet, at mid-century, when Davies published his verse, he significantly deviated from Dennis's formulation, explicitly taking issue with Dennis's exclusive notion of the subtle sublime. At the beginning of the century, Watts also addressed the problem of joining enthusiasm and refined taste in his own verse practices. As discussed in the Introduction to this book, Watts separated his verse into two tiers according to its appropriateness for those of higher and lower taste. He wrote lyric poetry in the manner of the religious sublime for his highest class readers, and he wrote hymns devoid of difficult images and prosody for what he called "the plainest capacity."[20] While both Watts and Davies also wrote within the shadow of a British poetic tradition, and therefore showed ambition toward a higher taste and cultivation of that taste, they did not eschew the firm belief that all needed poetry, just as all needed religion. For evangelically motivated poets like Watts and Davies, questions of poetic taste were secondary to the goals of the Kingdom of God, which included drawing all of mankind, including those of lower taste, to Christ.

Davies approached the problem of taste and enthusiastic Christian poetry differently than Watts. Instead of distinguishing between hymn and lyric according to the refinement of the audience, Davies dedicated his entire book of lyric and hymns to the benefit of those with "the plainest capacity." This is where he sharply parted ways with Dennis. For Davies, the primary authority for aesthetic judgment resided in the nature of salvation according to Scripture, whereas for Dennis members of the aristocracy remained the final arbiters. Dennis sought to protect poetry from religion when it threatened high notions of taste, while Davies sought to free poetry from elite aesthetics to take its rightful place as the partner of heaven.

This is clear throughout Davies's introduction to his book, in which he imagines himself writing for an audience of lower poetic taste, which he designates the *"Generality of Mankind."*[21] Davies begins his preface by addressing the commonly used trope of humility, or *"fashionable Modesty"* of speaking *"meanly"* of one's performance. The people he writes for, Davies bluntly states, do not require such a display because they are either partial to him or *"insensible to [the] imperfections."*[22] As for the *"critical and impartial Reader,"* he will realize Davies's sincere embarrassment because the blemishes cannot be hidden from an elite reader. This is no great matter because though *"persons of a refined and judicious Taste are conscious of peculiar Sensations"* when they encounter the rare poetry of genius and *"are captivated with the lively Images of Fancy, the Grandeur of Ideas, the Flowers of*

Language, the Pomp of Style, and the proper Arangement [sic] *of well-disposed Periods"* those of "*a coarse Relish*" take pleasure in those parts of verse that the refined ignore. These include "*the Jingling of Syllables, the Equality of Numbers, the ambiguous Punn, or witty Turn.*"[23]

Like Watts, Davies characterizes the higher forms of poetry primarily in terms of the difficulty of the images, while partitioning off issues of prosody for the lower forms. A quick allusion to arguments surrounding Milton's punctuation reveals Davies's fluency in poetic criticism and follows critics who designate jingling syllables and the stable use of numbers as mere ornaments for the common hearer. But, instead of using "jingle" pejoratively, Davies employs the term positively, believing its common appeal makes it particularly useful for the propagation of religion. Following George Herbert's lines, "A Verse may hit him whom a Sermon flies, / And turn Delight into a Sacrifice," Davies accords rhymed poetry and proportioned numbers their heuristic value by drawing on a long tradition of poetry as an avenue of education through memorization, including the acquisition of reading and the catechism.

Though these common readers cannot relish the most exquisite flavors of sublime poetry, they share with the rest of humanity "an innate Love of Harmony, *which gives those Things that are conveyed to their Minds in a poetical Vehicle a peculiar Relish.*"[24] The basic love of harmony opens the pleasures of poetry to everyone. This universal ability to enjoy poetry allows Davies to claim it as an instantiation of God's image in humanity, rather than a marker of taste and cultural standing. In Davies's words, "*This* harmonious Turn of Mind *is the Stamp of Heaven, the Image of the eternal Author of Order; and 'tis He that teaches us to feel the Charms of Poetry.*"[25] Davies's words succinctly bring together the vision of the religious sublime in which the poet "strove to visualize imaginatively the divine Being that suffuses creation" with the capacity to access poetic sound.[26] Davies employs synesthesia in his explanation: sound is image. To see the image of God in us requires one to have a mind attuned to sound; or, to have a mind attuned to sound is to have the image of God emblazoned on your person.

Davies's concept of the "harmonious Turn of Mind" comes directly from the acclaimed British poet and pietist Elizabeth Singer Rowe in her rendition of the music of the spheres in *Letters Moral and Entertaining* (1729–1732), which Davies quotes at length. Elsewhere, Davies designates her as his muse and follows Watts's directions to emulate her by declaring that he cannot read her without being moved to write poetry.[27] In the poem, she declares that "From Harmony to Harmony we rise" to the same skill that turns the spheres and gives rise to heavenly song and sacred poetry. According to Rowe's poem, "Th' inspiring GOD dwells in the mystic Sound, / And charms and captivates the list'ning Soul, / Thro' all her soft Capacities of Joy."[28] Echoing Rowe's vocabulary throughout the preface, Davies continues, "*The Generality of Mankind have neither Opportunity nor perhaps Capacity for [po- etic] Refinements; and yet are capable of a glorious Immortality, and the purer Joys of Paradise.—For the sake of such I write.*"[29] The mystic sound or under- current of harmony forms the base of poetry, which all can access, and upon which *"Degrees of Cultivation"*—or what would be called taste—are then built.[30] Prior to taste, then, resides sound, and it is this universally accessible aspect that makes poetry the most important evangelical tool.

When Davies declared this to be his project, he put himself at odds with Dennis by articulating a particular relationship of revival verse to harmony rather than the passions. Davies doesn't directly refer to enthusiasm in his in- troduction, but sticks to naming emotions in their particularity. Most impor- tantly, he emphasizes harmony, in contradistinction to Dennis's idea of an elite and refined enthusiastic poetry. In *The Advancement of Modern Poetry*, Dennis had dispensed with harmony in order to privilege the passions as the end and essence of poetry:

> That the Speech, by which Poetry makes its Imitation, must be pathetick is evident; for Passion is still more necessary to it than Harmony. For Harmony only distinguished its Instrument from that of Prose, but Passion distinguishes its very nature and character. For therefore Poetry is Poetry, because it is more passionate and sensual than Prose.... But Passion answers the two ends of Poetry better than Harmony can do, and upon that account is preferable to it: For first it pleases more, which is evident.... And ... a man may instruct without Harmony, but never without Passion."[31]

The particular refinement of the passions that Dennis holds out as the end of poetry, Davies refutes through an emphasis on harmony. Though elite poets and readers may deplore it, the basics of a universal harmony, including rhyme and simple jingle, are for him the essence of poetry and evangelical aesthetics.

Davies's poetry itself also engages with the heroes of early evangel- ical verse—Watts and Rowe—in order to defend and to expand a mid- dling revival poetry, *"these course Provisions."* Davies employs and refers to evangelical harmony throughout his poems. From the first verse of Davies's *Miscellaneous Poems*, the poet ecstatically declares the centrality of sound to the nature of both God and the relationship engendered by him:

> His Name is Music to my ravish'd Ears,
> Sweeter than that which charms the heavn'ly Spheres . . .
>   I spring from Earth, and Heav'n is my Abode,
> When I can say those charming Words, MY GOD;
> MY GOD!—Infinite Joys lie in the Sound:
> Be Thou but mine; and all the Sun goes round
> Without reluctant Murm'ring I resign;
> I have enough, if I can call Thee MINE.[32]

This brief excerpt typifies Davies's intensely affective meditative poetry, in which he induces emotional response through sublime imagery and the foregrounding of divine harmony. Proclaiming the unmatched delights that emanate from the sound of God's name, the poet relishes his relationship with his savior—an intimacy characterized by a sensuous aurality. Like the hymns of Watts and Doddridge and the poetry of Erskine and Rowe, Davies places a premium on heavenly music, and is enraptured by its cadences as his soul rises toward heaven. As Leigh Eric Schmidt has reminded scholars, "heavenly music was not merely a trope, not a geometrical or harmonial abstraction (as the music of the spheres often became in the new astronomy) but a highly tangible part of the evangelical imagination."[33]

The emphasis on sound flows from Davies's understanding of the nature of God and man as essentially poetic. Given man's nature, this middling sacred verse is not an afterthought, nor primarily an attempt to raise cultural proclivities, but a necessary tool of revivalism. A basic love of harmony in human nature opens the pleasures of poetry to everyone. This universal ability to enjoy poetry, rather than Dennis's restriction to the universal ability to enjoy only religion, Davies claims is an instantiation of God's image in humanity rather than a marker of taste and cultural standing. That is, more than a concept or belief, harmony was the instantiation of God's image in persons and in history. For revivalists, ecclesiology, eschatology, and soteriology all flowed from theology proper, the nature of God, and its implications for anthropology. Because humans partake of the image of God, they are privy to a particular relationship with God. For Davies and many revivalists, this meant that people were people because they had within them an innate love of poetry.

In addition to moving beyond earlier formulations of enthusiastic poetry that relied heavily on taste, Davies also employed harmony to shift more recent formulations of the sublime that focused on the visual toward sound. Addison popularized the religious sublime in America and profoundly influenced the New England poets of the sublime in the 1720s, a tradition Davies continued after it fell out of fashion.[34] These New England poets, like other practitioners of the religious sublime, primarily addressed the reader's imagination by meticulously rendering sensation because it was thought that the imagination interpreted sense impressions to produce emotion. Though mobilizing all of the senses generated the sublime, Addison, in his influential *Spectator* essays on the "Pleasures of the Imagination," clearly situated his discussion within the visual: "I mean only such Pleasures as arise originally from Sight."[35] Addison's famous passage on the polite imagination focalizes issues of class, ownership, and the cultivation of "the fine taste in writing" in relation to sight:

> A man of a Polite Imagination is let into a great many Pleasures, that the Vulgar are not capable of receiving. He can converse with a Picture, and find an agreeable Companion in a Statue. He meets with a secret Refreshment in a Description, and often feels a greater Satisfaction in the Prospect of Fields and Meadows, than another does in the Possession. It gives him, indeed, a kind of Property in every thing he sees, and makes the most rude uncultivated Parts of Nature administer to his Pleasures: So that he looks upon the World, as it were, in another Light, and discovers in it a Multitude of Charms, that conceal themselves from the generality of Mankind.[36]

Such polite taste unlocks exclusive pleasures and ownership through a cultivation of an aesthetics based on the visual. The one with a "Polite Imagination" discovers a new world concealed from the masses. The language is similar to Dennis's discriminating man who with pleasure "Ten thousand different objects . . . surveys."[37]

Davies's poetics differs substantially from taste as defined by Addison. Without simplifying Davies's poetics into a solely sonic approach to poetry— for he clearly engaged in a version of sublime aesthetics that mobilized grand images with the hope of inducing feelings of awe in the reader—his poetics explicitly comes at the sublime through an equalizing harmony. Rather than a vision of the world based on a type of exclusive sight that produces both pleasure and ownership, Davies prioritizes sound—that is, harmony—as a basic element of poetry that theoretically provides rather than obstructs aesthetic access to the majority of people.

Participating in this universal harmony required a revivalist outlook on the world, an idea Davies explored in his poem "The Universal Lamentation," for which he wrote the only other lengthy critical gloss outside of his preface. In his substantial footnote to the poem, the poet-minister defends the use of prosopopoeia as natural "for a Mind full of tender and vigorous Passions."[38] He admits that "a more exalted Muse" than his might be required to handle the subject more elegantly, but that none should "censure the Matter and Scope of the Poem, as favouring of fanatical Affectation."[39] This is one of the few times in the book that Davies directly addresses enthusiasm and fanatical affect.

It makes sense that he defends the poems with a lengthy explanation because the trope of personification, or prosopopoeia (sometimes distinguished by critics, sometimes not), was associated in the eighteenth century with emotion and madness. Lord Kames's *Elements of Criticism* (1762) advised against using the "insufferable" trope because it arose from the poet's passions and appeared "ridiculous."[40] As Shaun Irlam summarizes in his important work on enthusiast poetry:

> The apogee of this tendency to boldness, magnificence, and animation for the eighteenth-century poet is always personification, the animating of the inanimate, or corporealizing of the incorporeal. It is a device defined as the most flagrant violation of mimetic (and implicitly, rationalist) expectations, and the device regarded as being in consequence the unfeignable signifier of emotion and affective authenticity, and soon, of great Genius.[41]

Davies's footnote attempted to preempt responses that would reject the excessive emotion associated with the poetic device and, like Dennis, provide a positive connotation.

Davies's justification for why the poem does not promote fanatical affection involves the emotion's cause—the separation of the Divine Parent and the human soul—as appropriate to the ensuing emotion. Davies references Paul as the primary precedent for such a poetic practice (though both Thomson and Milton are noted as recent examples). The poem laments the degenerate state of the world, which Davies defends as a worthy and, more importantly, manly response:

> And can there be any Thing so moving, any Thing so just an Object for manly Sorrow, as this? It cannot be justly looked upon as an Instance of effeminate Softness, for the most exalted and dispassionate Mind, to dissolve into the tenderest Sorrows, when it is our common Humanity that demands the sympathising Fear, and prompts the lamenting Groan.[42]

For Davies, tears and lamentation in reaction to the state of sin comes from "our common Humanity" and can, therefore, be rightly designated "manly Sorrow," as opposed to "effeminate" or "fanatical Affectation." The intense response of the entire creation, to which Davies gives voice in the poem, entails an expansive sympathetic symbiosis between the world and the Christian believer. Importantly, it is declared universal and therefore manly, which is in keeping with the larger eighteenth-century culture of sensibility.

He ends the footnote by employing Jeremiah's words to express his own wish: "*Oh that mine Head were Waters! and mine Eyes Fountains of Tears.*"[43] In this biblical example, prosopopoeia functions in reverse. Instead of waters becoming a weeping head and a fountain crying tears, the objects already possess the emotional function that the poet desires. The waters, fountains, and teeming universe already respond appropriately to the separation of man and God. Prosopopoeia, which Davies stipulates must meet the emotional pitch demanded by the subject, is therefore a tool that befits sacred poetry and affective religion. It both reveals and enables a temperament cultivated by an evangelical disposition to the world.

The ease with which Davies participates in the lament of the universe, both in this poem and in his descriptions of his own spiritual practice, meshes with his sense of a universal harmony that is God's emanation to us. In a letter to John Holt dated March 26, 1751, Davies recounts his serious mood induced by time in the garden in which the creation praised God:

> The Verdure of the vegetative Tribes, the fragrance of the flowers, & the Harmony of the aerial Choir, who in various Forms were paying the grateful Tribute of Praise to the great Source of Life and Beauty, reproached the Languor of my Heart in Devotion, And the Silence of my Tongue in Praise. The inanimate World seemed to importune me to express their dumb Gratitude in human Language & be the Interpreter of the universal

Hallelujah; which suggests to me a stanza of Herbert which wants nothing but a modern Dress to render it truly poetical; "Man is the World's High=Priest who doth refrain, / Doth not refrain unto himself alone, / But robs a thousand who would praise thee fain, / And so commits a World of Sin in one."[44]

Synesthesia, or God's sound as his image in mankind, sets up a type of world in which the senses migrate to inflect each other and other objects. The attribution of senses to the creation partakes in a harmony of the universe and the senses; that is, synesthesia at some level attests to the harmony of the world—a world in which seeing a voice or hearing a vision proceeds from a universal (that is, manly) sympathetic passion. And it seems to compel Davies to turn to poetry. As Cowper later declared in *The Task* (1785), "There is in souls a sympathy with sounds."[45]

Davies cultivated the role of a sacred poet or poet-minister, rather than what he called "*playing the role of the Poet,*" in direct contrast to the poetic discourse on taste.[46] Yet, he does not leave behind taste completely. Instead, he reformulates its meaning in relation to the Lord's Table, rather than its association with bourgeois commensality that often defined taste philosophically.[47] He writes, "*Of those valuable Tracts of sacred Verse which are extant, there are but very few in this Colony in the Hands of common People; and in such a Famine, perhaps these coarse Provisions may not be disagreeable.*"[48]

Davies offers his collection as humble food for the common Virginian in need of spiritual sustenance amidst a shortage of sacred poetry. This is something Davies also highlights in his letters, requesting more verse, especially poetry by Watts, for his congregants and for converted slaves.[49] Describing his book in this manner works against the culture of taste, which requires that people have enough before they can perform discrimination. In the state of famine, coarse provisions satisfy and ideas of taste become less meaningful or absent altogether. For the pietistic Christian, hunger is in fact continual: it is her spiritual state. Believers yearn for the blood and body of Christ as they are brought low through their insufficiencies, they are urged to taste that the Lord is good, they are hungry for spiritual bread, they crave the fruits of the Spirit, they thirst for righteousness, they look forward to the banquet of the Lamb. And, in Davies's ministry to the spiritually barren fields of Virginia, the Lord's feast appeared as a humble morsel of poetry.

The Mad Black Poet-Minister and the
"No Language" of Revival

As an offer of humble victuals, Davies's book caused quite a stir. It was one of the few instances in the South when the public passionately engaged the new revival practices in print. Even George Whitefield never succeeded in galvanizing enough interest in Virginia to instigate a "media blitz" of pro- and anti-revival tracts as he did elsewhere.[50] Though previous scholarly treatments of the controversy recorded in the *Virginia Gazette* pursue the importance of the exchange for its religious dimensions while quickly losing sight of the poetry, Davies's verse did not serve merely as a ruse for anti-revival rhetoric. If Davies represented the acceleration of evangelicalism in Virginia, he also embodied an alternative to belletristic ambition. When revival came to Virginia accompanied by Davies's revivals and his poetry, Davies inserted religion where it did not belong—in the literary aspirations of the South.

Dymocke's criticisms of Davies's newly published book demonstrates that the evangelical poetics of "the plainest capacity" profoundly unsettled the poetics of the white, Anglican Virginian gentry. The first installment of Dymocke's essay in the *Virginia Gazette* (spanning seven separate issues over a total of four months) begins with a stinging critique of Davies's preface, in which Davies prioritizes the common reader over those educated in the nuances of great art:

> WHEREAS a very ingenious Writer has lately published two whole Books*
> of Divine Poems . . . with a learned Preface before them: Wherein he shews,
> that such Poets as *Virgil* and *Pope* can be of little or no Use to the World,
> because few are so refined, as to have a Relish for their Works; but such
> Writers as Himself must be of general and almost universal Benefit, because
> their Productions cannot but delight all People, who are not cursed with
> a good Taste; which makes up at least nine tenths of Mankind. Whereas
> he enforces this Reasoning by intimating, that it would be absurd to cram
> gross Feeders with nothing but Tarts and Cheese-Cakes; when they have
> Stomacks strong enough, to break their Fast with fry'd Hominy, and a
> greasy Rasher of fat Bacon.[51]

Dymocke bites into Davies's common poetics and turns his Eucharistic morsel of poetry into a feast fit only for rabble. Framing his criticism as though it were constructive praise, Dymocke goes on to show how Davies's book emphatically deserves publication under a poetic philosophy that promotes the worst writers. In the end, Dymocke declares, his extensive analysis of Davies's verse will produce a newfound confidence in the humble poet so that the next time he publishes he will be able to enter the world of typeface like a man instead of with "a great deal of Maidenly Bashfulness and Blushing."[52] Just as Davies had anticipated with his footnote, Dymocke wastes no time condemning Davies's evangelical harmony by transmuting an affective poetics of manly sorrow into effeminate fanaticism.

Dymocke continues his attack on Davies for collapsing the esteemed place of the poet with the debased needs of the commoner:

> No two Tallies can suit one another, as He is convinced, better than He and those for whom He Writes: They have no Taste for the greater Beauties of Poetry, such as *the proper Arrangement of well disposed Periods*. . . . He, *no Capacity* for them. . . . They love to hear Rhymes, or (as He elegantly expresses it) *the Consonance of final Syllables*. . . . He is of a *versifying Humour*. . . . They love to be entertained with *Variety and Confusion:* He to pack together a *Collection of Miscellanies; not digested into Order, according to the Nature of the Subject*.[53]

In these first paragraphs, Dymocke touches on several main complaints that return again and again in the same vivid language throughout his extensive harangue—Davies's lack of taste and its implications for the proper ordering of religion, class, gender, and race. His pseudonym serves to underscore this point: "Walter" echoes Walter Harte, the defender of Pope's satire *The Dunciad*, a poem which ridiculed poor performances of the sublime, while "Dymocke" evokes the role of the King's Champion, who, at the coronation of the British king, would throw down his gauntlet and fight anyone who challenged the king's right to the throne. At its most basic, Davies's mission to cultivate a poetic practice for the masses of the unlearned strikes Dymocke as ludicrous and treasonous. Dymocke, like other eighteenth-century literary critics, is preoccupied with defining taste, and, more importantly, with deciding who has the capacity to exercise it.

Davies, according to Dymocke, does not. He cannot even write English. Building on arguments against enthusiastic speech that gained ascendency after the English Civil Wars, Dymocke writes that Davies is "too poetical to write *English*, or, indeed, any other Language."[54] Instead, like the dim-witted Presbyterian knight, Sir Hudibras, of Samuel Butler's seventeenth-century mock heroic poem, *Hudibras*, Davies composes "hasty Noise" that only the ignorant masses recognize as legitimate speech. Several times Dymocke returns to the accusation that Davies's poetry resides outside of any proper language, including Davies's unique knack at translating poets, such as Pope, out of English into "no language."[55]

Dymocke's characterization of Davies's poetry as noise rather than language stems from its inextricability from Davies's religious practices. As many scholars have pointed out, revivals, both in the North and the South, were often characterized by both participants and suspicious observers as chaotic events notable for their sounds, which was part of a larger struggle over the voice of God during the enlightenment.[56] One versifier in *The New-York Weekly Journal* described those who embraced enthusiastic religion as celebrators of "the heavenly Sounds" that "Flow from [the] charming Tongue" of revival leaders, such as George Whitefield, while those who warned against such events described them as noisy and incomprehensible.[57] The rector of St. Paul's Parish in Hanover County, Virginia, complained in 1745 that New Light Presbyterian preachers would "thunder out" to the crowds, frightening them until they would "cry out fall down & work like people in convulsion fits."[58] The effect of enthusiastic preachers, according to one Anglican minister in Virginia, was "to screw up people to the greatest heights of religious frenzy, and then leave them in that wild state" until the next itinerant came along.[59] People in revivals were thought to behave wildly—they swooned, skipped, and danced, and they cried, howled, and ranted.[60] Engaging in such activities embarrassed polite society because it approached both the "uncivilized" state of natives, slaves, and the working classes, as well as the passionate excesses of femininity. Though Davies's revival services were extremely tame compared to Northern practices and the imminent Baptist revivals, Dymocke's characterization of Davies's poetry in the *Virginian Gazette* nevertheless deviates little from the general trend of banishing revival sounds from civilized society.[61] Harmony upholds civilization; evangelical noise does not.

Dymocke's critique, continued in the June 12, 1752 issue, crystallizes his argument that the structure of Davies's poems participates in evangelical forms of worship. Through summarizing the thematic shifts of Davies's poem "Conjugal Love and Happiness," Dymocke positions Davies as a minister of disorder and unintelligibility. The poem, according to Dymocke, implicitly provides a model for the type of ministry Davies performs, as well as instantiates the chaos of revival in written form:

What pleases me most in this Poem is, that it affords, I think, a most agree-
able Specimen of extempore Prayer. What a pretty Amusement it must be,
to pray after our Author! When he can pray and con-pray, for an Hour together, in such a cunning Manner, that his most sagacious Followers shall
not be able to know what they and he are asking, if they attend ever so
closely; until he come to the Conclusions.[62]

In this provocative moment, Dymocke links poetic form with evangelical
extemporaneous prayer, a critique that reveals more than just his position
against revival practices (for which the *Gazette* exchange has primarily been
mobilized), but a repulsion from the interpenetration of revival practice and
poetic form.

Dymocke's discomfort with the extemporaneous nature of evangelical
prayer is predictable given his Anglican ministry and practice. Anglicans
placed a premium on structure in their devotional exercises through utiliza-
tion of set prayers from *The Book of Common Prayer* to cultivate reverence,
communication with God, and the gradual transformation of the person. In
comparison, evangelical prayer sought to immediately place listeners in the
throes of an emotionally agitated self-examination that produced submission, conviction, and repentance.[63] New Light Presbyterian services, specifically, included singing, followed by a minister-led extemporaneous prayer
that could last upwards of 15 minutes. The purpose of the minister's Spirit-
led prayer, according to the Presbyterian Directory for Worship, was to cause
"hearts to be rightly affected with their sins, that they may all mourn in sense
thereof before the Lord and hunger and thirst after the grace of God in Jesus
Christ."[64] Rather than a unified recitation of prayer, the Presbyterian community participated through listening and affective response. Though officially
Presbyterians encouraged the use of the Lord's Prayer as both a means of
praying and as a model for spontaneous prayer, in actual practice American
Presbyterians avoided using all prewritten prayers.[65]

While it can be tempting to follow Dymocke's lead and divide revivalists
from other forms of Christianity based on an oral-textual divide, evangelical practices suggest a more variegated interpretation. Though evangelical prayer stressed a spontaneity that could not be replicated by prewritten
prayers, revivalists eagerly engaged print forms. In fact, for Dymocke, the
underlying problem with Davies's collection of poetry stems from the integration of print (that is, a set form) and evangelical practice. Rather than
the ephemeral noise of revival, Davies's printed poems authorize revival

language and their practices as compatible with print and its relation to upholding the state and society, like the set forms of Anglican prayer. It is Dymocke who seeks to detach revivalists from print by showcasing the "true" nature of Davies's poetry: incoherent sound.

Dymocke's assertion that disordered poetry provides a window into the inscrutability of Davies's prayers not only delegitimizes evangelical prayer, but also wrests the office of poet from would-be enthusiast bards. After he accuses Davies of fooling the ignorant with his noisy poems, Dymocke immediately paints him as a mad poet of "divine Enthusiasm" with questionable character.[66] Such statements collapse all difference between religious and poetic enthusiasm, which was a growing distinction in critical discourse since the aesthetic interventions of Dennis and Shaftesbury at the beginning of the eighteenth century.[67] Dymocke had already analyzed a series of poetic stanzas to show "our Author's Mind . . . to be as deep as the *Bathos* itself" and its various descents into madness.[68] Responding directly to the complimentary assessments of Davies that circulated among *Gazette* readers, specifically regarding his thoughtful nature as manifested through poetic descriptions of his intense stare, Dymocke insists on the opposite interpretation: "[Davies] intended no such Matter, but only some Delineation of that Amazement, which must discover itself in the Eyes of all Poets, who are blessed with any Thing of that noble Madness, and divine Enthusiasm, so necessary to Persons of their Character."[69] Here, Dymocke insists on an incompatibility between rational religious reflection becoming to the character of a minister and divine enthusiasm local to the office of a poet, whose character he questions.[70]

Davies's poetic madness and enthusiasm affects his ministerial character: for Dymocke, exposing Davies's illogical metaphors and chaotic style directly links to his religious practice that traffics in the same mistakes. Poetry functions as a barometer of his bad theology and ministerial practices; or to put it another way, revival practice is, at its root, enthusiastic poetry in its worst form. The most respected revival leader in Virginia, Dymocke would have his readers believe, is not an articulate, well-studied, thoughtfully premeditated minister himself suspicious of unlearned Methodists and Baptists (all of which Davies was), but rather a raving poetic lunatic, eyes ablaze with the madness of poetic and divine enthusiasm.

Furthermore, and more damning, he exemplifies a *common* poetic lunatic, whose poetry unsettles the world through its confused language, which rises when it should fall and falls when it should rise.[71] In Dymocke's words, "I know not whether the cloathing ordinary Thoughts with pompous Diction, or grand Sentiments with mean Language, ought to have the Preference: For it is equally diverting to see a Beggar dress'd like a King, or a King like a Beggar. Our Author is incomparably excellent in both."[72] Dymocke equates mismatching ordinary and exalted language with their proper objects to political and social upheaval. For Dymocke, Davies's revival poetics undermines societal structures that poetic taste helps hold in place.

This is why Dymocke must oust Davies from polite letters. According to Dymocke, Davies's "no language" poetry belongs in the realm of "common conversation" outside of polite society and conversations surrounding taste.[73] Though literary critics customarily compared writers with each other, Dymocke explains that Davies's passages have "no parallel in print," and he therefore must turn to "the Heroes of common Conversation; whose remarkable Actions and Sayings are in every Body's Mouth, and whose Sentiments and Diction are often more extraordinary and singular, than any which have appeared from the Press." He compares Davies's words to those spoken by "Culinary Ladies, *alias*, Kitchen Wenches," a carman driving oxen, and a Custom-House officer, all of whom use illogical images and ridiculous phrases.[74] Davies's lack of taste stems from the very commonness of his interlocutors, the exact opposite of Addison's influential recipe for cultivating poetic sense, which recommends "[c]onversation with Men of a Polite Genius" as a "Method for improving our Natural Taste."[75]

Dymocke's harangue rises to a feverish pitch as he not only equates Davies's poetry with the utterances of black slaves, but accuses Davies of aspiring to be black himself. Dymocke expresses his utter repulsion at Davies's intermixture of revival practice and poetic form by accusing the poet of promoting, even idealizing, the amalgamation of blacks and whites through his use of the marriage metaphor of Christ and the church.

There was already disdain among Anglicans for the sensuous marriage metaphor of Christ and the Church that Davies employs in his poem "On Conjugal Love." Dymocke's criticisms of the marriage metaphor follow a tradition of Anglican characterization of the image as "Nonsensick Raptures" and "Fulsome, Amorous Discourses," as well as a general disregard for plain preaching as nonsensical noise.[76] The deflation of affectionate ties that bound one to Christ accounted for part of the reason Davies regarded the reading of the Anglican John Tillotson and his modern divinity as dangerous to experimental religion.[77] Following in the tradition of Rowe, Watts, and Erskine, Davies cherished the conjugal metaphor and, like the Puritans, enjoyed the affections both for the vehicle (the earthly marriage) and the tenor (union with Christh).[78] Though Watts gracefully retreated from the image by the 1736 edition of his poems and with reservations defended its use in his preface to Rowe's *Devout Exercises* (1737), Davies embraced the image with the fervor of Rowe, Moorhead, and Erskine. Davies turns to the espousal of Christ and the believer to represent the apex of Christian experience. If the universe groans at the separation of Christ and believer, then their marriage embodies the fullness of affect promoted by experimental religion—and for Davies, the ideal poetic language as modeled in scripture. For this reason, to sustain one's relationship with God in terms of a conjugal union becomes the crucial point of contention between Dymocke and Davies.

For Dymocke, the metaphor functions as a barometer of the irrationality of enthusiasts and their dangers to social order. The poem on conjugal love infuriates Dymocke more than the others because it effectively undermines the hierarchies of God and man, man and woman, and man and slave—hierarchies that for Dymocke tasteful poetry upholds. Beginning an inflammatory familial attack, Dymocke points out that, though Davies compliments his wife by calling her the most beautiful of her sex, he ultimately undermines it by declaring that " 'God has a prettier Face than she' and that she is but a Glass, thro' which He views the more enchanting Features of the Deity." Dymocke chastises Davies by calling his behavior worse than "prophane Lovers" "who look into the Eyes of their Mistresses for Babies; and stupidly think of admiring nothing there so much as their own Image."[79] Here, Dymocke mocks the practice of double espousal (being married to one's earthly spouse and to Christ) and the way that it instrumentalizes the earthly spouse. In the case of Davies, it casts his beloved wife into an idealized vehicle of affective religion through which he can access God. And, because in the metaphor of espousal Davies would be the bride of Christ, when Davies looks at her, he sees merely himself. It is not lost on Dymocke that women revival poets are central to revival, and his critique points out not only the dangers of an idealized spouse of Christ, but also of a female muse.

The most odious insult occurs when Dymocke interprets a poetic passage employing the marriage metaphor. Dymocke introduces his reading of Davies's poem by surmising that the author is "somewhat mysterious" in it for good reason. The poem and Dymocke's criticism are worth quoting in full:

> Nor will my OTHER SELF refuse to own
> She finds her *Soul* to *perfect Stature grown*,
> And two *conjoin'd* but make a *finish'd* One

> The rougher Virtues of a manly Mind
> With her more tender female Virtues join'd;
> Form a well-tempered Compound.—So unite
> The *Glooms* of *Black*, and the *mild Streaks* of *White*,
> And form a well mix'd Picture, pleasing to the Sight. p. 59.)

(Was it not for the Word *Soul* in the second Line, I should conjecture, that our Author alludes here to his *Wife's first big Belly*, and to a certain Monster known to chaste Ears by the Name of the Monster with two Backs. But as the Passage stands, it is very *mysterious*; alluding, I think, to a Difference of Sex in Souls. The Simile at the End is extremely curious; and if He wears *dark*, and his Wife *light* coloured Cloaths; or if he have a *swarthly* Complexion and she a very fair one, could not have been more happily applied; except it had been used to represent the *Coalescence* of a *black* Man and a *white* Woman.)[80]

Dymocke refuses Davies's poetic rendition of the mysterious conjugal union and replaces it with another mystery; instead of a sacred poet culling the biblical text for his sacred images, Dymocke finds only base sensuality—allusions to both Shakespeare's mixed-race coupling in *Othello* and to the well-known early American pornographic text *Aristotle's Masterpiece*. The frontispiece of *Aristotle's Masterpiece,* which depicts a white hairy woman giving birth to a black boy as a result of the woman's glance at a picture of a black man during the moment of conception, displays blackness as transferable through the environment and sexual desire. According to Dymocke, Davies's poetics and revivalism, which drew hundreds of slaves, is a dangerous amalgam of erotic religious desire and black contagion. Dymocke makes starkly visible the association between black sensuality and the promiscuity of a revival verse for the masses. There is no question for Dymocke that the mad revival poet of no language has become black. Notably, he has become so through his attachment to the idealized spouse of Christ.

Attempting to exclude Davies from the polite world of genteel sociability, Dymocke goes so far as to veer outside the realm of acceptable conversation himself by broaching the taboo subject of racial mixing. Winthrop Jordan, in his seminal work on American attitudes toward blackness, found that only Charleston accepted public jesting about interracial sex, a point that both underscores the extreme (and possibly unique) nature of Dymocke's critique in the Virginia press and helps explain the silence this particularly odious attack met.[81] No respondent in the exchange, including Davies, addressed the startling comments.[82]

Unlike the *Virginia Gazette*, the *South-Carolina Gazette*'s publication of a verse on interracial sex in 1732 entitled "The Cameleon Lover" prompted a number of responses, including a poem in defense of the practice.[83] "The CAMELEON LOVER" warns white men against pursuing black lovers because they themselves would imbibe blackness and hinges their mistake on defiled taste:

> If what the *Curious* have observ'd be true,
> That the *Cameleon* will assume the *Hue*
> Of all the Objects that approach its *Touch*;
> No wonder then, that the *Armours* of *such*
> Whose *Taste* betrays them to a close Embrace
> With the *dark* Beauties of the *Sable* Race
> (Stain'd with the Tincture of the *Sooty* Sin,)
> Imbibe the *Blackness* of their *Charmer's* Skin.[84]

Through a taste that "betrays" them to desire "*dark* Beauties," the white men who take one of the "*Sable* Race" as lovers not only produce "stain'd" children, but actually become black themselves. The poem points out that such men's sexual taste has gone awry. A practitioner of true taste would recognize the correlation between morality and aesthetics; the skin darkened with "*Sooty* Sin" cannot, by implication, actually attain the status of beauty.[85] The association of whiteness with beauty and blackness with baseness precludes such lovers from attaining polite taste and instead marks them with the sinful hue.[86] Here, like *Aristotle's* frontispiece to which Dymocke alludes, the environment—the spaces one touches and passes through in the heat of desire—produces blackness to manifest one's interior state of sin. For Dymocke, Davies's ministerial and poetic face has been darkened by his communion with black slaves and his marriage that stands in for divine espousal, which disqualify any of his attempts to engage aesthetic discourse.

As expressed in the "Cameleon Lover," a complicated amalgam of desire and repulsion attended Southern white men in the common practice of sexually assaulting black women. This included an intense fear of black men assaulting white women. Paranoia over black male sexual agency routinely surfaced most forcefully whenever anxiety increased over potential slave revolts.[87] Dymocke links poetic and sexual agency when he insists that the production of verse for the pleasure of the uncultivated is akin to authorizing sexual potency in the black male slave. Furthermore, the unpredictability of print's reach, its circulation among the lower classes, attests to Davies's promiscuous and tasteless collection of verse that announces its desires to pleasure that population. Davies's revival poetics, according to Dymocke, promotes black sexual agency, and by implication, slave insurrection.[88] Or, as argued in other *Virginia Gazettte* articles, the natural end of religious tol-eration would be slave emancipation. Best not then tolerate Davies and his revival verse.

Dymocke's characterization of Davies's poetry reveals much about the imbrication of poetry with religion and social order in Virginia. According to him, Davies's poetics of common conversation reeks of extemporaneous prayers and sermons—that is, it is chaotic, illogical, feminine, and black. It is no language; it is effeminate black noise. While Dymocke's harangue grossly misunderstands and contorts Davies's poetics, his insistence that Davies's poetry embodies the core of his revival practice is entirely correct.

Harmony's Token

In a rhetorically powerful sacramental sermon, Davies proclaims the Lord's Supper as a type pointing to the marriage feast in heaven while urging listeners to "*come unto the marriage*" for "*there is room* for all that would come."[89] There is room, there is room, Davies repeats, as one distilling the Balm of Gilead from his lips after thundering the law with all the majesty and grandeur one would expect from a New Light minister hailed as one of the most dynamic orators of his generation.[90] "Come then, ye poor Africans; for yet there is room for you, and you are as welcome as kings and princes."[91]

The last words of the sermon marked the commencement of the cen-tral event of the communion season: the celebration of the Lord's Supper, which looks forward to the wedding banquet of Christ and the Church. Having prepared for the event through a week of prayer, inward retrospec-tion, Bible study, fasting, and catechism, congregants who considered them-selves worthy of partaking in the Lord's Feast would find a seat at the table by presenting their sacramental token. Carrying it with them as they left preparation services most likely the night before, the token issued to Davies's communicants encouraged them in original verse to meet their Lord and Friend at the memorial table (Figure 3.1):

Do this says Christ 'till Time shall end,
In Memory of your dying Friend,
Meet at my Table, and Record,
The Love of Your departed Lord.[92]

Davies's poem, inscribed in the center of the sacramental token, crystallizes the traditional scripture of this primary event through poetic paraphrase in hymnal form. As the congregants reflected with anticipation upon the meaning of the coming communion Sunday, not only reciting the poem but clasping it in the hand or tracing its edge that protruded from a book or pocket, poetry became a primary vessel of conversion and renewal, as well as a tangible symbol of one's connection with God and with his church.

Of the many extant communion tokens, Davies's stands out for its extensive design with words, including not only his name and the specific

Figure 3.1. Samuel Davies's poetry on his communion token.
William Smith Morton Library Special Collections, Union Presbyterian Seminary (Richmond, Virginia).

location, but also the four-line poem. Tokens came in different sizes and shapes throughout the transatlantic Presbyterian community and varied in their inscriptions. Most were square or circular, with the occasional heart shape, and included minimal inscriptions, such as the initials or name of the pastor, or the year or place, a scripture reference, or sometimes a symbol such as a heart.[93] Davies incorporated many of these usual elements in one token and replaced the scriptural reference with a poetic paraphrase of 1 Corinthians 11:23–26. Rather than use a small metal token, Davies used engraved cards in order to give himself enough space to include his poetry. Made from steel engravings that most likely came from England, Davies prepared the cards with the utmost care and placed a high value on them.[94] The detailed inscription reveals the priority Davies placed on poetry in his and his parishioners' religious practice, as well as materially modeling the relationship between Virginian social order and poetry.

The poem in italic script forms the centerpiece of the square token, with typeface bordering the verse on each side. This design of the token brings together print, as it connects to the state and law, with the manuscript poetry of gentry culture and places them both within the context of "the plainest capacity" of evangelical harmony. The words framing the poem clearly situate the verse in terms of locale and minister, with its font tending, if not to overwhelm the center, at least to compete equally with it. The top of the token reads "The Revd. Mr. Samuel Davies," followed by what might seem a redundant title down the right side of the token, "Minister of the Gospel." Upside down on the bottom of the token, and therefore a direct mirror of Davies's name, reads "To the Congregation of Hanover County." Reading up the left side of the token, "In the Colony of Virginia," becomes a further description of the congregation's location. If read as a mirror of the right side, the location underscores Davies's role as a minister of the Gospel in the colony of Virginia, a position he felt was needed in a colony filled with many Anglican ministers who were not preaching a lively gospel. The token, then, not only highlights Davies's actual struggle to attain the status of minister in Virginia; it acted as a symbol of the congregation's legitimacy. This was especially pertinent given that New Light communion ritual differed dramatically from Anglican Eucharistic practices, most notably in the "protracted nature of the event, its emotional journey from penitence to release, its exclusivity, and its resemblance to communal dining."[95] The token that traveled with the possessor after it was issued and before it was remitted on Sunday at the Lord's

Table declared a legitimate Presbyterian faith over a large swath of Anglican territory.

Leigh Eric Schmidt's foundational book on the influence of Scottish holy fairs in the development of early American revivals firmly established the central place of the sacrament in eighteenth-century Presbyterian-led awakenings, as well as the importance of ritual and visible symbols in such practices. For Schmidt, the sacramental season was "a crystallization of their religious world and a celebration of it . . . compress[ing] into a few days a series of transformations that helped give order, meaning, and definition to the lives of the faithful."[96] Serving as a corrective to histories that privilege the spoken word and the printed text over ritual action, Schmidt emphasizes the sacrament as a "*visible Gospel*," in the words of the popular catechist John Willison, through which Christ spoke "a Sacramental Dialect."[97]

Terming the visible sacrament a "dialect," however, returns us again to language, though with an expansive understanding of the phrase that is more in keeping with eighteenth-century Protestant uses—ones which engaged both the internal and external senses to become conversant in the language of the heart, the language of God, and the language of the sacrament. Davies's communion token literally inscribed the tool used to access the symbolic rite of Christ's sacrifice with verse, thereby inserting the language of poetry into the heart of New Light conversion and renewal practice. The token materializes the theory of sacred poetry Davies described in the preface to his poetic collection, reaching even those who could not afford a book or acquire the skill to read it. Or, perhaps more accurately, Davies's theology and practice of the Lord's Table produced a theory of revival poetry born out of an emphasis on this renewal time open to "all that would come."[98]

Davies used poetry for several purposes, from a mnemonic device for his congregants to a barometer for his own spiritual state. Like many New Lights, Davies understood his success as a minister to be rooted in his own spiritual life; to move other people's emotions, and hence their will, his own emotions needed to be stirred.[99] Many of the poems in the second part of Davies's collection serve not only to summarize his sermons, but also to mobilize his emotions. As he writes in his preface, after studying on a Saturday evening he would compose poems in order "to give [himself] a more lively Impression of the Subject of Discourse for the ensuing Day."[100] In addition to his own preparation and mediation, Davies viewed his poems as a type of sermon note or mnemonic device, or in his own words, "a Hint to my Hearers to help them to recollect the Discourses themselves."[101] Many of his poems, then, functioned either to prepare for, or to point to, the event of the sermon, an event which required the correct spiritual and emotional disposition on the part of the minister in order to inspire a deeply felt response in his hearers. These poems were not purposed simply to recall the words of the sermon, but to recall or to inspire (and re-inspire) the emotional disposition required to be moved to hear and then to do.

In the case of the token poem, which was dispensed before the Sunday of the Sacramental Sermon, the poem functioned closer to Davies's use as preparation for the sermon to come. Yet, the token paraphrases the scripture used during the celebration of the Lord's Table, not the specific sacramental sermon, which means the poem pointed the believer to the sacramental ritual. Choosing the sacramental scripture meant that Davies's tokens could be reused and were not specific to any number of sacramental sermons, surely a decision of necessity given their expense. Even so, the token as a commemoration of a memorialization service (the essence of the sacramental scripture "to remember Christ until he comes") functioned to prepare the congregant for the event of communion at the same time that it functioned to recall previous sacramental events.[102] The poem draws together both the bodily act of continually partaking of the sacrament and the act of recording the love of Christ experienced at the Table. The continual memorializing hinges on the frozen moment of Christ's death, "your dying Friend," who is continually dying for the sins of the people in each age. The poem serves as a visible record of this love like an epitaph carved into a miniature tombstone marking a grave that is no more. Unlike the poems annexed to sermons to help a person recall the discourse, the token poems would be absent after the sermon and the reception of the elements. The text of the poem acknowledges this absence, asking the congregant to meet at the table and then to record for herself the love of the departed Christ.

The token poem aided the parishioner in meditation and preparation, acts that themselves gave access to Christ's Table. The poem also acknowledges the repetitive and ritualized nature of the event—that they will repeat this process until Christ comes—meaning that the token poem will appear again. When it does, it will function both as a memorial of the past celebration and a preparation for the event to come. The ease of memorizing such a short poem meant that parishioners would have had a form of it at least loosely imprinted on their memories, calling them back to the table and back to their own memorialization of the event. In this sense, the token would appear and disappear, but the poem would become inscribed on the heart. The token was a physical reminder and sign of the heart transformed by Christ's sacrifice, and it was the poem that moved between the visible symbol of this process and the inward sign. Poetry was the tangible, imprintable essence of conversion.

The melding of poetry with the communion token reflected the very nature of the Eucharistic event by highlighting both the common and sacred nature of verse. Poetry could ornament a church-sanctioned symbol that designated the saints and gave them access to the table exclusively reserved for them. At the same time, the poetry was of lower taste, written by a non-canonical poet participating in an event open to anyone regardless of requirements of taste, class, or color. The Lord's Table, according to Davies's Sacramental sermon, was a table cast aside by the elite and available to any on the street, from the lowest sinner to the least significant slave. Davies's theory of poetry as an essential tool in the spread of the gospel stems from this basic understanding of the Lord's Table accessed by anyone through a token of poetry. In Davies's practice of fencing the wedding feast with his poetic token, we can see his theorization of poetic access in material form. The practice makes visible the work of poetry in creating a revival community focused on affective piety and experiential religion. It brings attention to issues of access—both the way verse aided the parishioner in her general journey toward God and in literally providing entrance to a specific Lord's Table, in contradistinction to the often inhibiting function of taste.

The political implications were not determined. Though no documentation exists regarding any slave's interpretation of Davies's token, it surely functioned in multiple registers. Much like a master's pass, slaves could have attached magical properties to the speaking paper, associated it with freedom of movement and eventual emancipation, delighted in its potentially subversive nature, used it toward literacy, or any combination of these and other affiliated meanings. The inscription of the minister's name and title over the geographical space claimed by the Anglican slave master, particularly, could have elicited a sense of escape from the plantation's dominion.[103] Davies would not have approved of any implications outside of the spiritual. But his authority to determine his message did not extend far. Neither did his control over the influences of his own poetics.

Davies ministry has been deemed by scholars as "the first sustained proselytization of slaves" in Virginia."[104] He had unusual success, both in intensity and scope, among those of African descent, with about 300 regular black attenders in his handful of congregations which he maintained and more than a thousand black visitors at various times. Differing dramatically from the position of the Anglican churches in Virginia, Davies insisted that slaves be taught to read, and he instituted a system of slaves teaching other slaves to maximize his efforts.[105] Hymns and poems were central to this process. Because of what he described as the slaves's "Ecstatic . . . Delight in . . . Psalmody," he requested verse, especially Watts, from his missionary sponsors for his work with black parishioners.[106] That Davies's poems appeared in print the same year that Virginia outlawed slave literacy did not help their reception.

But it was not just that slaves desired hymnals, it was also that Davies desired what he believed to be the more perfect harmony of slaves. Much of the excitement he exhibited surrounding the education of slaves came from his observation that they were more attuned to song and skilled in harmony than white people; he writes, they have the "best Voices & Ears for musick" and sing "the praise of God in perfect harmony" better than any white congregation.[107] Davies's characterization of black people as naturally attuned to sound participates in the construction of what Mark M. Smith calls the invention of " 'modern' racial stereotypes" through the use of "putatively premodern, proximate, nonvisual senses."[108] Davies's idealization of a natural black musicality led him to incorporate what he imagined was their solely heavenly inspiration into his own auditory religious practices while he distanced himself from their actual bondage. He recorded one such instance in a letter requesting books for slaves:

> Sundry of them [the Negroes] have lodged all night in my kitchen; and, sometimes, when I have awaked about two or three a-clock in the morning, a torrent of sacred harmony poured into my chamber, and carried my mind away to Heaven. In this seraphic exercise, some of them spend almost the whole night.[109]

Davies describes the slaves as the facilitators of his poetical and heavenly flight via their harmony, which he perceives as unconnected to their physical situation and thus fully accessible from his own subject position. While they take refuge from their normal slave quarters (and the attendant deprivations and debasements) in the servant's kitchen, Davies enjoys a flight into heaven from the comfort of his sequestered chamber. The slaves' experiences and accounts of the sources and meanings of their all-night singing evade Davies, as he imagines that the sounds signify only his religious tradition and his meanings of it.

Within these substantial limitations, he accepts the slaves as true spiritual mediators: with the angels they are priests to God who can lift this world and its inhabitants into the pulse of heaven. Like most revival ministers, Davies described affective experiences with the divine that were often facilitated by heavenly music. To rephrase Schmidt slightly, evangelical harmony, a concept that undergirded both music and poetry, "was not merely a trope . . . but a highly tangible part of the evangelical imagination."[110] This is evident in Davies's account of his reoccurring sense of God's beauty and his pleasure in it; or, in the words of Jonathan Edwards, "the sweetness" of an experiential knowledge of God's goodness. But here the facilitators of Davies's reoccurring heavenly aesthetic experiences were slaves. Davies's argument is clear: the "noise" of slaves and "kitchen wenches" is no less than the sacred harmony that undergirds all of evangelical soteriology, anthropology, and theology. His articulation of black slaves as having a greater ability to produce harmonious music underscores his insistence on their innate capacity for harmony; that is, the mark of being human, of bearing the image of God. And though he promulgates a general articulation of pre-modern races as identified with sound, his conception of harmony was not bounded by aurality; it was synesthetic—the stamp of heaven in the person, including the African slave and the white master. This is all to say that these appropriated night sounds point to how Davies found his poetics were not only confirmed but also influenced by his experience with the slaves he sought to educate and convert.

While Davies did not indulge or tolerate the democratizing ramifications of evangelical harmony and the mixing of slave sounds with the religious sublime, the political potential was not lost upon critics of revivalism in Virginia like Dymocke. Even with Davies's conservative application of his own theology, the rendition of evangelical harmony in his preface, combined with his idealization of slave harmony, makes the idea of Davies slipping into a black poetic persona seem not so farfetched. If evangelical experience regularly reveals one's internal emotional and spiritual transformations through outward signs of affective experience, Davies's momentary blackness confirmed the greater harmony within him.

While the acknowledgment is small and vexed at best, the moment in the poem opens up what scholars have come to recognize: enslaved and free African Americans were integral to the development of American revivalist religion, music, and literature. That Davies found his fellow black Christians exceeding in the virtues of feeling and harmony, as well as more

than competent at acquiring literacy, fundamentally influenced and confirmed his theory of poetry as a revival tool accessed by the generality of
mankind through sound. That poetry would fan the flame of revival, that
poetry was, in a sense, the essence of revival—these are clearly enunciated in
his preface. That the people seemingly naturally equipped to tune into this
mystic sound, filling pews, fields, and cabins, were black became apparent to
Davies through his experience. The sensorium that Davies produces through
his poetic language, rich in synesthesia, prosopopoeia, and the metaphor of
the conjugal union—all of which produce a world in which senses mingle
with each other—enables a migration of black harmony to infuse his own
sensorial capacities. While the imagination, taste, and the soul could be
used by Addison, Kames, and others to distinguish what we now call aesthetics from the bodily senses, and thereby exclude classes of people, evangelical harmony as practiced by Davies and many other evangelicals did not.
Because harmony was the stamp of heaven, the image of God in people, it
was in essence the mystery of the mixture of heaven and earth, the reflection
of the incarnation, and the perfected world to come. Harmony was basic to
understanding humankind, its past, its present, and its future.

Crucial to the evangelical story of the image of God in man, its marring
through Adam's sin, and its rebirth through Christ's atonement for sin, was
the singular event of one human race. Davies's harmony was a monogenic
aesthetics. As anthropology began to develop as a science based in large part
on the experiment of the "new" world, it became a primary avenue for deter-
mining racial equality or inequality. Most arguments for innate and perma-
nent inequality denied a singular origin for the human species and employed
aesthetic arguments to do so. The insistence of Dymocke's black noise to describe revivalists and their artistic expression was, in the context of an evangelical anthropology grounded in universal harmony, a refusal to accept this
mark of a universal image of God in humanity. As I have already indicated,
for many white evangelicals like Davies, the image of God in a person did
not translate to political and social freedom. Evangelical harmony broke out
in different directions around the political question of slavery. Even though
Davies insisted on the essential equality of black souls in heaven and the intellectual capacities of black people and their need for education, he still accom-
modated slavery, and his characterization of Africans as naturally attuned to
song still participated in the construction of race through the stratification
of senses. A world in which senses mingled and in which the revival poet
desired even the capacity of the rocks, mere objects, to praise God also set up

a logic that could idealize the harmony of slaves even as it relegated them as objects to be bought and sold. And clearly Davies's investment in the capacity of slaves to convert was more than interested—he made it starkly apparent that he saw the conversion of slaves as a way to shore up the British colonies against the French and Indians. In this way, both Dymocke and Davies saw aesthetics as necessary to a hierarchical social and political order that was raced and gendered and therefore underscored the imperative of raising poetry in an "uncultivated land."[111] The material presence of harmony through the bodily presence of slaves could confirm the universality of aesthetics and salvation, while also circumscribing it as religious affection which signaled one's freedom from sin, not civil laws and social practices. Even so, its democratic potential was clear. Davies's "course provisions" were ripe for criticism, to which the next chapter turns.

4

The Ethiop's Verse

The Limits of Poetic Capacity and Espousal Piety

Virulently denying the very possibility of a black woman inhabiting the position of the poet, Thomas Jefferson infamously wrote, "Religion, indeed, has produced a Phyllis Whately; but it could not produce a poet. The compositions published under her name are below the dignity of criticism. The heroes of the Dunciad are to her as Hercules to the author of that poem."[1] Jefferson's vicious rejection of Wheatley and her poetry, as many scholars have pointed out, positions her as a creature of sensuality and religion rather than an artist armed with imagination and intellect, as part of his ethnological project to ground slavery in insuperable differences between the races. If poetry was a sign of genius and imagination that was in itself a mark of one's right to liberty and enfranchisement—an idea that gained traction during the Revolution and early Republic—then Jefferson could never admit that African people wrote poetry. However, considering he was willing to admit that religion produced something parallel to but not actually poetry, it is worth asking: what did "a Phyllis Whately" signify to Jefferson, and why would he choose to separate religion as anathema to intellect and imagination?

A growing number of scholars have shown that aesthetic taste was central to early American thought and politics and to understanding citizenship in the early Republic.[2] Aesthetics became key to differentiating between not only people but also races and civilizations. These distinctions helped shape an exceptional history of the emerging and early nation, grounded in progress and the idea of a universal, modern liberal subject. David Waldstreicher, one of the most astute readers of Jefferson on Wheatley, convincingly argues that Jefferson dismissed Wheatley's obvious classicism because her poetry undercut claims of American progress by revealing the fact that American slavery was actually worse than ancient slavery. Waldstreicher concludes, "It was not just that she was an African and a slave writing, or writing poetry, or

Awakening Verse. Wendy Raphael Roberts, Oxford University Press (2020). © Oxford University Press.
DOI: 10.1093/oso/9780197510278.001.0001

writing Christian poetry: It is that she was writing neoclassical poetry, and in doing so bringing, by stealth (or by simile) her African and female experience to bear on various aspects of secular as well as religious life, including the politics of the Revolution."[3] The political implications of neoclassical poetry were clear and devastating.[4] Yet, we can't fully understand the extent of the critique her classicism performed without also grasping the importance of evangelical poetics to her thought and work.

When Wheatley became a famous transatlantic evangelical poet, she critiqued and transformed the tradition into which she wrote. The particular history of revival poetry that I have traced reveals that her interventions were multiple and significant. If we take into account the revivalist portion of her audience and the Whitefieldian practices in which she was immersed, her poetic choices materialize as stark and specific interventions in the poetics central to revivalist theology and experience. Most significantly, Wheatley's poetics entail subtle yet poignant critiques of both the limitations of the personae of white women poet-ministers built upon affective espousal devotion and of the political impotence of an anthropology based in evangelical harmony and appeals to the plainest capacity. An avid student of multiple poetic traditions, she knew evangelical verse extremely well and, as this chapter will argue, avoided many of the techniques revival poets employed precisely for the same reasons Jefferson wanted to blazon them on her: they were indications of low poetic capacity, not of eloquence, high literacy, genius, or one's rightful place in the social and political sphere. In fact, Jefferson's insistence that Wheatley's verse be religious and not classical shows that he recognized she brought them together in a politically threatening manner. Wheatley's classicism was not separate from her religious poetics; rather, it was a critique and remaking of revival poetics and its ambivalent relationship to slavery. In fact, it was precisely Wheatley's subject position that enabled her to critique revivalist poetics and its plainest capacity through classicism—even going so far as to reject its very premise. Recognizing the ways that Wheatley critiqued revival poetry brings into view how enslaved femininity became a site of dynamic exchange between religious and secular aesthetics and epistemologies. A history of revival poetry, then, not only reveals the full import of Wheatley's poetic choices in relation to slavery, but also how revivalism was integral to the often secularized story of the invention of race science.

Evangelical Anthropology and Jefferson's Race Science

By the time Wheatley began her poetic career, Watts's call for poets to write for the vulgar or "plainest capacity" had become part of an emerging scientific discourse of race. As Jefferson's argument makes explicit, poetry and aesthetics were giving shape to emergent anthropological inquiries and race science. The doctrine of human nature, or what the sixteenth century first termed "anthropology," in the eighteenth century became part of a widespread investment in natural history, a transformation that took place alongside the emerging scientific revolution, the slave trade, and European imperialism. At the same time that a modern proto-anthropology and an environmental theory of race emerged in the eighteenth century as part of the project of colonial modernity, what would later be termed "aesthetics" also became a predominant concern. Explorations of the nature of man and his origins turned not only to climate and to bodily characteristics, but also to poetry.[5]

It is imperative to recognize that when Jefferson suggested that religion produced Wheatley, he did not just mean any kind of religion, nor was he positioning the broad genre of religious poetry in contradistinction to classical verse. Various forms of English poetry had brought together religion and classicism, including the still popular Christian belletrism and religious sublime. To make clear his target, Jefferson leads into his pronouncement with a discussion of the racialized harmony that had come to identify black poetic capability in terms resembling those used by people like the Anglican priest Dymocke to discredit revival verse. Jefferson writes, "In music [the blacks] are more generally gifted than the whites with accurate ears for tune and time, and they have been found capable of imagining a small catch. Whether they will be equal to the composition of a more extensive run of melody, or of a complicated harmony, is yet to be proved."[6] By distinguishing between blacks and whites on the basis of sensuality and intellect, Jefferson designates not just media (aural verses textual) and degrees of musical difficulty (simple African tunes against complicated Anglo musical composition), but also poetic genres. The particular association of black slaves with revivalism and the hymnody of Watts places Jefferson's comments squarely within the continued battle between Southern belles lettres and revival verse geared toward the plainest capacity. Jefferson concedes, even insists, that slaves can produce revival hymns. What they cannot produce is poetry.

His ethnography, in other words, produced racialized genres. The evangelical harmony that Samuel Davies had espoused and that Dymocke had lambasted relied primarily on theology and the ideas of taste and sensibility that undergirded social structures and genres. Davies integrated experience to ground observable differences between the capacity of Africans and whites to access music and harmony, which participated in a general way in discourses of natural history, but he did not create an ethnography of race rooted in the body. His understanding of blackness was in keeping with the majority view of the colonialists in the eighteenth century, what Katy Chiles designates as "transformable race"—an exterior and flexible trait, rather than an internal and fixed biological category.[7] Jefferson advances Dymocke's earlier dismissal of Davies's revival poetics as a form of uncivilized black noise by interpolating it explicitly as ethnographic data, as part of a larger project in which a basic capacity for harmony became one characteristic among many that he permanently located in the bodies of lower races.

While most of the eighteenth century had seen one's capacity defined in terms of taste, which could be sharpened and refined through education or sensibility, Jefferson attempted to ground aesthetic difference in the body.[8] As William Huntting Howell points out in his reading of Wheatley's critique of the modern liberal subject, Jefferson "makes a sort of a racial science of the arts of poetry appreciation and performance."[9] Jefferson insists that "a Whately" is the category of people with religious capacity but not intellectual and refined aesthetic capacity. Though Wheatley may be able to mimic fine poetry through the extensive training of her master, she cannot produce an original piece because she does not have the capacity for genius—following David Hume's earlier claim that Africans do not have the intellectual capacity required for the kind of sentiment necessary to experience the beauty of the fine arts.[10] Though a romantic genius might instantly recognize and produce fine art sans education, Jefferson followed a developing line of argument that held that even if Africans could learn, they did not possess this deeper, innate capacity. Jefferson associated simple jingle or rhyme not only with childishness but also with impeded intellectual progress, while associating blank verse with the free liberal subject. For Jefferson, what a revival religion produced was an ideal slave, not a rights-bearing individual.[11]

As detailed in the previous chapter, evangelical harmony proposed a type of universal poetry immediately accessible to every person through the God-given sense of beauty. Though, as Davies said, "The Generality of Mankind have neither Opportunity nor perhaps Capacity for [poetic] Refinements," all people had the capacity for "a glorious Immortality, and the purer Joys of Paradise."[12] The "perhaps" performs a good amount of work: it allows that poetic refinement is limited to this world and of little matter to God and the ultimate pleasures of the soul that await the saved. Yet even without refinement, evangelical harmony asserted a meaningful and valuable universal poetic capacity that participated fully with God's image. Intellectual capacity or reasoning was not necessary to this equation. This anthropology was rooted in a commitment to theology and the biblical account of monogenesis.

There was an ironic edge to evangelicalism's more expansive offer of religious authority to a wide array of people. To be sure, the emphasis on authentic Christianity allowed a host of individuals to sidestep formal education and perform their piety in enthusiastic displays of the body that were already associated with disenfranchised groups, including women, slaves, and natives. Yet at the same time that evangelicalism provided access to authority for people across socially and historically produced inequities, it could also easily accommodate the debasement of peoples, since it acknowledged that affective religion was based in a common and basic aesthetic experience rather than creed or intellectual assent. For example, Samuel Stanhope Smith, a Presbyterian and president of the College of New Jersey, who was one of the best-known American anthropologists, exceeding even Jefferson in popularity, defended Wheatley against Jefferson's attacks.[13] Yet even though Smith's monogenic anthropology may have ensured the offer of salvation to all peoples through affirming the unity of the human race, it still proposed a hierarchical history of degeneration from Caucasians.

It is within this context that I consider Wheatley's strategic poetic choices as a matter of politics. If Wheatley was to be identified with religion, as Jefferson so adamantly insisted, it is important to consider why, enmeshed as she was in the world of revivalism, she would have chosen to avoid writing revival poems in the manner most typical of the Watts and Wesleyan tradition, those we might imagine slaves tutored in English via revival hymns would compose. The history of revival poetics elucidates the intense political significance of Wheatley's choice to embrace revivalism and its role of the woman poet-minister, yet to write primarily in the style of a Christian belletrist. In short, Wheatley sensed that her arguments for liberty would be encumbered by the accumulated racial associations embedded in revivalist poetry and its foundational anthropology expressed in Watts's mission to write for "the plainest capacity." Instead, she dramatically re-schematized the default relationship between the nature of black people and evangelical harmony to instead align Africans with culture and intellect. And though Jefferson attempted to expel Wheatley and other African Americans from literary history, his words undermine this effort because they inadvertently point to the fundamental influence African slaves had on the development of poetry in early America.

Jefferson cannot help highlighting the importance of this poetic history—a history that Wheatley deftly negotiated and reimagined to secure her own freedom and to argue for the freedom of other Africans. Davies and Jefferson represent two views of aesthetic anthropology that Wheatley engaged. Shrewdly maneuvering within and against them, she employed both a strategic politics of respectability and a finely tuned politics of refusal. She demanded to be considered as primarily a literary poet, even as she engaged revivalism in order to challenge the aesthetic hierarchies built to justify slavery. If Wheatley is the "radicalization of [political] enthusiasm," in Gregory Mac Gilgore's terms, she is at the same time the radicalization of religious enthusiasm and its revival poetics.[14]

Following this introductory section, this chapter moves through three sections to probe how Wheatley's verse engaged and critiqued evangelical poetics and its compliance with slavery. The next section establishes Wheatley's grounding in, and influence by, revival poetics by reading her George Whitefield elegy in light of the woman poet-minister tradition. I argue that this elegy resists the expected affect of a woman poet-minister and re-schematizes the relationship of slaves to harmony and mimicry. The subsequent section considers two formal and theological challenges Wheatley poses to revival poetics: plainest capacity and espousal piety. I maintain that Wheatley's hymns are a critique of Watts's plainest capacity and that her Christian belletrism amounts to an embrace of respectability politics, and that together these dynamics challenge the idea of a progressive Christian history. In the process, Wheatley engages and transforms espousal piety by inventing a new woman poet-minister persona, the Ethiop, which introduces the tensions of political freedom and chattel slavery into the Calvinist couplet and lived theology. The final section considers how Wheatley's hymns, in tandem with the Ethiop poet-minister persona, engage in a politics of refusal. I argue that her poetry exposes feminine sentimentalism and the domestic as underpinning white liberalism so that by refusing the domestic and the plainest capacity, she also rejects that which helps structure the capacities of liberal rights-bearing subjects. Ultimately, Wheatley's poetry deeply engages with revival poetics to critique the very category of capacity—whether low or high, evangelical or scientific, theologized or racialized—that sustained slavery.

In the Line of Women Poet-Ministers

When George Whitefield brought his brand of revivalism to the shores of British North America in the mid-eighteenth century, many people received him as a man sent directly by God. Poems, like the widely circulated "To the Rev. Mr. Whitefield On His Design for Georgia" (1737), placed him at the center of a grandiose vision of salvation history. It praised the "bles'd Prophet," who mastered the Atlantic like Jesus had once calmed the Red Sea, and would perform a feat no less than apocalyptic. He would ". . . from *Satan's* Pow'r whole Nation's free, / While half the World to JESUS bow the knee." The poem prophetically proclaimed that "Children, as yet unborn, shall bless your Lore, / Who, thus, to save them, left your *Native Shore.*"[15] The poet could never have imagined a precocious young girl renamed Phillis who, after being violently torn from her native African shore and sold into slavery, would bless the itinerant's lore, and in doing so not only save herself but also contribute to the work of freeing an entire nation. Yet, this is exactly what happened.

She was a small girl estimated to be about seven years old on the basis of her missing teeth when she stepped off the slave ship *Phillis* in 1761. Just six years later, Wheatley's first poem appeared in print as part of a revival upsurge in Newport, Rhode Island. It was soon followed by her career-making elegy for the Rev. Whitefield in 1770.[16] The elegy made possible the London printing of her first and only book *Poems on Various Subjects, Religious and Moral* (1773) a mere 12 years after her survival of the Middle Passage. The decades-older poem on Whitefield's designs for Georgia, which celebrated Whitefield's towering status in the evangelical eschatological imagination while unintentionally marking his largest moral failing—justifying and utilizing slave labor—was still available for the young slave to read. And she most likely did so, as she read every other major evangelical poem and occasional revivalist verse of the era with the encouragement of her mistress Susanna and her mistress's daughter Mary.

It took precious little time for Wheatley to grasp the religious and political force of revival poetry and to expect, like revival poets before her, monumental results in people and in Christian history from seemingly innocuous verse. Her expectations attached to her elegy for Whitefield, the largest international celebrity the world had seen, must have made it difficult to sleep as she quickly penned the lines and secured a printer within 11 days of the revered itinerant's death. The rapid composition, Vincent Carretta points out, bespeaks a profound knowledge of "Whitefield's cultural significance as a religious and political figure."[17] It also demonstrates an intimate familiarity with revival poetry. In the press, Wheatley had witnessed transatlantic and local revivalist leaders embrace publicity and perform their ministerial authority on the page. In the home, she served visiting itinerants, possibly Whitefield himself, who modeled evangelical conversation for her as they kept her abreast of revivalist news and culture. In others' homes, she performed her poetry and gained an intimate knowledge of the forms of religious grieving. All the while, she was eager to learn from the laypeople around her, primarily white women, who seized opportunities to shape the direction and culture of this powerful religious movement. Its poetry, Wheatley clearly observed, was a promising avenue for affecting masses of hearts and minds.

Her attraction and quick mastery of eighteenth-century colonial poetics points not only to her remarkable intellect, but also to the way that her own West African culture and Atlantic slavery experiences set her up to understand it. The social and political role of British North American eighteenth-century poetry was in many ways similar to West African poetry. Both were occasional, social, and imbued with political and religious import. Eighteenth-century British North American literature modeled itself in relation to the classical, which was concerned with the rise and fall of republics, the life and freedom of slaves, the power of gods and the dead, and the virtue and glory of eloquent poets and storytellers. Such themes resonated with the experience of Atlantic slavery. As a West African girl, part of the African diaspora, Wheatley would have already understood women's central role in ritual and mourning, as well as the value of women's eloquent words spoken to people in prominent positions.[18] The role of women poet-ministers as spiritual guides and models of religious speech would have been attractive because of its familiar contours.

Before becoming a transatlantic poetic sensation, Wheatley had already succeeded in gathering an audience of white religious women. Both Mary and Susanna avidly promoted their young protégé in local poetic culture. It was this larger female network that circulated her manuscript poetry and advanced her social status and poetic reputation.[19] It is not surprising, then, that Wheatley's elegy for Whitefield drew on the tradition of the woman poet-minister, and Sarah Moorhead's Whitefield poem in particular. By the time of Whitefield's death in 1770, a distinct poetic discourse had already developed around notable itinerants in Boston, and Whitefield in particular. Poets, both praising and mocking the great evangelist, displayed an awareness of each other's poems and utilized common motifs. The large body of poetry written about Whitefield, including those penned by women poets like Moorhead and Jane Dunlap, supplied Wheatley with a clear tradition and set of expectations on which to draw. That Wheatley's Whitefield elegy utilizes themes and images common to earlier poetry about Whitefield underscores how well-versed she had become in the culture of revival poetry, and how invested she was in the poetry of women poet-ministers. Whitefield's visits had long been associated with poetic productions, including Ralph Erskine's bestselling *Gospel Sonnets*, which continually circulated in awakening culture, and the "New-England Lady" and the transatlantic "spouse of Christ" who often accompanied it was not only a well-known example of a woman poet-minister, but also a close friend of the Wheatley family.

The Whitefield elegy marked Wheatley's sudden arrival on the international scene. When "A Poem, By Phillis, A Negro Girl, in Boston" appeared under the title "On the Death of the Reverend George Whitefield" (1770), it immediately became the most popular Whitefield elegy in the colonies and England, and Wheatley's name became known on the European continent. Wheatley's elegy appeared in broadside form in the revival-rich communities of New York, Philadelphia, and Newport and was republished in Boston four additional times by the end of the year.[20] It migrated immediately across the Atlantic, where it was printed to benefit a family most likely associated with Whitefield's Tabernacle. Its appearance a year later with the London reprint of Rev. Ebenezer Pemberton's memorial address in Boston indicates that it was either the elegy used during that service, or it had risen to the status of a de facto official elegy.

Wheatley's poem was not composed, promoted, and published on a lark, but with a clear sense of the poetic and religious terrain in which it was entering. Carretta has observed that the October 11, 1770, announcement of Wheatley's illustrated Whitefield elegy "was more appropriate for an established poet than for a seventeen-year-old enslaved girl" and that "the full title and headnote for the poem indicate the great expectations Phillis and her owner had for its reception."[21] Clearly, Wheatley, Susanna, and Mary could not have known the extent of her coming fame. Yet, they understood the miraculous place a slave poet like Wheatley occupied in the story of redemption and renewal that Whitefield preached.

While the majority of Whitefield elegies circulated anonymously, Wheatley's title page heralded the black slave girl's presence, making it essential to the act of memorialization. Unlike many revival poets, especially women like Sarah Moorhead who entered print with at least the appearance of anonymity, Wheatley's poetic celebrity depended crucially on her identity. The portrait that would appear three years later with Wheatley's collection of poems confirms what was already true of her circulating poems: they were, one might say, experienced ekphrastically.[22] That is, white audiences read and understood her poetry always in relation to the image her biography painted for them, which, as Eileen Razzari Elrod points out, was ethnographic in nature.[23] The elegy's announcement and each of the published poem's variants highlights Wheatley as an enslaved black poet, and two of the printings place her in spatial equality (if not outright competition) with the revered itinerant. The eight-page elegy printed by Russell and Boyles in 1770 includes a cover that in effect contains two images: a woodcut of the sleeping saint and another triggered in the imagination by the large type, "A Poem, By Phillis, a *Negro* Girl." While the single sheet print includes Wheatley's name subordinated to Whitefield's large type, Isaiah Thomas's single sheet broadside serves as a corrective fueled by popular response; Thomas, leaving off the biography, need only title the broadside "Phillis's POEM," followed by the much smaller print, "On The Death of Mr. Whitefield." The woodcut, which pictures Whitefield in the pulpit, not only illustrates the first line of the poem ("Hail happy Saint on thy immortal throne!") but also positions Phillis's name between Whitefield's death and his resurrection. In this space, Wheatley fashioned herself as a poet-minister. Like the graphic representation on the front page of her elegy, she quite literally arose "on the death of" Whitefield.

Elegiac competition had long been part of New England culture, but a colonial slave had never entered it in such a public manner. Such promotion of a slave as exhibited on the front page of the lengthy broadside evidently worked without transgressing the bounds of proper respect due the beloved minister. Rather, the elegy catapulted Wheatley to transatlantic fame and enshrined her image with that of the first cultic hero. That the poet who would soon be referred to as "a Wonder of the Age" appeared on the same broadside as the "marvel of the age" is astounding—an incredible historical collision that cannot be overemphasized.[24] At the same time, it is entirely in keeping with an evangelical milieu seeking grandiose demonstrations of God's new and expanding work of grace, which Whitefield's ministry represented. Wonder begat wonder; celebrity, celebrity. The miraculous image of the poet "Phillis" exceeded the limits of the imagination, exploding the boundaries of black and white, minister and child, male and female, slave and free in a way that approximated the awe due to the divine celebrity whose preaching pushed hearers to their psychological limits.[25]

The curiosity that had drawn thousands to hear Whitefield over three decades of itinerancy suddenly mobilized once again around a slave girl speaking from the pulpit of a revival poem. Wheatley signaled her authority as a poet-minister by employing the poetic discourse developed around Whitefield and actively building on previous poems. From a poet that mastered several verse traditions, this comes as no surprise. To ascend to the great itinerant's pulpit, she carefully crafts her steps, beginning with praise of the minister who called the pulpit his throne: "Hail happy Saint on thy immortal throne!" Celebrating his glorification in heaven, the line proclaims that Whitefield's ministry culminated in enduring joy. To the Boston poets who alternatively epitomized Whitefield as "happy" when they approved of him and "unhappy" when they satirized him, Wheatley provides the last word.[26] Readers familiar with the numerous poems for Whitefield, both praises and parodies, that appeared regularly during his American tours would appreciate Wheatley's next line, "To thee complaints of grievance are unknown," for its description of Whitefield's heavenly remove not only from his bereaved fans, but also from those who had criticized his ministry.[27]

Wheatley's opening stanza adeptly encapsulates Whitefield's auditory genius, which had already become a poetic convention when it came to addressing Whitefield in verse:

> Hail happy Saint on thy immortal throne!
> To thee complaints of grievance are unknown;
> We hear no more the music of thy tongue,
> Thy wonted auditories cease to throng.
> Thy lessons in unequal'd accents flow'd!
> While emulation in each bosom glow'd;
> Thou didst, in strains of eloquence refin'd,
> Inflame the soul, and captivate the mind.
> Unhappy we, the setting Sun deplore!
> Which once was splendid, but it shines no more;

He leaves this earth for Heaven's unmeasur'd height:
And worlds unknown, receive him from our sight:
There WHITEFIELD wings, with rapid course his way,
And sails to Zion, through vast seas of day.[28]

Wheatley repeats the near cliché references to Whitefield's sound, but she does so to inflect his rhetoric with a tint of poetic genius—"thy lessons in unequal'd accents flow'd"—thereby merging the itinerant's sermons with the meter of poetry.[29] Another broadside mistakenly attributed a Wesley hymn to Whitefield and, in essence, memorialized Whitefield as a great hymnist— a slip that speaks to the importance of the production of sacred verse as a marker of evangelical spiritual authority.[30] Wheatley's poem emphasizes Whitefield as a versifier, a gesture that elevates him to the position of a poet-minister.

The stanza not only creates a lineage for revival poetry by fashioning Whitefield as a poet, but also connects Wheatley specifically to the well-known revival poet of Boston, Sarah Moorhead. Styling Whitefield's eloquence as meter in the hands of a masterful poet, she also renders his listeners as aspiring poets themselves by describing the glowing in their breasts as "emulation," evoking the notion of classical imitation in which the artist copies the master in order to excel. That the poem highlights this relationship to poetic forebearers within the context of revivalism points also to the poem's relation to earlier Whitefield poems. In fact, Wheatley's 14-line stanza that opens the original Whitefield elegy pays homage to Moorhead by inverting the 14-line stanza that opens Moorhead's "In Honour of the Reverend Mr. *Whitefield*" (1744). Moorhead's poem begins:

Welcome dear *Whitefield* to these joyful Coasts;
Couragious Soldier of the GOD of HOSTS.
The Gospel Trump, seraphick Herald, sound:
The *Heavens* applaud; the *Earth* with Joy resounds.
The *infernal Regions* rage to hear thy Voice;
Convicts cry out for Help, and *Saints* rejoyce.
Erroneous Minds their hateful Notions leave,
Give Angels Joy, while piously *they* grieve,
To think they 'ere embrac'd such horrid Fiends,
Prov'd Foes to CHRIST, yet tho't themselves his Friends
Lethargick Souls like mine, start from their Sleep;

> Hear JESUS speak, by you, and love and weep;
> Abhor the carnal Ease indulg'd before,
> And trembling at the Feet of CHRIST, adore.[31]

While Moorhead's poem hails the return of Whitefield to Boston after a serious illness, welcoming him to "these joyful Coasts" as one returned from the dead with the full aplomb of heavenly sound and the loud despairs of hell, Wheatley's poem pronounces a profound silence as she bids him sail to his final shore, the "vast seas of day." Like Moorhead, who "composed upon hearing him preach," Wheatley praises Whitefield for moving the souls and minds of his hearers. While Moorhead closes her stanza by conflating Whitefield's voice with that of Jesus and then trembling at the feet of Christ, a common Christian image that explicitly enthrones Christ, Wheatley opens her stanza as one already under the feet of the exalted and enthroned Whitefield. Wheatley's elegy is, in essence, the inverse of Moorhead's poem: Moorhead literally welcomes him as one back from the dead after a severe illness and commissions him "Swift as seraphick Flame, bless'd *Whitefield* go, / Proclaim well-grounded Peace to Men below." Wheatley bids the angelic Whitefield to go quickly to heaven: "[wing] with rapid course his way."[32]

Though Wheatley was not yet born and therefore could not remember when the first itinerant poems were written and circulated in Boston, John Moorhead, the fiery Presbyterian minister who would later sign Wheatley's attestation for the publication of her book, certainly did. His wife's poems on the itinerants Davenport, Tennant, and Whitefield may have been direct inspiration for Wheatley to write an elegy for the great itinerant. From them she would have learned how poetry could enable the role of a female spiritual guide to address directly religious controversies through a refined poetic practice rather than humbler verse. Clearly, the Moorhead household cultivated art and poetry as part of their religious experience and understood them to be tools for steering the winds of revival. Given that Sarah Moorhead had taught her slave Scipio to paint, it would have been a natural extension of Sarah Moorhead's religious and artistic vision to take the young Wheatley under her wing as well.[33] Mather Byles and Joseph Green, both of whom were still closely connected to women in Wheatley's poetic circle, along with Nathan Fiske's wide literary circle, would all distinctly remember Moorhead's revival poetry. Hannah Mather Crocker, who was around the same age as Wheatley, clearly knew of Moorhead because she later wrote a history of Boston women's political poetry, in which she cast Moorhead as the most influential model for her own political poetry.[34] Though the exact nature of the mentorship is murky, it is clear that Wheatley's strategic choice to tacitly acknowledge Moorhead's poem plays to her primary supporters: white women. Wheatley builds on Moorhead's poetic legacy of authoritative female speech directed at skeptical critics and erring revivalists.

Moorhead, like many other Whitefieldian poets, often styled herself as a listener. She performed her spiritual authority through her emotional response to Whitefield's preaching and its resulting emulation: "O, that an equal Zeal, might fire my Breast."[35] Though Wheatley includes herself as a listener, she diverges from Moorhead's example, and does not perform an ecstatic experience. Rather, upon hailing Whitefield's "rapid course" to heaven, Wheatley proclaims him mute and deaf, opening the way for her own preaching. Her elegy ends with Whitefield in the tomb until "life divine reanimate his dust."[36] Her aural appreciation for Whitefield focalizes the community of Whitefield admirers on poetic language so that she may now enter into the persona of the woman poet-minister.

In the world of the poem, Wheatley has done just that. As Max Cavitch astutely observes, Wheatley's ventriloquism of Whitefield reanimated black voices that Whitefield had explicitly exhorted to remain silent: "There is an implicit logic of substitution at work here, whereby Whitefield's death—his silencing—enables the music of the poet's tongue to seek 'auditories' of its own."[37] Other critics have often noted Wheatley's use of the minister's voice. Astrid Franke singles out the Whitefield elegy as an example of how "a skilled artist might . . . shape her role as a public poet by drawing on the rhetorical predilections of the evangelical revival."[38] Wheatley did more than ventriloquize or utilize homiletic rhetorical styles; she specifically engaged the tradition of the poet-minister, which treated verse as a premier tool for activating revival and affecting the course of history.

Wheatley works skillfully toward the exact moment in the poem when she performs Whitefield's words from her pulpit. She begins with emotional rhetoric personal to Bostonian hearts: "When his Americans were burden'd sore, / When streets were crimson'd with their guiltless gore!" Whitefield came for them.[39] Most Whitefield elegists used the saint's death as an opportunity to create a Whitefield in their own image. Wheatley was no different. Employing the patriotic and, often, evangelical rhetoric of the pulpit, she invokes Whitefield as a symbol of patriotism in the wake of the Boston

Massacre before she embodies the fullness of her own status as a symbol of Whitefield's wonder-inducing ministry.

African converts became a symbol to white people of Whitefield's incredible mission early in his career. Revival journals and other reports of revivals often emphasized the number of black converts, and those critical of revivals often highlighted black participation as emblematic of the unruliness of enthusiasts. Whitefield, though a slave holder who admonished slaves to serve their masters as their Christian duty, not only preached to mixed audiences in the North and slave audiences on Southern plantations, but he is also said to have toured British North America with a black preacher.[40] The salvation of Africans signaled the great depth and breadth of the special dispensation of God's Spirit moving among the people, and as such, black preachers were enlisted by leaders like the Countess of Huntingdon to further the work.[41] Stories of black people who inhabited the persona of Whitefield and preached with power entered the imaginary of revivalists on both sides of the Atlantic. Boston lore during the 1740s revivals included not only black exhorters but also successful imitations of the renowned orator Whitefield. On October 17, 1741, *The Weekly History* reported one such incident in Boston, adding it to a larger transatlantic perception of black converts as markers of that which is "almost incredible, but certainly true" and confounders of "the Wisdom of the Wise."[42]

According to the account told by "an eminent Divine," a gentleman that hated religion, and Whitefield's preaching in particular, thought he heard the great preacher orating. Upon investigation, he found it was his own slave. The account continues:

The next Day the Gentleman had an Entertainment at his House, several Gentleman were there. After Dinner the Gentlemen said to his Company, *Come, I'll entertain you with Mr. W's Preaching: For my Negroe can preach as well as he.* The Pipes and Tobacco, Bottles and Glasses were brought, and a Joint-Stool for the Negroe to preach on. So the Negroe began and ended his Prayer: (the Negroe had the very Phrases of Mr. *Whitefield*) And then began his Sermon, the Company Laughing and Ridiculing at *Whitefield's* Doctrine. At last the Negroe came to his Exhortation, and explain'd himself thus. *I am now come to my Exhortation; and to you my Master after the Flesh: But know I have a Master even Jesus Christ my Saviour, who has said that a Man cannot serve two Masters. Therefore I claim Jesus Christ to be my right Master; and all that come to him he will receive. You know, Master,*

you have been given to Cursing and Swearing, and Blaspheming God's holy
Name, you have been given to be Drunken, a Whoremonger, Covetous, a Liar,
a Cheat, &c. But know that God has pronounced a Woe against all such, and
has said that such shall never enter the Kingdom of God. And now to conclude
(said he) *except you all repent you shall likewise perish.* The Negroe spoke
with such Authority that struck the Gentlemen to Heart. They laid down
their Pipes, never drank a Glass of Wine, but departed every Man to his
own House: and are now pious sober Men; but before were wicked profane
Persons. Such is the Work of God by the Hands of poor Negroes: We have
such Influences every Week from some Part of the Country or other.[43]

The story explicitly proves to be a lesson on the greatness of Whitefield's
preaching—even his words merely repeated by a slave can produce converts.
But, according to Nancy Ruttenburg, it also provides a striking illustration of
the powerful speech enabled by Whitefield.[44] If up until now the slave had provided entertaining "whiteface" by speaking the exact phrases of Whitefield,
his imitation ceases as he turns to deliver his exhortation. The slave's own personal testimony of freedom—in which Christ accepts him but condemns his
master—strikes the master to the core, something even Whitefield's preaching
had not been able to accomplish in the gentleman. The imitation of the itinerant, at first laughable, quickly becomes the biblical performance of the weak
shaming the wise, a lesson with which the editor concludes.

By speaking in Whitefield's voice, Wheatley invokes the black
Whitefield lore:

> Take HIM ye wretched for your only good;
> Take HIM ye starving souls to be your food.
> Ye thirsty, come to this life giving stream:
> Ye Preachers, take him for your joyful theme:
> Take HIM, "my dear AMERICANS," he said,
> Be your complaints in his kind bosom laid:
> Take HIM ye *Africans*, he longs for you;
> Impartial SAVIOUR, is his title due;
> If you will chuse to walk in grace's road,
> You shall be sons, and kings, and priests to GOD.[45]

The entire evangelical invitation to Christ's kingdom appears at first purely
a rendition of Whitefield's famed auditory appeals. However, the quotation

marks around Whitefield's phrase "my dear Americans," combined with Wheatley's interruptive phrase "he said," underscores the double-voiced nature of the exhortation. The quotations suddenly recast the poetic sermon in the voice of Wheatley—a young, black enslaved girl pronouncing the priesthood of all believers.

Only after Wheatley signals her performance of the black Whitefield does she address her black audience at length—an unusual move among Whitefield elegists. Using the authority of the poet-minister and the wonder of the black Whitefield performance, Wheatley insists that Christ deserves his full recognition as the "Impartial SAVIOUR." Extending Whitefield's invitation to black persons farther than Whitefield himself, Wheatley goes on to incorporate herself and fellow "*Africans*" into the citizenship not just of heaven, but of earth. Like the puissant sermon of the black slave thought to be merely imitating Whitefield but imbued with a rhetorically persuasive testimony in his own right, Wheatley claims that slaves can choose whom they will serve, and they will be transformed into "sons, and kings, and priests." Moving from her black Whitefield performance, she addresses the "Great COUNTESS!" directly as a unison of united American voices: "we *American's* revere / Thy name. . . . / We mourn with thee."[46] In doing so, Wheatley lodges her own iconographic value as a symbol of revivalism within Whitefield's growing association with America in order to claim a revolutionary identity for herself and her fellow black colonists and thus deserving of freedom.

Wheatley's poetic performance drew on an established lore of black people preaching under the influence of the itinerant and using his words to speak with authority to whites. But there is a significant difference. Unlike the white-authored lore, Wheatley never plays the fool; she does not speak like the illiterate black preacher whose mimicry provokes laughter, and she refuses to present herself as fringe, revival noise. Instead, she performs Whitefield as a masterful poet. In Wheatley, Whitefield's "lessons in unequal'd accents [flow]."[47] Wheatley's elegy transformed the black Whitefield lore into poetry and thereby re-schematized the relationship of black converts to revivalism. It was no longer the foolish shaming the wise, but quite the opposite. Her white audience found themselves required to imagine a black woman preacher whose rendition of Whitefield prompted not laughter but aesthetic appreciation, as she transformed his plain speech into graceful couplets. The epitome of revival noise, the black and the female, had become eloquent harmony. Further still, in the context of Wheatley's poetry collection, in which her Whitefield elegy also appeared, black and female revival noise had

become belles lettres. The Whitefield elegy reconfigures revival poetry in relation to black people as mimics and representatives of the plainest capacity
to challenge evangelical verse and its common harmony both socially and
politically.

Though it was early in her career, it was not the first time that Wheatley,
under the tutelage of white women, had reinterpreted revival poetics in the
context of black believers and their relationship to literacy and high literature. When Wheatley's first published poem appeared in the *Newport
Mercury* in December 1767, it did so in the context of a newly stirred revival
that had begun with slaves.[48] This was enabled by a women's prayer meeting
at Newport's First Church, founded in the 1740s by Sarah Osborn, an ad-
mirer of Whitefield and a convert under Tennent's preaching. After several
decades under Osborn, it remained the most significant evangelical influence in the congregation and served as the epicenter of a revival outbreak in
1766 and 1767.[49] At the time of Wheatley's publication, meetings included as
many as 525 attendants and included an Ethiopian Society for free blacks and
a Sunday evening fellowship for slaves.

Given Osborn's sudden status as a revivalist leader and the centrality of
slaves to the upswell of God's spirit, it would have been a natural gesture for
Susanna Wheatley to contact Osborn about her own piously educated slave.[50]
That Osborn was a schoolteacher, combined with the fact that the black
members of her meetings tended to call it "school," suggests a personal reason
for Osborn's interest in Phillis as a successful prodigy of the Wheatley family.
Additionally, a published poem "composed by a Negro Girl" would implicitly advertise the pious and civilized fruits of the revival under Osborn's roof
and, as such, serve as a decisive rebuttal to the remarks from Newport society
that Osborn was "keeping a Negro House."[51] Even if Wheatley's poem did
not make its way to Newport through Susanna's evangelical network, it most
certainly spoke to its concerns. The verse was religiously moving not only for
its particular subject matter (in this case, a near death experience prodding
one's salvation status), but also because the very fact of a slave writing poetry
testified to the power of God's work.

This early Wheatley poem, "On the Mssrs Hussey and Coffin," displays a
keen grasp of revival culture and poetics through its incorporation of evangelistic expectations for the power of verse. Wheatley employs the same
kind of sublime language as Davies, who often describes life's dangers as an
ocean and its risks in expansive language, such as an "unbottomed Cavity"
filled with "tribes that walk in [its] dark shades], as well as the bliss of God's

grace."[52] The clearest revivalist language occurs in the poet's interruption of herself and the two-line benediction. Breaking from the narrative couplets into first person prose, Wheatley unexpectedly halts the poetic form to insert her own testimony as an aspiring revival poet:

> Doubtless the Fear of Danger far had fled:
> No more repeated Victory crown their Heads.
> Had I the Tongue of a Seraphim, how would I exalt thy Praise;
>   thy Name as Incense to the Heavens should fly, and the
>   Remembrance of thy Goodness to the shoreless Ocean of
>   Beatitude!—Then should the Earth glow with seraphick
>   Ardour.
> Blest Soul, which sees the Day while Light doth shine,
> To guide his Steps to trace the Mark divine.[53]

In this prose interruption to her couplets, the poet intrudes on her own poetic voice which to this point has been pluralized. Instead of praising God in the voice of the poet, which in revival poetry written by ministers regularly partakes of the direct sermonic voice, Wheatley valorizes the lay voice that would often interrupt the preacher during revival gatherings. At the same time, the prose break echoes the elevated language of an experienced preacher reaching his pitch and winding his audience up into an ecstatic vision of the world alight with God's glory. The break, then, performs at least two purposes at once. It confirms the prophetic and eloquent voice of the lay exhorter speaking from the crowd. The feared inarticulate ravings of social underlings and black slaves do not materialize in Wheatley's representation of revival culture. At the same time, she prioritizes the common practice of lay interruption by placing sermonic prose in the margins of the poetic voice. That is, the break inserts the sermonic into the poem in order to recast the slave-poet's voice as from "the Tongue of a Seraphim."

Yet, the poet also resists being completely identified with revival language. The ecstatic language of the prose interlude and the praise that it describes is in the subjunctive: "Had I," "I would," "then should." Wheatley does not perform an ecstatic response to a minister in the manner of Sarah Moorhead. While she does perform an ecstatic interruption in this poem, the enthusiastic speech is not in response to another's sermon, but to her own religious moralizing and poetic performance. Additionally, the break highlights the fact that she has cast Hussey and Coffin's experience primarily in classical terms. Though Davies and Moorhead used some neoclassical forms and some belletristic conventions, they did not directly invoke the names of Greek gods, which Wheatley does.

From her earliest revival publication and her most famous elegy, it is clear that Wheatley was not only enmeshed in revival culture, but she was also actively pushing up against its limitations for her own uses as a slave invested in political freedom. Wheatley's poems were often circulated by white women in the context of black revivalism and literacy, which Wheatley engaged by way of revision and critique. As glimpsed in the poems so far, she resisted the expected affect of a woman poet-minister, realigned slaves with higher rather than common harmony and mimicry, and re-approximated the classical in relation to vulgar revival poetics. Always aware that her poems were by "a Negro girl," she leveraged her identity in the interplay between the belletristic and revivalist poetic cultures in which she fully and deftly engaged. The use of both poetics enabled her to engage in a politics of respectability as well as a politics of refusal.

This was especially true in the London-published *Poems on Various Subjects, Religious and Moral* (1773), which was the pinnacle of Wheatley's transatlantic success. Though it was sponsored by Whitefield's patron, the Countess of Huntingdon, and embraced by John Wesley, John Newton, and other evangelical leaders, it was markedly different from most revival poetry. The next section isolates two primary ways that Wheatley's poetry collection differed from the popular revival poetry I have traced thus far in British North America: her treatment of hymns and her use of espousal piety. I read these differences not as reasons to believe that Wheatley was not a revival poet, but as indications of Wheatley's deep engagement with revival poetics for the purpose of reforming its indifference to the practice of chattel slavery. In other words, following Waldstreicher's argument, I will argue that the threat of Wheatley was not just that she was a slave writing poetry or writing Christian poetry, nor even that she was a slave writing neoclassical poetry, but that she was a slave writing neoclassical poetry *as* a revival poet-minister.

The Hymn, Plainest Capacity, and the Progress of Christian History

The portrait of Wheatley that graced the frontispiece of her volume of poetry was as important as the poems themselves to her reception, then and now (Figure 4.1). Wheatley's portrait offered her and those promoting her work the opportunity to shape the black poet in their readers' imagination. The portrait styles Wheatley in a recognizable European tradition of high literature, and her reflective pose resembles representations of middle-class and elite women. It has been repeatedly emphasized by scholars that Wheatley's portrait is remarkable because it was the first to accompany a colonial woman's own writings. Most importantly, the portrait adds a unique element: the actual act of a woman writing. It was only after her "groundbreaking" frontispiece that "there occurred a sea change in the way that women writers and poets began to present themselves in British formal portraiture."[54] The slave writing—this is what the frontispiece highlights. But *what* the slave is writing, as Waldstreicher reminds us, was the more urgent and politically charged question. In fact, the portrait, in tandem with the collection of verse, emphasizes that very question.

Figure 4.1. Phillis Wheatley, *Poems on Various Subjects, Religious and Moral* (1773), Frontispiece.
Library Company of Philadelphia.

Wheatley's portrait elevates her into the realm of elite women's portraiture, but it does so as a distinctly Whitefieldian poet without classical flourishes. For instance, instead of the trumpet, lyre, scrolls, flowers, and flowing clothing that frame the portraits of women writers like Elizabeth Griffith and Elizabeth Singer Rowe, Wheatley sits in plain attire with only the elements necessary for writing—ink, quill, paper, and one unmarked book. The single elaborate aspect of the portrait is the length of the engraving that encircles it; rather than just her name, the frame emphasizes her status as a "negro servant to Mr. John Wheatley, of Boston." The choice of Wheatley's attire and pose intentionally styles her after Whitefield's patron, the Countess of Huntingdon, who had insisted that a portrait accompany the collection of poems.[55] The similarities are pronounced: though Wheatley's is significantly plainer, several features of their bonnets are the same and their breasts are both covered with a white fichu. One unattributed portrait of the Countess, circa 1770–1780, matches even the position of the hands—both to the chin with the pointer finger higher up on the face and the same colored small book with the same style binding.[56] The portrait places Wheatley firmly within the purview of the Countess, a powerful transatlantic evangelical leader, and enlists Wheatley in her army of itinerants and diverse missionaries.

With the portrait's clear homage to her patron, the untitled book on the table needed no further elaboration; it was a hymnbook, and as such, it clearly marked Wheatley as evangelical. The eighteenth-century hymnbook was an effective and at times divisive accessory that explicitly announced one's Methodist or Dissenter allegiances as it traveled with its owner between home, church, and even school.[57] Displaying Wheatley with the same style of bound hymnbook found in one of the Countess's own portraits incorporated Wheatley and her poetry into the transatlantic evangelical community in which reading, memorizing, and singing hymns were essential to the spiritual formation of the believer and the church.

With its use of a dignified, Huntingdon inspired pose and clothing, the posture of a fluent writer, and the accoutrements of religious devotion, the portrait promised to have an effect on the image of slaves. Watts's writings were on their way to surpassing the popularity of the Bible in the London-based Society for Promoting Religious Knowledge among the Poor's (SPRKP) own records.[58] For those who supported the SPRKP, who had supplied Davies and others with hundreds of Watts's hymnbooks to distribute to slaves for their instruction in religion and literacy, Wheatley's portrait as a civilized African was a celebration of success. It invited the looker to reconsider the black slave in relation to revival hymns: instead of seeing the riot-like chaos of outdoor meetings that was often invoked in relation to slaves, the portrait presented a slave in staid and thoughtful devotion at a proper writing table. By instead highlighting the quiet simplicity of reading and writing as the activity of the slave with a hymnbook, Wheatley appeared as the exemplum and promise of evangelical black literacy for whites: a civilized Christian.

Yet, even the Countess seemed concerned that Wheatley's poetry was not quite fully conformed to the evangelical mission. In a letter to the Countess, one colonist praised the "Christian Poetess" at the same time that he assured her that with age and experience Wheatley's "writings will run in a more Evangelicall Strain."[59] The African American hymnodist Jupiter Hammon knew of Wheatley—and he, like the Countess, also worried about her lack of evangelical focus.[60] In light of the portrait's stylization of Wheatley as a revivalist, the hymnbook attempts to fill in what the volume surprisingly lacks: Wheatley has not contributed a single hymn to the transatlantic evangelical community. Many scholars of Wheatley, especially prior to recent work on her neoclassical investments, assumed that because she was raised within an evangelical family, wrote in a pious vein, and published three poems explicitly titled hymns that her poems resided comfortably in the evangelical tradition. Yet, it does not take much prodding for these assumptions to fall apart. And the deviation certainly was not lost on her revival readers like the Countess and Hammon.

Of particular concern may have been the failure to include a type of hymn that was central to evangelical devotional life and its patterns of morning and evening prayer. Every major revival hymn writer in the eighteenth century composed these hymns, which were extensions of a long tradition of morning and evening Christian prayer. Wheatley would have known many of these hymns, including those by Watts and Wesley, and most likely by the Mohegan minister and hymn writer Samson Occom. Perhaps Wheatley also saw the circulating manuscript of poems by the well-known Elizabeth Scott Smith, an English woman of distinction who moved to the center of revivalism in Connecticut, which included a morning hymn that takes up the familiar themes of the genre.[61] Even so, as far as we know, Wheatley did not replicate them. She certainly did not in her published collection of verse.

The morning and evening hymns Wheatley does include deviate significantly from all of these evangelical hymns. First and foremost, they stand apart because they are in heroic couplets, not standard hymn meter. Second, hers address specifically and at length classical gods and muses, which was anathema in most revival poetry, let alone revival hymns. While some Christian belletrists who became part of revivalism crafted neoclassical poetry, neoclassical hymns were decidedly different from evangelical hymns, which had specific purposes in congregational, familial, and personal devotion. Wheatley's "An Hymn to the Morning" does not invoke Christ's inward light to pierce sin and ask for guidance in God's will for the day; it is not about Christ at all. Rather, it is a hymn to Aurora and a prayer for poetic inspiration. Wheatley does not write in response to the Christian God's directive to worship, but states that "Aurora now demands my song." While Watts briefly describes the sun's journey through the sky in one of his morning hymns, he defines it as a symbol of the Christian God, and when he does invoke muses in his poems, he follows Milton in Christianizing them first. In contrast, Wheatley's first line of her hymn—"Attend my lays, ye ever honour'd nine"—directly announces its inappropriateness for a hymnbook.[62] Watts had invented the first line index when he published his collection of hymns, which meant that the first lines of hymns became significant in terms of memorization and categorization.[63] No such first line would find its place in a revival hymnbook indexed according to the interests of evangelical life and devotion.

This is especially evident when both poems are read in sequence because they create a cycle focused only on songs for Aurora. Aurora begins and ends the poem series, as does the poet's writing and inspiration. When the poet speaks of God and virtue directly, it is communal or concerning others' faith; there never seems to be direct praise from the poet to God. In fact, the end of evening highlights the ceasing of the poet's song, which never entirely got off the ground in the morning because it was "abort[ed]" by the "king of day['s] . . . fervid beams." In these hymns the poet encourages others but never actually sings a hymn to God. She only directly praises Aurora: "Aurora hail."[64]

Rather than writing revival hymns, Wheatley wrote what John C. Shields specifies as "epic hymns" modeled from the classical tradition of hymns to gods, also practiced by Renaissance poets.[65] For elite poets, and women in particular, these classical hymns and odes performed one's class or helped to elevate one's class, as well as provided an avenue for political writing. For instance, Mary Leapor, who was a British kitchen maid, also wrote a "Hymn to the Morning" in which she takes up her own poetic ability while praising Aurora.[66] Not surprisingly, Elizabeth Singer Rowe also practiced this higher, neoclassical verse, but with an important difference from Wheatley—Rowe also wrote hymns suitable for hymnbooks and evangelical devotion.

The particular traction Wheatley gained as a symbol of both grace and wonder pleased those friendly to evangelical sensibilities, but it also positioned her to aspire to the literary fame cultivated by the Christian belletrists like Mather Byles. That she crafted her poetry collection so closely after his own *Poems on Several Occasions* (1744) speaks to her knowledge of, and vision to accomplish, the typical trajectory of an esteemed New England poet.[67] At the same time, she seemed to understand that international success would most likely come through capturing the attention of the transatlantic evangelical network that was the innovative engine of eighteenth-century print culture. She had witnessed Whitefield invent the modern press entourage and his resulting celebrity by bringing together oral performance and publication through his "preach and print" strategy.[68] Taking her cues from him, and from the audacious self-promotion of her mentor Byles, Wheatley used the press and her printed and manuscript performances to attract attention to herself and her unique position as the sable muse.

Wheatley's increasingly skilled couplets and classicism speak to her investment in belles lettres. Her choices emphasized her literacy in forms honored by cosmopolitan Bostonian society, rather than the common poetics that revival hymns ultimately represented. She followed Byles in his pioneering role of merging unlikely poetic fashions. The religious sublime, captured not only by belletrists like Byles but also by revival poets like Davies, in Wheatley becomes a hybrid practice of a cosmopolitan polite Christianity, neoclassicism, and revivalist aesthetics. That is to say, Wheatley aspired to Christian belletrism and its cultural benefits, borrowing many of its poetic practices and conventions, while also firmly cementing herself in the tradition of revival poetics, which traditionally esteemed lower verse.

Yet, even Byles included many proper Christian hymns in his book of poems. The first poem of Byles's collection, "The Almighty Conqueror" in fact explicitly rejects the muses in favor of Christ: "I glow in Raptures all divine / As with the Theme I rise, / Your tuneful Aids, fictitious Nine, No more shall tempt my Eyes."[69] Though it is not strictly a revival hymn, it is a Congregational hymn invested in personal devotion and the larger triumph of Christ, and it engages the sublime while keeping the classical muses at bay. There was no reason, whether she was following a Christian belletrist or evangelical mentor, not to include an exclusively Christian hymn.

Wheatley grew up enslaved in an evangelical household where she would have been required to participate in reading, reciting, and singing hymns. Because classicism rose to the level of national consciousness during the

Revolution, evangelicals may have embraced it more than they had in the past, though it always had an uncomfortable relationship to their version of Christianity.[70] Even in histories that merged classical and Christian history, and among families, such as the Edwardses, that read and learned classical literature, there was always the underlying sense that one should be careful not to accidently imbibe the spirit of the non-Christian ancients.[71] For the most educated revival ministers, classical poetry was among the areas of study, but evangelical hymns and poems always remained the priority.

Wheatley would have known the hymn's popularity, its uses among other black evangelicals at Newport and elsewhere, and its potential in abolitionist circles. Wheatley would even meet the famous slaver turned abolitionist Rev. John Newton, who wrote renowned hymns such as "Amazing Grace," which one scholar has argued drew upon Wheatley's own verse. If she wanted to appeal to evangelicals or if she wanted a sure-fire way to a second publication, hymns were in demand—and if white evangelicals supplied itinerants with Watts hymnbooks to give specifically to slaves, they would surely buy up a collection of hymns written by one of the most famous slaves. Yet she did not publish one. Given how Wheatley orchestrated her own emancipation and how her writings show an active investment in joining religious liberty to political liberty for those in bondage, there is every reason to believe this absence of evangelical hymns was well reasoned and intentional.

That Wheatley was received as a revival poet, actively engaging revivalists throughout her career and showing a keen grasp of Christian theology and experiential religion, yet did not write hymns, is a matter of great significance. By not including revival hymns, she implicitly criticized Watts's emphasis on writing for those with the plainest capacity. This highlights the paradox of Watts's evangelical anthropology, which, for all its emphasis on an idea of common harmony, could not translate spiritual freedom into political freedom. Participation in the harmony of heaven with one's plainest capacity could make one human, but this did little good if it did not also make one free. As demonstrated in the previous chapter, a revival minster could idealize the harmony of slaves, even model his own poetics after this idealization, but it did not compel him to free slaves.

Wheatley provided a corrective to poetic theories such as Davies's, which associated slaves with music and the harmony of poetry rather than cultivated aesthetics. Her poetry thematically underscored the revivalist call for egalitarian access to the liberty of Christ at the same time that her poetic form proclaimed the ways that evangelical verse emphatically inhibited a full response. One must have a certain amount of privilege, as Watts and Davies did, to idealize relinquishing one's performance of taste for the sake of common humanity. On the other hand, no one would expect a high level of engagement with aesthetics from a slave whose supposed aptitude for song linked her to uncultivated societies. The more accomplished and cultured Wheatley's verse, the more wonder she might produce in her white readers and the more she could chip away at the justifications for American-style chattel slavery that relied upon a matrix of racialized ideas about the ability of Africans to become civilized. Wheatley understood the crucial difference the type of poetry she practiced would make in issues of life, death, and freedom. Her emancipation, distilled to its simplest cause, was a matter of poetic form.

A woman in Wheatley's poetic coterie said as much. When Wheatley sent her collection of poems to London for publication, at least one of Boston's elite families clearly understood that its argument for the liberty of slaves depended upon the display of natural genius, which, of course, depended upon one's ability to perform the aesthetics valorized by the culture. The white Bostonian poet Ruth Barrell Andrews, member of a family of successful merchants some of which were well-known patriots, took it upon herself to circulate a manuscript poem that argued against "tyrant man['s]" enslavement of "half mankind" through "recent proof" of African intellect and humanity—Wheatley's poems (Figure 4.2). The poem forcefully presents Wheatley's collection of verse as an argument that "dignity of mind / Is not to color or to rank confin'd." Andrews points to the "elegance of thought" evident in Wheatley's poems that demonstrate her "genius," "rare abilities," and "nat'ral graces yet unrival'd," as well as confirm "the value of a soul within." Her "comprehensive poems . . . / . . . speak a soul beneficently great / A soul whose magnitude surmounts her fate." By emphasizing that freedom cannot be "wrest" from "the ingenious breast," Andrews seems to directly respond to Hume, who said of Jamaican poet Francis Williams that he had "no ingenuity."[72]

Reflecting arguments from Wheatley's own poems concerning the liberty and the imagination, Andrews proclaims Wheatley a poetic genius equal to or better than any white colonist. This is a bold statement coming from a woman well connected to Boston's poetic scene—Andrews was the niece of the well-known tavern poet Joseph Green (Byles's arch nemesis) and daughter of manuscript poet Ruth Green Barrell. Andrews's argument also served a clear rhetorical purpose: if colonists were worthy of political freedom based on their refined intellect and culture, then so were Africans. She appeals to

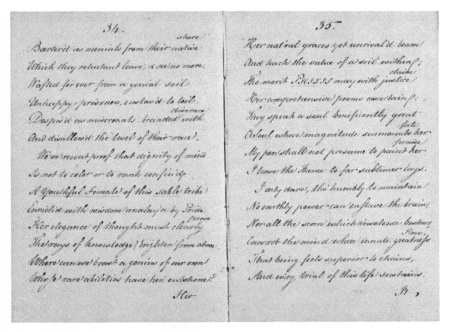

Figure 4.2. Middle portion of Ruth Barrell Andrews's poem concerning Phillis Wheatley entitled "Slavery" (1772). Commonplace-book of poems by Ruth Barrell Andrews, 1791.

Massachusetts Historical Society.

the art of poetry as a sign of genius and imagination that marked full political liberty. It is decidedly not an appeal to the value of Watts's vulgar hymns for the plainest capacity. In fact, at the close of the poem she issues a threat—that in the future their "untutor'ed blacks" will also display the same virtue that Wheatley has and that heaven will take note. Wheatley's performance at the highest level of poetics enabled such a claim.

Andrews, like Wheatley, collapsed the distinction between political bondage to England and chattel slavery, as was then common in revolutionary rhetoric. Many whites who described colonists as slaves to England tried desperately to deny the travesties suffered by the actual referents in need of political redress. To defend the difference between black slaves and white colonists, some of the first systematic arguments about the mental, rather than the cultural, inferiority of blacks surfaced. Some white writers went as far as to claim "that political slavery, a slavery of the mind, was far worse than racial slavery, a slavery of the body."[73] Andrews inserts Wheatley into these arguments by arguing that she retains an inextinguishable liberty within herself because "No Earthly power can enslave the brain." Andrews extends this idea over several lines focalized through Wheatley's experience:

> Nor all the scorn which insolence bestows,
> Can rob the mind where innate greatness flows
> That being feels superior to chains,
> And every tryal of this life sustains.
> It dignifies a freedom nought can wrest
> Or ever tare from the ingenious breast.
> This consolation only can appease
> Sorrows extensive and enlarged as these.[74]

The poem argues that Wheatley's sorrows are made bigger by benevolence, which sees the person who is the object of generosity as less powerful. Yet, Wheatley's "inborn fortitude" "repels" this because she does not internalize the fact that she is of lesser status. It is important that Andrews claims that Wheatley "feels superior to chains," as this incorporates sentimental language on the cusp of romanticism, in which feeling rather than reason grounds one's rights. The final couplets describe Wheatley as a classical hero who "surmounts fate" and who deserves a sublime poet to relate it. The poem displays the tensions heightened in this period as neoclassical ideas shifted toward romantic concepts between the "vogue for natural geniuses and abolitionist desire to prove [mental] equality."[75]

Yet, as Waldstreicher argues, it wasn't just that Wheatley's neoclassical poetics displayed her mental equality with whites. It was that her use of classicism inserted doubt into the political project that colonists were beginning to imagine. Wheatley's classicism threw the imagined relationship between the ancients and the moderns and historical progress into turmoil; in short, she "showed that modern, American slavery was worse than the ancient kind precisely insofar as it did not celebrate or even free individuals like Wheatley. She raised the distinct possibility that history was going backwards, nor forwards, in America."[76] This was debilitating not only for colonists who were more deist in outlook, but also for those of an evangelical persuasion. It had been Jonathan Edwards who had proclaimed the likelihood that God's movement in the latter days would begin in America. For those evangelicals who embraced the spirit of the New Divinity movement, in which Wheatley was enmeshed, the Revolution promised a moral awakening and birth of a virtuous society. Rev. Samuel Hopkins, who led this revitalization of a moral or "consistent Calvinism," "the antislavery cause [became] the nexus between religious and secular idealism, between the Awakening and the Revolution, between the millennium and the virtuous republic."[77]

The tension between Wheatley's neoclassical poetics and the progress of modern civilization helps explain how her use of classical in place of revival hymns served as a critique of evangelicalism for its ambivalence about slavery. If classical poetics written by a slave impugns the progress of American civilization, then classical hymns written by a slave in place of revival hymns similarly casts evangelicalism in a disconcerting light. The ancients were credited with moving God's plan for humankind forward by centralizing language, which was later used to spread Christianity. If evangelicals were more morally corrupt than the ancients, how were they moving forward to the promised perfection and glory of God's kingdom? Wheatley's classical hymns introduced the possibility that rather than accelerating toward the millennium, evangelicals were slowing down God's plan for the entire world. Several scholars have convincingly demonstrated that classicism in Wheatley's hands was a powerful and complex engagement and critique of the political and world economic system. In the context of revival poetics, it was also a critique of a religious movement that for the most part promoted, enabled, and justified an emerging American empire founded on social and economic inequalities.[78] But Wheatley doesn't just critique and then leave revival poetry and its evangelical readers behind. Instead, she remakes the meanings of the central forms used in revival poetry.

This impulse comes through in Wheatley's "Hymn to Humanity," which offers to undo the haywire chronology of Christian history caused by chattel slavery in British North America. Like her classical hymns to morning and evening, this Wheatley hymn is also explicitly concerned with her own poetic inspiration. Some scholars have argued for purely classical interpretations of this hymn; yet, Wheatley often incorporates several poetic traditions and inflections at once. This hymn, more than her others, highlights Christian discourse by centering it on a theme dear to evangelicalism—the story of Christ's incarnation and its experiential, visible, and punctiliar application in the individual's life. In fact, it is because Wheatley particularizes this experience to the extreme—naming the individual to whom this awakening occurs and how it affects the poet's life in particular—that the hymn becomes unfit for use in evangelical devotion. The hymn cannot be a prayer to God from one's own lips, expressing one's own sentiments. Wheatley focalizes the universe-altering fact of Christ's incarnation by sending it like a bolt through time into S. P. Gallowy's heart that awakens him to the reality of "the rushing God" and "enlarge[s] [his] close contracted mind."[79] The result is not that S. P. Gallowy becomes an itinerant minister or performs the stages of conversion, but that he takes pity on "*Afric's* muse" and calls the muses to her aid. That is, the hymn is about the humane act that has enabled her poetry, which is itself part of God's larger purpose. Notably, it is an awakened man's direct experience with Christ in the manner of an evangelical conversion that prompts him to merge the political power of classical verse with God's plan for justice. "Hymn to Humanity" reimagines what Watts and other revivalists called "evangelic day"—the hope and salvation of Christ for all nations for all times, made real in the coming of Christ and culminating in the eschaton—as the redemption of the African muse who stands in for the beginning of the abolition of slavery. Bringing the classical muses in line with this vision corrects the lapse in Christian progress represented by the disjunction of the superior morality of the ancients in regard to slavery. It was a call for Christians to right the wrong that threatened to thwart the progressive movement of God in history.

What kind of figure is this "*Afric's* muse" who distances herself from revival hymns and its plainest capacity and instead highlights her poetics as the direct concern of God and as a repair for a Christian history thrown violently off course? To answer this, we must explore the poem in which Wheatley most clearly and forcefully foregrounds her role of the woman poet-minister and directly spiritually guides and corrects ministers and potential ministers, "To the University at Cambridge, in New-England."

This poem has often been used to situate Wheatley within the broad religious rhetoric of New England and evangelicalism because she clearly takes up the role of the preacher. This is certainly true. Yet, by placing this poem in the context of British North American Calvinist revival poetics specifically, its irregularities immediately stand out. First, it is in blank verse, which was not the normal verse form in which Wheatley wrote, nor the preferred verse form of most revival ministers. And second, Wheatley's revivalist milieu, which wedded the couplet and doctrine, magnifies another absence: espousal piety. If Wheatley takes on the personae of the woman poet-minister, where is the spouse of Christ and her affect? Even more, where is it in the entire volume of poetry? Not one of the poems directly and explicitly takes up the *Song of Songs* or the believer as the bride of Christ. Wheatley's metrical paraphrase of Isaiah 63 perhaps broaches the imagery when Zion "serenely on thy bosom lies," but the passage's dominant imagery is not marital but martial.[80] Even if one were to argue that there are allusions to espousal in various poems, it is nowhere near the emphasis that would be usual for a revival poet, especially a woman in Boston under the tutelage of Moorhead and the like, and in a culture in which *Gospel Sonnets* routinely circulated. Many scholars have pointed out the lack of emotional displays in Wheatley's verse and have interpreted the emotional distance as a strategic choice on the poet's part. These choices to occlude espousal imagery and affect and to use blank verse in a poem in which a woman poet-minister directs the most esteemed male ministers in the community forcefully assert a new woman poet-minister persona.

To begin, "To the University at Cambridge" combines both neoclassical and revivalist enthusiasm with careful attention to her audience of ministers. For instance, rather than refer to classical names, she relies on a Miltonic invocation in which the classical muses have been clearly Christianized: "While an intrinsic ardor prompts to write, / The muses promise to assist my pen."[81] The use of blank verse, the name University at Cambridge, and the word "ardor" written within the context of inspired poetry and education all conjure poet John Milton. Rather than a "noble ardor," the goal of virtuous education according to Milton, Wheatley writes with an "intrinsic ardor," which places her on equal footing with the students. The phrase also invokes Milton's usage of ardor as a singing choir of angels, which situates Wheatley's inspiration to write in heavenly origins. At the same time, it evokes the enthusiastic passion of the sublime as it had been reclaimed by not only John Dennis but also Watts, Rowe, and Jonathan Edwards.[82] In keeping with the religious sublime, she focuses on biblical rather than classical themes. The poet recalls Eden with the line "blooming plants of human race divine" as well as the warning to "suppress the deadly serpent in its egg." The poet figures herself as an Ethiop who has crossed over from "the land of errors," the place of the fall of humankind, and into God's safety. She echoes the Miltonic language of *Paradise Lost* and the messengers from heaven who move through "revolving worlds" to protect and give warning to humankind of their coming fall. As one such messenger with direct ties to the climactic scene of original sin, she warns the students of Cambridge, "ye sons of science," to be on guard against sin that sinks the entire soul into "immense perdition."

Just as Wheatley altered her relationship to the poet-minister by refusing black mimicry as it was expressed through Whitefield lore, the poem announces her powerful inhabitation of the spouse of Christ. At the center of Wheatley's poetic and religious authority is her claim to being an Ethiop poet-minister. The Ethiop instantiates various traditions for Wheatley— clearly the African woman prophet and the classical slave and poet Terrance. Additionally, for a revival audience whose affective piety was intimately bound up with the *Song of Songs* metaphor of espousal, the Ethiop bespoke the original bride of the biblical text: "I am black, but comely, O ye daughters of Jerusalem" (1:5). The Ethiop, associated through Moses with the giving of the law, through *Song of Songs* with the typological fulfillment of the law in Christ, and with the great evangelical mission to the world leading to the eschaton through the *Book of Acts*, was firmly grounded in the evangelical imagination of salvation history. Watts's hymns refer to Ethiopia whenever referring to evangelizing Africa, and *Psalm 68*—"Princes shall come out of Egypt; Ethiopia shall soon stretch out her hands unto God"— predicts the great and glorious final movement of God in history. Wheatley's line—"an Ethiop tells you"—mobilizes this entire salvation history to create an originary rather than a recursive claim to biblical history and poetic inspiration.

If the Ethiop is at the center of espousal and at the center of African Christianity, then Wheatley asserts herself as a poet deeply rooted in African and Western traditions. Reaching back to the past and historicizing the spouse of Christ resists the direction of Wattsian hymn language, which he had explicitly justified through the need to dehistoricize the *Psalms* in order to gain the proper height of affection during worship and to glimpse "evangelic day." It also creates a speculative kinship through the genealogy and history of biblical figures. Again, we are swimming in language that, as Waldstreicher argues, in the Revolutionary moment pits modern against ancient in uncomfortable relation to America and its progress toward liberty. If in the poem, the Ethiop speaks from Eden, that is, from the origins of humankind, and is the originary model of affective religion, the spouse of Christ, she also does so with prophetic clarity and unrelenting urgency at the origins of the American Republic—best to kill slavery, the serpent in the egg, than to experience the sure judgment of God and history.

The Ethiop's words concerning the paradox of a revolution for freedom argued and fought by slave holders have a particular salience in the context of a new upswell in revitalizing Calvinism by those called "consistent Calvinists." Wheatley was connected with Newport's revivalism and the benevolent Christianity espoused there by the Rev. Hopkins, which defended

Calvinism by wrestling with its moral import, especially in regard to slavery. This is why her verse form is important to consider, not just in relation to classicism and the Popian couplet but also in relation to the Calvinist couplet as Erskine defined it. Given the popularity of Erskine's *Gospel Sonnets*, the espousal poetics embedded in the Calvinist couplet, and the New England preoccupation with refiguring Calvinism, it is of special significance that Wheatley's moral preaching to Cambridge University students was in blank verse. As I argued in Chapter 1, revivalist soteriology was fused with rhyme in such a way that the couplet expressed the divine metaphor of Christ's espousal. The manner in which Erskine formulated the couplet expressed the very tensions and paradoxes that believers must internalize and balance in order to successfully inhabit Calvinist belief and practice, especially law and grace, sovereignty and will, saint and sinner, freedom and slavery. Yet, in the poem in which Wheatley performs most like a poet-minister, she also deviates from this expected form.

The figure of the Ethiop in the role of the woman poet-minister proclaiming a theology of consistent Calvinists in a poem that asks its audience to "scan" the heights like a poem announces itself as a reformatory revival poetics. When we scan it, we find neither the Calvinist couplet nor the universal and ethereal spouse of Christ persona. Instead, the Ethiop intrudes as a highly individualized and bodily presence whose origin elicits truth, beauty, and intellect through its association with not only the biblical text, but also Milton's high and unfettered blank verse. At the same time that the spouse of Christ is entirely recast as an African persona, the couplet to which Erskine wed Calvinist paradox is suspended. When Wheatley returns to her preferred form of the couplet, she does so with a difference. For the evangelical, the Ethiop that grounds the authority of her verse casts the paradoxes of living out Calvinism not just in terms of law and grace, God's sovereignty and man's will, spiritual freedom and slavery, but most importantly, political freedom and slavery. Wheatley remade the spouse of Christ and inserted Africa into the foundation of the evangelical structure of affect, theology, and poetics.

If Wheatley distanced herself from replicating the affective espousal that evangelical readers were encouraged to internalize as their own, while at the same time instantiating the originary singer, the Ethiop, at the center of her poetics, her investment in the couplet, within the context of revival poetics, functions as a critique. Couplets (sans revival hymns) both move her verse into the belletristic rather than the plainest capacity and also associate her verse with a critique of slavery through its constant iteration of classicism. At the same time, as the revival poet whom the Countess and the Wheatleys promoted, her couplets reconfigure the meaning of the espousal metaphor of the Calvinist couplet. The espousal metaphor imbues her verse with the *"Afric's muse"* at every turn—and hence the paradoxes of Calvinism become bound up in the pull between spiritual and political bondage. These are replicated through multiple binaries and paradoxes in the revolutionary moment, including democracy and tyranny, chattel slavery and colonial liberty, civilized and barbarian, modern and ancient, Christian and pagan history, genius and imitation, and plainest capacity and belletrism. These are problem binaries, paradoxes that interrupt the successful living out of theological schemas if not properly reconciled as consistent Calvinists aspired to do. In her verse forms, Wheatley's poetry consistently brings to the fore these life-and-death tensions and casts them on a personal and social scale, demanding an answer to the question: How to eradicate the evil at the center of an unfolding Christian history?

To Refuse Capacities of Religion and Science

When Jefferson enrolled Wheatley in his ethnographic project, he made "a Whately" into a specimen of verse that correlated to what he deemed to be the capacities of her race. She did not have the capacity for intellect, genius, originality, imagination, or civilized feeling. Her greater capacities were limited to harmony and memory. By taking up belletristic and classical verse forms, Wheatley engaged in a politics of respectability in which she offered her verse as proof of African intellectual, reflective, and creative capacities. This demanded that she distance herself from revivalist poetics and its mission to appeal to the plainest capacity, which first became identified with the Wattsian hymn and then with other forms of revival verse. Yet, her poetry remained invested in revivalism and its liberatory potential as she brought classicism to bear on its inconsistencies.

Wheatley, like most of her black contemporaries, fought for liberty on multiple fronts, often at odds or in outright contradiction with each other. By deploying a politics of respectability, she was able to critique revivalist poetics and other colonial supports to slavery, while at the same time refusing the most basic premise upon which her respectable belletristic verse depended—the concept of capacity itself. The utter effacement of revival hymns from her volume of poetry published under the patronage of the evangelical leader the Countess of Huntingdon strongly hints that Wheatley maintained an intentional distance from the plainest capacity. This absence of hymns, combined with the presence of the Ethiop where the universal and invisible white female body of the spouse of Christ had been, points toward a rejection of the category of capacity itself and the type of liberal subject it underwrote. This is because the category of capacity was part of an aesthetic and scientific discourse reinforcing exclusion and hierarchy that had become crucial for deciphering who were rights-bearing individuals. By placing the Ethiop at the center of espousal and the domestic, Wheatley disrupted the structure of liberalism, which depended on white women as representatives of the private, domestic sphere.[83] In this final section, I turn to one last poem, "On Recollection," to show how Wheatley exposed the depths of evangelical hypocrisy and refused "on the lower frequencies" to participate in a poetics whose structure inhibited her full participation in the body politic.

Wheatley's poem "On Recollection" addresses two of the capacities Jefferson attributed to Africans: harmony and memory. Turning again to Christian eschatology, classicism, and African history, Wheatley rejects both revivalist and neoclassical aesthetics of harmony and instead remakes harmony in the image of Mneme. The poem speaks directly to both the shortcomings of revival harmony and the hubris of neoclassical writing as a civilizing tool.

Both Wheatley and Davies used the phrase "ravished ears" in their poems. The phrase was one that had traction in two discourses—one in neoclassical arguments about harmony, and the other in revival poetry. The first poem of Davies's poetry collection, "My God!" inspired by Job 21:17 and written in conjunction with a sermon he preached on that verse, showcases the heights of Davies's ecstatic pietism in fervent pursuit of God. In it, he proclaims, "[Jesus's] Name is Music to my ravish'd Ears, / Sweeter than that which charms the heav'nly Spheres."[84] Here is a quite orthodox proclamation of the enthroned Christ higher than all creation and hence the most exquisite sound, above even the music of the spheres. He seems to place the "ravish'd Ear" in contradistinction to "ravish'd Sight" in another poem in which Solomon unsuccessfully turns to the aesthetics of architecture (reminiscent of neoclassical forms) for ultimate meaning and comfort.[85] Within Davies's explicit emphasis on evangelical harmony, he appears to be remaking the neoclassical purpose of poetry expressed in Edmund Waller's poetic preface to Horace's *Art of Poetry*:

> Poets lose half the praise they should have got,
> Could it be known, what they discreetly blot
> Finding new words, that to the ravish't Ear
> May like the Language of the Gods appear,
> Such as of old, wise Bards employ'd, to make
> Unpollish't men their wild retreats forsake,
> Law-giving-Heroes, fam'd for taming Bru'ts,
> And raising Cities with their Charming Lutes,
> For rudest minds, with Harmony were caught,
> And civil Life was by the Muses taught, . . .[86]

Dymocke's attack on Davies's common harmony places the disgruntled Anglican priest in line with Waller's thought—the purpose of the poet and poetry is to promote civilization. Davies's evangelical "ravish'd Ear" is decidedly different than what Waller is describing—that the ear has been deceived into thinking it hears the sound of the Gods, but it is only the poet's ruse in order to civilize.

Wheatley takes up the phrase "ravished ear" in her neoclassical poem "On Recollection," which was solicited as a performance piece by a member of her coterie. In "On Recollection," Wheatley celebrates Mneme for her justice:

> Mneme, enthron'd within the human breast,
> Has vice condemn'd, and ev'ry virtue blest.
> How sweet the sound when we her plaudit hear?
> Sweeter than music to the ravish'd ear,
> Sweeter than Maro's entertaining strains
> Resounding through the groves, and hills, and plains.
> But how is Mneme dreaded by the race,
> Who scorn her warnings and despise her grace?[87]

For Wheatley, a "ravish'd ear," like Davies's hearing the sweet music of heaven, or like Waller's hearing the civilizing harmony of the poets, cannot compete with the sweet sound of applause to Mneme. That is, to reckon with the past and with God's acts to make all things just is sweeter than the music of any ravished ear. That this poem is dedicated to someone active in Wheatley's circle designated A.M. is an enticing mystery. Could it be Agnes Moorhead, daughter of the fiery revivalist John Moorhead and the transatlantic poet-minister Sarah Moorhead; or possibly Abigail Mather, sister of poet and historian Hannah Mather Crocker and relative of Christian belletrist Mather Byles?[88] These possible dedicatees represent two different poetic approaches, but for either the message would be equally relevant. It is not the power of belletristic poets to civilize the "rudest mind" through harmony, which is the sweetest sound—the elite Mather circle could stand to be reminded of this. But neither is it evangelical harmony that is the highest virtue, the sweetest sound and employment of heaven, as the Moorheads would have claimed. Rather, it is the sound of justice as the history-shaking failure of evangelical harmony—slavery—is made right.

Even further, Mneme, unlike ideas of intellectual capacity, whether elite or plain, belongs to all people and nations. Even Jefferson thought slaves had prodigious capacities for memory—it was what he claimed made them great imitators. The poem is less concerned with harmony and aesthetics as a kind of equal access to God and more concerned with an Augustinian notion of memory, "a universal moral faculty that is not reserved for any particular race and by which anyone can recollect divine truth," in order to establish that all people will be judged.[89] The emphasis is on benevolent Christianity—that is, accountability as universal—and feeling oneself sheltered from judgment through divine recollection. Yet, the poem does not perform personal religious affect as the white woman poet-minister would. Nor does the relationship that Wheatley sets up between memory and feeling look the same as that expressed by white women in her poetic circle.

This is particularly clear through a comparison of another poem entitled "On Recollection," written by a white woman who participated in the same poetic circle as Wheatley (Figure 4.3). In a book given to Jane Tyler (sister of playwright Royall Tyler) by Ruth Barrell Andrews, Tyler recorded another poem "On Recollection," written in response to the same prompt given to Wheatley, perhaps at the same event, and most surely in poetic competition with each other.[90] Both Wheatley's poem and the poem attributed to Portia, a cognomen for Deborah How Cottnam, present the verse as part of the same scenario.[91] Wheatley's poem, published in the London magazine, dates the circumstances of the poem's writing to a prompt within a gathering of young ladies on January 1, 1772: "The following was occasioned by her being in company with some young ladies of family, when one of them said she did not remember, among all the poetical pieces she had seen, ever to have met with a poem upon RECOLLECTION. The *African* (so let me call her, for so in fact she is) took the hint went home to her master's, and soon sent what follows."[92] The scene of writing for Portia's poem is quite similar. Jane Tyler

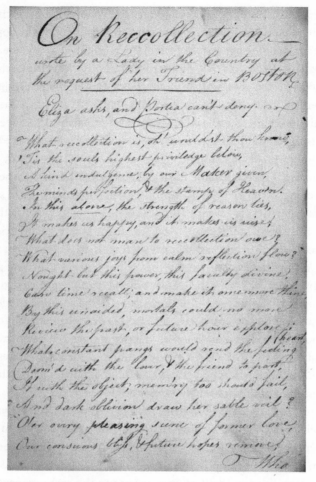

Figure 4.3. "On Recollection" by Deborah How Cottnam in Jane Tyler Book.
Royall Tyler Family Collection, Vermont Historical Society.

copied it with the following subheading "wrote by a Lady in the Country at the request of her Friend in Boston. Eliza asks, and Portia can't deny." When Cottnam's poem appeared in print in the early nineteenth century, its title indicated it was written after someone said they had never heard of a poem on recollection.

Portia's poem figures white women's domesticity and sentiment upholding reason and republican virtue, while Wheatley's poem concerns itself with how morality demands universal justice. The difference in the two poems is stark from the first lines. Portia's begins "What reccollection is, oh! would'st thou know / 'Tis the souls highest privilege below."[93] Rather than a performance of emotion, Wheatley's begins with a classical invocation and a reference to her status as an African poet: "Mneme, begin; inspire, ye sacred Nine! / Your vent'rous *Afric* in the deep design."[94] Portia highlights the social situation of the poetic play (the request for the poem) and elevates the diction through heightened affect. Wheatley focuses on the classical context and its relationship to Africa, the source of poetic inspiration, and begins with an assertive command to one of the three original muses. Wheatley invokes the classical, the Christian, and the African to give a sweeping account of God's judgment for slavery. Though the view is of all of history and every nation, only the gods and the poet appear as individualized, and their relationship is one that produces empowerment to critique and to prophesy—in the biblical sense of warning to avoid sin and judgment. Portia frames recollection primarily in terms of how it enables familial relationships through the ability to remember past loved ones and imagine a future in heaven with them. Without the future of heaven, familial relationships would truly be lost at death and, as a result, virtue would be lost to the tyranny of passions.

Notably, Portia's poem expresses the loss of recollection in racial terms—it is like a "sable veil."[95] In fact, the poem imagines the situation that a slave like Wheatley experienced when she was ripped away from all her familial and social relations. Portia imagines lack of family in this life and the next as a vale of blackness, suggesting that Wheatley's white women readers thought of her in relation to their own mourning, as Joanna Brooks has argued, and as a symbol of the person cut off from all hope and observable memory.[96] The sable veil is the nothingness of social death and the erasure of memory and future. Interestingly, Portia places memory as "the minds perfection, and the stamp of Heaven" and declares, "In this alone, the strength of reason lies."[97] That is, women (associated with memory) are the strength of men (associated with reason). Wheatley might almost be inclined to agree with her that memory is the stamp of heaven, except that Portia mobilizes it to reinforce the family. Wheatley is interested in memory far beyond the bounds of family and nation, the aims to which it was most normally applied.[98] For Wheatley, if the soul is calmed and resigned, it is not because of the promise of familial restoration anchored by white femininity, but because universal memory results in universal justice.

Her poetic coterie recognized that Wheatley's poetry aimed not to affirm the ties and aims of the sentimental family, but to transform the relation of blacks to the literary and the political. As Andrews's poem "On Slavery" indicated, a correct response to Wheatley should be a changed summation of black capability and its implications for abolition. Classism was a necessary and strategic way to critique domestic verse by a figure that could literally not embody it. According to Andrews's husband John, Wheatley's persistent neoclassical flourishes impeded her familial ties and marked her as outside the closest emotional bonds of family and friends.[99] And in fact Wheatley didn't need to write in neoclassical form to participate in her elite white woman's poetic coterie in Boston—doing so actually made her verse visibly quite different from theirs.

The difference between Wheatley's and Portia's "On Recollection," which had everything to do with the domestic, returns us to the conspicuous absence of revival hymns in Wheatley's book. This absence inflects the meaning of the Ethiop that Wheatley inserts at the center of espousal piety. In addition to critiquing the plainest capacity and evangelical harmony, Wheatley's absence of revival hymns also critiques the domestic imagery upon which the woman poet-minister personae depended. The absence of revival hymns, especially in relation to the hymnbook in her portrait, asserts a different relation to the domestic. The hymn and the hearth went together. In the home and in small prayer meetings, the hymn was part of women teaching children and other family members how to conduct the pious life upon which virtuous social and political bodies depended. Wheatley, as a house slave, was necessary to the work of the domestic, but she was not central to its pious leadership. Her virtue was not her own, and her relationship to the reproductive work, both of piety and of a lineage through children, was cut off. Wheatley's refusal of the revival hymn vividly underscores this reality through absence. None of Wheatley's poems could be used by the family at the hearth. At the very center of the feminine domestic was the hymnbook, and Wheatley's hymnbook was empty.

In a culture in which hymnbooks materially connected families and communities of worship and in which white women were often the keepers of this memory and knowledge, Wheatley's rejection is a refusal of sentimental kinship; in its place she practices speculative kinship. The Ethiop as the spouse of Christ invoked a biblical genealogy that grounded "an imaginative project of mapping descent . . . across the African diaspora that did not hinge upon the Atlantic slave trade," which according to Britt Rusert was a precursor to the black ethnographic work that she identifies as "fugitive science" in the nineteenth century.[100] This speculative kinship responds to both audiences that

Wheatley negotiated—the ethnographic science of those like Jefferson and the anthropological poetics of evangelicalism.

Rusert positions Jefferson's *Notes* as a sort of Ur-text for fugitive science—which she defines as a kind of dynamic and vernacular engagement of black cultural producers with race science in the late eighteenth and nineteenth centuries. Wheatley's critique of evangelical harmony shows that her poetry is both a fugitive theological and scientific argument to which Jefferson must respond. She offers up evidence of both genius and intellectual capacity, while refusing its very categories through refashioning key aspects of theological anthropology and poetics. Jefferson's ethnography and its racialized genres tried to undercut the powerful work Wheatley had done. She had redirected revival poetics and its anthropology so as to affirm the primary relation of Africans to espousal through both biblical genealogy and capacity. She had positioned abolition as the crucial issue for the millennial progression of Christian history. In addition to challenging racialized ideas of the plainest capacity, Wheatley set up the Ethiop, not white femininity, as the center of evangelical espousal and experience. Wheatley's persona as the Ethiop, the original spouse of Christ, not only rearranged the assumption of the white universal subject at the heart of revival verse and sentimentalism, but also challenged racial science like Jefferson's that cast her off as derivative. The black female body became a charged site of contestation between evangelical and secular epistemologies and their attendant anthropologies and aesthetics. Given that sentimentalism was becoming tied to and enabling the race science that would proliferate in the nineteenth century, Wheatley's critique, rejection, and remaking of both were highly prescient.[101]

As I argued in Chapter 1, the most ubiquitous domestic image in evangelicalism was the pervasive metaphor of the believer's espousal to Christ, which was embedded even in the couplet. Rowe put pious verse and espousal affect together to become in effect an early version of the poetess whose words of feeling were not wholly her own but were instead available to everyone to make as their own. Even though Wheatley took up the role of the woman poet-minister, she departed from Moorhead, the New England spouse of Christ, and other women poet-ministers in their performance of affect, and she insisted on the presence of her marked body and the persona of the Ethiop, a difference that asserted her actual relation to the domestic that undergirded the imagery of revival religion and threw its universality into question. Eighteenth-century pleasures of the imagination were carefully separated from the body, which created a universal, non-material field in which black bodies could not escape their physicality.[102] This is why placing the Ethiop in the metaphor of espousal was so potentially disruptive: it demanded that, in the evangelical imagination, the universal pleasures of the soul embodied through the espousal metaphor were black, a move that undermined the universality (whiteness) of that imagination.

Recognizing that Wheatley's abolitionist verse came with a devastating critique of the domestic and its relationship to evangelical poetics introduces new elements to the way that we understand her centrality to the poetry of abolition. The end of the eighteenth century saw the sudden rise of white women's sentimental abolitionist verse, much of it by evangelicals, which depended upon white women's feelings and the availability of the slave to affective piracy. If the fundamental metaphor of affective piety was espousal, how did slaves fit in, particularly given that stable marriage was denied by the institution of slavery? It is as if the tireless output of sentimental verse reasserted the place of the universal spouse of Christ at the white hearth through a compulsion to fill the empty hymnbook of the Ethiop. That is, Wheatley's unavailability accelerated the affective piracy of anti-slavery sentimental poetry typical of the nineteenth-century white poetess. Wheatley positioned herself as one most in touch with mourning, loss, and the experience of death and social death—a mediator of this for white people. She often told white people how to feel, but she didn't give them her words in which to do it. Her refusal to create a language that could be put in the mouth of the reader to perform affective piety is not only a distancing of her own emotion, not only an explicit critique of harmony and capacity and its relation to genius and barbarity, but also a refusal to lend her words to affective piracy. Whatever else white readers could use her poetry for, they could not collapse her language into their own, as Watts had suggested all Christians do with Rowe's writings. Rowen Ricardo Phillips very aptly asks, "Who has put Phillis Wheatley's poems to heart, or thinks to use any of her lines to describe a situation that is not Phillis Wheatley's situation?"[103] Wheatley's refusal of the "heavenly singer" role set off a reactionary chain and, we might say, produced a field of white "heavenly singers" into the nineteenth century.[104] The nineteenth-century white poetess became bound up in an almost compulsive response to the Ethiop's affective vacancy—a vacancy that was predicated on black women's prophetic speech, the call of universal justice, and an original grounding and authority in biblical history.

On the eve of the American Revolution, Wheatley was in many ways the culmination of colonial revival poetics and its potential, as well as its severest critic. She was a shrewd reader of revival verse not only for its Dymockian and Jeffersonian tactics, but for the structural shortcomings of revival poetics that inhibited its liberatory potential for slaves. Wheatley not only challenged revival poetics for its reliance on a schema of capacity but also questioned the white and domestic metaphor of espousal. The final chapter turns to another, though very different, reinterpretation of the poet-minister and its relation to espousal piety. Unlike Davies who embraced espousal, a later white itinerant preacher in Virginia, James Ireland, recoiled from its feminine affect and espousal piety. His poetics of conversion helps situate evangelical sociability and poetic form as part of the construction of white masculinity in an expanding network of both male-dominated evangelical itinerancy and women poet-ministers.

5

A Revivalist *Ars Poetica* for an Itinerant Coterie

Evangelical Wit, Punctiliar Revision, and Poetic Address

At the same time that Samuel Davies's *Miscellaneous Poems* (1752) blanketed the colony of Virginia and advanced Presbyterianism in the South, manuscript verse fanned the flames of Baptist revival in the woods of Virginia. One young man, James Ireland, was caught up in this burgeoning evangelical poetic culture, converted to the Baptist sect, and became an itinerant minister. As Ireland tells it, it was poetry that saved him. In the late 1760s, the Scottish-born immigrant and back-slidden Presbyterian "Jemmy" Ireland had established himself in the social milieu of the young Virginia gentry through his exceptional dancing, exemplary wit, manuscript poetry, and bawdy songs. His poetry circulated in manuscript throughout Shenandoah County, where he served as a schoolmaster; by night he was the life of the party, whipping up verse and performing it on demand. Meanwhile a Baptist minister set his sights on Ireland and invited the young man not to take up his Bible, but rather to take up a poetic challenge: compose religious verse. The result of the ensuing battle of wits was Ireland's salvation—and that, most surprisingly, by his own poem. Soon, Ireland was the revered poet-minister and leader of a band of young evangelical itinerants.

Among the thousands of early evangelical conversion narratives, *The Life of the Rev. James Ireland* (1819) is quite extraordinary for its incredible detail, as it recounts the conversion of a sociable bard into a revival poet (Figure 5.1). Deviating from the typical early evangelical conversion narrative, which rarely includes more than a stanza or two of verse scattered here and there, Ireland's book not only includes several full-length poems within and following the body of the conversion narrative, but draws upon the force and significance of poetry as the controlling subject and structure of the first half of the narrative. Ireland's narrative provides a rich description of how

Awakening Verse. Wendy Raphael Roberts, Oxford University Press (2020). © Oxford University Press.
DOI: 10.1093/oso/9780197510278.001.0001

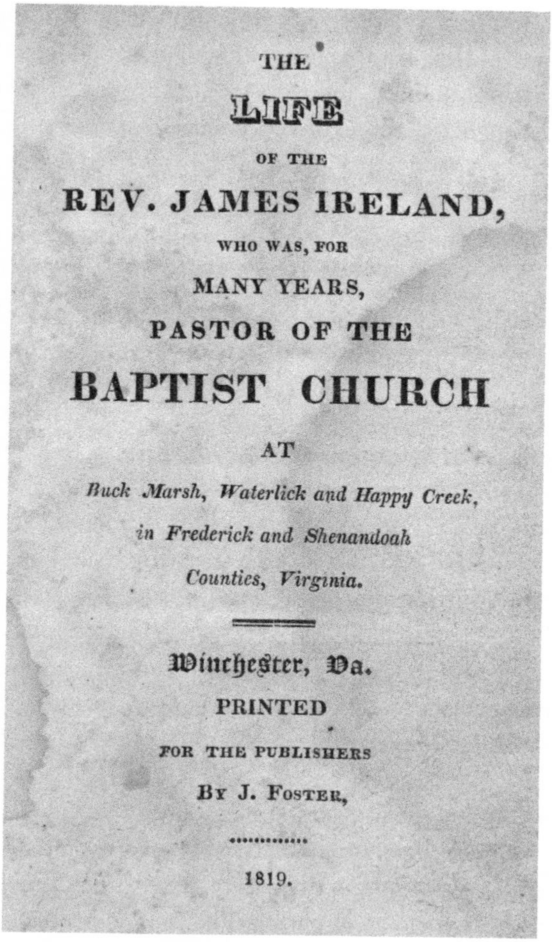

THE

LIFE

OF THE

REV. JAMES IRELAND,

WHO WAS, FOR

MANY YEARS,

PASTOR OF THE

BAPTIST CHURCH

AT

Buck Marsh, Waterlick and Happy Creek,

in Frederick and Shenandoah

Counties, Virginia.

Winchester, Va.

PRINTED

FOR THE PUBLISHERS

BY J. FOSTER,

1819.

Figure 5.1. James Ireland's conversion narrative.
The Newberry Library.

potential converts read and were converted through poetry, as well as an extended account of the uses and practices of revival poetry by itinerants.

Ireland's account shows how enmeshed revival poetry was in the larger practices of poetic culture, while at the same time enumerating its differences. Literary games, wit, sociability—these are all alive in Ireland's account of secular and evangelical verse. As one would expect, the subject and focus of revival verse differed from its counterparts, favoring values like repentance and Christian joy over empty frivolity and promiscuous earthly entertainments.

Less obvious are the strict differences Ireland delineates in regard to revision practices and both the type and function of poetic address. Ireland links revision and poetic address to the nature of evangelical conversion, which revivalists conceptualized and experienced as a discrete point in time that participated in an eschatological history deeply invested in the everyday life of the individual.

This extended account of conversion through poetry speaks to not only how revival verse interacted with the larger culture, but also how it mediated differences within evangelicalism itself. Wheatley's first published poem, in tandem with the Newport revival initiated by free and enslaved blacks, appeared just a year or so prior to Ireland's conversion. Her revival poetics exposed the paradoxes of Calvinism, espousal piety, and evangelical anthropology to advocate for the centrality of African freedom to the millennial progress of Christian history in America. As such, she was part of a growing transatlantic movement and rift within evangelicalism for the abolition of slavery. Ireland's poetics worked in the opposite direction. Ireland emphasizes how revival poetry produced a successful coterie of white and muscularized itinerants fighting and suffering for religious freedom. Ireland's narrative reveals how male converts could engage verse and its attendant forms of sociability to negotiate a religion they experienced as uncomfortably feminine and racially threatening.[1] Revival poetry, including hymns, provided a pious avenue for white brotherly sociality that could recontextualize, mitigate, and contain espousal affect and the pervasive influence of praying, exhorting, and versifying women. Just as women poet-ministers found ways to expand their ministries through revival poetry by taking up gendered personae, itinerants like Ireland practiced forms of revival poetics that helped secure white masculinity within religious freedom and its protection from the state.

Ireland was most representative of the larger culture of revival verse in that he was largely unknown outside of his regional sphere and wrote in popular forms. Unlike the other poets highlighted in this book, all of his poems appear to have been composed in ballad and hymn meters. His account emphasizes that hymns were part of larger poetic practices in the eighteenth-century culture and in evangelicalism that often go missing when placed only within the context of the hymnal or pious worship. The pervasive poetic cultures alive in coffeehouses, taverns, salons, churches, prayer closets, kitchens, fields, and on street corners were not pure and distinct. These aspects of Ireland's story have significant implications for how literary and religious historians understand and regard the contribution and importance of the large archive of verse that early evangelicals crafted. James Ireland's narrative is a window into a prolific early American revival poetry and the continuing role of the evangelical poet-minister so crucial to the culture, work, and vision of revivalism and the larger poetic landscape.

To avoid severing Ireland's poetry from the story into which it was embedded, this chapter proceeds more narratively than previous chapters. The next section argues that Ireland's conversion story underscores practices of literary games, wit, and imitation as crucial to the conversion process and for sustaining evangelical masculinity. Once this has been established through a reading of the account, the following section returns to Ireland's religious conversion and the beginning of his Baptist itinerancy to argue that itinerant networks should be understood as new forms of poetic coteries, which required particular transformations of the revival poet-minister that were crucial for establishing a pious and robust white evangelical masculinity. Though wit and sociable literary games and manly competition continued after conversion, some practices, such as revision, were altered to conform to the theology of conversion itself. The final section turns again to imitation, this time as a kind of mockery, and its relationship to the hyper-personal address of evangelical conversion rhetoric to argue that revival verse and poetic conversion laid a foundation for an emerging lyric address.

Poetic Conversion

Ireland's autobiography is typical of Baptist conversion narratives in many respects: it follows a Calvinist conversion morphology, it includes intense bodily experiences, and it painstakingly distinguishes between activities in the world and pietistic pursuits. What is exceptional is that poetic games explicitly drive the plot of the first half of the autobiography. Ireland crafts the narrative to bring attention to the centrality of poetry in Southern and evangelical sociability and to articulate what he sees as crucial differences between them—differences stark enough to require a conversion from one poetics to the other. At the same time, the narrative consistently foregrounds literary activities central to genteel sociability that are remade to activate conversion and to provide suitable entertainment for itinerants instead. Though Baptists painted conversion as a complete rejection of the profane practices of much of the social world, Ireland does not detail a conversion from bawdy wit into pious sentimentalist, but a redemption of verse to its rightful purposes, which includes not only the display of religious feeling but also the performance of evangelical wit. Ireland's narrative contextualizes evangelism and conversion within the sociable world of poetic games; that is, he brings the Augustan values of imitation and wit into the service of a poetics of religious passion. In doing so, he schematizes a poetics of evangelical conversion that weaves a purposeful role for imitation, wit, and feeling within the typical evangelical conversion morphology. Gregory Jackson takes up the relationship of homiletic novels and board games in the process of nineteenth-century evangelical spiritual development, which he identifies as a pew-to-parlor shift in religious practices. He argues that the use of games shows that the experience of evangelical reading, unlike most theories of the novel, was socialized.[2] My argument situates poetic games as an earlier evangelical social reading practice—what might be termed a parlor-to-pew shift in eighteenth-century revivalism.

The phrase "evangelical wit" can sound like an oxymoron given that the eighteenth century's proto debate between Alexander Pope and John Dennis once stood in for a stable division that scholars marked between wit and pathos, neoclassicism and enthusiasm. As discussed in previous chapters, the Virginian Anglican priest who harangued Samuel Davies for years in the 1750s defended just such a distinction to condemn Davies and other evangelicals as the equivalent of Pope's failed bathetic dunces—a distinction Jefferson defended. For Pope, Dymocke, and Jefferson, Augustan verse, which celebrated wit as the well-placed and well-timed image or metaphor that displayed inventiveness on one's feet, was the opposite of enthusiastic revival verse. Yet wit permeated revival culture under another name: extemporaneous speech.

Just as the eighteenth-century stage and verse celebrated the performance of wit, so also did the evangelical revivals. Whitefield, whom Harry Stout dubbed the "divine dramatist," brought the affect and techniques of the stage into the pulpit and helped make extemporaneous preaching the standard for evangelical preachers as he encouraged them to create experiences for their audiences rather than merely reiterate lifeless theology. This revival experience often resulted in more extemporaneous speech, which would erupt from the audience and mark the commencement of conversions. Nancy Ruttenburg locates the first instantiation of "the democratic personality" in the Whitefieldian revivals, which she argues produced a newborn self whose "dominant characteristic was the aggressive uncontainability of its speech" authorized by "the prohibitions of established authority."[3] Part of the culture of this evangelical extemporaneity included the condemnation of an ecclesiastical authority "polished with Wit and Rhetorick," in the words of Gilbert Tennent.[4] Extemporaneity was often a marker of the Spirit's presence working through an evangelical minister and his or her sermon or exhortation, rather than dead tradition and human learning. As such, expectations for powerful and affective preaching were so strong that an itinerant who buckled under the pressure could be instantly ruined. For instance, a young itinerant who coughed while preaching, and so was forced to look down at his notes, gave up in shame, having lost all of his credibility.[5] A truly converted preacher displayed his authority through Spirit-inspired words—the right words, at the right time, to the right effect. He channeled God, the ultimate wit. Such did "the eloquent David Thomas," "a country bard," who began his itinerant ministry a year before Samuel Davies's book saw press and who was part of the first sustained surge of Baptists in Virginia.[6] What exactly was a country bard? And what did it have to do with being an eloquent Baptist itinerant minister who valued extemporaneity? The oxymoronic term conjures what Brook Hollifield recognized as two conflicting images of the Southern minister who was supposed to exhibit both the sentiments of the common folk and the erudition and elevated stature of the gentleman.[7] James Ireland's narrative is particularly important for what it reveals about these conflicting images in Baptist poetic practices in the woods of Virginia.

Ireland's narrative provides a view into how wit manifested itself in the poetic practices of those immersed in a revivalist culture of conversion. From the beginning of his narrative, Ireland intertwines his religious rebirth with his pre-conversion poetic practices. Ireland is careful to make sure that the reader of his autobiography understands that in the late 1760s, he had established himself in the social milieu of the young Virginia gentry who relished competitive performances—from dancing, to boxing, to writing verse—in order to fashion and to display their masculinity.[8] Because part of the education of a Southern gentleman included the art of writing poetry, this became a means of performing one's class as well.[9] Long before Ireland immigrated to Virginia, Southern gentry had cultivated various poetries appropriate to the social, political, and personal spheres. It was the respected William Byrd who brought the practice of belles lettres to the Southern colonies at the beginning of the eighteenth century through his prolific writing, including manuscript self-publication of his verse among his circle of friends.[10] Southern gentlemen such as Robert Bolling continued the practice with a rich circulation of manuscript verse, as well as printed verse, that underscored his wit. Even a simple advertisement in the paper for his lost horse was an opportunity to practice his wit and invite a public display of genteel sociability.[11]

One of Bolling's self-published manuscript poems makes clear the active and competitive poetic culture of much Southern verse as well as its stakes: the would-be poet risked being ridiculed as a fool rather than respected as a dignified gentleman. In "Occlusion, or final Poem if ever my Compositions be published," Bolling bemoans his relegation to a lineage of failed bards in light of the success his favorite dunce, the future governor of North Carolina Thomas Burke, has achieved:[12]

> From Rhyme twas always vastly hard
> By counsil to reclaim a Bard.
>
>   . . .
>
> Ye Gods, ye Gods, what Fate is mine!
> Why Burke gains Glory from the nine
> And must I judge in the same Class
> With Paisly, Davis, Randolph, Grymes,
> And Exposed to Laughter for my Rhymes,
> And, tho no Knave, confirmed an Ass!
> Thanks to my worthy Friend;
> Here ends my Poem, here my Follies end.[13]

Realizing that he has been made a fool while dunces have been esteemed, Bolling's poem questions the legitimacy of the entire poetic enterprise. He asks, why would one "toil and rack his Brain / For pleasing Rhymes and but to gain / From every one who reads a Curse!"?[14]

Prior to his conversion, Ireland aggressively participated in the poetic economy that Bolling describes. In such a scheme, the end game is status and respect; all else is beside the point. To this end, sentimental verse often invited mockery, which could be a chance to display manly wit. For instance, Bolling turned Burke's sentimental poem on inoculations into a sexual farce in his manuscript poem "Civil Dudgeon," which turns the new technique of inoculation via needle into a sexual pun. Though no pre-conversion poems of Ireland's are extant, a few lines of Bolling's harangue give a sense of the type of humor and wit the pre-converted Ireland would have aspired to in his bawdy poems:

> Come prick us Sir the Ladies cried,
> To hight Dalglesih, and turn'd aside
> The sacred Lawn. To work he went
> And, lugging forth his Instrument,
> 'Gan soft Palpation on their Skin,
> To find how it shou'd enter in.[15]

Like so many other young Southern white men, he performed his masculinity through such manly contests, including the cultivation of wit.

Like these other Southern men, Ireland's poetry circulated in manuscript throughout the local area; in Ireland's case this drew the attention of a Baptist minister, Reverend Nicholas Fane. This minister, like Samuel Davies and many others, valued the special role of verse in revival and so recognized Ireland's poetic talent as a gift from God that "should be improved for Him and not in the service of the Devil."[16] The Baptist minister, who Ireland later reveals had followed him all the way from Scotland, sought to speak with Ireland several times about his salvation while Ireland attempted to dodge him. At one point, the Baptist minister tried to engage Ireland at a corn husking, which to Ireland's horror, put his status as the reigning master of wit at risk. Corn huskings were lively heterosexual social rituals complete with dancing, drinking, and courting games. In the poetic description of Joel Barlow: "A frolic scene, where work, and mirth, and play, / Unite their charms, to chase the hours away."[17] As Ireland describes it, they were also a chance to perform his masculinity through battles of wit:

> Being invited to a certain gentleman's house to what is called a husking, and being divided in different parties, [the Baptist minister] made choice to be close by me, and the general subject that he was upon, was briefly about religion; as he told me afterwards, I was a youth that might be led, but could not be drove, and possessing some strange and unusual impressions towards me, which at that time he said he could not account for, led him [to] come from the city and place of my nativity, with to make that subject a topic between us. Every ingratiating method that he could take, he pursued in order to acquire my confidence. It happened when we were conversing

together, that a man who conceived himself pretty active in dissipation and burlesque, was running blackguard upon the rest of the company; I was all on nettle to be at him, but this good man's presence had such an awe upon me, that I could not encounter the other, whilst standing along side of him; for a few minutes I avoided his company, and retired, in order to engage the other, and caused some of my companions to form a line between that good man and me, in order to prevent him from seeing what I was about. I then got upon my knees to prevent being seen, encountered this wicked champion, and run him aground in a few minutes. I only mention this in order to show what commanding influence the presence of a gracious man will have over a wicked person's conduct at such a period.

After having executed my purpose I returned to his company immediately, he very well knew my voice, and heard what I was about, yet never made the least mention of it to me.[18]

The incompatibility of the two worlds—evangelical conversation and the poetry of wit—causes Ireland literally to construct a human barrier and to drop to his knees in order to lampoon the "wicked champion" and restore the social order under him. The bodily excess recalls his earlier days of ruckus boxing in which he could subdue a young man in half a minute or take on three schoolmates, while it also foreshadows his approaching repentance in which he will find himself upon his knees without knowing how he got there.[19]

Though Rev. Fane's attempt to corral Ireland into a religious conversation fails at the husking, he later seizes the opportunity at a chance meeting on the road to set the young man upon the right course: the minister challenges Ireland to compose a poem on brotherly love. Neither the Baptist minister's seemingly random poetic game nor the proposed subject were happenstance, but explicitly engaged the contest culture on display at the husking and translated it into an evangelistic tool. The topic itself—brotherly love—underscores that Rev. Fane understood the importance of masculine sociability to Ireland's poetic performances. Shields has shown how games of literary skill in the seventeenth and eighteenth centuries became "rites of initiation" into the art of poetry, while also serving "both sociability and self-cultivation" as one strove "for mastery and reputation in society and art."[20] The minister's invitation to Ireland to try his skill at revival poetry transforms the conventional battle of the wits into an evangelical call to repentance,

which conversion narratives often characterized as a strenuous and prolonged contest between themselves and God.

The competitive Ireland was not one to turn down a friendly challenge.
Though he admits his knowledge on the religious subject of brotherly love is
limited, he confidently completes the poem by making inferences about the
Baptist sect from a meeting he once attended. Ireland composes 11 stanzas
in long meter that begin by directing the reader to God's love through the
sacrifice of Christ on the cross. It then instructs the reader on the correct
affective response to such a sacrifice, which in turn creates a community of
peace and brotherly love between those saved from hell. In comparison to
Ireland's post-conversion poems printed at the back of the narrative, this
verse is stilted in its use of a forced first-person moralism to describe religious enthusiasm:

> Again how ought our bowels move
>   In streams of sympathetic love,
>   To Christ the Son of God on high,
>   Who to redeem our souls did die;
>   Our faculties should be all fire
>   Flowing to Him with love's desire.
>
> Secondly, from our love to God,
>   Let us return to earth's abode,
>   Where, if we see and doth perceive
>   Any that in our Lord believe,
>   It ought to make our bowels move
>   On them with a brotherly love.[21]

Here, Ireland's attempt to understand the relationship between Christ's sacrifice, religious enthusiasm, and love for other Christians comes out as a
rote moralism, "should be all fire," in a clunky poetic voice that has to explicitly mark the links between his ideas—"secondly . . . Let us return to
earth's abode." In his role of the exhorter or preacher who encourages love
of Christ and brother, he takes up the bodily image of the deepest emotions
being moved, yet awkwardly as if a third party, especially in comparison
to the great Methodist poet Charles Wesley—"To me, to all, thy bowels
move."[22] Though he tries to use their language, and none of the Baptists in his

narrative takes offense, its clumsy phrasing tips into a Swiftian image of religious enthusiasts: believers spewing their bowels on each other. The social
wit who was still, in Ireland's own words, in a "natural and wicked state," can't
quite escape his bawdy humor.

Ireland proceeds in the poetic game as he would any other poetic challenge
and so expects a social tribunal, which he seeks at a barn raising. Like other
literary contests, the play initiated by the Baptist minister proceeds from
poetic challenge to composition to performance and then to judgment.[23]
The minister gathers the barn raisers together to witness a duet as he turns
the poem into a display of spontaneous Christian worship and fellowship.
Ireland accompanies the minister without hesitation, well-practiced in the
art of both poetry and song, but the minister's effeminate body language—
prolonged hugging around the waist—proves difficult to bear. In the social
context of a barn raising, a space often associated with manly contests, the
minister's demeanor shames Ireland, who is expecting to assert his poetic
prowess and win the game through public applause.

The choice of brotherly love as the subject of the minster's challenge forces
the performance of masculinity into the center of the competing poetic
cultures of evangelicalism and Southern gentility. Ireland immediately genders
the experience, describing the poet-minister as the cultivator of a feminized religious feeling and the sociable poet as a conduit for masculine displays of wit.
After giving the poem to the Baptist minister to read, Ireland writes:

> As we were singing together, [the minister] kept his left arm around my
> waist, and feeling affected at some passages as he sung them, he would
> hug and press me up to him; I felt ashamed at such effeminacy, as that of
> one man to be hugging another; and I must confess, it stretched my mod-
> esty to bear with it.—When we had finished singing, the eldest son of the
> Pastor of the Church (of which the old Gentleman was a member) who was
> somewhat advance [sic] in years, and had a tolerable numerous family, at
> the same time possessing a tolerable degree of low satirical wit attempted
> to make me the object of his burlesque, before the people—I immediately
> broke through all restraint, and lampooned him before the old Gentleman
> and every person present, without receiving from my old friend the least
> admonition or rebuke.[24]

Here, Ireland counters his uncomfortable experience with the perceived
effeminacy of Baptist worship and its sentimental and physical displays of

brotherly love by exercising a decisive blow of satire to reaffirm his mascu-linity. The episode marks the sociable poetry that the pre-converted Ireland practiced as dependent upon, and productive of, a masculine affect incom-patible with revival poetry.

The eldest son clearly recognizes Ireland as first and foremost a bawdy poet whose incommensurability with revival verse produces a humorous com-bination overripe for burlesque because it already seems a mock-imitation of itself. The pastor's son, accustomed to Ireland's dominant role at dances, races, fights, and other social gatherings, cannot resist the opportunity to at-tempt to topple the reigning wit. Ireland, not able to tolerate such an affront, lambasts him in the middle of the spontaneous worship. Given Ireland's lan-guage in the passage—"satiric wit," "burlesque," "lampoon"—as well as the fact that he is defending his reputation in light of his newly composed reli-gious poem, Ireland's harangue most likely takes the form of verse. It was, after all, only when one could compose poetry spontaneously that one could rightly claim the title of a wit.

The burlesque response by the local Pastor's son returns the barn-raising space to its traditional purpose, dramatically distinguishing secular socia-bility from evangelical fellowship. The immediate dissolution of Ireland's poem on brotherly love and its accompanying performance of revival into a lampoon on the Pastor's son forcefully marks Ireland's ineptitude as a revival poet.[25] The judgment rendered by the audience only affirms Ireland's success as a profane wit. The minister's silence speaks to the alternative rules of en-gagement for the poet-minister: only God's voice rules over the social field, overthrowing the heart and replacing it with lively piety.

Though the first game only confirms Ireland's success as a social wit who can both imitate revivalist poetry and mock its adherents, the minister feels God's work is imminent and so proposes a new game in which the rules are slightly altered:

> Before I parted with [the minister], he made a second request, which was to this effect—That I would compose him one piece more, with which I com-plied, and believe I shall have reason to bless God to all eternity for it, its being the means, in the hand of the Spirit, of my awful convictions for sin before God. My old friend also informed me afterwards that he was unusu-ally impressed, that God was about to do something on me or in me, that disposed him to solicit a second composition. When I applied to him to know upon what subject I should make it, he replied he had none to give

me, but left it to myself. I felt myself more at a loss what subject to choose, than I was to know his meaning of the word charity [or brotherly love], in the first piece.[26]

While the first poem proved easy to write, the second came with a new twist: the choice of topic. The changed rules of the game reflect the minister's sense that a more spontaneous format was in order. The minister's retreat from the position of challenger and judge signals his belief that God will transform the game from everyday poetic play into a cosmic battle for the soul.

The extemporaneous nature of this second poetic challenge provides space for God to intercede in Ireland's poetic process. While walking through the woods, anxious to determine a topic for his composition, Ireland's subject comes to him through divine intervention:

in an instant of time it appeared as if these words were articulate [sic] into my heart, and that so forcibly as if another person had spoke them, viz., "Make one on the naturally [sic] man's dependence for heaven." An inquiry arose in my breast immediately, what is the natural man's dependence for heaven? Like two contrary voices questioning and answering, the reply was, "What is your own dependence for heaven?"[27]

Ireland quickly replies that he personally plans to continue in the pleasures of sin until he nears the end of his life, when, by his own power he will repent for a few weeks to secure his salvation. The voice returns to confirm that this is, for many people, the natural man's dependence for heaven. "From this conclusion," Ireland writes, "I immediately set about the performance of my piece."[28]

The poem Ireland writes employs a persona that, juxtaposed to his determination to remain in sin until his deathbed, highlights his poetic performance as hollow religiosity. Content to mimic a minister who warns against "the natural man's dependence for heaven," Ireland seems unconcerned that he indicts himself. Stanza two, in fact, versifies his profane sentiments exactly, while stanza three mimics a ministerial call to repent of those views:

2
O! how their consciences they'll bribe,
Under such base pretences,

To gratify their sinful pride,
Committing gross offences;
They'll acquiesce—
There is a bliss
Where righteous men will enter;
Likewise they'll tell
There is a hell,
Where wicked men shall center:
But say they, we're here on earth,
We'll spend our time in Jovial mirth,
And when our youthful pleasure's past
We'll then turn unto God at last;
Few weeks repentance will secure,
Making to us salvation sure,
And save us from
The eternal doom
Or wrath and indignation.

3
But sinners O! whoe'er you are,
Possess'd with such a notion,
That dreadful day will soon appear,
When all things will have motion;
When heaven will roll
Up like a scroll
And vanish with a mighty noise,
And the earth sweat
With fervent heat,
Melting at the great God's voice:
When the archangel will be sent
To raise the dead to judgment,
At God's tribunal to appear,
To answer at His awful bar,
For deeds they've done here on earth,
And their doom pronounced forth;
Either to go
To bliss or woe
And there to dwell for ever.[29]

The poem strikingly avoids a personal response to the voice that asked him, "What is your own dependence for heaven?" Instead, Ireland writes in the third person, as if talking only of other "wicked men" who spend their earthly life in "Jovial mirth."[30] His religious training in Scotland enables him to parrot a Calvinist call to repentance as he rightly schematizes the ways and ends of the wicked and the saved, but it does not equip him to perform a crisis of faith or evangelical repentance.[31] Ireland's disinterested religiosity is on display through his concern about rhyme. He writes, "the jingle of sound was more the object of my pursuit than the matter contained in it: yet I have often seen since, the overruling hand of Providence in the matter it contained."[32] Ireland's description of his compositional demeanor as one concerned with "the jingle of the sound," accurately describes the final product, whose six stanzas each follow an intricate rhyme scheme (ababccdeedffgghhiid) generally consistent throughout. Yet, while Ireland tinkered with sound, God serendipitously ordained the content. Or, as Ralph Erskine put it in *Gospel Sonnets*, the power of the verse's form causes fools to see "their Wit, and Wits their Folly see."[33]

Immediately, God exposes Ireland's poetic imitation by seizing his poet-minister persona for himself and infusing the words with life. Ireland writes, "So soon as I had finished this poem, these words in the last verse, viz. 'The law does breathe nothing but death to slighters of salvation,' kept continually running through my mind."[34] After a day and a half of unceasing agitation provoked by the poetic voice lodged in his head, Ireland takes the poem to the Baptist minister, who after reading it and "look[ing] solemnly and steadfastly" into Ireland's countenance, can only say, "O! Man."[35] Rev. Fane's grave biblical phrase announces that the initial game of wit has ceased and the Lord's conviction of sin has begun.

Unable to understand the reason for the incessant poetic voice or to comprehend the minister's prescient response, Ireland resolves to "drive that foolish notion (as I took it to be) out of my mind."[36] The dramatic scene that follows dramatizes the oppositional nature of sociable and revival poetry on his body:

When I had got at a proper distance so as not to be heard, I began to sing wicked and lascivious songs, of which I had a great number; but although I exerted my voice to its utmost power and highest pitch still the words— "The law does breathe nothing but death to slighters of salvation," sounded louder in my mind than the audible exertion of my voice; I would then form my body in to a bending position and putting a hand upon each knee, would exert all the force of nature within me, shake my head and endeavor to force other objects and subjects upon my mind, but nothing could avail to dispossess me of that impression; I therefore, gave over the attempt.[37]

Here, Ireland presents his initial experience with God's convicting work as a new duel of wits. Yet as much as he attempts to render his own mock revival verse mute through a crescendo of bawdy songs, the ministerial poetic voice Ireland imitated was now beyond his control. He finds his bawdy wit and physical strength shamefully impotent to counter God's poetic harangue. Walking away in his first defeat of wit and wrestling, he retires to a dance where he finds himself "inadvertently . . . inform[ing] the company that [he] expected that was the last time [he] should ever dance amongst them."[38] His words forecast the exchange of one bodily performance and pleasure, the socializing of polite society, for another, the work of conversion.[39]

The next day, God finally condescends to interpret the poet's lines for Ireland, who appears a mere dunce wandering around in a stupor of confusion. The awakening appears like a bolt of lightning and hinges entirely upon the personalization of the poet-minister's address:

I felt an unusual conflict within; the aforementioned words running through my mind, all at once I was made as it were to stand!—God was pleased to manifest light to my understanding, and brought it home to my conscience that I was the slighter and contemner of the salvation of Christ; and that the law of God was then breathing death against my soul. The impression was so forcibly brought home to my conscience, that it never become [*sic*] obliterated from that period until I had reason to believe that Christ was formed in my soul the hope of Glory.[40]

Ireland presents the writing and interpretive practice of his revival poems as entirely the divine work of God sending the natural man into a state of mental and physical confusion. God's work of conviction extends and transforms the initial game of wit, beginning with God's repetition of a single line of Ireland's verse—a move that at first berates Ireland's impotent imitation of a revival poem. Soon, the unrelenting repetition renders imitation obsolete; it begins to undo the original context and authorship until the words are stripped bare, to their essence, a divine logos that speaks into existence Ireland's rebirth into eternal life.

This spectacular account of conversion begins with a revivalist's admonition to participate in a poetic game of wit. Specifically, the Baptist minister invites Ireland to imitate and to best the poet-minister. Among a people that embraced Thomas a Kempis *Imitatio Christi* as an ideal of the spiritual life, which emphasized solitude, silence, and rejection of the world as a true internal devotion to Christ, this may appear strange. Yet, imitation was a practice that extended beyond the believer imitating Christ and into the evangelistic invitation to Christ. Ireland's narrative demonstrates that poetic imitation could produce the believer's *imitatio Christi*.

This efficacy is one reason why many revivalists embraced forms of neo-classical imitation long after ideas of poetic genius became fashionable. In 1772, Sir William Jones's "Essay on the Arts Called Imitative" represented the general tenor of the times, which identified emotion, not imitation, as the essence of the art of poetry. Evangelical poets were criticized often (then and now) for missing the mark for both the neoclassical and the Romantic ideals of poetry: they were accused of being both slavishly imitative as well as excessively emotional.[41] One of William Wordsworth's critics who abhorred what he thought to be an echo of Methodism in the poet's verse warned that such pulpit effusions were unfit companions of true poetic inspiration:

> Moral and religious enthusiasm, though undoubtedly poetical emotions, are at the same time dangerous inspirers of poetry; nothing being so apt to run into interminable dullness or mellifluous extravagance without giving the unfortunate author the slightest intimation of his danger. His laudable zeal for the efficacy of his preachments, he very naturally mistakes for the ardour of poetic inspiration;—All sorts of commonplace notions and expressions are sanctified in his eyes, by the sublime ends for which they are employed; and the mystical verbiage of the Methodist pulpit is repeated, till the speaker entertains no doubts that he is the elected organ of divine truth and persuasion.[42]

Such criticism of Methodist verse applied to James Ireland and his coterie of Baptist itinerant poets who were also considered unoriginal enthusiasts. Or using the words of John Stuart Mill, Ireland and his lot were not writing the truest form of poetry, lyric poetry, because "it is the poetry most natural to a really poetic temperament, and least capable of being successfully imitated by one not so endowed by nature."[43] Yet, in the hands of the Baptist minister, the seemingly imitability of revival poetry made it a successful evangelistic tool. Ireland's salvation came about because Rev. Fane invited him to imitate revival verse. At the same time that revivalists wrote thousands of poems with little to distinguish them from each other, they reserved an inimitable poetic element, the original genius of God.

A Poetic Coterie of Itinerant Ministers

Ireland understood that Baptist conversion required him to undergo radical personal and social alteration. Instead of enjoying the pleasures of society, he would willingly throw aside his social position and become a religious spectacle to his former friends by joining a community that conflicted with the dominant Anglican and gentry culture. Sacrificing his reputation for being the best dancer in the region and a sociable poet, he would become an outcast—an enthusiastic Baptist who wrote, to quote the Anglican Dymocke, an effeminate and black "no language." His verse would now instigate the work of the Lord and cause bodies to bend and contort under conviction for sin like it had his own. This was not looked upon kindly by his friends. Changing the rules of poetic engagement—from that which propped up the sociability of genteel culture to that which sustained and spread the upside-down world of Baptist life—was a provocative proposition. Converting into a Baptist was one thing; taking poetry with you was quite another.

According to Ireland it was a painful transformation. He had once moved adeptly between diverse social settings, even boasting, "I possessed certain qualifications by which I could accommodate myself to every company; with the religious I could moralize a little; with the well bred I could be polite; with the merry I could be antique [*sic*]; and with the obscene I could be profane."[44] Now he hid from his friends—some who shunned him and others who continuously attempted to drag him back from his descent into disrepute. On one particular occasion a former friend, whom Ireland notes would later become "a governor, a general and a member of congress," found Ireland noisily groaning in the woods and declared, " 'Jemmy, you have turned a fool, you are certainly distracted and raving in despair.' "[45] The possibility of another encounter with his "teasing acquaintance" terrorized Ireland so much that he moved his lodging next to the Massanuttin Mountains where he "retire[d] every morning with [his] bible and hymn book . . . under the anxious concern of [his] soul" for "a considerable number of days."[46] During one of these lonely retreats, his anxiety over the sociable world produced his ministry as a revival poet and his new poetic fellowship:

> My sense of guilt appearing to me gone, and the lonesome distresses I then felt, together with the reflections my companions made drew from me the following composition, which I addressed to the Lord.

P1
Come Lord in mercy 'suage my grief
And from me not depart
But send some comfort or relief,
To ease my wounded heart.

. . .

5
Which makes all those of earthly minds,
Strange stories on me raise;
And also my young carnal friends,
Have turn'd my enemies.

6
For I do but by them walk
They say I've turn'd a fool;
Then I become their common talk,
In scorn and ridicule.

7
Where'er they see me griev'd or sad,
Walking myself alone;
Poor thing they say, I know he's mad,
His senses are all gone.

8
They say they're sorry for my case,
And likewise will declare,
Telling me plainly to my face
I'm raving in despair.

9

Therefore O Lord, their hearts do smite
With a sore sense of sin;
And make them feel the dreadful state
By nature they are in.

10

That they may know such madness too,
Themselves must also find,
If e'er Thy grace do bring them through,
To holiness inclin'd.
        . . .[47]

Unable to ignore the social milieu that enabled his poetic fame, Ireland boldly claims a new role as the raving fool rather than the composed wit. He has become the talk of the party, the butt of satiric jokes, and the victim of poetic lampoons. Ireland does not retreat from competition, even though he now occupies the upside-down value system of the Kingdom of God in which the weak are strong, and the foolish wise. If anything, he becomes emboldened in his war of words, heralding the gospel across the countryside of Virginia. Rather than a witty harangue, Ireland writes an evangelical poem in which he strikes back by cursing his former crowd with the same conviction of sin that he had undergone.

With this new poem in hand, Ireland targets for conversion a young man who had loved Ireland dearly and relentlessly sought for his friend to return to polite society. The young man grieved that Ireland "had resigned up all that sprightly behavior which was pleasing to company, lost [his] senses and become a fool."[48] When Ireland hears his friend utter these words, he simply hands his newly composed poem to his friend as proof of his "folly."[49] Knowing that the verses include the same language that the young man had just used to describe his religious foolery, Ireland watches closely for a response. The young man reads the manuscript once, then twice as he begins to show physical signs of spiritual agitation. Suddenly, the man rises and declares before absconding, " 'I believe that we are all fools, and you are the only wise man amongst us.' "[50] Though his friend wanted to save Ireland from folly and bring him back into the sociable world, Ireland's verse turns the tables. Post-conversion, the stakes of wit change: the dire consequence being the possibility of an "awful" conviction of sin.[51]

The episode outlines the new sociality of poetic exchange within a revivalist worldview. With the first transfer of the manuscript, Ireland signals his poetry's participation in a topsy-turvy literary play whereby he stages the opportunity to display his folly rather than his wit. It is as if holding the poem activates its curse, for the friend begins to react physically to the verses—a clear indication that God has begun to "smite" him "[w]ith a sore sense of sin."[52] Recanting the judgment of their genteel fraternity, the friend suddenly affirms the reversed values of evangelical community and declares Ireland's dominion over it. With the return of the manuscript, the friend both acknowledges and affirms the new rules of poetic engagement. Ireland's role as the fool becomes an esteemed position: he is once more the reigning poet of wit, and the beginning of his male evangelical coterie is born.

It is unusual for scholars to situate itinerant ministers within the eighteenth-century poetic culture of exclusive coteries and salons.[53] Even so, evangelical itinerant ministers trafficked in the century's most prolific verse communities and were descended from a long line of British dissenters and separatists for whom verse was essential. At first, this might seem to be for good reason. Poetic coteries were often private affairs fashioned out of a system of courtly patronage. Most itinerant ministers eschewed traditional elite markers such as classical rhetoric and education and chose to take up a life associated with peddlers and vagrants—extemporaneous preaching and hymn singing. They existed to serve the unknown, unsaved masses, not to cultivate manners among an exclusive circle of friends. This is why they have often been mobilized to support narratives of democratization. In fact, later traveling poets, such as the eccentric Jonathan Plummer, were not regarded as serious poets because they lived an itinerant lifestyle that associated them with enthusiastic itinerant ministers. Such poets were called ballad mongers—a label that had everything to do with class and respectability, rather than the form of their poetry.[54] Likewise, itinerant ministers who wrote together and circulated their enthusiastic poems between each other while living a life on the road certainly were not to be equated with respectable poetic coteries.

Such an elision overwrites the history of poetic coteries that is closely bound up with the history of conventicles, or private religious meetings, which birthed evangelicalism and remains a central practice today. This is particularly important because the emergence of private groups has been considered central to eighteenth-century society and politics and the century's cultivation of civility through pleasure, taste, and manners. Following Jürgen

Habermas, accounts of the public sphere have shifted toward the exclusion of religion, including a firm split between private, secular societies and conventicles.[55] Yet, both private religious meetings and private secular societies were concerned with formulations of community, aesthetics, and poetry. Unthinking the conventicle and the eighteenth-century poetic coterie as oppositional makes more sense out of the influence of common-sense philosophy on evangelicalisms, enlightenments, and the public sphere, and the centrality of aesthetics to politics and religion in an emergent secularism.

Evangelical itinerant poetic circuits or fellowships were types of eighteenth-century poetic coteries that, like their non-evangelical iterations, followed an arch-poet, were efficacious circulators of verse, enjoyed competition and play, pursued patronage, and considered their pursuit of poetry essential to the flourishing of society.[56] Itinerants often saw themselves on the typical trajectory of an eighteenth-century poet who circulated manuscripts among his coterie, published occasional poems and hymns, and then wrote epics and other long forms. Itinerant poet-ministers considered themselves under the tutelage of Watts and Wesley. Joshua Marsden, missionary to England, Nova Scotia, Bermuda, and the United States, memorialized Methodist itinerant preachers as followers of the greatest poets since David. They carried out what Watts had commissioned—saving poetry from its worldly applications and returning it to its godly uses; that is, they redeemed verse in order to redeem souls.

At a more local level, arch-poets arose among itinerants that met en route as well as through their yearly conferences. Joshua Marsden defended the idea that one could devote his entire life to only writing evangelical poetry, though he and others chose to write in their spare time while itinerating.[57] They often composed while traveling, relaxing after preaching, or preparing for a meeting, as Joseph Craig and others recorded.[58] Itinerant ministers often served the communities they entered as poets, writing occasional poems, solidifying affections through verse, and engaging in poetic games. They sometimes aided each other's compositions even if they were not of the same denomination. For instance, one of Joseph Thomas's poems was dictated to a Methodist preacher who asked him to write it.[59] At other times, itinerants lambasted each other's theologies in verse and performed apologetics in rhyme, such as the infamous John Peck who took part in many poetic battles, with one of the responses in print titled "The Wrestler" (1814).

Ireland's narrative emphatically underscores that literary play was not the exclusive domain of the sociable poet who delighted in salons, coffeehouses, taverns, and the like. Just as he "was much taken up in those [pre-conversion] times with making songs and satirical poems, which had a pleasing influence on the generality of the settlement, which highly gratified [him]," Ireland continued to enjoy his reputation as a poet and worked to cement it in his new evangelical poetic coterie.[60] He writes:

> And now, as many of my religious friends are fond of poetical compositions, and know that I possess measure of talent that way, I will entertain them with one in this place. The origin of which belongs to Mr. Thomas Buck Jr. Being at his house one evening, in our younger days, and both being fond of spiritual songs, he mentioned one he would sing; it was called "The Minister's Hymn." After hearing it sung, I observed, I thought it greatly deficient. That the minister's duty, work and reward was but barely touched on in it; but if he would learn me the tune, I would compose him one that would better comport with that title, which was accordingly done, and the hymn is as follows.[61]

Reminiscent of Rev. Fane's poetic contest, this time Ireland initiates the game for himself: he will write a better hymn on the subject of a minister's duty. Ireland's bardic boasts have not changed with Baptist conversion, nor has he lost his pleasure in writing poems for another's judgment. That his friends already knew of his talent indicates that Ireland cultivated a new social circle to judge and applaud his poetic skill. As Ireland's editor writes in the preface to his autobiography, "I have heard [Ireland] say, that in his leisure hours, when he got on a vein of poetry, he could follow it up almost at pleasure."[62] The boast, suited to the sociable world in which Ireland first earned his poetic reputation, transferred to the evangelical community Ireland served and molded without censure. The story suggests that Ireland's criticism and rewriting of the hymn was not an unusual activity for an evening of mutual edification. In an environment in which evangelicals placed a premium on their own "freshly written" hymns, in which the gentry promoted poetic mastery through extemporaneous wit, and in which many believers both pre- and post-conversion were acquainted with sociable verse, the collision of piety with literary play was not just inevitable, but common.[63] There was a time and place for displaying one's poetic talents, even by directly challenging another's composition.

Ireland stages his poetic skill through composing hymns and poems—forms that often blur because evangelicals experienced them together. For instance, the collection of poems printed in the back of Ireland's autobiography includes the prefatory remark: "Here follows a few of Mr. Ireland's poems which we presume will be read with pleasure."[64] Among them are elegies—clearly a traditional poetic form. Yet, after the second poem we are informed that "the above was frequently sung by Mr. Ireland and congregation in meeting."[65] The reading of poems and the singing of hymns were often practiced with the same text. As such, one cannot assume that the presence of a hymn meant the absence of a literary poem.[66] Rather, evangelical poetry was a flexible category that encompassed a wide range of verse that could accommodate and stimulate various religious experiences and needs.

Games of wit were particularly important in Ireland's coterie of itinerant poet-ministers because it helped neutralize some of the sting of what they perceived to be a transition from masculine to effeminate behavior in Baptist conversion. According to Ireland's account, moving from polite letters to composing revival hymns and poetry was an emasculating process; yet, what is remarkable about Ireland's narrative is that he remakes masculine literary play into an evangelical pastime. That is, he narrates how to perform Baptist piety without giving up all of the markers of Southern masculinity, many of which revolved around contests of wit. Baptist men may have to give up boxing, drinking, dancing, gambling, and the like but, Ireland emphasizes, they need not give up poetic wit.

While scholars have understood the communal nature of hymns through their variations in different regions and churches, Ireland's narrative shows that a more deliberate practice of rewriting also occurred in social settings that adapted sociable literary games to evangelical fellowship.[67] The poetics of conversion, however, was a distinct practice from these revisionary games because it demanded a particular reverence for the original composition. Because Ireland intentionally includes poetry within the text of the conversion narrative, he not only provides an example of the way poetry worked in the conversion process, but how it functioned differently than prose and other types of poems. The self-revision necessary in the conversion process and in the writing of autobiography came to bear on Ireland's conversion poetics in ways that illuminate revival poetry's particular relationship to the refined world of belles lettres and its attendant coteries. Polite literature, both in manuscript and print, aspired to an elevated presentation and perfected skill. Though Erskine and Davies apologized for their humble verse, they nonetheless revised it. Ireland revised many of his other poems as well. But he, along with many other poet-ministers, did not revise their pre-conversion poems for theological reasons.[68]

Three times in the narrative Ireland makes a specific assertion about revision before he includes a poem. Taken together, they reveal a firm commitment to keeping pre-conversion poems in their original form. Before the first poem, "Of all the passions," he gives an explicit rationale for including the original version:

> Were I disposed to correct the following piece, I could make it appear more consistent with the form of sound words; but being then in my natural and wicked state, I choose, therefore, to give it in the ideas I then possessed; and as there will be a variety of compositions interspersed in my narrative, they will appear more consistent with soundness, as I became some further enlightened [sic].[69]

Ireland chooses to include unrevised poems within his narrative in order to demonstrate the trajectory of his religious transformation. The poems, pieces of his pre-converted self plucked from the past, serve as historical evidence for God's work in his life. Following his third poem, "Come Lord in mercy," which he presents to his friend, he boasts, "Whatever poetical compositions are here related, I choose to make them appear in their original dress as I composed them, or there would be no difficulty in making them appear with a better gloss."[70] The comment suggests that prior to his deathbed composition in the early nineteenth century he had faithfully kept the poems in their original state. Even against his persistent competitive flair, the poems would remain unrevised.[71]

The nature of Baptist and evangelical conversion prompted him to retain and display his original versions. Evangelicals remade the morphology of conversion from a gradual process into a punctiliar event—that is, a tangible moment in which God broke into history and transformed the past self into the new.[72] As a result, evangelicals spent a great deal of energy and ink trying to account for the exact moment of their salvation. In Ireland's formulation, poems become punctiliar placeholders that serve to identify God's transforming grace.

This punctiliar conversion was part of a larger impulse in eighteenth-century revivalism to account for God's action in time:

> The movements of renewal and revival of the eighteenth century sought their legitimation in the hand of God in history; their characteristic achievement was not, like the Reformers of the sixteenth century, to offer a

confession of faith for public discussion, but to accumulate archives which would support their understanding of history.[73]

Ireland's narrative forms part of this historical archive, but it is poetry that he mobilizes as a distinct artifact of the soul's regeneration. Serving as a physical record for God's work, Ireland situates the poems, not in an otherworldly space, but as valuable markers of a very real religious journey that occurs in the body and in time. A more perfected theology or a more elevated poetics could not justify erasing this fingerprint of God's redeeming work. Ireland's account, then, reveals both the inclusion of sociable forms in his conversion and ensuing role as a revival poet, as well as the limits of their transmutability. Literary games in evangelical poetic culture were, in the end, very serious ones. And, unlike the resistance to memorialization in belletristic manuscript culture, conversion poems were meant to last.

As unique as Ireland's conversion narrative might be, it provides a window into the broader uses of literary play that underscored the salvific efficacy of poetry in the Baptist, and larger evangelical, experience.[74] Autobiographies traced the life of an individual believer, but they also mapped the religious terrain of the community. For example, the consistent corporeal emphasis of Baptist conversion narratives points to a corporate recognition of the body's centrality to Baptist experience.[75] Similarly, though poetic conversions like those described in Ireland's account are not mandatory elements of the revivalist autobiography, Virginian Baptists and many other evangelicals often named hymns, songs, or other poetic experience as essential to their conversion process.[76] Ireland portrays the community that he writes about in the 1760s in order to model an investment in the power of poetry for the nineteenth-century community for whom he writes. As Jewel Spangler and others have pointed out, conversion narratives were not only representative but prescriptive.[77]

His conversion in the late 1760s was part of a transatlantic evangelical poetic culture that reached even to the woods of Virginia and entered the separatist culture of the emerging Baptists. Remarkably, though Ireland grew up in a rich poetic world, he effectively presents it as a local practice under the dominion of his rhyme. Even so, Ralph Erskine and Samuel Davies hover in the background. For instance, Ireland mentions in passing that his closest school friends were the sons of Ralph and Ebenezer Erskine, the "faithful and pious ministers of Scotland."[78] Ireland could not have been raised Presbyterian in Edinburgh with personal connections to the Erskine family and remain ignorant of the *Gospel Sonnets*. That Ireland fails to mention Samuel Davies's poetry does not seem surprising given that his autobiography works to establish his identity as a persecuted Baptist. From the earliest Baptist histories written in America, Baptists claimed their distinctiveness through their fight for religious liberty. Mentioning Davies, a vocal Presbyterian advocate for toleration, would muddle the story. However, given that Presbyterians distributed a large number of Davies's books and that Ireland mingled with Presbyterians both pre- and post-conversion, means that Ireland likely knew of Davies's collection. Perhaps during one of his many visits with Presbyterian acquaintances to seek the latest family news from Edinburgh, or during his extended stay with an "old Presbyterian friend" at whose home he composed "Come Lord in mercy," the conversations turned to some great Presbyterian minister who used poetry to revive Virginians at services that resembled the holy fairs they knew in Scotland.[79]

Or, perhaps, Ireland's silence on Davies had more to do with a widening gap over slavery among white evangelical poets. The publication of Ireland's narrative did, after all, appear the same year that Virginia removed restrictions from interstate slave trade and forbade the education and gatherings of all black people whether slave or free. Unlike Davies, who idealized slave harmony and explicitly credited slaves singing in his kitchen at night for his own religious and poetic inspiration, Ireland figures slaves as at once beleaguered and dangerous. Slaves surface in his narrative as eager revival participants and as amorphous threats of slave rebellion. In fact, Ireland attributes the event that precipitated his deathbed narrative to his own slave woman who poisoned him, the effects of which resulted in a long-term deterioration of his health. His kitchen appears in his narrative not as a site of inspiration, but of imprisonment and coercion. He locks her in it to produce her confession; never does he consider any viable reasons for her violence toward her master. Wheatley was already a well-known poet at the time of Ireland's early ministry, and at the time of his deathbed narrative she was firmly part of evangelical abolitionist literature. Yet, she also remains absent. Nevertheless, Ireland's text, which immortalizes his white, muscular Christianity, remains haunted by the story of his own female slave. It raises the still unresolved issue of evangelical anthropology and, as Wheatley underscored, a regressive Christian history with an ambivalence toward evil at its core.

Ireland's exclusion of other poets also points both to the separatist impulse of Baptists and to a consistent thread in his self-presentation: his commitment to poetic entertainment and competition. Ireland's autobiography should be understood, at least in part, as an attempt to provide a history, not only of Baptist persecution, but also of the region's revival poetry and its importance to the new revivals of the nineteenth century.[80] As such, it addresses the premier Baptist elder John Leland, who wrote in his account of the Baptists in Virginia, *The Virginia Chronicle* (1790):

> Dr. Watts is the general standard for the Baptists in Virginia; but they are not confined to him; any spiritual composition answers their purpose. A number of hymns originate in Virginia, although there is no established poet in the state. Some Virginia songs have more divinity in them, than poetry or grammar; and some that I have heard have but little of either.[81]

Ireland's narrative nominates himself as the founding revival bard; it attests to the mid-century poetic eruption in Baptist circles and lays claim to his status as a foundational poet-minister during the early days of Baptist itinerancy and poetics in Virginia. The editorial commentary in Ireland's edition suggests that Ireland's poetry circulated prolifically. Gathering Ireland's poems, the editor explains, would be a herculean task because his constant itinerancy meant that his poetry circulated as often and as far as he did. By his death, the editor writes, his poems "were much scattered, and but few could be come at. It has been said, that Mr. Ireland had lent [*sic*] about sixty of his poems to a friend of his beyond the Allegheny Mountains."[82] Ireland had a reputation to memorialize and, even at the end of his life, he vied for the position of arch-poet.

It was not only a bid at recognition among Baptists, but an attempt to add his name and the Baptist poetic presence to the active multidenominational poetry of the region. For instance, the same printer who issued Ireland's narrative in the town of Winchester, Virginia, in 1819 also published works by the famous itinerant of the Christian Connexion, Joseph Thomas, known as the White Pilgrim. In addition to several hymn books, Thomas wrote *A Poetical Descant on the Primeval and Present State of Mankind or the Pilgrim's Muse* (1816), and a year later published his autobiography, *The Life of the Pilgrim Joseph Thomas* (1817). At the end of the autobiography, Thomas included several poems, one of which graciously acknowledges a Methodist minister who took time to read it—a comment that points to a continuing active poetic community among traveling itinerants across multiple denominations.[83]

Ireland portrays his Baptist itinerant community in the 1760s as one invested in the power of poetry. Taken together with the uses of evangelical poetry discussed throughout this book, Ireland's description appears well founded. Part of this corporate appreciation of poetry had to do, of course, with the turn to hymnody. Baptists in America experienced the same controversial hymnal shift that occurred among other evangelicals in Britain and America at the beginning of the eighteenth century, though they lagged behind their English counterparts. By mid-century most Baptists in North America accepted singing in worship, and it became standard by the nineteenth century. The Separate Baptists in the South, with whom Ireland identified, were known in his time as particularly enthusiastic hymn singers. By the 1790s, Baptists in America began to use their own compilations rather than relying on standard hymnals.[84] The turn to Baptist-produced hymnals corresponds more or less to the first attempt at an American-produced anthology of poets in the United States, Hubbard E. Smith's *American Poems* (1793).

Yet, the rise of hymns did not encompass the entire story of Baptist poetics. What traditional histories of Baptist hymnody do not include is the broader literary poetic tradition that developed alongside hymns and in tandem with a general proliferation of poetry during the Revolution and into the early Republic. Perhaps most emblematic of the joint hymnal-poetic tradition emerging from Baptist revivalists is the career of Elhanan Winchester. Earning the distinction as the most prolific hymn compiler of the young Republic with Baptist ties, Winchester wrote hymns as well as a swath of traditional poetry.[85] A year after his first hymnic publication, *A Collection of Psalms, Hymns, and Poems* (1772), he published *A New Book of Poems, on Several Occasions* (1773), which followed the forms expected of an aspiring young poet's first book. His poetic masterpiece, a prophetic poem in 12 books entitled *The Process and Empire of Christ*, appeared in London in 1793, followed by its posthumous printing in Vermont in 1805. Though Winchester evolved into a Universalist and helped to found that transatlantic denomination, his poetry and hymn writing career began as a Baptist minister who served in both the Northern and Southern regions of America. That his poetic career has been ignored by both scholars of hymnody and poetry points to the pervasive sense that evangelicals wrote hymns, not poetry.

But an early anecdote of Baptist history puts the lie to this. When hymn writing reappeared among British North American Baptists after a long hiatus, it surfaced by the hand of a Virginian layman along with a poem.[86] Samuel Newman, Esq., wrote two poetic compositions in 1755 at the request of the itinerant John Gano, who knew "Mr. Newman to possess a poetical turn."[87] One was a hymn to celebrate Gano's ministry; the other was a traditional poem composed in couplets that authorized the itinerant to pass through the countryside during the French war.[88] The everyday uses of hymns and poems point to their imbricated histories and practices in evangelicalism and in the broader culture of eighteenth-century verse.

Coda: Conversion and Evangelical Poetic Address

Ireland's conversion is not easy to forget—this infectious tale of a cheeky lad who finds himself thrashing about in the forest desperately trying to escape his own poetic line stands on its own. It is an extraordinary scene that directly speaks to the kind of historical narrative I have tried to write: one that forestalls skeptical interpretations that find the most important meanings beneath the trappings of the religious.[89] And one that is not looking for when "bad" (in Tracy Fessenden's sense) religious poetry will finally turn in to something else more politically palatable.[90] This is especially important for historical poetics because, as Jordana Rosenburg underscores, the role of poetry has been "the repository of religious feeling" in secularization narratives that place "the vestiges of religion . . . within poetry's exquisite address."[91] To these ends, let me return briefly to the moment of Ireland's conversion for what it reveals about evangelicalism's robust and enduring poetic address.

In addition to the unrevised poem as an artifact of God's work, Ireland's conversion by poetry closely aligns with another key structure found in many evangelical conversion narratives. While stories of sincere seekers abound, many trace an inverse relationship between mockery and repentance by representing the convert as an antagonist who falls under God's conviction. Just as authoritative prohibitions against revivalists authorized "democratic speech," mockery catalyzed conversions. Imitators of Whitefield often found themselves saved by their own satirical rendition of the great itinerant. The passionate investment required of successful mockery, such as the internalization of the rhetorical moves of preaching and conversion, could quickly tip into enthusiastic practice. This inversion, in fact, flows from the very heart of evangelicalism, which is founded on the distinction between outward forms (mockery) and inward religion (authentic experience). The majority of white evangelicals were Christians who converted, not to an entirely different religion, but to a different experience of the same form. Evangelical conversion makes personally meaningful a set form, whether this form is Puritan conversion morphology or, as in Erskine's *Gospel Sonnets*, the riddle and the couplet. This is one reason why most revivalists did not so much innovate new poetic styles and forms as direct energy into making them meaningful through personal experience.

Whether a saving encounter with an itinerant's sermon or a poet-minister's verse, the transformation of mockery and imitation into experiential conversion depended upon a hyper-personal address. Again and again, evangelicals attest to a moment in which the religious message directed at anonymous crowds suddenly becomes excruciatingly personal. Often this is the sudden feeling that the minister is speaking directly to the potential convert, their eyes locked with electric intensity. For instance, the black loyalist and minister John Marrant writes a skilled rendition of this recurring trope into his own conversion narrative. He pushes into a revival meeting at the goading of a friend with the intent of interrupting the gathering by blowing his French horn. But before he has the chance to mock the noise of revivalists with his loud blast, Whitefield appears to look directly at him and says, "Prepare to meet thy God, O Israel." In an instant, Marrant is knocked off his feet and rendered speechless and senseless.[92]

It is not the hyper-personalized address alone that defines evangelicalism. In his analysis of the evangelical public sphere, Michael Warner argues that what makes evangelicalism new in the history of Christianity is "the conversionistic address to the stranger."[93] Rather than speak to their own parishes, God called evangelical ministers to "make the world their parish" and to convert the stranger. The poetic address that Ireland depicts in his conversion narrative helps locate this new conversionistic address to the stranger within the story of revival poetry and its relation to the development of the modern lyric.

What is so fantastic about Ireland's narrative is not so much that his imitation suddenly flips into personal religious experience, but that his own verse is the instrument. It could be tempting to imagine the conversionistic address of the poetic lines and Ireland as two parts of the same personality—that is, his narrative is a story of a man speaking to himself. That the two dichotomous roles of the preacher and the convert have collapsed into one person seems to point toward a type of extreme self-authorization. This would map onto a general move over the eighteenth century and early nineteenth century from the sovereignty of God found in Calvinism to the increased volition of man expressed in Arminianism. It makes sense in the lyrical imagination of Mill in which the poet is insular and self-sufficient: the poet who is "feeling confessing itself to itself," not to a priest. For G. W. Hegel, the lyric was the embodiment of modern subjectivity; the poem itself was a particular instantiation of the poet who was now "a self-bounded subjective entity."[94] Charles Taylor mobilizes this development of the modern lyric as evidence of the secular self he describes as buffered; that is, a self upon which the world, including magic and religious forces, does not impinge.[95]

Yet, Ireland does not describe his experience in this way. He does not imagine that he is speaking to himself or that the words he hears are his own, but instead finds his poem entirely alien—even though it is thoroughly ordinary and reproducible. In Ireland's account the poem becomes loosed from his authorial control and aimed at his very soul, which results in contortions, profanity, and the like as he tries to escape its grasp. The poetic line is made unfamiliar and the poet himself made a stranger to his own poem. Ireland's verse, like other evangelical poetry, is activated by sermonic address, and as such it situates the audience as a stranger who then must come into a personalized address through God's intervention. The repetition of Ireland's own poetic line estranges him so that he is like one who overhears a sermon and then is suddenly individuated by God's direct address. His account is particularly provoking because it shows how revivalists crafted a circuit of poetic address based on the distinction of the preacher and the stranger that was strong enough to separate the poet from his own preacher's address. Eighteenth-century belletrists followed the Earl of Shaftsbury's maxim that "wit makes a stranger into a friend"; in Ireland the formulation is reversed: evangelical wit first makes the friend into a stranger.

At the same time as evangelical itinerants directed their sermons to strangers, the history of poetry seemed to be headed in the opposite direction. Scholars of historical poetics point to the nineteenth century as a period in which literary critics began to create a transcendental poetry increasingly removed from its actual scenes of circulation.[96] The most common definition of this new lyric genre was "utterance overheard"—an idea taken from John Stuart Mill's 1833 essay "What Is Poetry?" in which he famously declared: "eloquence is heard; poetry is overheard." Rather than a modern definition of lyric, however, Mill was much more concerned with the type of speech the poet performed. For Mill, poems should not have a direct address, especially a political one, but should indirectly address the audience: "the peculiarity of poetry appears to us to lie in the poet's utter unconsciousness of a listener."[97] Although the speech should be overheard, instead of directed rhetoric like that of a sermon or political speech, Mill assumes no personal connection to the listener—he or she is a stranger.

While Mill separates direct and indirect speech according to the positionality of the speaker in order to distinguish between genres, revivalists mediated these two experiences of speech within the convert. It is not a far leap from a conversionistic address to the stranger to a poetic address overheard by a stranger. The constellation of poetries codified into the lyric and the hymn becomes especially apparent when the creation of the secular and the religious is viewed as a mutually constitutive relationship. What appears to be a shutdown of revival verse—the turn in poetics from the directed speech of the sermon to the indirect address of the lyric—is not. Part of revival poetry's innovation was the conversionistic schema embedded in its address that depended upon flipping overheard speech into directed speech.

Ireland's narrative reveals how revivalist poetic address was invested in the historical, punctilliar moment of salvation to the stranger in what might at first appear to be the impersonal address of the modern lyric. As in most instances, evangelicalism was not at the helm, nor at the mercy, of historical change, but inextricably bound up in it with non-evangelicals. Eighteenth-century poetry and its address to the stranger played an early role in what would become the modern lyric, at the same time that its own insistence on its separateness from secular poetics and high literariness helped efface its own presence in that history.

Conclusion

Conversions of Poetic History

In 1770 a manuscript poem began its journey along Lost River in Hardy County, Virginia. It exhorted readers to avoid the blind "unconverted man, / Altho' he be a preacher" and to seek out those "call'd of God," who could lead people into an experience of saving grace.[1] The poem's author, James Claypool, directed his words methodically at each type of unconverted person the homiletic poem might come in contact with, from the hedonist to the self-righteous. The closing lines invited the reader to seek by faith whether the verse "be truth or no." If for some reason the poem began but did not complete its conversionistic work, Claypool bid the person to seek out the poet himself. He concludes:

> If aught you find disturb your mind,
> You think the same not true;
> When me you see pray tell to me,
> I'll take it kind from you.*
> You'll find me out you need not doubt,
> While I'm in time and place;
> For now it seems my name is James
> And of the Claypool race.
>
> *If delivered in a spirit of meekness.
> December, 17th, 1770.
> Hardy County, Lost River.[2]

Claypool knew it would take just one line lodged in the mind to agitate an unconverted person into conviction, setting off a saving work. His lone and seemingly insignificant manuscript poem, along with many others like it written by both ministers and laypeople, helped catapult a modern

Awakening Verse. Wendy Raphael Roberts, Oxford University Press (2020). © Oxford University Press.
DOI: 10.1093/oso/9780197510278.001.0001

movement of Christianity into what is now described as a "majority world religion."[3]

Poetry saved. Early evangelicals knew this through personal and communal experience. They located profound aesthetic experiences in a particular moment in time that determined their eternal future and furthered the work of God in history. Even when this moment was not directly induced by verse, it was punctuated by it—they called this moment conversion.

The advent of evangelicalism was as much, if not more, a shift in an emphasis on aesthetics and its correct uses than it was a specific change in any theological tenet. For its adherents, the feeling of being more authentically religious than others depended not so much upon a correct creed or course of study as on a personal experience of God's goodness and beauty, or, in Jonathan Edwards's words, of God's "sweetness." Though verse was not the media of everyone's conversion, it was definitely its most discernible product. In this life and in the life to come, verse marked the salvific and glorious work of God. For evangelicals, the Holy Bible was saturated with the world's oldest poetry; Christ, the very Word of God, moved the passions as sacred verse should; and the Holy Spirit's travails birthed those fluent in its language and form. Verse produced, testified to, and served as evidence of the experience of the immediate presence of God for a great number of people who insisted on its divine origins. Though the suturing of enthusiasm with poetry that John Dennis promoted in the early eighteenth century meant to exclude enthusiastic forms of religion and politics in order to rehabilitate enthusiasm as a high aesthetic form, there arose a revitalized and persistent strain of poetics that insisted on the God-ordained unity of enthusiastic religion and verse and aspired to be a universally accessible aesthetic form, elevated only by the message of the gospel itself. Conversion as an aesthetic experience entailed that all people had the capacity to appreciate poetry—the very language of God and of heaven—which necessitated verse tailored even to the most vulgar of capacities.

The creation of evangelical verse in British North America coincided with, among other things, the expansion of a white middle class, a rising book trade and printing industry, a political revolution spurring new interpretations and institutions of Christianity, and a rethinking of the justifications for slavery, which became increasingly based in racialized science and bodily capacities. The emergence of this new evangelical verse corresponded to wider concerns in the eighteenth century about aesthetics, natural science, political and social systems, and the nature of empire, colonialism, and slavery. This is also to say that evangelical poetics was as much a part of the age and its contours as Pope, Hume, or Smith.

Awakening Verse has highlighted one stream of this eighteenth-century revival poetry in British North America that people across continents and languages immersed themselves within. By exploring a specifically Calvinist manifestation of a larger evangelical poetics in the eighteenth century, this book has aimed to undo a persistent myth in American literary studies: that Calvinism was at odds with poetry and aesthetics and that it was waning by the early nineteenth century. Instead, this book helps situate how a Calvinistic strain of evangelicalism informed early American verse form, meaning, and expansion and became a central part of nineteenth-century verse practices— practices which were extended and transformed well into the twentieth and twenty-first centuries.

In the culture of early revivalism, itinerancy and affective conversion brought the sermon and the poem, minister and the poet, the itinerant and print, closer together. Poems became itinerating sermons. Evangelicals extended and transformed a longer Dissenter history of using George Herbert's well-known lines that figured poems as sermons. Benjamin Keach, who transformed Baptist worship in the seventeenth century, drew on Herbert to argue that "A Verse may catch a wandring Soul, that flies / Profounder Tracts."[4] In the eighteenth century, the bestselling poems of Michael Wigglesworth and Edward Young helped popularize the idea of the poet-minister and itinerant poem. Peletiah Chapin was one of many lesser known revival poet-ministers who referred to Herbert's lines, choosing to place Young's version on the title page to his *Evangelical Poetry* (1794).

> Ye Sons of Earth! (nor *willing* to be more!)
> Since *Verse* you think from Priestcraft somewhat free,
> Thus, in an Age so gay, the Muse plain Truths
> (Truths, which, at Church, you *might* have heard in Prose)
> Has ventur'd into Light; . . .[5]

The poem and sermon became so closely linked that one of the most famous English novels of the century, Samuel Richardson's *Pamela*, justified itself through Herbert's lines by likening the novel, a form of amusement in the service of reforming Christianity, to that of the poem's sermonic function. This idea became foundational for evangelicals who embraced itinerancy and affective sermons, and it galvanized the revivalist's pen. The vast number of circulating poems that described and produced the fires of revival could be printed, scribbled, peddled, declaimed, sung, nailed to trees, or stealthily slipped into books or pockets. The poem's combination of pleasure, accessibility, and mobility constituted an ideal itinerant minister.

It was not only that poems acted like sermons, but also that revival sermons functioned like poems in that they drew people's interest. The exemplary revival sermon, like the pleasures of a poem, was not one from which, but to which, people ran. Nathan Cole famously recorded in his journal the cloud of dust billowing for miles as crowds hurried to reach Whitefield's next venue.[6] Such sermons captivated and raised the passions through dramatic and poetic language. When Prudence Nye Bates, with whom this book began, placed a cut-out newspaper poem inside Joseph Bates's Bible to facilitate his conversion, she participated in these mutually constitutive practices of revivalism.

The merging of the poet and minister within the culture of evangelicalism entailed reconstituting the meaning of verse form itself. One of the most famous and enduring revival poems, *Gospel Sonnets*, has not sustained its presence in literary history like other beloved evangelical poems, such as those by Thomson and Young, mostly due to the fact that rather than a nascent Romanticism, it is biblical paraphrase and allegory in plain-style poetics saturated in theological didacticism. Yet, it was essential for forging the relationship between the couplet and Calvinist theology for a large segment of revivalists. Erskine's poem makes explicit how broad espousal piety was in evangelical culture—infusing the couplet not with Popian rationalism, but with the marriage of the believer and Christ, which itself wed multiple paradoxes of Calvinist theology and practice through sound. When a radical revivalist like James Croswell, lay itinerant and brother of the infamous Rev. Andrew Croswell, vowed to recite by memory daily the entirety of the *Song of Songs*, he may well have declaimed sections of Erskine's poem, just as many others did.[7] Verse form mattered in the successful formation of Calvinist believers. Changes in verse form could signal important alterations in key aspects of evangelical lived theology, while enduring verse form could also serve to maintain continuity with the past even as experiences and the concepts to explain them changed. As Catherine Brekus has pointed out, "If evangelicals had realized that they were creating a new type of religiosity, they would have been alarmed, but because their religious practices seemed to connect them to the past, they were able to ignore the theological shifts that had begun to separate them from their Puritan heritage."[8] Close attention to the practices of revival poets, then, is crucial for understanding evangelical history and culture, and the larger history of American literature.

Verse evangelism abounded. The fusing of the poem and sermon quickly blurred the lines between preaching clergy and exhorting laypeople, which produced an array of verse ministries and opportunities for those outside the official pulpit. Evangelical women used and created diverse poet-minister personae—including the evangelical muse, the spiritual director, the spouse of Christ, and the Ethiop—as part of a broader practice of revival ministry and, in doing so, contributed not only to its conversion numbers and growing momentum, but also to its foundational theologies, which were grounded in aesthetics. Women's revival verse, which often drew authority from the performance of affective auditing of revival ministers, functioned not as some kind of derivative sermon notes, but effectively as sermons—catching those readers that the minister's sermon did not. For instance, the poems in Jane Dunlap's collection of verse on Whitefield's sermons, which perform both her authority as a listener of the sermon and her affective authority as the spouse of Christ, act as versified sermons itinerating to convert new hearts.[9]

When the sermon failed, poetry succeeded—early evangelicals believed and documented this notion time and time again. The White Pilgrim, Joseph Thomas, explained that "it was forcible with him that were the topic rehearsed in a *poetical strain*, it would better suit the design of the work, and be the more extensively beneficial, as many are excited to read poetry who have but little taste to read a subject of the nature were it to appear in prose."[10] The use of verse had as much to do with God's special interest in poetry and its unique relationship to the passions as it did with God's call to preach to all people. Poetry was the image of God in humanity, and as such, all people had the ability to experience God through it. For this reason, there needed to be poetry for the vulgar and common capacity. This seemed to inspire William Marsh, who wrote in *A Few Select Poems on Free Grace* (1797), "I don't pretend in poetry, / To any skill or art, / But I do mean to let you see / The prospect of my heart."[11] Evangelicals expected to hear God through the everyday language and cadence of poetry, not just the exceptional poet.

For those invested in poetry and aesthetic taste as the property of the white upper classes, this position was unacceptable. Samuel C. Loveland wrote, in a poetic response to a lowbrow revival poem:

> One thing is true, but strangely true indeed,
> That poems vile and rude, more converts lead

>Among the baser sort, and weaker hearts,
>Than the sound reas'ing of the man of parts.[12]

A poem published in *The Mercury* in 1740 mocked Whitefield's "68 preachments in 40 days" and insulted those who had begun to support him by comparing "their Matchless Poetry" to the "Genius & Sense" of Whitefield, whose "pious Arts" consisted "of crazing Noodles and of Cobbling Hearts."[13] These kinds of criticisms were commonplace. The liberatory potential of revival aesthetics was clear to its critics, and its chaotic implications earned revival poetry the status of "no language," or effeminate black noise. In contrast, a poet-minister like Samuel Davies treated black harmony as a conduit for heavenly flights and poetic inspiration. Even so, the idealized black capacity for harmony was part of a racialization of the senses and capacities that helped neutralize the radical social implications of evangelical harmony.

Evangelicalism arose as a form of authentic Christianity in tandem with eighteenth-century preoccupations with aesthetics and natural history. As such, conversion, conceived as a modern event based in new ideas of aesthetic perceptions and Lockean sense experience, was shaped by, and contributed to, the rights-bearing liberal subject who was white and male. Yet, it also contained routes for activism and resistance. Phillis Wheatley's poetry offered a thorough critique of revival verse, especially of its evangelical harmony based on the plainest capacity and its espousal piety. She critiqued evangelical anthropology, embedded as it was in aesthetics and verse form, through the routes of respectability and refusal. Situating Wheatley fully in the context of revival poetics underscores how enslaved femininity became a site for competing notions of anthropology, which ultimately made revival verse a potent locus for addressing slavery and for reinforcing white women's affect.

For some white male itinerants, the saturation of revivalism in espousal piety and affect was too effeminate, and its liberatory potential was too threatening. Within their coteries, a robust culture of wit and competitive literary games served as a bulwark to white masculinity. These muscular aspects of secular verse needed to be retained, while other aspects, including revision practices and poetic address, required transformation in accord with conversion morphology and evangelical homiletics. Though these originally marked a difference from secular verse, they laid a foundation for an emerging lyric address that would come to define poetry itself. Though extemporaneous sermons and itinerant circuits were part of the eighteenth-century poetic coteries and wit, a strict division between religion and the secular has often separated these practices. In fact, much of revival poetry's perceived separateness from secular, literary history was an evangelical invention.

The revitalization of religious poetry in the eighteenth century hinged upon a story of the decline of pious verse. John Dennis leaned on this story when he argued for the importance of enthusiastic poetry and the religious sublime in elite verse culture. A poem on Edward Young's *Night Thoughts* repeated Watts's declension model, and like him and a host of evangelicals, longed for the great day when the virtuous arts would return:

> Thus did the muses sing in early times,
> Ere skill'd to flatter vice, and varnish crimes:
> Their lyres were tun'd to virtuous songs alone,
> And the chaste poet, and the priest, were one.[14]

The itinerant Joshua Marsden also emphasized Young's pairing of the poet and priest.[15] The revival poet-minister was a millennial ministry of God in these last miraculous days. That revival poetry has been undervalued in American literary histories, which have followed Whitman's credo "the priest departs, the divine literatus comes," speaks to the success of its own story of decline and its aspirations to a lower form of aesthetics for the masses.

In the nineteenth century, as in the eighteenth, to commit one's life to evangelism was to embrace aesthetics and the power of verse. As Benjamin Allen wrote in *Urania, or the True Use of Poesy* (1814), poetry was "almost unbounded" and the poet had "a greater power over the mind of the world, than any other mortal."[16] And it was the gospel that was the most "boundless ocean of excellence open to poesy."[17] Like other evangelical poets after Watts, Allen recounted a narrative of the decline of truly pious verse and longed for its resurrection. He names the most esteemed modern poets as Young, Cowper, and Watts—a trio that became increasingly important to evangelicalism over the eighteenth century and into the nineteenth. But Watts, Allen writes, has been the most important to humankind because he was so "deeply imbued with the evangelical temper."[18] As Allen and other revivalist declared, "I had rather have the deathbed thoughts of Watts, than all the fame, of all the heroes, that ever descended from Adam."[19] He ends his introduction with a prayer: "Let my writings, like those of Watts, be but grateful to the humble christian in his retired cottage, and I shall esteem it nobler praise than if they were hung in letters of gold in every senate house in the universe."[20] For a great number of evangelicals, loving Watts also meant loving his heavenly muse, Rowe. She continued to hover over espousal devotion and helped create a woman poet-minister persona whose words were not her own, but the pious language of every Christian. Though men, like Allen, would often name male revival poets, evangelical women poet-ministers became the most plentiful and popular.

By the early nineteenth century, many evangelical churches tamped down on socially disapproved activities that challenged white male ministerial authority. Clamoring for middle-class approval, they prohibited people of color and women from preaching, and began to use more elevated verse, even in hymns. For instance, Asahel Nettleton's *Village Hymns* (1824) reverses Watts's definition of hymns as lower poetry by declaring that his collection of hymns is necessary because so many revival hymns "are entirely destitute of poetic merit."[21] The preface to *Airs of Palestine* (1817) by John Pierpoint makes his case for a more refined Christian poetry against its demise in the hands of fanatical believers:

> I am sure it will render to my sleep of death peaceful and triumphant to know, that I have succeeded even partially in restoring to virtue the beauties of which dogmatists have plundered her;—and to religion the evidences of her claim to the love of the refined and the veneration of the learned— claims which have been withheld from her by the ignorance, or the arts, or the fanaticism of those, who arrogate to themselves the character of exclusively religious, while they are strangers to learning, taste and refinement, and to the intimate friend of them all—Christian Charity.[22]

Though many objected to the ever present and expanding doggerel verse of revivalists, there was no squashing it. As the well-known Calvinist poet-minister John Peck wrote:

> What if the Author is no bard,
> But writes a dogg'rel song;
> What if the muse her aid refuse
> While he doth creep along?
> The squalling winds may clear the air,
> And drive the fog away;
> My grov'ling rhymes may hit the times,
> And truth and light convey.[23]

Evangelicals were invested in poetry and aesthetics because they were committed to conversion. Spreading Christianity through individuated, heartfelt conversion required innovative tactics that drew not only crowds but affections. Women poet-ministers filled their letters, manuscript books, local papers, and printers with itinerant poems that could travel farther than they generally could. Itinerant ministers, some of whom were women, spread verse across large swaths of land and spent their evenings engaged in practices of verse sociability. Even the rise of large tract societies did not displace the importance of verse as an evangelical tool. The "heavenly Singer of Connecticut," Lydia Huntley Sigourney, wrote a poem about the function of the evangelical religious tract—a form that often included verse. She describes tracts as "light-wing'd birds" that never tire as they "rove . . . from zone to zone" even "check[ing]" the sailor's "ribald song." That is, she figures these "links of love" that "enchain the world / To Mercy's changeless throne" as revival poems.[24]

As revival verse flowered in the "Second Great Awakening," one thing surely did not change: revival poetry did things. It sought to move the affections, convert the soul, fan the flames of revival, and guide believers in daily life. It could enable conversion and record conversion; it could extend and even replace the sermon; it could help one parse theology or cause the body to contort under conviction of sin. It was an array of poetries, including the hymn, that sought to engage a common rather than a cultivated aesthetic. It helped popularize the sublime, solidified the association of feeling with verse, melded the poem with the pulpit, separated even the poet from his own address, and encouraged high expectations for both the heavenly and earthly work of poetics. Early evangelicals traded in the verse forms of their day and bequeathed to later practitioners a seemingly intractable commitment to populating the most popular commodities with their divine function, rather than searching to invent new art forms to awaken the soul.

While this book follows the Calvinist strain most popular in the early eighteenth century, various trajectories of revival poetries flourished in the eighteenth century and especially into the early nineteenth century, which are ripe for fuller analysis. Revival poets influenced, and were influenced by, major poetic developments in sometimes clear, but often unquantifiable ways. I have emphasized how revival poetry drew upon and transformed more elite practices of verse and have resisted emphasizing connections to the Romantics and other later poets who supposedly cast off their Puritan predecessors. The poet-ministers I take up were not important to literary history primarily because they laid a groundwork for Romanticism (though they surely intersected in meaningful ways with poets as diverse as Blake, Wordsworth, Whitman, and Dickinson, among many others),[25] but because they were precursors to sweating laborers of the gospel who traversed thousands of miles on horseback and foot to save and nourish the soul through verse; and to those who, within the confines of their home and town, proclaimed the gospel both far and near through poems that altered countless readers' lives. They were the popularizers of the ubiquitous belief, the widespread experience, of poetry as the avenue to the deepest yearnings of the heart and the facilitator of an immediate experience of God's love. They made the writing of verse a natural outflow of a converted soul and the love of a verse of feeling impossible to expel from nineteenth-, twentieth-, and twenty-first-century religious sensibility. They did this because they wholeheartedly believed that God broke into history through the words of poetry.

Poet-ministers, like the early nineteenth-century itinerants James Ireland and Elhanan Winchester, would tell us that the evangelical God spoke through poetry even in the midst of a supposedly enlightened, romantic, and secular world, at the very dawn of "American" literary history and culture in the new Republic. What, then, will the modern historian, who derives all meaning from the social and the privileged position of absence, do? The gods, I imagine, perch close to hear.

Selected Revival Poets and Poetry

The following is a selection of eighteenth-century revival poets and poems written in English by British North American inhabitants before 1830. Works that are primarily identified as hymns are not included. Some samples of manuscript poems are included. Printed works can be read in Early American Imprints. For the most complete list of all printed verse in books in North America, see Roger E. Stoddard and David R. Whitesell's *A Bibliographical Description of Books and Pamphlets of American Verse Printed from 1610 through 1820* (University Park: Penn State University Press, 2012). Also see J. A. Leo Lemay, *A Calendar of American Poetry in the Colonial Newspapers and Magazines and in the Major English Magazines Through 1765* (Worcester, MA: American Antiquarian Society, 1972).

Allen, Benjamin. *Urania, or The True Use of Poesy.* New York: A. H. Inskeep, and Philadelphia: Bradford & Inskeep, 1814.
Allen, Benjamin. Under name "Osander." *Miscellaneous Poems, on Moral and Religious Subjects.* Hudson, NY: Wm. E. Norman, 1811.
Allen, John. *Thoughts on Man's Redemption, as Exhibited by Christ.* . . . Utica, NY: Merrell & Seward, 1805.
Anon. *An Account of the Remarkable Conversion of a Little Boy and Girl.* Boston: Fowle & Draper, 1762. Reprints: New London, CT, 1770; Dover, NH, 1792; Bennington, VT, 1794.
Anon. "A Brief Representation of the Approaching Judgment." Boston, New Haven, or New London, CT: between 1746 and 1771(?).
Anon. *The Dagon of Calvinism, or the Moloch of Decrees, A Poem, in Three Cantos. To Which is Annexed A Song of Reason.* Cincinnati: John W. Browne, 1811. Several editions. Also printed with John Peck and Lemuel Haynes.
Anon. *Nebuchudnezzar, A Poem.* From Isaac Backus Library. Manuscript. American Antiquarian Society.
Anon. "A Poem Occasion'd by the Late Powerful and Awakening Preaching of the Reverend Mr. Gilbert Tennant [sic]. By some young lads much affected therewith. Boston: 1741(?).
Anon. *A Poem Occasioned by the Spreading in this Province the Result of a Consociation in a Neighbour Government.* . . . Boston: Rogers and Fowle, 1742.
Anon. "A Poem, on the Joyful News of the Rev. Mr. Whitefield's Visit to Boston." Boston: October 1754.

Anon. *Lover of their precious souls. History of the Holy Jesus . . . Being a Pleasant and Profitable Companion for Children.* 1745. Numerous editions.

Anon. "On the Reverend Mr. Gilbert Tennent's Powerful and Successful Preaching in Boston, and Other Neighboring Towns. Boston, 1741(?).

Anon. *The Surprizing Appearance of a Ghost, with the Message he Brought from the Unseen and Eternal World.* Boston: Fowle and Draper, 1759.

Arooawr. *The Wanderer. Trenton Falls.* Utica, NY: William Williams, 1823.

Branagan, Thomas. *Avenia: Or, A Tragical Poem, on the Oppression of the Human Species, and Infringement of the Rights of Man.* Philadelphia: Silas Engles and Samuel Wood, 1805. New edition: Philadelphia: J. Cline, 1810.

Branagan, Thomas. *The Penitential Tyrant: A Juvenile Poem, in Two Cantos.* Philadelphia, 1805.

Branagan, Thomas. *Penitential Tyrant; Or, a Slave Trader Reformed. A Pathetic Poem, in Four Cantos.* New York: Samuel Wood, 1807.

Brewster, Martha. *Poems on Divers Subjects.* New-London, CT: John Green, 1757. Reprint, Boston: Edes & Gill, 1758.

Brewster, Martha. Manuscript Poems. Wheelock Papers. Letters. Dartmouth.

Brockway, Thomas. *The Gospel Tragedy.* Worcester, MA: James R. Hutchins, 1795.

Chandler, David. *The Miscellaneous Works.* Schenectady, NY: Riggs & Steven for Price, 1814.

Chapin, Pelatiah. *Evangelic Poetry. For the Purposes of Devotion, Excited by Spiritual Songs, and Conviction Urged by Gospel Truth.* Concord, NH: Geo. Hough, 1794.

Chapin, Pelatiah. *Jamy and Hervey's Second Dialogue Among the Tombs.* Windsor, VT: Alden Spooner, 1795.

Chaplin, John. *A Journal Containing Some Remarks Upon the Spiritual Operations, Beginning About the Year Anno Domini, 1740 or 1741.* Boston(?), 1757.

Chaplin, John. *War, Temporal and Spiritual, Considered.* Boston, 1762.

Claypool, James. *Original Poems.* Winchester, VA: J. Foster, 1811.

Cottle, Jabez. *The Life of Elder Jabez Cottle.* Manuscript. Harris Collection of American Poetry and Plays. Brown University Library.

Crowell, Simeon. Commonplace-book of Simeon Crowell, 1790–1824. Massachusetts Historical Society.

Dow, Peggy. *A Collection of Poetry. Selected by Peggy Dow.* Philadelphia: Griggs & Dickinsons, 1815.

Dunlap, Jane. *Poems, Upon Several Sermons, Preached by the Rev'd, and Renowned, George Whitefield, While in Boston.* Boston: Ezekial Russell, 1771. [John Hay Library holds the complete book; last poem missing from Early American Imprints.]

Enoch, David. *Offers of Christ No Gospel Preaching. To which is added, A Word of Advice to a Young Gospel Minister.* Philadelphia: Henry Miller, 1770.

Fenn, James. *Hymns and Poems on Various Subjects.* Schenectady, NY: Van Veghten & Son, 1808.

Fenn, James. *A Poem on Friendship and Society to which is added Remarks on the British and French Nations. . . .* Schenectady, NY: Riggs and Stevens, 1815.

Fenn, James. *A Humble Plea for the Benevolence of God in the Restoration and Final Happiness of All Men.* [Poems pp. 75–88]. Schenectady, NY, 1816.

Fenno, Jenny. *Original Compositions, in Prose and Verse.* Boston: Bumstead, 1791.

Fisher, Elijah(?). *A Poem on the American Revolution.* Kennebeck, ME: 1804(?).

Frisbie, Levi. "Cohos: The Wilderness Shall Bloom as the Rose." New London, CT, 1769.

Griswold, Martha. "Death Triumphant and Hell Following After, or The Doom and Downfall of all Impenitent Sinners under the Gospel: by way of dialogue." CT(?), 1751(?).

Hamilton, Adam. *The Confession and Lamentation of a Leper, While Shut Out of the Camp of God's Spiritual Israel. With Other Poetic Labours, Respecting His First Awakenings, Conversation, Call to and Success in the Ministry of the Gospel.* New London, CT: J. Springer, 1795.

Hammon, Jupiter. "An Address to Miss Phillis Wheatley, Ethiopian Poetess, in Boston, who Came from Africa at Eight Years of Age, and Soon Became Acquainted with the Gospel of Jesus Christ." Hartford, CT: n.p., 1778.

Hammon, Jupiter. *An Evening's Improvement. Shewing the Necessity of Beholding the Lamb of God. To Which is Added, A Dialogue, Intitled, "The Kind Master and the Dutiful Servant."* Hartford, CT, 1783.

Hammon, Jupiter. *An Evening Thought. Salvation by Christ, with Penetential Cries.* [United States: s.n., not before 1760].

Hammon, Jupiter. "An Essay on Slavery, with Submission to Divine Providence, Knowing that God Rules Over All Things." Ms. Hillhouse Family Papers. Yale University.

Hammon, Jupiter. "A Poem for Children With Thoughts on Death." *A Winter Piece.* Hartford, CT, 1782.

Harmon, Nathaniel. *Poetical Sketches, on Various Solemn Subjects, Composed by Deacon Nathaniel Harmon, late of Bennington, of Pious Memory. Written a Short Time Before His Death.* Bennington, VT: Anthony Haswell, 1796.

Haynes, Lemuel. "A Poem, Occasioned by the Sudden Death of Mr. Asa Burt." Hartford, CT: Ebenezer Watson, 1774.

Lamb, Jonathan. *Gospel Sonnets, or Poems, On Various Subjects, in Three Parts, Designed Principally for Youth.* Burlington, VT, 1830.

L***, Mrs. "Invocation to Religion," in Jonathan Lamb, *Gospel Sonnets.* Transcribed from a volume (missing) of manuscript poems.

Lamb, Nehemiah. *Hymns and Poems, On Various Subjects.* Utica, NY: T. Walker, 1807.

Le Mercier, Andrew. *The Christian Rapture: A Poem.* Boston: Rogers and Fowle, for D. Gookin, 1747.

Lomis, Mary. Manuscript Poem, 1798. John Hay Library.

Marsh, William. *Few Select Poems, Composed on Various Subjects, Especially on the Doctrine of Free Grace.* Bennington, VT: Anthony Haswell, 1797. Reprint, Windsor, VT: Nuhum Mower, 1802.

Maffitt, John. *Tears of Contrition; or Sketches of the Life of John N. Maffit: With Religious and Moral Reflections. To which are Appended Several Poetic Effusions.* New London, CT: Samuel Green, 1821.

Man, Mary and Thomas. Various poetry notebooks. *The Mary Man Literary Manuscripts.* 1765(?)–1812(?). John Hay Library.

Marsden, Joshua. *Amusements of a Mission; or Poems, Moral, Religious, and Descriptive. Interspersed with Anecdotes.* 1818.

Marsden, Joshua. *The Backslider: A Descriptive Moral Poem in Four Books.* Plymouth-Dock, England: J. Johns, 1815.

Marsden, Joshua. *Forest Musings; or, Delineations of Christian Experience in Verse.* London: W. Ross, 1821.

Marsden, Joshua. *Leisure Hours; or Poems, Moral, Religious, & Descriptive.* New York: Griffin and Rudd; Paul & Thomas, 1812.

Marsden, Joshua. *The Mission: A Poem, With Copious Notes and Illustrations.* 1816.

Marsden, Joshua. *The Narrative of a Mission to Nova Scotia, New Brunswick, and the Somers Islands with a Tour to Lake Ontario. To Which is Added The Mission, an Original Poem, with Copious Notes; Also, a Brief Account of Missionary Societies. . . .* Plymouth Dock, England: J. Johns, 1816 [2nd ed., London: J Kershaw, 1827].

Moorhead, Sarah Parsons. "A Poem, Dedicated to the Rev. Mr. Ralph Erskine, by a Lady in New England, upon reading his Gospel Sonnets." Ralph Erskine. *Gospel Sonnets.* Edinburgh: John Gray and Gavin Alston, 1762. [First printed appearance]. Manuscript copy with attribution at Princeton University Library.

Moorhead, Sarah Parsons. "A Poem in Honour of the Reverend Mr. Whitefield." Boston, November 28th, 1744.

Moorhead, Sarah Parsons. "The Spouse of Christ Returning to her First Love. An Hymn compos'd (as 'tis tho't) by a Lady in New-England. *Boston Gazette,* July 1751.

Moorhead, Sarah Parsons. "To the Revd Mr Byles Upon his Enquiring about a Leather Belt." May 29, 1753. Manuscript. Massachusetts Historical Society.

Moorhead, Sarah Parsons. "To the Rev. Mr. Gilbert Tennent, Upon Hearing Him Display Both the Terrors of the Law and Blessed Invitations of the Gospel, to Awaken Sinners, and Comfort Saints." *New England Weekly Journal,* 1740.

Moorhead, Sarah Parsons. "To the Reverend Mr. James Davenport on His Departure from Boston, by way of a Dream. To which is added, a postscript to the Rev. Mr. A--d--w C--w-ll." Boston: Charles Harrison, 1742.

Muzzy, Harriet. *Poems, Moral and Sentimental.* New York: F. W. Ritter, 1821.

S. M. "The Triumphs of Faith Manifested to the World or, Abraham Offering up his Son Isaac as a Sweet Sacrifice upon Mount Moriah to the Lord. [New London, CT]: T. Green, 1749.

N. N. *Awakening Calls to Early Piety.* Boston: Kneeland and Green, 1738.

Palmer, Mary. *Miscellaneous Writings on Religious Subjects.* Windsor, VT: Alden Spooner, 1807.

Peck, John. *Description of the Last Judgment . . . Also, a Poem on Death, and One on the Resurrection.* Boston: E. Russell, 1773. Several printings.

Peck, John. *Devil's Shaving Mill; or, Poem in which the Devil is Personated.* Tauton, MA: A. Danforth, 1815.

Peck, John. *Poem, Containing a Descant on the Universal Plan.* Keene, NH: John Prentiss, 1801. Several printings. Sometimes with Rev. Lemuel Haynes's sermon.

Philodemus. A Minister of the Gospel. *Serious Reflections on the Times: A Poem.* Philadelphia: James Chattin, 1757.

Philomuse. [most likely Levi Frisbie] *Reflections of a Saint, Under a View of the Presence of an Infinitely Holy and All-Seeing God.* Boston: J. Kneeland, 1772. Reprint, Norwich, CT: Green & Spooner, 1773, 1776.

Shaw, Thomas. Manuscript Poems [Various copies and books]. Maine Historical Society.

Smith (Scott), Elizabeth. *Poems.* Ms. Connecticut Historical Society, and *Hymns and Poems,* 1740, and *Poems on Several Occasions,* 1750. Ms. Yale Beinecke.

Scales, William. *The Quintessence of Universal History; or, An Epitomial History of the Christian Era. A Poem.* MA, 1806.

Shippen (Livingston), Anne Home. *Sacred Records Abridged in Verse: Consisting of Some of the Parables and Miracles, the Life, Death, Resurrection and Ascension of the Blessed Saviour.* Philadelphia: T. S. Manning, 1817.

Sigourney, Lydia. *Moral Pieces, In Prose and Verse.* Hartford, CT: Sheldon and Goodwin, 1815.

Stryker, Mary Elizabeth. Notebook, ca. 1819. John Hay Library.

Thacher, William. *Battle Between Truth and Error.* Middletown, CT: T & J. B. Dunning, 1808.

Thayer, Caroline Matilda. *Religion Recommended to Youth . . . To Which is Added, Poems on Various Occasions.* New York: Thomas Bakewell, 1817.

Throop, Josiah. *Sacred Poetry.* Utica, NY: Ira Merrell, 1811.

Thomas, Joseph. *A Poetical Descant on the Primeval and Present State of Mankind, or, The Pilgrim's Muse.* Winchester, VA: J. Foster, 1816.

Thomas, Joseph. *Poems, Religious, Moral and Satirical. To which is Prefixed a Compend of the Life, Travels and Gospel Labours of the Author.* Lebanon, OH, 1829.

Vaill, Joseph. *Noah's Flood: A Poem. In Two Parts.* New London, CT: Samuel Green, 1796.

Waterous, Timothy. *The Battle-Axe, and Weapons of War; Discovered by the Morning Light: Aimed for the Final Destruction of Priest-Craft.* Groton, CT, 1811.

Wheatley, Phillis. *Poems on Various Subjects, Religious and Moral.* London: A. Bell, 1773.

Winchester, Elhanan. *New Book of Poems, On Several Occasions.* Boston: Isaiah Thomas, 1773.

Winchester, Elhanan. *The Process and Empire of Christ, From his Birth to the End of the Mediatorial Kingdom: A Poem, in Twelve Books.* Brattleboro, VT, 1805.

APPENDIX B

Selected Verse

Anne Dutton

An HYMN *Compos'd upon copying something for the Press.*[1]

1. Give this *Service* LORD, to *Thee*;
   Myself I dedicate:
Accept myself, my feeble Work,
   And *grant* thy Blessing great.

2. O Prince of Grace, *Send from above*,
   And take and bless this Bread:
That so thy needy *Children* dear,
   By Thousands may be fed!

3. Oh All-sufficient God, Thou dost
   None of my Service need:
Ten Thousand Thousand, LORD, Thou canst
   Without thy Creatures Feed!

4. But such thy *Condescending Grace,*
   To Men and Angels is,
That thou'lt *employ them in thy Work;*
   Which, LORD, is *perfect Bliss!*

5. O Thou who art of *Jacob,* GOD,
   Thy *feeblest Worm regard;*
Accept the *Mite* I give in Love;
   And grant a *free Reward;*

6. O LORD, I love Thee for thy SELF!
   Thy Work to me is sweet:

And had I *all created Strength,*
   I'd *lay it at thy Feet!*

7. But LORD, thy Worm has but a *Mite.*
   Thou know'st I'm *weak* and *poor*:
But Thou'lt accep't of *Turtle-Doves*
   When Thine can *give no more.*

8. Then LORD, accept my little *All,*
   And grant me what I *crave*:
That Thou Great *Glory,* Thine great *Good*
   By what I've *wrote* may have.

Sarah Moorhead

A POEM, dedicated to the Reverend Mr RALPH ERSKINE, by a Lady in *New-England*, upon reading his Gospel-Sonnets.[2]

ERSKINE, thou blessed herald sound,
Till sin's black empire totter to the ground.
Well hast thou *Sinai's* awful flames display'd,
And rebel's doom before their conscience laid:
From sin, from self, from trust in duty fly,
Commit thy naked soul to Christ, or die.
Go on and prosper in the name of God,
Seraphic preacher, through the thorny road;
The gracious Christ thy labours will reward;
His angel bands be thy perpetual guard;
Though hell's dark regions at the present hiss,
The God of glory thy strong refuge is.
Mere moral preachers have no power to charm,
Thy lines are such my nobler passions warm;
These glorious truths have set my soul on fire,
And while I read, I'm love and pure desire.
May the black train of errors hatch'd in hell
No longer on this globe in quiet dwell;
May more like you be rais'd to show their shame,
And call them by their diabolic name.

Exalt the Lamb in lovely white and red,

Angels and saints his lasting honours spread;

My trembling soul shall bear her feeble part,

'Tis he hath charm'd my soul, and win [sic] my heart.

Bless'd be the Father for electing love,

Bless'd be the Son who does my guilt remove,

Bless'd be the Dove who does his grace apply.

Oh! may I praising live, and praising die!

The following Lines are humbly dedicated to the Rev. Mr. GILBERT TENNENT, *by Mrs. S. M. upon Hearing him display both the Terrors of the Law and blessed Invitations of the Gospel, to awaken Sinners, and comfort Saints.*[3]

S E E Heaven-born TENNENT from Mount *Sinai* flies,

With flaming Targets, light'ning in his Eyes!

 Hear him, with bless'd Experience, tell,

The Law can do no more than doom to Hell!

He rends the Cov'ring off th' infernal Pit,

Lest tho'tless Souls, securely, drop in it.

Welcome, dear thund'ring Herald of the Lord!

GOD prosper in thy Hand the flaming Sword:

Its Office now is chang'd: Our JESUS be ador'd.

It once was set to guard Life's lovely Tree,

But now, sweet CHRIST, to drive home Souls to thee.

Yet, O dear sacred *Tennent*, pray beware,

Lest too much Terror prove to some a Snare:

Lest stupid Scoffers be provok'd to say,

They were by awful Curses drove away:

And while the snarling Dogs bark at the Whip,

Some frighted Sheep shou'd in the Mire skip.

By Love divine, draw them from black Despair;

For 'tis hard rising once we're plunged there:

A cursed Nature, and a frowning GOD,

A guilty Conscience: Oh most dreadful Load!

'Tis Hell begun, when these sad Sights we see;

Without a precious CHRIST, the Remedy.

O sacred Surgeon! ply the healing Balm,

Lest deep Incision should weak Grace disarm.

Thus does our LORD a blessed Mixture use,

He wounds and heals the Soul he deigns to chuse.
Heroic Champion! mount Love's blazing Car,
Brandish the Sword where hardned Sinners are:
Lest they, to their eternal Sorrow, know
 All you can say, comes short of endless Woe.
 O where's the Mortal, that has Eyes to see,
 More than a Glance of vast Eternity?
But O! how can I bear to write or speak!
Unwelcome News! My Tho'ts Connexion break;
That blessed T E N N E N T should so soon depart,
Has rais'd a Palpitation in my Heart:
A fav'rite Prophet of the blessed GOD,
A Blessing purchas'd by the SAVIOUR's Blood.
O! that I could his Vertues live and speak;
For GOD couragious, to his Foes is meek.
Tho' Demons rage, when ere he comes in Sight,
CHRIST's Lambs surround his Feed with bless'd Delight;
Repeat the awful Musick of his Tongue,
And strike with Pleasure all the list'ning Throng.
Let cursed Scoffers now with Anguish mourn,
Alas! from us he goes; but ah! from you he's torn.
You shall no more behold the slighted Prize;
GOD takes him now, in Justice from your Eyes.
But GOD's dear Saints throw Nature's Tears away,
'Tis Sin to mourn this Resurrection Day:
'Tis now a glorious Spring of blooming Joy,
When Birds of Paradice their Tongues imploy.
Tho' all our outward Blessings should depart,
We're ever near our dear REDEEMER's Heart.
LORD, tune my Heart, accept my feeble Song,
Oh that each Nerve were made a praising Tongue!
    Forgive these Lines, wash all that I profess,
I'd praise thee with each Atom of my Flesh.
    Let Angel Bands dear *Tennent*'s Guards appear,
And strike his Foes with Blindness, or with Fear.
On now, bless'd Champion! let thy Courage raise,
Thou'rt safe in CHRIST, tho' many Hells should blaze.

To the REVEREND Mr. *James Davenport* on his Departure from *Boston*, By Way of a DREAM: With a Line to the *Scoffers* at Religion, who make an ill Improvement of his naming out our worthy Ministers. To which is added, A Postscript to the Rev. Mr. *A—d— w C—w—ll. By a Female Friend.*[4]

ASSIST celestial Powers my grieved Heart,
For Love and Sorrow bear an equal Part;
I love the Zeal that fires good DAVENPORT's Breast,
But his harsh Censures give my Soul no rest;
Our worthy *Guides* whom GOD has much inflam'd,
As unexperienc'd Souls, alas, he nam'd;
Hence giddy Youth a woful Licence take;
A mock at reverend hoary Heads they make,
Despite the blest Instructions of their Tongue,
Conversion is become the Drunkard's Song;
GOD's glorious Work, which sweetly did arise,
By this unguarded sad Imprudence dies;
Contention spreads her Harpy Claws around,
In every Church her hateful Stings are found
But as these Thoughts my troubled Mind opprest,
Sleep sweet Cessation instantly refresh'd,
My Tumults calm, and new-born Pleasure rise,
A charming VISION swims before my Eyes.

The sacred Man is to his Shade convey'd,
On Cammomile his aking Temples laid;
Here Roses, Honey-Suckles, Jessamine
In beauteous Arches o'er the Champion twine;
Here Nature does her flowery Glories spread,
Sheets of white Lillies dress the lovely Bed,
With rich Cor'nations for his Coverlid;
Here pretty Birds employ each smiling Hour
In noble Toyls to deck the charming Bower;
Arabia Trace for Spices in the Bloom,
And with enamel'd Branches straw the Room;
Here gilded Clouds *Ambrosia* Drops distill,
And all the Air with matchless Odors fill;
Here gentle Zephyrs fan the fragrant Flowers,

While singing Angels guard his sleeping Hours:
Now as the shining Warriors watch his Bed,
These *gentle Checks* they whisper in his Head;
'Favourite of Heaven! How came it in thy Mind?
'That Grace was so much to thy self confin'd;
'Crush the proud Thought, and kill it in the Bud;
'Too long you have in this sad Error stood;
'Let Charity unclose thy drowsy Eyes;
'You'll see a Train of faithful Pastors rise,
 'Thousands of happy Souls surround their Feet,
 'Which you in Realms of Glory soon shall meet;
 'The timorous Christian to his great Surprize,
 'Sees himself there, tho' he himself despis'd;
 'So the censorious Wonders when he views
 'Souls there he thought GOD surely would refuse:
 'What has the Enemy provok'd you too?
 'Success is not confin'd, dear Man, to you,
 'O let not Fancy turn thy Zeal aside,
 'Free Grace in others must not be deny'd;
 'No more attempt to touch the Judgment Throne,
'*Soul Secrets* to the LORD alone are known.'
    The Heraulds rise & touch him with their Wings;
Now in his Breast a holy Shame there springs;
He starts with rosy Blushes in his Face,
And weeping sweetly sings to sovereign Grace;
'Praise to Free Grace, that kept my erring Breath,
'Nor sent me, swiftly to eternal Death:'
Down his Cheeks the chrystal Showers flow,
He wrings his Hands in penitential Woe,
Cryes, 'What have I vain-glorious Mortal done,
'Strove to Eclipse the Influence of the Sun,
'Made false Report a Bandage for my Eyes,
'And boundless Grace in Numbers vast despise;
'The very End my Zeal pursu'd the most,
'The glorious End untemper'd Zeal has lost:[']
In lovely Language here his Lips impart
The blest Contrition of his pious Heart;
His shining Guardians listen to his Tongue,

And smiling upwards bear his mournful Song:
I'll hearken too, as yet he does not cease;
'FATHER, he cries, Creator of my Peace,
'Forgive my Guilt, I'll censure so no more,
'Thy Pardon on my Knees I here implore;
'Unite the Churches I have rashly rent,
'To heal the Breaches O let some be sent;
'My Error in my Mind I ever keep,
'Unhappy Shepherd thus to scatter Sheep;
'COLMAN and SEWALL I in hast exprest,
'I clasp as first rank Worthies to my Breast;
'Now all I've wrong'd, or have too rashly nam'd,
'Freely forgive, as I myself have blam'd:'
In folded Arms of Love the Prophets meet,
GOD's Work goes on by Unity most sweet.

     Round him again his heaven'ly Guardians fly,
With Love and Pleasure sparkling in each Eye;
In Language here too sweet to be exprest
They still the Self-Reflections of his Breast;
One holds before a burnish'd golden Shield,
One graves his Love and Zeal upon the Field,
One from the Living Greens which ever spread,
Twists up a Lawrel for his sacred Head,
One holds the fainting Hero in his Arms
With heav'nly Cordials his blest Bosom warms;
And all by turns their golden Harps employ
To banish Sorrow and encrease his Joy:
No more, blest Man, do thou thy self upbraid,
Atoning Blood has Reparation made;
The glorious SAVIOUR shews the Crimson Flood,
And bids him welcome to his smiling GOD:
Now joyful Thoughts in blissful Torrents role,
And fill with Raptures his dear labouring Soul:
The Vision ends, pleas'd and refresh'd I wake,
And long my Rev'rend Friend the *Hint* should take.

     But I must leave the Pleasures of my Dream,
And turn my Thoughts to a more awful Theme,
To Souls immers'd in the black Gulph of Sin,

Who sporting drink the deadly Poison in;
Pleas'd with the fancy'd Freedom of their Will,
They seek their crying Conscience to still;
Nor can they bear dear Nature to deface,
Pride will not Beggar be to sov'reign Grace;
Array'd in moral Duties, gaudy shew,
They for a Saviour little have to do;
They wonder any such Complaints should make,
In Reformation they a Shelter take:
Dare you appear before th' eternal Throne
In this vile Cob-webb Garment of your own!
Oh no! my Friends, repent, reform ye must,
And trust Free-Grace, or be for ever curst:
A Sovereign Saviour, all in all must be;
His Gifts, his Grace, his glorious Mercy free;
We merit nothing by our utmost Cares,
But plead the Scars his human Nature wears;
This boundless Deep no Angel fathom can,
The perfect Sacrifice is GOD and Man;
The noblest Theme that golden Harps employ;
No wonder Mortals faint beneath the Joy:
While at the *worthy Man* you railing stand,
Say, should such Truths as these your Minds offend?
For this you ought him highly to esteem
These Truths were often his beloved Theme,
'My worthless Works I banish from my Breast,
'And on the blest incarnate Myst'ry rest;
'Yet let a holy Life dear JESUS shew
'My humble Faith and high Profession true;
'A helpless Worm in thy kind Arms I fall,
'Be thou my Prophet, Priest, my King and all;
'Command dear Sovereign every flying Hour,
'But with thy Precepts give the doing Power:'
Now let the Scoffers at the Word of GOD,
Tremble, for *Gabriel* brandishes his Sword;
Your raging Hearts shall feel the burning Steel,
And GOD his Terrors in your Soul reveal;
Think not the Frailties of a Man forgiv'n,

Gives you a Licence thus to storm at Heav'n;
Turn your dire Hissings into Songs of Praise,
Leave off your Railings, and amend your Ways;
Fly to the purple Steams on Calv'ry shed,
There bathe your Souls, or Vengeance strikes ye dead:
But ah, in vain I bid you thither go,
Of this blest Fountain yet ye nothing know;
Poor blinded Nature can't her Danger see,
Unless the optick Scale removed be,
Much less descry the blessed Remedy.

    O glorious JESUS! the poor Sinner's Friend,
Our Sins, black Mountains, come and condescend
To show the charming Beauties of thy Face,
And stop the Rebels in their woful Race;
In sleeping Conscience fix thy piercing Spear,
And make them bow to thee with trembling Fear.
When they have inwards turn'd a weeping Eye,
Oh! sovereign GOD thy cheering Grace apply;
When e'er they do their Nakedness confess,
Adorn them with thy perfect Righteousness;
O shew the Sacrifice thou didst provide,
That Justice is compleately satisfy'd;
O let the Sinners see the cleansing Flood,
Their Sins all cancell'd in the Blood of GOD:
Celestial Dove! Their Bosoms now inspire,
Then shall they praise thee on, and never tire.
Lord pour a radiant File of Angels round
To guard our Levites on their sacred Ground;
In Life and Doctrine may they pure appear,
Of Fellow Mortals make them void of Fear;
Ho'd them as shining Stars in thy right Hand,
While they display thy Counsels and Commands
O! Grant the Promise thy blest Word has giv'n,
Let Satan fall as Lightning quick from Heav'n;
His Legions fright thy Sheep with dreadful roar,
Confine them down that they may rise no more:
We long to see, sweet CHRIST, thy rising Throne,
That Praise and Vict'ry should be thine alone:

Lord sanctify these worthless feeble Lays,
O glorious TRINITY accept the Praise!

A Postscript

To the Rev. Mr. A—d—ew C—w—ll, On his writing against some of the worthy Ministers of the Gospel.

GO dear lov'd *C—w—l* rest on *D—p—t*'s Bed,
To ease the Pains that seize your lab'ring Head,
There let your tuneful Soul with Angels join;
There let your Sentiments and Stile refine.
May heavenly Language from your Lips distill,
And Love's soft Hand guide your ingenious Quill,
Then worthy *F-x—ft* you no more will blame,
Or so reflect on gentle *T—r—l*'s Name,
Your Fathers and your Brethren don't despise;
Tho' you'r array'd with *Argus* shining Eyes:
An Optick-fold turn inward, you may view,
Some Imperfection that remains in you.
Excuse the Freedom real Friendship takes,
And let your Wisdom just Improvement make:
How can Reflections those blest Lips employ,
That Heav'n has form'd to raise immortal Joy,
You have the Art to win with melting Words;
You need not use Granadoes, Darts and Swords;
Let rougher Minds these hostile Weapons take;
By Love divine hard Hearts in Pieces break.
My Soul by you it's glorious Power has felt.
My Bosom warms all my Affections melt:
I should not think a thousand Winters long,
While Jesus Love sounds sweetly from your Tongue
Many such Times has Sovereign Love return'd:
By many Instruments my Heart has burn'd;
Then blame me not if I should take the Part
Of all, whom GOD has made to reach my Heart;
I cannot bear a Mortal should reflect

Or treat our precious Guides with cold Neglect:

I beg on bended Knees, with flowing Tears,

You may not give me ground for future Fears;

GOD does their mutual pious Labours bless,

Don't Methods take to lessen their Success;

But Hand in Hand the glorious Work pursue,

There's sweet Employ for many more than you:

Each faithful Shepard does perform his Part;

Some rouse the Conscience, others chear the Heart;

Some from mount *Sinai* throw the awful Flame;

While some sweet Peace in *Jesus* do proclaim.

Each have their different Talents from the Lord,

And each to wandring Souls their help afford.

If I should perish, them I cannot blame;

But my deceitful Heart must take eternal Shame.

A POEM in Honour of the Reverend Mr. *Whitefield*.
Composed upon hearing him preach with so much Flame the Truths of the blessed Gospel of the SON of GOD.[5]
Boston, November 28th 1744.
By a GENTLEWOMAN.

WElcome dear *Whitefield* to these joyful Coasts;

Couragious Solider of the GOD of HOSTS.

The Gospel Trump, seraphick Herald, sound:

The *Heavens* applaud; the *Earth* with Joy resounds.

The *infernal Regions* rage to hear thy Voice;

Convicts cry out for Help, and *Saints* rejoyce.

Erroneous Minds their hateful Notions leave,

Give Angels Joy, while piously *they* grieve,

To think they 'ere embrac'd such horrid Fiends,

Prov'd Foes to CHRIST, yet tho't themselves his Friends.

Lethargick Souls like mine, start from their Sleep;

Hear JESUS speak, by you, and love and weep;

Abhor the carnal Ease indulg'd before,

And trembling at the Feet of CHRIST, adore.

What anxious Thoughts possess'd each pious Mind,

While the dear Man by Sickness lay confin'd?

For fear the Fav'rite should be snatch'd away;

As a black Prelude of a dreadful Day:
When Sinners shou'd to their Hearts Lusts be giv'n,
And Judgments like a Deluge rush from Heaven:
But O! the wise forbearing sovereign GOD;
Who lifted up, but laid not on the Rod!
The wrestling *Jacobs* prostrate at his Throne,
Confessing Sins in general, with their own:
With Hearts dissolv'd in penitential Tears,
To CHRIST they bring him, and declare their Fears:
 Mark, when the LORD gives Grace and Faith to pray,
He never sends a Soul deny'd away.
To Him, let us our thankful Voices raise,
 And let our answer'd Prayers end in Praise:
Behold! another glorious Day begun!
Improve the shining Moments while they run.

   Swift as seraphick Flame, bles'd *Whitefield* go,
Proclaim well-grounded Peace to Men below,
JESUS in all his charming Beauties show.
GOD, and GOD's SON, who from Eternity,
Did in the glorious FATHER's Bosom lie,
Became a Child, a Man, for sinful Men to die.
Come Sinners now of every Age and Size,
Fly to this lovely perfect Sacrifice;
Banish your Fears, and wipe your weeping Eyes:
Justice is pay'd in Streams of heav'nly Blood,
The Dragon's chain'd, the Earth has drank his Flood,
The INCARNATE GOD has for our Surety stood.
The fiery Law has now no more to claim;
JESUS has rose, and put his Foes to Shame:
Angels and Saints exalt his lovely Name.

O, that an equal Zeal, might fire my Breast;
And my Corruptions have no future Rest.
I'd rather feel Convictions sharpest Sting,
Than rest or play in the wide Fields of Sin.
My naked Soul to JESUS I commit;
O may he make me for his Service fit:

I feel in *Adam*, I have fouly fell;
That I by Nature am a Lump of Hell:
Nor 'till GOD gave 'em, had I Eyes to see
My dire Condition, or my Remedy.
Come SACRED DOVE, bless'd promis'd SPIRIT come;
Renew my Heart, and take the chiefest Room:
ETERNAL FATHER, justify my Claim;
I plead no Right, but in my SAVIOUR's Name;
Heal my Backsliding, and thy Joys restore;
Say CHRIST is mine, and I desire no more.

May GOD his favour'd *Whitefield*'s Life prolong;
Increase his Zeal, and make his Nature strong;
Prosper his feeble Body, as his Soul;
May all his Years in heavenly Pleasures roll:
May Angel-Bands the lovely Charge that bear;
Display their flaming Banners in the Air;
And shew the Prophet has his Guardians there:
Shew to his Foes the Chariot's pav'd with Love;
And guilty Prejudice, shall soon remove.
May *Levi*'s sacred Tribe that round him wait,
Dear *Whitefield*'s Zeal and Plainness imitate:
Lay moral Themes, scholastick Terms aside;
And sin-sick Souls, by Faith to JESUS guide:
Call Error by its diabolick Name,
Nor fear the Rage of Hell, nor Mortals blame:
But tell from sweet Experience, what they know:
Say CHRIST is Love; for they have found him so.
Then shall the Doves unto their Windows flock,
And scoffing Rebels be asham'd to mock.

The Spouse of CHRIST *returning to her first Love. An Hymn* compos'd (as 'tis tho't) by a LADY in *New-England*.[6]

THrise happy were the golden Days,
When JESUS tun'd my chearful Lays,
Unveil'd to me his shining Face,
Disclos'd the Riches of his Grace;
When, by an Instinct all divine,

I knew, and call'd my SAVIOUR *mine*:
With Joy I clasp'd *the heavenly* GUEST,
A Joy too great to be express'd.
Nor Art nor Language could impart,
The glowing Transports of my Heart;
'Till, like a Wretch, with trifling Toys,
And empty Sounds of fleeting Joys,
(Ah how I blush! asham'd to say,)
By these I griev'd my Lord away,
And now, alas! my plaintive Moan,
My Sighs and Sobs declare him gone.
How sad the Change! How vast my Woe!
My melting Eyes, like Fountains flow:
Yet still I'll seek his lovely Face:
My highest Hopes are in his Grace,
And all my Heaven in his Embrace.
My GOD, with conscious Guilt oppress'd,
Fain would I fly to *Thee* for Rest:
But ah! my trembling Steps will slide,
Unless Thou stoop to be my Guide.
Vouchsafe, dear LORD, one shining Ray
Of Light divine to point my Way,
Or I shall ever from thee stray.
Let not my Soul, dear bought by thee,
To Sin a wretched Captive be:
My great REDEEMER, set me free!
Let me once more behold thy Grace,
And view thy reconciled Face;
Then I'll resume the chearful *Lyre*,
And imitate the heavenly Choir,
While all my Soul thy Praise conspire.

Martha Brewster

Barnardston [] September 18th: 1769[7]

Imboldn'd [ ] Sir from former Clemencies
I send my rent. my bond un-cancel'd lies

So great so just the obligations are
My time my talents fail my debt to clear
Except my wishes Sir they shall not fail
Being well Insur'd by a Devine Intail
Tis that the Sovereign of the Universe
Fit and Accommadete each various Case
Of your Dear selves. Illustrious progeny
And each domestick as his gracious eye
Sees most Conducive to his Glory and
Best Calculated to Subserve your end
And may the School Sir under your Direction
Still flourish and Increase by Heavens protection
The Great Redeemers Kingdom to Advance
Our mutual peace and Comfort to Inhance
And your Eternal honour, Sir to raise
And sparkle in your Crown more Rich then bays_____
That hand that Spread the Earth and Arch't the skie
That Guides the worlds below and worlds on high
That thought of me before Creation Rose
Doth this Last period of my Life dispose
He Call'd me forth to A new Settlement
Which I obey'd not knowing where I went
Some most endearing Comforts Left behind
My Reverend. pastor. freinds. [sic] my Children kind
So was the Ark brought home unto its place
By willing hinds [sic] yet mourning all their race
But may not I some blessed news Impart
The Lords been here he whispers to my heart
His visits more than fill each vacance
Oh Sanctifie Transform And humble me
Dear Sir though our Injoyments often blast
By foiling much of what our hopes Suggest
But Lo: tis otherwise all things Exceed
My expectations here's a Smile Indeed
I beg your prayers for help in evry case
Body and Soul: And Long to Se your face
I crave your kind protection for my Son
And his dear family Sir evry one
Wishing your Exit still delayd may be

Till thousands more to Christ may weded be
Great Sir by your Instrumentalite
What though a while a Starry Crown you wait
Eternal Bliss will Amply compensate
Swiming in boundless seas of Loves delight
Glorious Beattitudes Attract the sight
Each Apprehension shall Emencely grow
As new Sceens open all the way we go—

Notes

Introduction

1. Joseph Bates, *The Autobiography of Elder Joseph Bates* (Battle Creek, MI: Steam Press, 1868), 180–182.
2. Some may reasonably object to the wide variety of denominations included in this list of revival poems, especially if they proceed from a definition of evangelicalism based on doctrinal content. However, even with a more restricted definition of evangelicalism, the poetic output is still extensive.
3. Claudia Stokes details the influence of the Great Awakening on a whole host of women writers often classified as sentimentalists, many of whom made hymns and other poetries popular in *The Altar at Home: Sentimental Literature and Nineteenth-Century American Religion* (Philadelphia: University of Pennsylvania Press, 2014). In the nineteenth century an invisible Protestantism often precludes attention to such verse as religious. See Tracy Fessenden, *Culture and Redemption: Religion, the Secular, and American Literature* (Princeton, NJ: Princeton University Press, 2007), for the history of secular formation in the United States as invisible Protestantism.
4. See Appendix A for an extended list of British North American revival poets.
5. Max Cavitch, *American Elegy: The Poetry of Mourning from the Puritans to Whitman* (Minneapolis: University of Minnesota Press, 2007), 13.
6. David S. Shields, *Civil Tongues and Polite Letters in British America* (Chapel Hill: Published for the Institute of Early American History and Culture Williamsburg Virginia by University of North Carolina Press, 1997).
7. William C. Spengemann, *A New World of Words: Redefining Early American Literature* (New Haven, CT: Yale University Press, 1994).
8. Virginia Jackson, *Dickinson's Misery: A Theory of Lyric Reading* (Princeton, NJ: Princeton University Press, 2005).
9. Susan M. Stabile, *Memory's Daughters: The Material Culture of Remembrance in Eighteenth-Century America* (Ithaca, NY: Cornell University Press, 2004); Patrick M. Erben, *A Harmony of the Spirits: Translation and the Language of Community in Early Pennsylvania* (Chapel Hill: University of North Carolina Press, 2012); Colin Wells, *Poetry Wars: Verse and Politics in the American Revolution and Early Republic* (Philadelphia: University of Pennsylvania Press, 2018); Christopher Phillips, *The Hymnal: A Reading History* (Baltimore, MD: Johns Hopkins University Press, 2018). The nineteenth century has seen field-changing work by an array of historical poetic scholars, including Virginia Jackson, *Dickinson's Misery*; Meredith McGill, ed., *The Traffic in Poems: Nineteenth Century Poetry and Transatlantic Exchange* (New Brunswick, NJ: Rutgers University Press, 2008); and Michael C. Cohen, *The*

Social Lives of Poems in Nineteenth-Century America (Philadelphia: University of Pennsylvania Press, 2015).

10. David Morris pointed out decades ago that "[t]o ignore the more than 7,000 hymns written during the period—whether or not supported by the curious argument that hymns are not poems—is to write history which conforms to one's own taste for literature." Morris, *The Religious Sublime: Christian Poetry and Critical Tradition in 18th-Century England* (Lexington: University Press of Kentucky, 1972), 79.

11. Richard J. Mouw and Mark A. Noll, eds., *Wonderful Words of Life: Hymns in American Protestant History and Theology*, Calvin Institute of Christian Worship Liturgical Studies Series (Grand Rapids, MI: W. B. Eerdmans, 2004).

12. Isaac Watts, "Preface," in *Horae Lyricae, Poems, Chiefly of the Lyric Kind* (London: S and D. Bridge, 1706), [viii].

13. Isaac Watts, *Hymns and Spiritual Songs* (London: J. Humphreys, 1707), xiii–ix.

14. Morris, *The Religious Sublime*, 106; Isaac Watts, *Hymns and Spiritual Songs*, 2nd edition (London: J. H. Lawrence, 1709), ix.

15. Recent work on the culture and function of early American hymns include Christopher Phillips, *The Hymnal*; Claudia Stokes, *Altar at Home*; Mark A. Noll and Edith L. Blumhofer, eds., *Sing Them Over Again to Me: Hymns and Hymnbooks in America* (Tuscaloosa: University of Alabama Press, 2006); Mark A. Noll and Edith L. Blumhofer, eds., *Sing the Lord's Song in a Strange Land: Hymnody in the History of North American Protestantism* (Tuscaloosa: University of Alabama Press, 2004); on British hymns, see Isobel Rivers and David L. Wykes, eds., *Dissenting Praise: Religious Dissent and the Hymn in England and Wales* (Oxford: Oxford University Press, 2011).

16. John Knapp, "Isaac Watts's Unfixed Hymn Genre," *Modern Philology* 109.4 (2012), 463–482.

17. Shaun Irlam and John D. Morillo transformed the place accorded by scholars to the poetics of enthusiasm in Britain during the eighteenth century by resuscitating the forgotten Dennis. Shaun Irlam, *Elations: The Poetics of Enthusiasm in Eighteenth-Century Britain* (Stanford: Stanford University Press, 1999); John D. Morillo, "Poetic Enthusiasm," in *A Companion to Eighteenth-Century Poetry*, ed. Christine Gerrard (Oxford: Blackwell, 2006).

18. Morris, *The Religious Sublime*, 67, 82.

19. According to Morris, scholars usually trace the sublime in English literary history through Newtonian science, physic-theological thought, and Lockean epistemology. However, at the beginning of the century, English poets and critics established a relationship between the sublime and religion not through Newton or Locke, but through Longinus, Milton, and the Bible. Morris, *The Religious Sublime*, 2–3. More recently, Abram Van Engen has traced the history of sentiment through Puritan fellow feeling rather than Scottish moral sense philosophy. Van Engen, *Sympathetic Puritans: Calvinist Fellow Feeling in Early New England* (Oxford: Oxford University Press, 2014).

20. Morris, *The Religious Sublime*, 59.

21. Jon Mee, *Romanticism, Enthusiasm, and Regulation: Poetics and the Policing of Culture in the Romantic Period* (Oxford: Oxford University Press, 2005), 17.

22. There are some recent notable exceptions. Colin Jager explicitly tries to counter the literary replacement of religion narrative by positing the literary as a third term rather than as a binary. Jager, *The Book of God: Secularization and Design in the Romantic Era* (Philadelphia: University of Pennsylvania, 2007). Jon Mee expands enthusiasm beyond Romanticism and takes up the dissenter poet Barbauld. Yet, he seems less interested in this larger enthusiasm and its poetics than its relation to the privileged Romantics. Mee, *Romanticism, Enthusiasm, and Regulation.* Jasper Cragwell's work takes seriously the presence of evangelicalism on Romantic poetics. Jasper Cragwell, *Lake Methodism: Polite Literature and Popular Religion, 1780–1830* (Columbus: Ohio State University Press, 2013). And the work of Emma Salgård Cunha follows Dennis into Methodist poetics. Emma Salgård Cunha, *John Wesley, Practical Divinity and the Defence of Literature* (London: Routledge, 2018). Recent work on British dissenter poets, especially women, by Sharon Achinstein, Paula Backscheider, Christine Gerrard, Timothy Whelan, and others has been important for an expanded sense of British poetry in the eighteenth century. Sharon Achinstein, *Literature and Dissent in Milton's England* (Cambridge: Cambridge University Press, 2008); Paula R. Backscheider, *Eighteenth-Century Women Poets and Their Poetry: Inventing Agency, Inventing Genre* (Baltimore, MD: Johns Hopkins University Press, 2005); Christine Gerrard, ed., *A Companion to Eighteenth-Century Poetry* (Oxford: Wiley-Blackwell, 2014); Timothy Whelan, *Other British Voices: Women, Poetry, and Religion, 1766–1840* (New York: Palgrave Macmillan, 2015). Enthusiastic eighteenth-century American poetics and its relationship to Romanticism has been less studied. The most thorough and recent account of literary enthusiasm in early America by John Mac Kilgore is laudable, timely, and necessary. Yet, it too cleaves religious from political enthusiasm in favor of the latter. Mac Kilgore, *Mania for Freedom: American Literatures of Enthusiasm from the Revolution to the Civil War* (Chapel Hill: University of North Carolina, 2016). More generally, there has been a turn to reimagine the secular and the religious in the eighteenth century, some of which is concerned with complicating, but keeping intact, the secularization narrative and some of which refuses the binary. See Lori Branch, *Rituals of Spontaneity: Sentiment and Secularism from Free Prayer to Wordsworth* (Waco, TX: Baylor University Press, 2006); Sarah Eron, *Inspiration in the Age of Enlightenment* (Lanham, MD: University of Delaware Press, 2014); Eric Parisot, *Graveyard Poetry: Religion, Aesthetics and the Mid-Eighteenth-Century Poetic Condition* (New York: Routledge, 2013); Jordana Rosenberg, *Critical Enthusiasm: Capital Accumulation and the Transformation of Religious Passion* (Oxford: Oxford University Press, 2011); Misty G. Anderson, *Imagining Methodism in Eighteenth-Century Britain: Enthusiasm, Belief, and the Borders of the Self* (Baltimore, MD: Johns Hopkins University Press, 2012); Joseph Ā. Josephson-Storm, *The Myth of Disenchantment: Magic, Modernity, and the Birth of Human Sciences* (Chicago: University of Chicago Press, 2017).

23. Contrary, for example, to John Sitter, the eminent scholar of eighteenth-century poetry, who claims that the religious put less faith in poetry's redemptive power than those who did not believe in religion. Sitter, "Questions in Poetics: Why and How

Poetry Matters," in *The Cambridge Companion to Eighteenth-Century Poetry*, ed. John Sitter (Cambridge: Cambridge University Press, 2001), 141.

24. John Wesley, *A Plain Account of Christian Perfection* (Fenwick, MI: Alethia, 2006), 36.

25. Linford Fisher, "Evangelicals and Unevangelicals: The Contested History of a Word, 1500–1950," *Religion and American Culture* 26.2 (2016): 184–226.

26. Perhaps the most used doctrinal definition has become known as the "Bebbington quadrilateral," which identifies four characteristics shared by evangelicals: biblicism, crucicentrism, conversionism, and activism. D. W. Bebbington, *Evangelicalism in Modern Britain* (New York: Routledge, 2004).

27. Douglas L. Winiarski, *Darkness Falls on the Land of Light: Experiencing Religious Awakenings in Eighteenth-Century New England* (Chapel Hill: Omohundro Institute and University of North Carolina Press, 2017), 14–16.

28. For instance, the German Pietists who had a profound influence on the evangelical revival taken up by Patrick Erben in *A Harmony of the Spirits*, as well as verse in Native American languages. For the most recent work focused on British evangelical literary culture, see Isabel Rivers, *Vanity Fair and the Celestial City: Dissenting, Methodist, and Evangelical Literary Culture in England 1720–1800* (Oxford: Oxford University Press, 2018).

29. John Lardas Modern argues that attention to how people came to feel religious should be central to religious studies in the nineteenth century. Lardas Modern, *Secularism in Antebellum America* (Chicago: University of Chicago Press, 2011). Abram Van Engen argues for a Puritan history of feeling, which provides a longer context for feeling and American evangelicalism. Van Engen, *Sympathetic Puritans*.

30. W. R. Ward's *Early Evangelicalism: A Global Intellectual History, 1670–1789* (Cambridge: Cambridge University Press, 2006) traces evangelicalism from the German Pietists for whom poetry was a central religious practice. Whitefield and Wesley were influenced by them and their ensuing passion for verse. See Catherine Brekus, "Writing as Protestant Practice: Devotional Diaries in Early New England," in *Practicing Protestants: Histories of Christian Life in America*, eds. Laurie F. Maffly-Kipp, Leigh E. Schmidt, and Mark Valeri (Baltimore, MD: Johns Hopkins University Press, 2006) for how Christian practices can often function to obscure dramatic changes in its own history and provide an illusion of continuity.

31. Noll and Blumhofer, eds., *Sing Them Over Again to Me*; Stephen A. Marini, *Sacred Song in America: Religion, Music, and Public Culture*, Public Expressions of Religion in America (Urbana: University of Illinois Press, 2003).

32. Edmund Burke, *A Philosophic Enquiry into the Origins of Our Ideas of the Sublime and the Beautiful* (London: R and J. Dodsley, 1757), 48.

33. In this sense, *Awakening Verse* constitutes a first step toward not only a fuller and richer literary history but, what Robert Orsi has called for, an "abundant history." This type of historical work seeks to reorient an "inherited . . . ontology in which all events derive their meaning from the social and which is aligned with the modern privileging of absence." Orsi's challenge to the historian, and I include here the literary historian, is not simply to balance the number of religious and secular topics in the list of important events and developments in modern history, but "to find a place for the gods in our

histories of the modern world," which requires accounting for people "in the modern world who live in ways beyond the conceptual range of modernist epistemology and historiography" without "enrolling them as further evidence of the inevitability of modernity's pervasive disenchantment" or as simply elements of what will become preferred forms of religion. Orsi, "Abundant History: Marian Apparitions as Alternative Modernity," *Historically Speaking*, September 2008, 12–16. See also Robert Orsi, *History and Presence* (Cambridge, MA: Belknap Press of Harvard University Press, 2016).

Chapter 1

1. Sarah Pierpont Edwards, "The Spiritual Narrative of Sarah Pierpont Edwards," in *The Silent and Soft Communion*, eds. Sue Lane McCulley and Dorothy Z. Baker (Knoxville: University of Tennessee Press, 2005), 2.
2. Jonathan Edwards, "To the Rev. James Robe of Kilsyth, Scotland (May 12, 1743)," in *The Works of Jonathan Edwards*, Volume 4: *The Great Awakening*, ed. C. C. Goen (New Haven, CT: Yale University Press, 1972), 538.
3. Edwards, "Spiritual Narrative," 6.
4. This was part of the broader eighteenth-century "cult of sensibility," in which affect and refinement of emotions became the preeminent value of the arts. G. J. Barker-Benfield, *The Culture of Sensibility* (Chicago: University of Chicago Press, 1996).
5. See Sharon Achinstein, *Literature and Dissent in Milton's England* (Cambridge: Cambridge University Press, 2003), for the extent of *Song of Songs'* and George Herbert's influence on seventeenth-century Dissenter verse.
6. This is a play on Puritan minister Thomas Shepard's seventeenth-century book of the same name, which was still being reprinted during the eighteenth-century revivals. Thomas Shepard, *The Sound Believer: A Treatise of Evangelical Conversion* (Boston: Green, Bushell, and Allen in Cornhill, 1742). Leigh Eric Schmidt also places an emphasis on evangelicals as "sound believers" within the context of an eighteenth-century effort to train enlightened ears not to hear God. Leigh Eric Schmidt, *Hearing Things: Religion, Illusion, and the American Enlightenment* (Cambridge, MA: Harvard University Press, 2000).
7. *The New England Weekly Journal* appears to have taken the Franklin edition as the basis for its printing, providing the first preview for an American audience and serving as an advertisement. Franklin most likely placed it there; the paper attributes the request to an unnamed gentleman. *New England Weekly Journal*, 669, February 12, 1740, *America's Historical Newspapers*, Readex.
8. Four days before Whitefield's second visit to America ended, *The New England Weekly Journal* published a second excerpt from *Gospel Sonnets*. *New England Weekly Journal*, 718, January 20, 1741, *America's Historical Newspapers*, Readex.
9. I know of no literary treatment of *Gospel Sonnets* in twentieth- or twenty-first-century scholarship. Very few religious historians have bothered to mention the book.
10. While Franklin maintained an ambivalent relationship to revivalist religion, he nevertheless actively published scores of revival material attesting to, if nothing

else, his keen business sense. Franklin's personal relationship with Whitefield proves a fascinating study with which scholars continue to wrestle. Frank Lambert importantly observes that the "unlikely friendship" proceeds from a false dichotomy often advanced by scholars in which Franklin represents the Enlightenment and print, while Whitefield stands in for the world of religion and oral culture. Contrary to this understanding, "Franklin and Whitefield entered into a mutually profitable relationship that blurs the boundaries between the spoken and printed word as well as between revivalism and enlightenment." Frank Lambert, "Subscribing for Profits and Piety: The Friendship of Benjamin Franklin and George Whitefield," *The William and Mary Quarterly* 50 (1993), 530. Franklin's timing with Whitefield's tour helped not only to boost the sales of the *Gospel Sonnets*, but also to promote the sale of Franklin's newly published Whitefield journal. Toward this end, Franklin inserted in his edition "A Letter From the Reverend Mr. Ralph Erskine to the Reverent Mr. Geo. Whitefield," penned in 1741, in which Erskine praises Whitefield's journals. For more on Whitefield's use of media, see Harry Stout, *The Divine Dramatist: George Whitefield and the Rise of Modern Evangelicalism* (Grand Rapids, MI: William B. Eerdmans, 1991); and Frank Lambert, *'Pedlar in Divinity': George Whitefield and the Transatlantic Revivals* (Princeton, NJ: Princeton University Press, 1994). For an extensive treatment of the use of transatlantic publishing on the creation of a transatlantic revival community, see Frank Lambert, *Inventing the "Great Awakening"* (Princeton, NJ: Princeton University Press, 1999); and Jonathan Yeager, *Jonathan Edwards and Transatlantic Print Culture* (Oxford: Oxford University Press, 2016).

11. Frank Lambert, *Inventing the "Great Awakening,"* 163.

12. James N. Green, "English Books and Printing in the Age of Franklin," in *The Colonial Book in the Atlantic World*, Volume 1, eds. David D. Hall and Hugh Amory (Cambridge: Cambridge University Press, 1999), 267.

13. Thomas continues, "Mr. ERSKINE'S Poems, as Dr. BRADBURY says, are greatly to be esteemed; and above all, for that which animates the whole, the favour of divine and experimental knowledge." Isaiah Thomas, "Advertisement" in *Gospel Sonnets*, 2nd American edition (Worcester, MA: Isaiah Thomas, 1798).

14. Quoted in Donald Fraser, *The Life and Diary of the Reverend Ralph Erskine, A.M. of Dunfermine, One of the Founders of the Secession Church* (Edinburgh: William Oliphant & Son, 1834), 318. Ralph Erskine's brother Ebenezer Erskine published sermons and catechisms.

Whitefield first contacted Erskine in April 1739, initiating a correspondence that continued until Whitefield's controversial visit to Scotland and subsequent banishment from the Presbyterian churches there.

15. "Advertisement for Gospel Sonnets," *Weekly History, or, An Account of the Most Remarkable Particulars Relating to the Present Progress of the Gospel*, London, July 4, 1741, *Eighteenth Century Journals*, Sage; "Advertisement for Gospel Sonnets Reprinting," *Boston Evening-Post*, 303, May 25, 1741, *America's Historical Newspapers*, Readex.

16. Fraser, *Life and Diary of the Reverend Ralph Erskine*, 285.

17. In 1708 a much smaller poem of Erskine's, *The Believer's Dowry*, was published anonymously; it is an early version of "Part II: The Believers Jointure" in *Gospel-Canticles* (1720). Erskine, *The Believer's Dowry* (Edinburgh: John Moncur, 1708).

18. Neonomianism designated the gospel as a new law whose requirements could be met through exercising faith and repentance. The view is usually associated with the theologian Richard Baxter (1615–1691), who interprets the Christian's relationship to Christ as a contract that requires certain performances in order to receive its benefits. Baxter wrote, "Our first faith is our Contract with Christ. . . . And all contracts of such nature, do impose a necessity of performing what we consent to and promise, in order to the benefits. . . . Barely to take a Prince for her husband may entitle a woman to his honours and lands; But conjugal fidelity is also necessary for the continuance of them; for Adultery would cause a divorce. . . . The Covenant-making may admit you, but it's the Covenant-keeping that must continue you in your privileges." Baxter, *Of Justification* (London: R. W., 1658), 123–124. Fisher's *The Marrow of Modern Divinity* was meant to navigate between the extremes of Neonomianism and antinomianism.

19. Ralph Erskine, *Gospel-Sonnets: Or, Spiritual Songs*, 2nd edition (Edinburgh: John Briggs, 1726), vii.

20. Erskine, *Gospel-Sonnets*, 1726, viii–ix.

21. Erskine, *Gospel-Sonnets*, 1726, x.

22. Erskine, *Gospel-Sonnets*, 1726, viii. Italics in the original.

23. Erskine, *Gospel-Sonnets*, 1726, 6; Ralph Erskine, *Gospel Sonnets*, 1st American edition (Philadelphia: Benjamin Franklin, 1740), 10.

24. The poem was also enlisted in a transatlantic feud between Whitefield's Calvinism and John Wesley's Arminianism. To headline the controversial public break between the two famous revival figures, *The New England Weekly Journal* published an excerpt from *Gospel Sonnets* juxtaposed to the anonymous poem "A Poem, In Imitation of the Rev. Messr. John and Charles Wesley, on Universal Redemption" as soon as the news of their argument broke at the end of Whitefield's tour. *The New England Weekly Journal*, 718, January 20, 1741, *America's Historical Newspapers*, Readex.

25. See Richard Cullen Rath, *How Early America Sounded* (Ithaca, NY: Cornell University Press, 2003).

26. Alexander Garden, *Take Heed How Ye Hear: A Sermon Preached in the Parish Church of St. Philip Charles-Town, in South Carolina on Sunday the 13th of July, 1740: With a Preface, Containing Some Remarks on Mr. Whitefield's Journals* (Charleston, SC: Peter Timothy, 1741), 20–21.

27. George Whitefield, *Directions How to Hear Sermons*, 3rd edition (Boston: G. Rogers and D. Fowle, and also by B. Eliot, 1740), 14.

28. Mark A. Noll, *The Rise of Evangelicalism: The Age of Edwards, Whitefield and the Wesleys*, Volume 1 (Downers Grove, IL: InterVarsity Press, 2010), 13.

29. Erskine, *Gospel Sonnets*, 1740, iii. Italics in the original.

30. Erskine, *Gospel Sonnets*, 1740, iii–iv.

31. In the American printing of *Song of Solomon* in 1743, Erskine treats poetic taste at length in terms of a food metaphor. He also refers to Watts's flights of figurative language, which had initiated the creation of *Horae Lyricae* as a separate book from Watts's collection of hymns. Erskine doubts that he has soared like Watts; he has instead created a work of poetry for the vulgar. Erskine, *A Paraphrase, or Large Explicatory Poem Upon the Song of Solomon* (Boston: G. Rogers, 1743).

32. Erskine, *Gospel Sonnets*, 1740, iv, v.

33. Erskine, *Gospel Sonnets*, 1740, iv.

34. Isaac Watts's preface to the second edition of *Horae Lyricae* details the qualities of Hebrew poetry and argues for the ability of Christian subject matter to revitalize contemporary poetry. Isaac Watts, *Horae Lyricae*, 2nd edition (London: J. Humfreys, 1709). John Dennis promotes Longinian principles in his works, arguing for a poetry of the religious sublime and using scriptural poetry as its precedence. Dennis, *The Advancement and Reformation of Modern Poetry* (London: Rich. Parker, 1701); Dennis, *The Grounds of Criticism in Poetry* (London: Geo. Strahan and Bernard Lintott, 1704). The idea that Hebrew poetry sanctioned poetic language for Christian uses was already an argument that revival poets routinely mentioned by the time Robert Lowth's *Lectures on the Sacred Poetry of the Hebrews* appeared in English in 1787, which attained wide currency earlier under the Latin title *De Sacra Poesi Hebraeorum* (1753). William Keach, "Poetry, After 1740," in *The Cambridge History of Literary Criticism*, Volume 4: *The Eighteenth Century*, eds. H. B. Nisbet and Claude Rawson (Cambridge: Cambridge University Press, 1997).

35. Erskine, *Gospel-Sonnets*, 1726, iii–iv.

36. Erskine, *Gospel-Sonnets*, 1726, v.

37. Erskine, *Gospel-Sonnets*, 1726, iv.

38. Erskine, *Gospel Sonnets*, 1740, ix.

39. Erskine had already prepared the text of *Job's Hymns* for printing before his death and its posthumous publication.

40. Ralph Erskine, *Job's Hymns, or a Book of Songs upon the Book of Job* (Glasgow: J. Newlands, 1753), 9.

41. Erskine, *Job's Hymns*, 10.

42. Erskine, "Heavenly Strife," *New England Weekly Journal*, 669, February 12, 1740, 1.

43. Erskine, "Heavenly Strife," 1.

44. Erskine, *Gospel Sonnets*, 1740, 71–72.

45. Fraser, *Life and Diary of the Reverend Ralph Erskine*, 422.

46. Fraser, *Life and Diary of the Reverend Ralph Erskine*, 498.

47. Patricia Roberts-Miller, *Voices in the Wilderness: Public Discourse and the Paradox of Puritan Rhetoric* (Tuscaloosa: University of Alabama Press, 1999), 2.

48. Charles Chauncy, "Man's Life Considered Under the Similitude of a Vapour," in *American Sermons: The Pilgrims to Martin Luther King Jr.*, ed. Michael Warner (New York: Library of America, 1999), 283.

49. Chauncy, "Man's Life Considered," 292.

50. Chauncy, "Man's Life Considered," 291.

51. Jonathan Edwards, "Sinners in the Hands of an Angry God," in *A Jonathan Edwards Reader*, eds. John E. Smith and Harry S. Stout (New Haven, CT: Yale University Press, 1995), 90–91.

52. George M. Marsden, *Jonathan Edwards: A Life* (New Haven, CT: Yale University Press, 2003), 222.

53. Edwards, "Sinners," 97–98. Given *Day of Doom*'s popularity, it seems likely that Edwards would have read it; however, there is no proof that he did; his father owned Wigglesworth's *Meat Out of the Eater* but not *The Day of Doom*. Additionally, the Puritan divine Thomas Shepard used the imagery of hanging by a thread, an image he culled from the punishment of hanging (itself a focus of poetry in both the seventeenth and eighteenth centuries). The image was, then, available through multiple strains. However, the popularity of Wigglesworth's poem suggests that even if Edwards did not intentionally reference *The Day of Doom*, many of his auditors would have heard it that way. Regarding the popularity of the poem, Amy Morris reports that *The Day of Doom* overtook the *Bay Psalm Book* as the bestselling book in seventeenth-century New England, and it was memorized and recited extensively through the eighteenth century, especially by women and children. Morris, *Popular Measures: Poetry and Church Order in Seventeenth-Century Massachusetts* (Newark: University of Delaware Press, 2005), 52 and footnote 75.

54. Michael Wigglesworth, *The Day of Doom: Or, A Poetical Description of the Great and Last Judgment*, 2nd edition (Cambridge, MA: Samuel Green, 1666), 88.

55. Edwards preached "Sinners" in multiple locales, the most famous instance being in Enfield, Connecticut, where the emotional outburst it provoked precluded his ability to finish the sermon. Philip F. Gura, *Jonathan Edwards: America's Evangelical*, 1st hardcover edition (New York: Hill and Wang, 2005), 117–119.

56. For more on Edwards's metaphors and their influence on homiletics, see Gregory S. Jackson, *The Word and Its Witness: The Spiritualization of American Realism* (Chicago: University of Chicago Press, 2009).

57. Edmund Burke, *A Philosophic Enquiry Into the Origins of Our Ideas of the Sublime and the Beautiful* (London: R and J. Dodsley, 1757), 48.

58. Louis FitzGerald Benson, *The English Hymn: Its Development and Use in Worship* (New York: Hodder & Stoughton, 1915), 208.

59. Morris, *Popular Measures*, 24. Morris argues that Wigglesworth's presentation of himself in *The Day of Doom* (and other poems) as a minister and a poet and his characterization of his poems as poetic sermons should be understood as a defensive posture rather than an acceptable norm. Puritan ministers were not poets. Her stance regarding the Puritan suspicion of poetic language, however, is not entirely convincing. My argument is not, like Morris's, that Puritans distrusted poetry, but that for a number of historical and cultural reasons, it appears that in the eighteenth century verse became a more central extension of the pulpit as it was reconfigured into a revivalist enterprise. In many ways, the conversionist potential of revival poetry came from the wider expectation that devotional texts, so coveted by Puritans, were a means of grace by which transformation could be effected. For a compelling argument for this type of reading practice, see Matthew P. Brown, *The Pilgrim and the Bee: Reading Rituals and Book Culture in Early New England* (Philadelphia: University of Pennsylvania Press, 2007). For a Puritan minister's poem on conversion, see Cotton Mather, "Conversion Exemplified in Verse" (Boston, 1703).

60. The verse is from the prefatory poem by James Mitchell, "On the Following Work, and Its Author," in Wigglesworth, *Day of Doom*.

61. Espousal to Christ was central to Pietist religious thought and experience, including poetry. See Patrick Erben, "(Re)Discovering the German-Language Literature of Colonial America," in *A Peculiar Mixture: German-Language Cultures and Identities in Eighteenth-Century North America*, eds. Jan Stievermann and Oliver Scheiding (University Park: Penn State University Press, 2013): 117–149, for a comparison of the poetry of the Puritan Edward Taylor and the German Radical Pietist Johannes Kelpius.

62. Fraser, *Life and Diary of the Reverend Ralph Erskine*, 57.

63. See Leigh Eric Schmidt, *Holy Fairs: Scottish Communions and American Revivals in the Early Modern Period* (Princeton, NJ: Princeton University Press, 1989).

64. Thomas S. Kidd, *George Whitefield: America's Spiritual Founding Father* (New Haven, CT: Yale University Press, 2014), 165.

65. *A Faithful Narrative of the Suprizing Work of God in the Conversion of Many Hundred Souls in Northampton* (London: John Oswald, 1737); Sandra M. Gustafson, *Eloquence Is Power: Oratory and Performance in Early America* (Chapel Hill: Published for the Omohundro Institute of Early American History and Culture, Williamsburg, Virginia, by the University of North Carolina Press, 2000), 64.

66. Andrew Fuller, *The Complete Works of Rev. Andrew Fuller: With a Memoir of His Life, by Andrew Gunton*. Volume 1, Reprinted from the 3rd London edition (Philadelphia: American Baptist Publication Society, 1845), 2.

67. Fuller, *Complete Works*, 3.

68. Fuller, *Complete Works*, 5–6.

69. Erskine, *Gospel Sonnets*, 1740, 187.

70. Ralph Erskine, *Gospel Sonnets*, 2nd American edition, 1798, 18.

71. See Sue Land McCulley and Dorothy Z. Baker, eds., *The Silent and Soft Communion: The Spiritual Narratives of Sarah Pierpont Edwards and Sarah Prince Gill* (Knoxville: University of Tennessee Press, 2005). Interestingly, *Pamela* appeared in London in 1740 and though its popularity warranted an American printing, Benjamin Franklin could not complete it until 1742 because of the volume of revival publications coming through his press. Green, "English Books and Printing in the Age of Franklin," 268.

72. That a pietistic, religious poem relies on the mystery and emotional experience of the marriage union for its controlling image may not be remarkable; yet, it recalibrates scholarly narratives that trace the popularity of sentimentalism in America through secular novels.

73. John Hubbard, *A Poem Occasioned by the Death of the Honourable Jonathan Law Esq; Late Governor of Connecticut* (New London, CT: Timothy Green, 1751), 4–5.

74. Ruth H. Bloch, "Changing Conceptions of Sexuality and Romance in Eighteenth-Century America," *The William and Mary Quarterly* 60.1 (2003), 29.

75. Bloch, "Changing Conceptions," 40.

76. John Tillotson, *The Works of the Most Reverend John Tillotson, In Ten Volumes*, Volume 8 (Edinburgh: Wal Ruddiman, 1772), 437.

77. Michael P. Winship, "Behold the Bridegroom Cometh! Marital Imagery in Massachusetts Preaching, 1630–1730," *Early American Literature* 27.3 (1992), 176.

78. See Robert Orsi, *History and Presence* (Cambridge, MA: Belknap Press of Harvard University Press, 2016), in which he argues against the secular and modern assumption of absence, which turns the lived reality and physical presence of God into metaphor.
79. Erskine, *Gospel Sonnets*, 1740, 1.
80. Erskine, *Gospel Sonnets*, 1740, 1.
81. Erskine, *Gospel Sonnets*, 1740, 1.
82. Erskine, *Gospel Sonnets*, 1740, 1–2.
83. Erskine, *Gospel Sonnets*, 1740, 2.
84. Erskine, *Gospel Sonnets*, 1740, 133.
85. Erskine, *Gospel Sonnets*, 1740, 132.
86. Erskine, *Gospel Sonnets*, 1740, 132.
87. Erskine, *Gospel Sonnets*, 1740, 132.
88. Erskine, *Gospel Sonnets*, 1740, 133.
89. Erskine, *Gospel Sonnets*, 1740, 133.
90. Erskine, *Gospel Sonnets*, 1740, 133.
91. Erskine, *Gospel Sonnets*, 1740, 133.
92. Erskine, *Gospel Sonnets*, 1740, 133.
93. Erskine, *Gospel Sonnets*, 1740, 135.
94. Erskine, *Gospel Sonnets*, 1740, 135.
95. Erskine, *Gospel Sonnets*, 1740, 134.
96. Erskine, *Gospel Sonnets*, 1740, 134.
97. Erskine, *Gospel Sonnets*, 1740, 134.
98. Erskine, *Gospel Sonnets*, 1740, 134.
99. Erskine follows Watts's defense of rhyme as a crucial form as long as it does not degenerate into jingle, or sound without content.
100. Erskine, *Gospel Sonnets*, 1740, 135.
101. Erskine, *Gospel Sonnets*, 1740, 135.
102. This includes heroic couplets and hymnal long meter with couplets.
103. Richard Bradford details the historical developments of prosodic theory in the eighteenth century. One tendency was to regard the couplet "as the vehicle of reason." Richard Bradford, *Augustan Measures: Restoration and Eighteenth-Century Writings on Prosody and Metre* (Farnham, UK: Ashgate, 2002), 200. Elsewhere, Bradford argues that the Augustans employed the closed couplet strategically as a way to shape the world through an elaborate sophisticated linguistic structure. Bradford, "Rhyming Couplets and Blank Verse," in *A Companion to Eighteenth-Century Poetry*, ed. Christine Gerrard (Oxford: Blackwell, 2006), 343. Margaret Anne Doody characterizes the eighteenth century's use of the couplet as "the enactment of appetite as well as the perfect expressive form for stylistic self-consciousness. . . . In the couplet the deep figure of Augustan thought, its oxymoron, finds perfect form and it can produce debate, through paradox, antithesis and parallel. Through the operation of the couplet various languages can play, and the double-voices [*sic*] statement finds a natural pattern." Doody, *The Daring Muse: Augustan Poetry Reconsidered* (Cambridge: Cambridge University Press, 1985), 232–233.
104. Erskine, *Gospel Sonnets*, 1740, 2.
105. John Wesley, *A Plain Account of Christian Perfection* (Bristol: William Pine, 1766), 9.

106. Samuel Davies, *Miscellaneous Poems, Chiefly on Divine Subjects* (Williamsburg, VA: William Hunter, 1752), viii.

107. McCulley and Baker, eds., *The Silent and Soft Communion*, 23.

108. Edward Godwin, *A Brief Account of God's Dealings with Edward Godwin*, 2nd edition, corrected (Bristol: Felix Farley, 1744), v–vi. The versified account was also published in Rhode Island in 1772.

109. John Allen, *Thoughts on Man's Redemption* (Utica, NY: Merrell and Seward, 1805), 6.

110. The book, like Erskine's, also features a female revival poet to introduce the work. For the importance of these female poet-ministers, see Chapter 3.

111. *The Christian Journal*, Utica, NY, Oct. 9, 1829, 1.

112. Christopher Phillips, one of the few scholars to notice the prolific abolitionist and revival poet Thomas Branagan, makes the incisive point that Branagan intentionally wrote a bad epic. Christopher N. Phillips, "Epic, Anti-Eloquence, and Abolitionism: Thomas Branagan's Avenia and the Penitential Tyrant," *Early American Literature* 44.3 (2009), 609. The early history of revival poetry provides more context for why he did so.

113. The Lay Preacher, *Bee*, July 19, 1797, New London, CT; reprinted in *Federal Gazette*, Baltimore, MD, August 18, 1797. Both credit *The Farmers Weekly Museum*.

114. Jon Mee, "Blake and the Poetics of Enthusiasm," in *The Cambridge Companion to English Literature, 1740–1830*, eds. Thomas Keymer and Jon Mee (Cambridge: Cambridge University Press, 2004), 200.

115. "The Farrago," *The Federal Mirror*, Concord, NH, June 21, 1796, 191, 1.

116. Charles Wesley's copy of *Night Thoughts* by Edward Young, Methodist Printed Collections, MA 1977/582, John Rylands Library, Manchester, England. Jack Lackington, *Confessions of J. Lackington, Late Bookseller, At the Temple of the Muses* (New York: Ezekiel Cooper and John Wilson, 1806).

117. See Wendy Raphael Roberts, "Demand My Voice: Hearing God in Eighteenth-Century Poetry," *Early American Literature* 45.1 (2010).

118. Phillis Wheatley, who is the focus of Chapter 4, was owned by Mary Wheatley, who married into the evangelical Lathrop family.

119. Christopher N. Phillips, *Epic in American Culture: Settlement to Reconstruction* (Baltimore, MD: Johns Hopkins University Press, 2012). 67.

120. *Nebuchandezzar: A Poem*, Isaac Backus Papers, Mss. Misc. Boxes B, folder 1, American Antiquarian Society, Worcester, MA.

Chapter 2

1. William Williams also published his *Llythyr Martha Philopur* in 1762, a prose work that featured an archetypical revival woman writing a letter to an itinerant minister, which was followed a year later by the itinerant minister's response. Williams, like other leading British revivalists, placed his local revival in the context of the Scotland, New England, and Georgia revivals. See David Ceri Jones, Boyd Stanley Schlenther, and Eryn Mant White, *Elect Methodists: Calvinistic Methodism in England and Wales, 1735–1811* (Cardiff: University of Wales Press, 2012).

2. Susan Juster, *Disorderly Women: Sexual Politics and Evangelicalism in Revolutionary New England* (Ithica, NY: Cornell University Press, 1994); Sandra M. Gustafson, *Eloquence Is Power: Oratory and Performance in Early America* (Chapel Hill: Published for the Omohundro Institute of Early American History and Culture, Williamsburg, Virginia, by the University of North Carolina Press, 2000); Sarah Rivett, *The Science of the Soul in Colonial New England* (Chapel Hill: Published for the Omohundro Institute of Early American History and Culture, Williamsburg, Virginia, by the University of North Carolina Press, 2011).

3. Jon F. Sensbach, *Rebecca's Revival: Creating Black Christianity in the Atlantic World* (Cambridge, MA: Harvard University Press, 2005); Moira Ferguson, ed., *The Hart Sisters: Early African Caribbean Writers, Evangelicals, and Radicals* (Lincoln: University of Nebraska Press, 1993); Catherine Brekus, *Strangers and Pilgrims: Female Preaching in America, 1740–1845*; Catherine Brekus, *Sarah Osborn's World: The Rise of Evangelical Christianity in Early America* (New Haven, CT: Yale University Press, 2013); Natasha Duquette, *Veiled Intent: Dissenting Women's Aesthetic Approach to Biblical Interpretation* (Eugene, OR: Pickwick, 2016); Timothy Whelan, *Other British Voices: Women, Poetry, and Religion, 1766–1840* (New York: Palgrave Macmillan, 2005).

4. Extended treatment of women evangelicals is essential given the centrality of women to Puritan piety, including the edges of its transformation into evangelicalism as detailed by Marilyn J. Westerkamp, *Women in Early American Religion* (London: Routledge, 1999), and Bryce Traister, *Female Piety and the Invention of American Puritanism* (Columbus: Ohio State University Press, 2016); the performance of the feminine at the heart of evangelicalism demonstrated by Gustafson, *Eloquence Is Power*; and the primacy of female religious piety to the developing liberal public sphere, argued by Elizabeth Maddock Dillon, *Gendering Freedom: Fictions of Liberalism and the Literary Public Sphere* (Stanford, CA: Stanford University Press, 2007).

5. Scholarship on Rowe has begun to restore her place in literary history: Henry F. Stecher, *Elizabeth Singer Rowe, the Poetess of Frome: A Study in Early English Pietism* (Frankfurt: Peter Lang, 1973; Sarah Prescott, *Women, Authorship and Literary Culture, 1690–1740* (Basingstoke, UK: Palgrave Macmillan, 2003); Melanie Basingstoke Bigold, *Women of Letters, Manuscript Circulation, and Print Afterlives in the Eighteenth Century: Elizabeth Rowe, Catherine Cockburn and Elizabeth Carter*, Palgrave Studies in the Enlightenment, Romanticism and Cultures of Print (Basingstoke, UK: Palgrave Macmillan, 2013); Paula Backscheider, *Elizabeth Singer Rowe and the Development of the English Novel* (Baltimore, MD: Johns Hopkins University Press, 2013); Deborah Plymouth Kennedy, *Poetic Sisters: Early Eighteenth-Century Women Poets* (Lewisburg, PA: Bucknell University Press, 2013); and several other book chapters and articles.

6. Paula R. Backscheider, *Eighteenth-Century Women Poets and Their Poetry: Inventing Agency, Inventing Genre* (Baltimore, MD: Johns Hopkins University Press, 2005), 123–174.

7. Isaac Watts, "Preface," in Elizabeth Singer Rowe, *Devout Exercises of the Heart in Meditation and Soliloquy, Prayer and Praise*, 3rd edition (London: R. Hett and Brackstone, 1738), 15–16.

8. Isaac Watts, "To Mrs. Singer. On the Sight of Some of her Divine Poems Never Printed" in *Horae Lyricae, Poems, Chiefly of the Lyric Kind*, 2nd edition (London: J. Humfreys, 1709), 293.
9. John Dennis, *The Grounds of Criticism in Poetry* (London: Geo Strahan and Bernard Lintott, 1704), 37.
10. Watts, "Preface," in Rowe, *Devout Exercises*, 9.
11. Rowe so successfully represented herself as the idealized pious poet that, according to Sarah Prescott, her actual writing, especially its non-religious elements, has been almost entirely overlooked. Sarah Prescott, "Elizabeth Singer Rowe (1674–1737): Politics, Passion and Piety," in *Women and Poetry, 1660–1750*, eds. Sarah Prescott and David E. Shuttleton (Basingstoke, UK: Palgrave Macmillan 2003), 71.
12. Elizabeth Singer Rowe, *The Miscellaneous Works in Prose and Verse of Mrs. Elizabeth Rowe, Volume 1* (London: R. Hett and R. Dodsley, 1739), 2–3.
13. Rowe, *Miscellaneous Works*, 3.
14. See David Morris, *The Religious Sublime: Christian Poetry and Critical Tradition in 18th-Century England* (Lexington: University Press of Kentucky, 1972).
15. David S. Shields, *Civil Tongues and Polite Letters in British America* (Chapel Hill: Published for the Institute of Early American History and Culture Williamsburg Virginia by University of North Carolina Press, 1997).
16. Elizabeth Singer Rowe, *The History of Joseph, A Poem* (London: T. Worrall, 1736), 3.
17. David S. Shields, "British-American Belles Lettres," in *The Cambridge History of American Literature*, Volume 1: *1590–1820*, ed. Sacvan Bercovitch (Cambridge: Cambridge University Press, 1994), 326.
18. See Timothy E. W. Gloege, "The Trouble with *Christian History*: Thomas Prince's 'Great Awakening,'" *Church History* 82.1 (2013): 125–165.
19. See, among others, Virginia Jackson and Yopie Prins, "Lyrical Studies," *Victorian Literature and Culture* (1999): 521–530; Virginia Jackson, "Poet as Poetess," in *The Cambridge Companion to Nineteenth-Century American Poetry*, ed. Kerry Larson (Cambridge: Cambridge University Press, 2011): 54–75. Paula Bernat Bennett distills the different directions studies in nineteenth-century women's poetry have taken over the poetess. Paula Bernat Bennett, "Emily Dickinson and Her American Women Poet Peers," in *The Cambridge Companion to Emily Dickinson*, ed. Wendy Martin (Cambridge: Cambridge University Press, 2002): 215–235.
20. Sarah Pierpont Edwards, "The Spiritual Narrative of Sarah Pierpont Edwards," in *The Silent and Soft Communion*, eds. Sue Lane McCulley and Dorothy Z. Baker (Knoxville: University of Tennessee Press, 2005): 2, 15.
21. Backscheider credits Rowe with the expansion of the various poetries and their uses by women in the eighteenth century. Backscheider, *Eighteenth-Century Women Poets*, 122.
22. Kennedy, *Poetic Sisters*, and Laura Henigman, *Coming into Communion: Pastoral Dialogues in Colonial New England* (Albany: State University of New York Press, 1999), explore Rowe's influence on Turell through the poem "To My Muse."
23. Jane Colman Turell, "To My Muse," in Benjamin Colman, *Reliquiae Turellae* (Boston: Kneeland and Green, 1735), 75.

24. Rowe in *The Miscellaneous Works*, 1–2; Turell in *Reliquiae Turellae*, 75.

25. Turell in *Reliquiae Turellae*, 73.

26. Sarah Pierpont Edwards, "The Spiritual Narrative," 15.

27. Rowe, *Letters Moral and Entertaining, in Prose and Verse*, 2nd edition, Volume 1 (London: Worrall, 1733), 23.

28. Several studies have focused on the poetic coteries of Rowe and Steele, including Timothy Whelan, *Other British Voices*; <<<REFO:BK>>>Deborah Kennedy, *Poetic Sisters*; Cynthia Y. Aalders, *To Express the Ineffable: The Hymns and Spirituality of Anne Steele* (Eugene, OR: Wipf and Stock reprint of Paternoster, 2008); Marjorie Reeves, *Pursuing the Muses: Female Education and Nonconformist Culture, 1700–1900* (London: Leicester University Press, 1997).

29. It is quite common to characterize Pietistic hymns as focused on the personal in contrast to traditional Protestant hymns that stress doctrine or ecclesiastical matters. Stecher, *Elizabeth Singer Rowe*, 200. It is this difference that drives Aalders to contrast the personal and emotive poems of Rowe with the theological focus of Dutton's verse. Aalders, *To Express the Ineffable*, 55. It is important to remember, though, that Pietistic poets could move between these two registers and that evangelicalism, as a Pietistic movement, also cherished and needed theological hymns. This is also true of Christian belletrism and plain style verse. Though poets tended to write in one vein, they read both. For example, poets in Steele's belletristic circle cite *Gospel Sonnets* and the revivalist poet Samuel Davies. Jane Attwater's *Copies of Poems by Mary Steele and Others*, c. 1772, D/ATT 2/1, Angus Library and Archive, Regent's Park College, University at Oxford; *Poems of Mary Steele Wakeford, Poems on Devotional Subjects*, 1748–1769, D/STE 10/2 Angus Library and Archive, Regent's Park College, University at Oxford.

30. Michael Warner, "The Preacher's Footing," in *This Is Enlightenment*, eds. Clifford Siskin and William Warner (Chicago: University of Chicago Press, 2010), 382.

31. "An Hymn Compos'd upon copying out something for the Press," *The Weekly History* [London], 69, July 31, 1742, 3.

32. Jennifer Snead, in her important article on the evangelical public sphere, explicates the hymn to show how print did not always embody "rationality, human agency, and stability in its constitution of publics." Snead, "Print, Predestination, and the Public Sphere: Transatlantic Evangelical Periodicals, 1740–1745," *Early American Literature* 45.1 (2010), 112. The hymn can be identified as Dutton's verse from one of her later collections in which it serves as prefatory material. Anne Dutton, *Letters on Spiritual Subjects and Divers Occasions Sent to Relations and Friends* (London: J. Hart, 1743).

33. Frank Lambert's study of the transatlantic evangelical imaginary as constituted through revival journals is foundational for studies of evangelical print culture. Lambert, *Inventing the "Great Awakening"* (Princeton, NJ: Princeton University Press, 1999).

34. Susan [O'Brian] Durden, "A Transatlantic Community of Saints: The Great Awakening and the First Evangelical Network, 1735–1755," *American Historical Review* 91 (1986), 827.

35. Michael D. Sciretti, "Feed My Lambs": The Spiritual Direction Ministry of Calvinistic British Baptist Anne Dutton during the Early Years of the Evangelical Revival," Dissertation (Baylor University, 2009), 294. Sciretti is the first and as of yet only

book-length study of Dutton. Bruce Hindmarsh dramatically gestures to the spiritual role and impact of Anne Dutton: "If Catherine of Siena was a Third Order Dominican, then Anne Dutton must be reckoned something of a Third Order Baptist mystic." Hindmarsh, *The Evangelical Conversion Narrative: Spiritual Autobiography in Early Modern England* (Oxford: Oxford University Press, 2005), 299.

36. Sciretti, "Feed My Lambs," 5.
37. Dutton, *Letters on Spiritual Subjects and Divers Occasions*, front matter.
38. Dutton defended the appearance of women in print by invoking the privacy of the reading relationship: "what is printed is published to the World, and the Instruction thereby given, is in this regard Pub-lick, in that it is presented to every ones View: Yet . . . Books are not Read, and the Instruction by them given in the public Assemblies. . . . But visit every one, and converse with them in their own private Houses. And therefore the Teaching, or Instruction thereby given is private: and of no other Consid-eration than that of Writing a private Letter to a Friend." Dutton, "A Letter to Such of the Servants of Christ, Who May Have Any Scruple about the Lawfulness of Printing Any Thing Written by a Woman," *Selected Spiritual Writings of Anne Dutton; Autobiography*, Volume 3: *The Autobiography*, ed. JoAnn Ford Watson (Macon, GA: Mercer University Press, 2006), 254.
39. Dutton, "A Brief Account of the Gracious Dealings of God with a Poor, Sinful, Unworthy Creature . . . Part III," *Selected Spiritual Writings*, Volume 3, 167.
40. Dutton, "A Brief Account," 191.
41. Dutton, "A Brief Account," 183.
42. Dutton, "A Brief Account," 187.
43. Stephen J. Stein, "A Note on Anne Dutton, Eighteenth-Century Evangelical," *Church History* 44.4 (1975), 485.
44. JoAnn Ford Watson, ed., "Introduction," *Selected Spiritual Writings of Anne Dutton: Eighteenth-Century, British-Baptist, Woman Theologian*, Volume 1 (Macon, GA: Mercer University Press, 2003), 95; Joseph Ivimey, *A History of English Baptists*, Volume 4 (London: Isaac Taylor Hinton and Holdsworth and Ball, 1830), 510.
45. Dutton, "A Brief Account," 209.
46. Dutton, "A Brief Account," 161.
47. *A Narration* appeared in London in 1734, followed by a second the same year, and then subsequently in 1735, 1818, 1831, and 1833.
48. Dutton, "A Brief Account," 205.
49. Anne Dutton, *A Narration of the Wonders of Grace, in Verse* (London: Printed for Dutton, 1734), iv–v.
50. Dutton, *A Narration*, 9.
51. Dutton, *A Narration*, 9.
52. Dutton, *A Narration*, 10.
53. The first and second London printings of *A Discourse upon Justification* do not include the author's name. The 1740 edition includes "By the Author of *The Discourse Concerning the New-Birth*," which was anonymous. Anne Dutton, *A Discourse Upon Justification* (London: John Oswald and Ebenezer Gardner, 1740); Anne Dutton, *A Discourse upon Justification* (London: J. Hart, 1743).

54. Dutton, "A Brief Account," 169.

55. Dutton, "A Brief Account," 202–203.

56. Dutton, "A Brief Account," 204–205.

57. There is an established scholarship that has identified early American women's poetry as an act of political intervention in the public sphere, including Pattie Cowell, *Women Poets in Pre-Revolutionary America, 1650–1775* (Troy, NY: Whitson, 1981); Paula Bennett, *Poets in the Public Sphere: The Emancipatory Project of American Women's Poetry, 1800–1900)* (Princeton, NJ: Princeton University Press, 2003); Carolyn Eastman, *A Nation of Speechifiers: Making an American Public after the Revolution* (Chicago: University of Chicago Press, 2009); and Natasha Duquette, *Veiled Intent*. The limited scholarship on Sarah Moorhead's poetry generally focuses on her verse for its political and feminist intervention, which can appear quarantined from her investment in radical evangelicalism.

58. Sarah and John Moorhead were married in Boston in 1727 by Rev. Colman. Sarah Moorhead's genealogy is unknown other than her designation as English. Her children are nearly as difficult to follow. Eric Slauter provides the most extensive information about Sarah Moorhead and her artistic influence on her slave Scipio Moorhead. Slauter, "Looking for Scipio Moorhead: An 'African Painter' in Revolutionary North America," in *Slave Portraiture in the Atlantic World*, eds. Agnes Lugo-Ortiz and Angela Rosenthal (Cambridge: Cambridge University Press, 2013): 89–116; Vincent Carretta, *Phillis Wheatley: Biography of a Genius in Bondage* (Athens: University of Georgia Press, 2014).

59. Leigh Eric Schmidt, *Holy Fairs: Scottish Communions and American Revivals in the Early Modern Period* (Princeton, NJ: Princeton University Press, 1989), established the particular importance of Scottish piety and practices on the development of revivals in colonial America.

60. Jonathan M. Yeager's *Enlightened Evangelicalism: The Life and Thought of John Erskine* (Oxford: Oxford University Press, 2011) provides the first extended treatment of John Erskine's centrality to evangelical transatlantic print exchange. John Fea provides a convincing account of the primacy of Eleazar Wheelock in the circulation of revival manuscripts in New England in Fea, "Wheelock's World: Letters and the Communication of Revival in Great Awakening New England," *Proceedings of the American Antiquarian Society: A Journal of American History and Culture Through 1876*, 109 (1999): 99–144.

61. "The Copy of a Letter from a Minister of the Gospel at Boston in New-England, to his Friend near Glasgow, in Scotland," May 14, 1742, *The Weekly History* (London) Number 77, September 25, 1742. Ralph Erskine's early biographer Donald Fraser refers to this same letter transcribed in shorthand, most likely by Henry Erskine (eldest son of Ralph), which is there addressed to Ralph Erskine. In it Moorhead also praises *Gospel Sonnets* and its recent American publication. Fraser, *The Life and Diary of the Reverend Ralph Erskine, A.M. of Dunfermine, One of the Founders of the Secession Church*, 282.

62. Ann Taves, *Fits, Trances, and Visions: Experiencing Religion and Explaining Experience from Wesley to James* (Princeton, NJ: Princeton University Press, 1999), details the different responses and interpretations of the bodily expressions of revivalism.

63. Gilbert Tennent, *The Danger of an Unconverted Ministry* (Philadelphia: Benjamin Franklin, 1740).

64. Lisa Smith, *The First Great Awakening in Colonial American Newspapers: A Shifting Story* (Lanham, MD: Lexington Books, 2012), 96.

65. Sarah Moorhead, "To the Rev. Mr. GILBERT TENNENT, upon hearing him display both the Terrors of the Law and blessed Invitations of the Gospel, to awaken Sinners, and comfort Saints," *New England Weekly Journal*, Number 726, March 17, 1741. Also reprinted by Benjamin Franklin in April 1741; *General Magazine and Historical Chronicle* (Philadelphia: Franklin, 1741), reproduced by The Facsimile Text Society (New York: Columbia University Press, 1938), 281–282. Franklin's version corrects spelling and changes punctuation, including increasing the number of exclamation points from two to 14. Quoted material comes from Franklin's version. Full poem printed in Appendix B.

66. Moorhead, "Tennent," 281.

67. Moorhead, "Tennent," 282.

68. Moorhead, "Tennent," 282.

69. Smith's *The First Great Awakening in Colonial American Newspapers* pinpoints 1742 as a year that saw increased negative publicity concerning the revivals.

70. Lambert, *Inventing*,187.

71. Sarah Moorhead, "To the Reverend Mr. *James Davenport* on his Departure from *Boston*, By Way of a DREAM: With a Line to the *Scoffers* at Religion, who make an ill Improvement of his naming out our worthy Ministers. To which is added, A Postscript to the Rev. Mr. *A--d--w C--w-ll. By a Female Friend*" (Boston: Charles Harrison, 1742).

72. Moorhead, "Davenport," 2.

73. Kenneth B. E. Roxburgh, "Female Piety in Eighteenth-Century Scotland," *Evangelical Quarterly* 74.2 (2002), 173–174. Hindmarsh, *Evangelical Conversion Narrative*, also discusses the edited McCulloch MS at length.

74. Moorhead, "Davenport," 1.

75. Moorhead, "Davenport," 2.

76. Moorhead, "Davenport," 2.

77. Moorhead, "Davenport," 2, 3.

78. Moorhead, "Davenport," 4.

79. Gloege, "Trouble with Christian History," 129. Prince was committed to a more cosmopolitan and polite Christianity and downplayed enthusiasm, including visions. Gloege argues that Prince started his revival journal, *The Christian History*, in an effort to reign in the excesses of awakening culture represented by Davenport (whom Prince refuses to acknowledge in the magazine, even though the infamous book burning incident in New London occurred at the same time as the first issue appeared).

80. Shields, *Civil Tongues and Polite Letters*.

81. John Moorhead was ridiculed for his support, most notably in the pamphlet *The State of Religion in New-England* published in Glasgow by A.M., most likely a Boston opponent of the revivals. It describes John Moorhead as an "ignorant, stupid, conceited,

impudent, ill-natured, and turbulent" man who ministered to the "poor Irish" and "common Sailors" and "is, and always has been, despised by every body of tolerable sense." A.M., *The State of Religion in New-England, Since the Reverend Mr. George Whitefield's Arrival There* (Glasgow: Robert Foulis, 1742), 11. He became the target of satirical poems, including "On John M------d's stiling himself, the Rev'd John M-----d," *Boston Evening-Post*, December 27, 1742; and "Unlucky Jack. A Tale," *Boston Evening-Post*, January 10, 1743.

82. "Copy of a letter from a Gentleman in the Country to his friend in Boston," in *A Collection of Miscellaneous Tracts,* manuscript book inscribed Boston, 1764, Massachusetts Historical Society, 7.

83. Moorhead, "Davenport," 2; Shields, *Civil Tongues,* 262.

84. Shields, *Civil Tongues,* 260, attributes the poem to Green. Leo Lemay discovered and analyzed at length Joseph Green's poem, "The Disappointed Cooper," written in 1743 as the controversy over unconverted ministers continued. The controlling imagery of the poem is the drunkard's song. Lemay identifies the play on the word "Heading" as John Moorhead. The line also seems to refer to more than one Moorhead. Given Sarah's intervention in the revival controversies, it would make sense that Green is also referring to her. See Lemay, "Joseph Green's Satirical Poem on the Great Awakening," *Resources for American Literary Study* 4 (1974), 180.

85. "Hail! Davenport," *Boston Weekly Post-Boy*, July 19, 1742, 3.

86. Moorhead, "Davenport," 4–5.

87. This complex rhetorical positioning is again displayed in the broadside's postscript "To the Rev. Mr. A—d—ew C---w-ll, On his writing against some of the worthy Ministers of the Gospel." Moorhead invites Croswell to "rest on D---p—t's Bed" where he can join his "tuneful Soul with Angels" and "refine" his "Sentiments and Stile" with "heavenly Language." Moorhead, "Davenport," 7. Croswell, like Davenport healed by poetry, is transformed into a poet. Whether he becomes a Christian belletrist or a revival poet depends upon the reader.

88. Sarah Moorhead, *A Poem in Honour of the Reverend Mr. Whitefield: Composed Upon Hearing Him Preach with So Much Flame the Truths of the Blessed Gospel of the Son of God* (Boston: Kneeland and Green, 1745), i.

89. Moorhead, *Whitefield,* iv.

90. The attribution of the poem to Moorhead comes from an inscription on the copy held at the Newberry Library in Thomas Prince, Sr.'s hand that ascribes it to "Mrs. Moorhed," as well as indicates its avenue of acquisition: "Rev. Mr. [John] Erskine of Kirkintilloch [Scotland] á T[homas] Prince Junr." Slauter, "Looking for Scipio Moorhead," suggests that this inscription points to the book's Scottish publication.

91. Research assistant Toni Armstrong of Clark University, under the direction of Meredith Neuman, helped collect and analyze the material aspects of the extant copies. Elizabeth Pope of the American Antiquarian Society located the advertisement of the poem's lone publication. "Advertisement," *The Boston Weekly News-Letter*, January 3, 1745. Will Hansen of the Newbery Library helped analyze their copy and provided images. John Hay Library at Brown University also provided images.

92. This would not be unusual. For instance, the sammelband of the entire year of *The Christian History* held by the Massachusetts Historical Society was bound with a printed hymn. *The Christian History*, E187, Massachusetts Historical Society. There are extant sammelbands of anti-Whitefield materials as well. See Thomas Church, "A serious and expostulatory letter to the Rev. Mr. George Whitefield," bound with other titles, C 6557.172, Newbury Library.

93. Congregational Church in Fairfield, *Invitations to the Reverend Mr. Whitefield, from The Eastern Consociation of the County of Fairfield* (Boston: Kneeland and Green, 1745), 8, 6.

94. Congregational Church in Fairfield, *Invitations*, 6.

95. Ralph Erskine, *Gospel Sonnets*, 4th edition (London: J. Oswald . . . and sold by the booksellers in Edinburgh and Glasgow, 1734), 2011-0310N, Department of Rare Books and Special Collections, Princeton University Library.

96. John Mitchell, "On the following Work, and its Author," in Michael Wigglesworth, *Day of Doom*, 2nd edition (Cambridge, MA: Samuel Green, 1666).

97. Sarah Moorhead, "A Poem, Dedicated to the Rev. Mr. Ralph Erskine, by a Lady in New England upon reading his *Gospel Sonnets* in *Gospel Sonnets*, Ralph Erskine (Edinburgh: John Gray and Gavin Alston, 1762), preface. Gray and Alston printed "win" instead of "won," which is fixed elsewhere.

98. Moorhead, "Erskine."

99. Moorhead, "Tennent," 282.

100. The fact that John Erskine and Prince exchanged Sarah Moorhead's 1744 poem on Whitefield and, as early as 1742, conversed about women's responses to Whitefield's preaching on the espousal to Christ, points toward one very likely avenue through which the poem may have traveled to Scotland. See MS S-377, Massachusetts Historical Soicety. Ralph Erskine was a close friend of John Erskine's relatives. See Fraser, 35. Additionally, John Moorhead corresponded with Scottish revival leaders, including John Erskine, and could have easily circulated her poem on *Gospel Sonnet*, perhaps sending it to John Erskine or directly to Ralph Erskine himself. Though the records are harder to trace, the role of Scottish women in the manuscript should be considered. Because John Erskine was so prolific in his facilitation of revival news and print, he may have been instrumental in the poem's much later appearance in the 1762 Edinburgh edition of *Gospel Sonnets* printed by John Gray and Gavin Alston. In fact, just a few years after Sarah Moorhead's poem appeared in *Gospel Sonnets*, John Erskine worked to have Jonathan Edwards's *Life of Brainerd* published in Edinburgh by Gray and Alston in 1765 for William Gray. Gray and Alton would go on to print two more editions of *Gospel Sonnets*, both with "A Lady" poem, with other publishers soon following their lead.

101. Sarah Moorhead, "*The* Spouse of CHRIST *returning to her first Love. An Hymn compos'd* (as 'tis tho't) by a LADY in *New-England*," *The Boston Gazette*, July 9, 1751.

102. Nathan Fiske Papers, 1750–1799, Box 1, Notebook 17, American Antiquarian Society.

103. An almost identical series appears in Benjamin Church's commonplace book held at the Houghton Library but is directed at the Harvard tutor Flynt. According to

Jeffrey Walker, Church authored the first poem, "The Author's Advice," followed by "His Dental Majesty's Soliloquy" and "Muse," both penned by Samuel Quincey. These two poems by Quincy are nearly verbatim to "J---M---'s Soliloquy" and "Muse." Church was never short on derision for New Lights. Later, in "Elegy on the Death of the Revered Jonathan Mayhew, D.D" (1766), Church praises Mayhew's strong anti-revivalist sentiments and parodies new lights. He relentlessly parodies enthusiasts in "A Poem Occasioned by the Death of the Honourable Jonathan Law Esq; Late Governor of Connecticut," including a direct reference to the revival poem *Gospel Sonnets*. It is not clear that Church wrote the Law elegy. Walker attributes the elegy to Church but gives no reason, while it is attributed to John Hubbard in the *Proceedings of the American Antiquarian Society* 36 (1926): 193–195. Walker, "Benjamin Church's Commonplace Book of Verse: Exemplum for a Political Satirist," *Early American Literature* 15.3 (1980/1981): 222–236.

104. Fiske Papers, American Antiquarian Society; Moorhead, "*The* Spouse of CHRIST."

105. Nathan Fiske Papers, 1750–1799, Box 1, Folder Misc., American Antiquarian Society. This copy says "For Mrs. Abigail Badger Resident in Natick Cambridge Weston." Another copy of the poem says "For the Rev.d Mr. Byles." Thomas Wallcut Papers, 1671–1866, Misc. Papers, Massachusetts Historical Society.

106. Eileen Hunt Botting, "Theorizing Women's Political Agency from the Margins of Hannah Mather Crocker's *Reminiscences and Traditions of Boston*," *Early American Literature* 49.1 (2014), 167.

107. Isobel Grundy, "Poet as Poetess," in *The Oxford Handbook of British Poetry, 1660–1800*, ed. Jack Lynch (Oxford: Oxford University Press, 2016), 254.

108. While I have focused on the Pietists who trace their genealogies to the evangelical revivals of the eighteenth century, Quaker women were avid versifiers and several participated in coteries that had high visibility, such as Hannah Griffitts. Elizabeth Graeme Fergusson headed a salon in Philadelphia, which included Annis Boudinot Stockton. See Carla Mulford, ed., *Only for the Eye of a Friend: The Poems of Annis Bouinot Stockton* (Charlottesville: University Press of Virginia, 1995). The poets on whom this book focuses wrote in English; however, another large repository of colonial evangelical verse resides in Moravian archives. For biographies of nonconformist British poets, see Whelan.

109. See Sandra Roff and Douglas Duchin, "Mrs. Muzzy—Who Was She? In Search of a Nineteenth-Century Woman Editor," *American Periodicals* 8 (1998): 45–59.

110. Mary Man Literary Manuscripts, Box A, Folder 7, John Hay Library, Brown University.

111. Bethiah Parker, Manuscript book containing an introductory passage entitled "Narrative of the trials which I had when I left the Congregational Church," followed by verse, MS, John Hay Library, Brown University.

112. Lucinda Read, Journal and Commonplace-books, 1815–1824, MS, Massachusetts Historical Society.

113. Martha Brewster, *Poems on Divers Subjects* (New-London: John Green, 1757), 20.

114. Brewster, *Divers Subjects*, 22.

115. The original appears to be "Home" but is difficult to read. "Hinds" appears where the context indicates it should be "Hands." Wedding Poem to Eleazar Wheelock By

Martha Brewster, December 4, 1747, 747654, Papers of Eleazar Wheelock, Rauner Library, Dartmouth College.

116. Letter, Martha Brewster to Eleazer Wheelock, September 18, 1769, 769518, Papers of Eleazar Wheelock, Rauner Library, Dartmouth College.

117. Mindwell Brewer, "Watchfulness Over the Tongue; or, Prudence and Zeal," Commonplace book, [ca. 1801–1825], MS 12.57, John Hay Library, Brown University.

118. Letter from Hannah Dunham to Eleazar Wheelock, August 10, 1769, 769460.2, Papers of Eleazar Wheelock, Rauner Library, Dartmouth College.

119. Levi Frisbie, "Poem . . . In Praise of Wheelock and the Grand Design," May 15, 1768, 768315.1, Papers of Eleazar Wheelock, Rauner Library, Dartmouth College.

120. See Joanna Brooks, "Six Hymns by Samson Occom," *Early American Literature* 38.1 (2003): 67–87.

121. Sarah Smith Papers, Writing and Poetry, Box 3, *Bryant-Mason-Smith Family Papers*, Massachusetts Historical Society. One of the extant manuscript poems by Martha Brewster is not in the poet's hand, but was copied by a daughter of Eleazar Wheelock. Wedding Poem to Eleazar Wheelock By Martha Brewster, December 4, 1747, 747654, Papers of Eleazar Wheelock, Rauner Library, Dartmouth College.

122. Fea, "Wheelock's World," 110.

123. Though correspondence between Brewster and Sarah Moorhead has not been discovered, they may have shared a publisher. The broadside "The Triumphs of Faith Manifested to the World" (1749) was issued by Brewster's publisher with the initials "SM," who may have been Sarah Moorhead. The poem is in a much different style than Moorhead's other poems, but she could have paid tribute to the plain style poetic tradition still popular in many broadsides.

124. Ralph Erskine, *Gospel Sonnets* (Glasgow: James Know, 1762), Princeton Theological Seminary Library.

125. "Invocation to Religion," in Jonathan Lamb, *Gospel Sonnets, or Poems, on Various Religious Subjects, Designed Principally for Youth* (Burlington: Printed for the Author, 1830), 5, 6.

126. Lamb, 5, 8.

Chapter 3

1. Though the *Gazette* regularly printed poems and general literary essays, it did not make a practice of issuing supplements. The next supplement would not occur until December 7, 1754, in an effort to recruit men for the expeditions against the French on the Ohio.

2. The exchange ignited by the Davies supplement continued for at least two years. There were likely more responses, but the *Virginia Gazette* issues are missing between 1752 and 1755. Richard Beale Davis, ed., "Preface," *Collected Poems of Samuel Davies* (Gainesville, FL: Scholars' Facsimiles & Reprints, 1968), xi.

3. In Davies's response to Dymocke, he writes that he could easily defend all of his poems but does not want to "encumber the Press, and clog the Public with such unsuitable Entertainment, as they will account both your Criticisms and mine.

However, if you leave the *Gazette*, and fall a Pamphleteering, I shall amuse myself at Times in trifling with you." His statement is footnoted in the paper: "This is approv'd of by the Printer, as a more proper Vehicle than the *Gazette*." However, I know of no evidence that the argument ever migrated to the pamphlet.

4. Abram Van Engen, "Eliza's Disposition: Freedom, Pleasure, and Sentimental Fiction," *Early American Literature* 51.2 (2016): 297–331, provides a succinct description of Edwards's aesthetics in relation to conversion and literature.

5. Edward Cahill, *Liberty of the Imagination: Aesthetic Theory, Literary Form, and Politics in the Early United States* (Philadelphia: University of Pennsylvania, 2012), 54.

6. For a biography of Davies, see George William Pilcher, *Samuel Davies: Apostle of Dissent in Colonial Virginia* (Knoxville: University of Tennessee Press, 1971). The best recent treatments of Davies's ministry to slaves are Jeffrey Richards, "Samuel Davies and the Transatlantic Campaign for Slave Literacy in Virginia," *The Virginia Magazine of History and Biography* 111.4 (2003): 333–378; and Shevaun E. Watson, "'Good Will Come of This Evil': Enslaved Teachers and the Transatlantic Politics of Early Black Literacy," *CCC* 61.1 (2009): 66–89.

7. Louis B. Wright, "Literature in the Colonial South," *Huntington Library Quarterly* (1947), 312.

8. J. Markland, *Typographia: An Ode, on Printing* (Williamsburg, VA: William Parks, 1730), 6–7.

9. Markland, *Typographia*, 11.

10. Richard Beale Davis, *A Colonial Southern Bookshelf: Reading in the Eighteenth Century* (Athens: University of Georgia Press, 1979), 116–117.

11. John Dennis, *The Advancement and Reformation of Modern Poetry* (London: Richard Parker, 1701), preface/no page.

12. Dennis, *Advancement*, 26.

13. John Dennis, *The Grounds of Criticism in Poetry* (London: George Strahan and Bernard Lintott, 1704), 126–127.

14. Phillip J. Donnelly offers an extended treatment of the nuanced uses of the term: "The political dimensions of 'enthusiasm' in England during the latter half of the seventeenth century are difficult to overemphasize" as it "threatened to destabilize the Anglican church-state by subjecting the wider social structure to . . . subjective imaginings." Phillip J. Donnelly, "Enthusiastic Poetry and Rationalized Christianity: The Poetic Theory of John Dennis," *Christianity and Literature* 54 (2005), 237.

15. J. G. A. Pocock, "Edmund Burke and the Redefinition of Enthusiasm: The Context of the Counter-Revolution," in *The Transformation of Political Culture 1789–1848*, eds. Francois Furet and Mona Ozouf, Volume 3: *The French Revolution and the Creation of Modern Political Culture*, ed. Keith Michael Baker (Oxford: Pergamon Press, 1989), 25.

16. John Mac Kilgore, *Mania for Freedom: American Literatures of Enthusiasm from the Revolution to the Civil War* (Chapel Hill: University of North Carolina, 2016).

17. Dennis, *Advancement*, 173.

18. For a fuller treatment of how Dennis's version of enthusiasm becomes exclusive, see John D. Morillo, *Uneasy Feelings: Literature, the Passions, and Class from Neoclassicism to Romanticism* (New York: AMS Press, 2001), 38.

19. Dennis, *Grounds*, 18.

20. Isaac Watts, *Horae Lyricae, Poems, Chiefly of the Lyric Kind* (London: S and D. Bridge, 1706), xvi.

21. Samuel Davies, *Miscellaneous Poems* (Williamsburg, VA: William Hunter, 1752), vii.

22. Davies, *Miscellaneous Poems*, iii, v.

23. Davies, *Miscellaneous Poems*, v.

24. Davies, *Miscellaneous Poems*, iv.

25. Davies, *Miscellaneous Poems*, iv.

26. David S. Shields, *Civil Tongues and Polite Letters in British America* (Chapel Hill: Published for the Institute of Early American History and Culture Williamsburg Virginia by University of North Carolina Press, 1997), 239.

27. In the same letter, Davies also encloses a poem for Holt and tells him it "consists chiefly of Thot's borrow'd from Mrs. Rowe." Samuel Davies, "Undated Letter to John Holt," Seventeen Letters from Samuel Davies to John Holt, Benjamin Rush MSS, Historical Society of Pennsylvania, Philadelphia.

28. Quoted in Davies, *Miscellaneous Poems*, iv.

29. Davies, *Miscellaneous Poems*, vii.

30. Davies, *Miscellaneous Poems*, v.

31. Dennis, *Advancement*, 24–25.

32. Davies, *Miscellaneous Poems*, 4.

33. Leigh Eric Schmidt, *Hearing Things: Religion, Illusion, and the American Enlightenment* (Cambridge, MA: Harvard University Press, 2000), 64.

34. Shields, *Civil Tongues*, 231.

35. Joseph Addison, "Pleasures of the Imagination," in *Selections from the Tatler and the Spectator of Steele and Addison*, ed. Angus Ross (London: Penguin, 1982), 369.

36. Addison, "Pleasures," 369.

37. Dennis, *Advancement*, 173.

38. Davies, *Miscellaneous Poems*, 32.

39. Davies, *Miscellaneous Poems*, 31.

40. Lord (Henry Home) Kames, *Elements of Criticism* (New York: F. J. Huntington and Mason Brothers, 1854), 359.

41. Shaun Irlam, *Elations: The Poetics of Enthusiasm in Eighteenth-Century Britain* (Stanford, CA: Stanford University Press, 1999), 56.

42. Davies, *Miscellaneous Poems*, 31–32.

43. Davies, *Miscellaneous Poems*, 33.

44. Samuel Davies, "Letter to John Holt," March 26, 1751, Seventeen Letters from Samuel Davies to John Holt, Benjamin Rush MSS, Historical Society of Pennsylvania, Philadelphia. The letter can also be found printed: Samuel Davies, "An Original Letter," in *The General Assembly's Missionary Magazine or Evangelical Intelligencer for 1805*, Volume 1, ed. William P. Farrand (Philadelphia: Farrand, 1806), 425–426.

45. William Cowper, *The Task* (Philadelphia: Dobson, Thomas, 1787), 151.

46. Davies sometimes privately expressed more cosmopolitan desires writing in a poem to his brother-in-law John Holt that he lived in an "uncultivated Land" and wished to "pass o'er the boisterous Ocean" and "The Works of Nature & of Art . . . explore."

Seventeen Letters from Samuel Davies to John Holt, Benjamin Rush MSS, Historical Society of Pennsylvania, Philadelphia. When he finally did travel to England, he cultivated an ecumenical poetic community (glimpses of which can be seen in his journal) whose conceptions of poetry and taste were informed by evangelism rather than high criticism. Samuel Davies, *The Reverend Samuel Davies Abroad; the Diary of a Journey to England and Scotland, 1753–55*, ed. George William Pilcher (Urbana: University of Illinois Press, 1967).

47. Denise Gigante writes, "Philosophically, the culture of taste involved elevating eating, the most basic of all human drives, into bourgeois commensality or dining; in practice, this meant civilizing appetite through the developing etiquette of manners." She continues by citing Kant's *Critique of Judgment*, "Only when men have got all they want can we tell who among the crowd has taste or not." Denise Gigante, *Taste: A Literary History* (New Haven, CT: Yale University Press, 2005), 8.

48. Davies, *Miscellaneous Poems*, x.

49. Samuel Davies, "Letters from the Rev. Samuel Davies, Shewing the State of Religion in Virginia, Particularly among the Negroes," in *The Colonial Period*, ed. Timothy Lockley, Volume 1: *Slavery in North America: From the Colonial Period to Emancipation*, eds. Mark M. Smith and Peter S. Carmichael (London: Pickering & Chatto, 2009).

50. Richard Beale Davis, *A Colonial Southern Bookshelf: Reading in the Eighteenth Century* (Athens: University of Georgia Press, 1979), 75.

51. Walter Dymocke, "Remarks on the Virginia Pindar," *Virginia Gazette*, March 20, 1752. The Huntington Library.

52. Dymocke, "Remarks," March 20.

53. Dymocke, "Remarks," March 20.

54. Walter Dymocke, "Remarks on the Virginia Pindar Contd.," *Virginia Gazette*, April 30, 1752. The Huntington Library.

55. Walter Dymocke, "Remarks on the Virginia Pindar Contd.," *Virginia Gazette*, May 8, 1752. The Huntington Library.

56. See Schmidt, *Hearing Things*; Peter Charles Hoffer, *Sensory Worlds in Early America* (Baltimore, MD: Johns Hopkins University Press, 2003); Richard Cullen Rath, *How Early America Sounded* (Ithaca, NY: Cornell University Press, 2003).

57. Juventus, "On the Rev. Mr. WHITEFIELD," *New-York Weekly Journal*, November 1739.

58. Patrick Henry, *Henry to Dawson*, February 1745. Dawson Papers, Library of Congress.

59. Quoted in Hoffer, *Sensory Worlds in Early America*, 173.

60. Charles Woodmason, *The Carolina Backcountry on the Eve of the Revolution: The Journal and Other Writings of Charles Woodmason, Anglican Itinerant* (Chapel Hill: University of North Carolina, 1969), 56.

61. Davis describes Davies's preaching style as hortatory but not given to enthusiasm: "[Davies] employed a variety of sounds and a whole spectrum of sublime imagery; but his effect was somewhere between the cool rationalism of the New England pre-Unitarians or Virginia Anglicans, and the extreme emotionalism of Whitefield and certain of Davies' evangelical countrymen, especially among the Baptists." Richard Beale Davis, *Literature and Society in Early Virginia, 1608–1840* (Baton Rouge: Louisiana State University Press, 1973).

62. Walter Dymocke, "Remarks on the Virginia Pindar Contd.," *Virginia Gazette*, June 12, 1752. The Huntington Library.

63. Jewel L. Spangler, *Virginians Reborn: Anglican Monopoly, Evangelical Dissent, and the Rise of the Baptists in the Late Eighteenth Century* (Charlottesville: University of Virginia Press, 2008), 62.

64. *The Confession of Faith: Agreed Upon by the Assembly of Divines at Westminster* (Edinburgh, 1966), 158.

65. Spangler, *Virginians Reborn*, 62.

66. Dymocke, "Remarks," April 30, 1752.

67. For instance, Shaftesbury's "The Sociable Enthusiast" (1704) and "A Letter Concerning Enthusiasm" (1708) and Dennis's *The Advancement and Reformation of Modern Poetry* (1701), *A Large Account of Taste* (1702), and *The Grounds of Criticism in Poetry* (1704).

68. Dymocke, "Remarks," April 30, 1752.

69. Dymocke, "Remarks," April 30, 1752.

70. Hoffer explains that revivalists were often considered afflicted with a madness or disease that could be detected in their countenance. He quotes Charles Chauncy: "A certain wildness is discernable in their general look and air, especially when their imaginations are moved and fired." Hoffer, *Sensory Worlds in Early America*, 180.

71. Aligning himself with Pope's satire of bad sublime writing, Dymocke names Davies the Virginia Pindar, ridiculing him as the "anti-Sublime poet" who sinks into banal and laughable verse: "It is an unvariable Rule with those, who have the true Spirit of the *Bathos*, to [*sink*] where a sublime Writer would *soar*; and to *rise* where He would fall" as "our Author has observed with admirable Constancy." Dymocke, "Remarks," April 30, 1752.

72. Dymocke, "Remarks," April 30, 1752.

73. Dymocke, "Remarks," April 3, 1752.

74. Dymocke, "Remarks," April 3, 1752.

75. Addison, "Pleasures of the Imagination," 366.

76. Michael P. Winship cites several examples: "Dissenters' sermons [were] no longer plain at all, but rather 'gibberish and canting (Glanvill 74), 'squeaking and roaring' (Eachard 119), 'unsavoury, clownish, and indecent' (Patrick 20). 'They trifle [the Precepts and Duties of the Gospel] away by childish Metaphors and Allegories, and will not talk of Religions but in barbarous and uncouth Similitudes' (Parker, *Discourse*, 75)." Winship, "Behold the Bridegroom Cometh! Marital Imagery in Massachusetts Preaching, 1630–1730," *Early American Literature* 27.3 (1992), 176.

77. Davies cautioned Holt against reading Tillotson and Sherlock because their liberal theology was a poison for both the people of the Church of England and Presbyterians. Davies suggested reading Doddridge instead. "Davies Letter to Holt," September 12, 1751, Seventeen Letters from Samuel Davies to John Holt, Benjamin Rush MSS, Historical Society of Pennsylvania, Philadelphia.

78. Richard Godbeer explores the Puritan use of marital imagery, concluding that such metaphors did not "undermine the Puritan rehabilitation of marriage through their denigration of earthly relations in comparison to those with Christ. In fact, affirming

the importance of divine espousal as a model for its human equivalent helped ministers and their flocks to rid marriage of its primal taint through its resanctification in the second Adam. Marital, romantic, and erotic conceptions of Jesus Christ could thus assume a positive and significant role as part of the New England clergy's reinvention of their faith toward the end of the seventeenth-century." Godbeer, "'Love Raptures': Marital, Romantic, and Erotic Images of Jesus Christ in Puritan New England, 1670–1730," *The New England Quarterly* 68.3 (1995), 383.

79. Dymocke, "Remarks," April 17, 1752.

80. Dymocke, "Remarks," April 17, 1752.

81. Winthrop D. Jordan, *White over Black: American Attitudes toward the Negro, 1550–1812* (Chapel Hill: University of North Carolina Press, 1968), 146.

82. Davies avoided, for the most part, addressing personal insults and instead focused on defending against Dymocke's blasphemous charges against God and his word. The treatment of his wife by Dymocke, however, must have particularly enraged him as he had expressed anxiety before publication about presenting his intimate life in print. In an undated latter, Davies writes to Holt: "The Poem on conjugal Love is wholly my own not only as to Invention, but Intention. . . . If ever I wrote anything with tender Emotion & Sincerity, it was this. My Thot's were turned toward it by occasion of some pleurely [sic] symptoms. I had not long since, which thro' Divine Goodness are removed. The weeping Tenderness of my dear other self at that Time wounded my Heart with the quickest Sensations—I should think myself happy to promote conjugal Affection in the World where the Indifferency of Neighbors, or the Malignity of Friends too often substituted in its stead . . . but I am doubtful it is too large for the Gaz. Be if I should [?] publish it in a Vol. with other Poems, its particular Reference to my own Circumstances would be probably discovered, which I would rather conceal. Perhaps were it printed in sheets by itself it would best answer the Purpose, but it awaits its doom wholly from your Determination." Davies, "Undated Letter to John Holt," Seventeen Letters from Samuel Davies to John Holt, Benjamin Rush MSS, Historical Society of Pennsylvania, Philadelphia.

83. Jordan, *White over Black*, 146.

84. "The Cameleon Lover," *South-Carolina Gazette*, March 11, 1732.

85. The realm of aesthetics had already excluded sexual desire from notions of true beauty. Both Shaftesbury and Addison associated morality and aesthetics promoting a refined sociability that could sustain political conversation and produce moral interactions. Part of refining one's aesthetic response included recognizing female beauty as an intellectual enterprise rather than a sensual one. As Bindman explains, "the impolite," for Shaftesbury, "by definition cannot conceive of a beauty that is not sensual." David Bindman, *Ape to Apollo: Aesthetics and the Idea of Race in the 18th Century* (Ithaca, NY: Cornell University Press, 2002), 57. In so many words, Davies's response is the same when he asks Dymocke if he is "too much of a Sensualist" to have heard of "moral Beauty" before. Davies, "Davies Response," *Virginia Gazette*, July 3, 1752.

86. Eighteenth-century ideas of human variety included the possibility of the transmutability of race, or what Katy Chiles calls "transformable race: a contemporaneous

understanding of race as a condition incrementally produced by external factors and continuously subject to change." Chiles, *Transformable Race* (Oxford: Oxford University Press, 2014), 139. Whether one's race reflected the true interior of the person was still contestable. See Jordan, *White over Black*, 216–265.

87. Jordan, *White over Black*, 153.

88. In the March 5, 1752, issue of the *Virginia Gazette*, another debate heatedly ensued regarding religious diversity and toleration. A response in the March 20, 1752, issue (the same week of the Dymocke-Davies supplement) associated the establishment of religious toleration with the inevitable outcome of slave emancipation. Davies's identity as the foremost promoter of religious toleration in the colony, then, clearly associates him with social unrest, including emancipation and the inevitable racial mixing that was feared would ensue. For an extended treatment of this debate and its relationship to Davies's ministry, see: Randolph Ferguson Scully, *Religion and the Making of Nat Turner's Virginia: Baptist Community and Conflict, 1740–1840*, The American South Series (Charlottesville: University of Virginia Press, 2008), 19–49.

89. Samuel Davies, "Sermon 55: A Sacramental Discourse," in *Sermons on Important Subjects*, Volume II (Boston: Lincoln and Edmands, 1811), 449.

90. Clarence Edward Noble Macartney, *Sons of Thunder, Pulpit Power of the Past* (New York: Fleming H. Revell, 1929), 209.

91. Davies, "Sermon 55," 450.

92. Samuel Davies, Token, in "Preface," of *Collected Poems of Samuel Davies*, ed. Richard Beale Davis (Gainesville, FL: Scholars' Facsimiles & Reprints, 1968), 157.

93. Leigh Eric Schmidt, *Holy Fairs: Scottish Communions and American Revivals in the Early Modern Period* (Princeton, NJ: Princeton University Press, 1989), 108–111.

94. George William Pilcher, *Samuel Davies; Apostle of Dissent in Colonial Virginia*, [1st] ed. (Knoxville: University of Tennessee Press, 1971), 93. Also see Mary McWhorter Tenney, *Communion Tokens, Their Origin, History and Use* (Grand Rapids, MI: Zondervan Publishing House, 1936).

95. Jewel L. Spangler, *Virginians Reborn: Anglican Monopoly, Evangelical Dissent, and the Rise of the Baptists in the Late Eighteenth Century* (Charlottesville: University of Virginia Press, 2008), 65.

96. Schmidt, *Holy Fairs*, 85.

97. Quoted in Schmidt, *Holy Fairs*, 67.

98. Davies, "Sermon 55," 449.

99. Davies recorded in his journal several instances of the presence or absence of a correct "Spirit of Preaching" and its correlation to the audience's response. For instance: "The Materials of the Sermon were very solemn, and Nothing appeared to me a more un-natural Incongruity, than to speak the most solemn thing with a trifling Spirit. Indeed the Incongruity appeared to me so great, that I was obliged to omit sundry Things, tho' written before me in my Notes, for Want of a Heart to express them with suitable Tenderness and Fervour. There appeared some small Solemnity among the Hearers; but oh! how far short of what I have seen in this Place in the Days of the Right Hand of the most High!" ("Diary," 10). Later, he recorded his surprise that many responded at a time when he did not have the "Spirit of Preaching" and accords it to the power

of God. Samuel Davies, *The Reverend Samuel Davies Abroad: The Diary of a Journey to England and Scotland, 1753–55*, ed. George William Pilcher (Urbana: University of Illinois Press, 1967), 10.

100. Davies, *Miscellaneous Poems*, iii.

101. Davies, *Miscellaneous Poems*, xi.

102. It could also recall the ritual of confirmation and first communion. Schmidt, 84–85.

103. Anglicanism was associated closely with the ruling elite of Virginia and the maintenance of slavery. As Scully summarizes, "The vision of the Anglican establishment was orderly, hierarchical, and integrative. . . . Religious dissent fit uneasily into this idealized world. Because of the close link between the establishment and the social order, breaking with the established church was not merely a matter of private conscience or theological particulars." Part of the attraction of blacks to dissenter religions included some of its practices that resembled African religious rites as well as its status as outsider to the Anglican Church. Additionally, in the seventeenth century, many slaves gained their freedom by being baptized. Though Virginia law had changed by the second half of the century, associations of baptism with freedom lingered among both masters (who expressed suspicion over slave desires for the rite) and among slaves (as evidenced by an uprising in 1730 caused by rumors that the King of England had declared all baptized slaves free). The formalized entrance to the Lord's Supper through an authoritative piece of printed paper could have accumulated many of these meanings. Scully, *Religion and the Making of Nat Turner's Virginia*, 27, 40–43.

104. Philip D. Morgan, "Slave Life in Piedmont Virginia, 1720–1800," in *Colonial Chesapeake Society*, eds. Lois Green Carr, Philip D. Morgan, and Jean B. Russo (Chapel Hill: University of North Carolina Press, 1988), 472.

105. Davies estimated that about 300 slaves gave "a stated attendance" in his ministry, with about 100 of them baptized by 1755. However, the total number that attended his ministry in various places numbered above a thousand. Davies, "Letters from the Rev. Samuel Davies, Shewing the State of Religion in Virginia," 201, 7. Davies's emphasis on teaching slaves to read was particularly impressive and, according to Richards, "if his own account can be trusted, no white person in colonial America was as successful as Davies in stimulating literacy among slaves in the South." Jeffrey H. Richards, "Samuel Davies and the Transatlantic Campaign for Slave Literacy in Virginia," *Virginia Magazine of History and Biography* 111.4 (2004), 334.

106. Samuel Davies, "To" Letter, Huntington Library.

107. Samuel Davies, "To" Letter, Huntington Library. The published version of this letter in 1757 does not include this line.

108. Mark M. Smith, *How Race Is Made: Slavery, Segregation, and the Senses* (Chapel Hill: University of North Carolina Press, 2006), 4.

109. Davies, "Letters from the Rev. Samuel Davies, Shewing the State of Religion in Virginia," 204.

110. Schmidt, *Hearing Things*, 64.

111. Samuel Davies, "Barbarities of the French," in *Collected Poems of Samuel Davies, 1723–1761*, ed. Richard Beale Davis (Gainesville, FL: Scholars' Facsimiles & Reprints, 1968).

Chapter 4

1. Thomas Jefferson, "Notes on the State of Virginia," in *Thomas Jefferson: Writings*, ed. Merrill D. Peterson (New York: Library of America, 1984), 267.
2. Among them, Jay Fliegelman, *Declaring Independence: Jefferson, Natural Language and the Culture of Performance* (Stanford, CA: Stanford University Press, 1993); David S. Shields, *Civil Tongues and Polite Letters in British America* (Chapel Hill: Published for the Institute of Early American History and Culture Williamsburg Virginia by University of North Carolina Press, 1997); Eric Slauter, *The State as a Work of Art: The Cultural Origins of the Constitution* (Chicago: University of Chicago Press, 2009); Nicole Eustace, *Passion Is the Gale: Emotion, Power, and the Coming of the American Revolution* (Chapel Hill: Published for the Institute of Early American History and Culture Williamsburg Virginia by University of North Carolina Press, 2008); Edward Cahill, *Liberty of the Imagination: Aesthetic Theory, Literary Form, and Politics in the Early United States* (Philadelphia: University of Pennsylvania Press, 2012); Catherine E. Kelly, *Republic of Taste: Art, Politics, and Everyday Life in Early America* (Philadelphia: University of Pennsylvania Press, 2016); and John Levi Barnard, *Empire of Ruin: Black Classicism and American Imperial Culture* (Oxford: Oxford University Press, 2018).
3. David Waldstreicher, "Ancients, Moderns, and Africans: Phillis Wheatley and the Politics of Empire and Slavery in the American Revolution," *Journal of the Early Republic*, 37.4 (Winter 2017), 732.
4. Work on Wheatley's neoclassicalism includes John C. Shields, *Phillis Wheatley's Poetics of Liberation* (Knoxville: University of Tennessee Press, 2008); John C. Shields and Eric D. Lamore, *New Essays on Phillis Wheatley* (Knoxville: University of Tennessee Press, 2011); Eric Ashley Hairston, *The Ebony Column: Classics, Civilization and the African American Reclamation of the West* (Knoxville: University of Tennessee Press, 2013); and Barnard, *Empire of Ruin*.
5. Roxann Wheeler, *The Complexion of Race: Categories of Difference in Eighteenth-Century British Culture* (Philadelphia: University of Pennsylvania Press, 2000); Bruce Dain, *A Hideous Monster of the Mind: American Race Theory in the Early Republic* (Cambridge, MA: Harvard University Press, 2003; George Boulukus, *The Grateful Slave: The Emergence of Race in Eighteenth-Century British and American Culture* (Cambridge: Cambridge University Press, 2008); Andrew Curran, *The Anatomy of Blackness: Science and Slavery in an Age of Enlightenment* (Baltimore, MD: Johns Hopkins University Press, 2011); Katy Chiles, *Transformable Race: Surprising Metamorphoses in the Literature of Early America* (Oxford: Oxford University Press, 2014); Sharon Block, *Colonial Complexions: Race and Bodies in Eighteenth-Century America* (Philadelphia: University of Pennsylvania Press, 2018); Greta LeFleur, *The Natural History of Sexuality in Early America* (Baltimore, MD: Johns Hopkins University Press, 2018).
6. Jefferson, "Notes on the State of Virginia," 266.
7. Chiles, *Transformable Race*.

8. G. J. Barker-Benfield, *The Culture of Sensibility: Sex and Society in Eighteenth-Century Britain* (Chicago: University of Chicago Press, 1992); Sarah Knott, *Sensibility and the American Revolution* (Chapel Hill: Published for the Institute of Early American History and Culture Williamsburg Virginia by University of North Carolina Press, 2009).

9. William Huntting Howell, *Against Self-Reliance: The Arts of Dependence in the Early United States* (Philadelphia: University of Pennsylvania, 2015), 55.

10. David Hume, *An Enquiry Concerning the Principles of Morals*, 1751, Section 1.

11. Eric Slauter, "Neoclassical Culture in a Society with Slaves: Race and Rights in the Age of Wheatley," *Early American Studies*, 2.1 (2004): 81–122; Cahill, *Liberty of the Imagination*.

12. Samuel Davies, *Miscellaneous Poems* (Williamsburg, VA: William Hunter, 1752), vii.

13. Samuel Stanhope Smith, *An Essay on the Causes of Variety of Complexion and Figure in the Human Species*, 2nd edition, 1810.

14. Gregory Mac Kilgore, *Mania for Freedom: American Literatures of Enthusiasm from the Revolution to the Civil War* (Chapel Hill: University of North Carolina Press, 2016), 88.

15. "On His Design for Georgia" appeared in the *Gentleman's Magazine* in November 1737. It was appended two years later to Whitefield's popular sermon, "The Almost Christian," published in London and Boston. The sermon and appended poem were a part of the Prince Library donated to Old South Church in Boston and therefore available for Phillis Wheatley to read.

16. Vincent Carretta, *Phillis Wheatley: Biography of a Genius in Bondage* (Athens: University of Georgia Press, 2011), 65.

17. Carretta, *Phillis Wheatley*, 73.

18. David Waldstreicher, "Ancients, Moderns, and Africans," summarizes this scholarship and makes these points. Also see Katherine Clay Bassard, *Spiritual Interrogations: Culture, Gender, and Community in Early African American Women's Writing* (Princeton, NJ: Princeton University Press, 1999); Stephanie Smallwood, *Saltwater Slavery* (Cambridge, MA: Harvard University Press, 2007); Ruth Flanagan, *The Oral and Beyond: Doing Things with Words in Africa* (Chicago: Chicago University Press, 2007); Shields, *New Essays on Phillis Wheatley*; and the one reference to Wheatley's practice of her mother's African ritual in the family lore, written by Margaretta Odell, "Memoir," in *Memoir and Poems of Phillis Wheatley, a Native African and a Slave* (Boston, 1834), 11.

19. Joanna Brooks, "Our Phillis, Ourselves," *American Literature*, 82.1 (2010), 1–28. For a new approach to women's relational writing and Wheatley's elegies, see Caroline Wigginton, *In the Neighborhood: Women's Publication in Early America* (Amherst: University of Massachusetts Press, 2016).

20. Carretta, *Phillis Wheatley*, 78.

21. Carretta, *Phillis Wheatley*, 72.

22. Gwendolyn DuBois Shaw, *Portraits of a People: Picturing African Americans in the Nineteenth Century* (Seattle: University of Washington Press, 2006), 27.

23. Eileen Razzari Elrod, "Phillis Wheatley's Abolitionist Text: The 1834 Edition," in *Imagining Transatlantic Slavery*, eds. Cora Kaplan and John Oldfield (Basingstoke, England: Palgrave Macmillan, 2010), 98.

24. Carretta, *Phillis Wheatley*, 92; Harry S. Stout, *The Divine Dramatist: George Whitefield and the Rise of Modern Evangelicalism* (Grand Rapids, MI: W. B. Eerdmans, 1991), xv.

25. Here, I paraphrase Betsy Erkkila's argument regarding the extraordinary political implications of Wheatley's writing: "Within the discourse of sexual and racial inequality in the eighteenth century, the fact of a black woman reading, writing, and publishing poems was itself enough to splinter the categories of male and female, white and black and undermine a social order grounded in notions of sexual and racial difference." Erkkila, *Mixed Bloods and Other Crosses: Rethinking American Literature from the Revolution to the Culture Wars* (Philadelphia: University of Philadelphia, 2005), 78.

26. "Mr. Whi----d's Soliloquy" (Boston, 1745); "A Poem on the Joyful News of the Rev. Mr. *Whitefield's* Visit to *Boston*" (Boston, 1754).

27. In the book version, Wheatley changes the second line to "Possest of glory, life, and bliss unknown," which moves away from the earlier Whitefieldian controversies that came to matter less at his death. It also points to the difference her transatlantic audience makes—an audience that most likely would not have noticed the first line's allusion to the controversial "Wh---t---d's Soliloquy."

28. Phillis Wheatley, "An Elegiac Poem, on the Death of That Celebrated Divine, and Eminent Servant of Jesus Christ, the Reverend and Learned George Whitefield" (Boston: Russell and Boyles, 1770).

29. The book version makes this clearer with its change from "lessons" to "sermons." Phillis Wheatley, *Poems on Various Subjects, Religious and Moral* (London: A. Bell, 1773), 22.

30. George Whitefield, *Two Funeral Hymns* (Boston: Russell and Boyles, 1770). Though the title of the broadside announces Whitefield as the author of two funeral hymns, the first is a Watts hymn, which casts some doubt on the authorship of the second. Another broadside issued a hymn by Charles Wesley in one column with a poem by Whitefield next to it: Wesley, *To the Reverend Mr. George Whitefield . . . A Poem* (Boston, 1774).

31. Sarah Parsons Moorhead, "A Poem in Honour of the Reverend Mr. Whitefield" (Boston, 1744), i–ii. John Hay Library.

32. The transatlantic versions, both the broadside and the book, drop the direct references to the Boston poet Moorhead, and the broadside's stanzas are removed. The version Wheatley includes in her book drops the last three lines, which erases the inversion of Moorhead's stanza. Wheatley also removes the word "emulation," which had signaled her indebtedness to previous Boston poets and larger practices of poetic imitation.

33. Eric Slauter, "Looking for Scipio," in *Slave Portraiture in the Atlantic World*, eds. Agnes Lugo-Ortiz and Angela Rosenthal (Cambridge: Cambridge University Press, 2013), 89–116.

34. Eileen Hunt Botting, "Theorizing Women's Political Agency from the Margins of Hannah Mather Crocker's *Reminiscences and Traditions of Boston*," *Early American Literature* 49.1 (2014), 167.

35. Sarah Moorhead, *A Poem in Honour of the Reverend Mr. Whitefield: Composed Upon Hearing Him Preach with So Much Flame the Truths of the Blessed Gospel of the Son of God* (Boston: Kneeland and Green, 1744), iii.

36. Wheatley, "An Elegiac Poem," 8.

37. Max Cavitch, *American Elegy: The Poetry of Mourning from the Puritans to Whitman* (Minneapolis: University of Minnesota Press, 2007), 50.

38. Astrid Franke, "Phillis Wheatley, Melancholy Muse," *New England Quarterly: A Historical Review of New England Life and Letters* 77.2 (2004), 231.

39. Wheatley, "Elegiac Poem," 6.

40. Frank Lambert, " 'I Saw the Book Talk': Slave Readings of the First Great Awakening," *The Journal of Negro History* 77.4 (1992), 185–198, 190; Carretta, *Phillis Wheatley*, 33.

41. In addition to Wheatley, the Countess of Huntingdon promoted James Albert Ukawsaw Gronniosaw, John Marrant, and Olaudah Equiano.

42. *The Weekly History*, October 17, 1741, 3–4.

43. *The Weekly History*, October 17, 1741, 3–4.

44. Nancy Ruttenburg, "George Whitefield, Spectacular Conversion, and the Rise of Democratic Personality," *American Literary History* 5.3 (1993), 429–458.

45. Wheatley, "Elegiac Poem, 7.

46. Wheatley, "Elegiac Poem, 7.

47. Wheatley, "Elegiac Poem, 5.

48. Mary Beth Norton, " 'My Resting Reaping Times': Sarah Osborn's Defense of Her 'Unfeminine' Activities, 1767." *Signs* 2.2 (1976): 515–529, 519.

49. Charles E. Hambrick-Stowe, "The Spiritual Pilgrimage of Sarah Osborn (1714–1796)," *Church History* 61.4 (1992), 408–421, 410; Thomas S. Kidd, *The Great Awakening: The Roots of Evangelical Christianity in Colonial America* (New Haven, CT: Yale University Press, 2007), 99.

50. Carretta, *Phillis Wheatley*, 65.

51. Carretta, *Phillis Wheatley*, 23; Norton, "My Resting Reaping Times," 520; Phillis Wheatley, "On Messrs Hussey and Coffin," in *Phillis Wheatley: Complete Writings*, ed. Vincent Carretta (New York: Penguin, 2001), 72.

52. Samuel Davies, "The Messiah's Kingdom" in *Miscellaneous Poems* (Williamsburg, VA: Hunter, William, 1752), 74.

53. Wheatley, "On Messrs Hussey and Coffin," 73.

54. Shaw, *Portraits of a People*, 37–38.

55. Shaw, *Portraits of a People*, 37–38.

56. See at National Portrait Gallery, https://www.npg.org.uk/collections/search/portraitExtended/mw03325

57. Christopher N. Phillips, *The Hymnal: A Reading History* (Baltimore, MD: Johns Hopkins University Press, 2018), 33.

58. Phillips, *The Hymnal*, 112.

59. Richard Cary, "Letters and Proposals," in *The Poems of Phillis Wheatley*, ed. Julian D. Mason (Chapel Hill: University of North Carolina Press, 1966), 186n.

60. Jupiter Hammon, "An Address to Miss Phillis Wheatly [*sic*]," ed. Carretta, *Phillis Wheatley: Complete Writings*, 204.

61. Elizabeth Scott W. Smith, "Poems," MS 94014, Connecticut Historical Society.

62. Wheatley, "An Hymn to the Morning," in Carretta, *Phillis Wheatley: Complete Writings*, 32.

63. Phillips, *The Hymnal*, 89.

64. Wheatley, "An Hymn to the Morning," 32.

65. John C. Shields, *The American Aeneas: Classical Origins of the American Self* (Knoxville: University of Tennessee Press, 2001), 236.

66. Mary Leapor, *Poems Upon Several Occasions*, 1748.

67. John C. Shields, "Phillis Wheatley and Mather Byles: A Study in Literary Relationship," *College Language Association Journal* 23 (1980), 377–390.

68. Stout, *Divine Dramatist*, 1991.

69. Mather Byles, *Poems on Several Occasions* (Boston: Kneeland and Green, 1744), 3.

70. Barnard, *Empire of Ruin*, 26.

71. Caroline Winterer, *The Mirror of Antiquity: American Women and the Classical Tradition, 1750–1900* (Ithaca, NY: Cornell University Press, 2007), 27–28.

72. Ruth Barrell Andrews, "Slavery," *Poems, Interspersed with Prose*, 1770, MS, Boston Public Library. Earliest known copy. Later copied into Theodore Barrell, Jr.'s book: Commonplace-book of poems by Ruth Barrell Andrews, 1791, Massachusetts Historical Society. Also see Wendy Raphael Roberts, "'Slavery' and 'To Mrs. Eliot on the Death of Her Child': Two New Manuscript Poems Connected to Phillis Wheatley by the Bostonian Poet Ruth Barrell Andrews," *Early American Literature* 51.3 (2016): 665–681.

73. Slauter, "Neoclassical Culture," 82.

74. Andrews, "Slavery," 1770.

75. Slauter, "Neoclassical Culture," 105.

76. Waldstreicher, "Ancients, Moderns, and Africans," 727.

77. Joseph A. Conforti, *Samuel Hopkins and the New Divinity Movement* (Eugene, OR: Wipf & Stock, 1981), 126. For influence of covenantal theology and importance of Calvinism for early African American abolitionists, see John Saillant, "'This Week Black Paul Preach'd': Fragment and Method in Early African American Studies," *Early American Studies* 14.1 (2016): 48–81 and Christopher Cameron, *To Plead Our Own Cause: African Americans in Massachusetts and the Making of the Antislavery Movement* (Kent, OH: Kent State University Press, 2014).

78. Barnard, *Empire of Ruin*, 47. For centrality of African Americans and Native Americans to evangelicalism, see Edward E. Andrews, *Native Apostles: Black and Indian Missionaries in the British Atlantic World* (Cambridge, MA: Harvard University Press, 2013).

79. Wheatley, "Hymn to Humanity," in Carretta, *Phillis Wheatley: Complete Writings*, 50. SPG, Esq. to whom the poem was dedicated is "S.P. Gallowy: who corrected some Poetic Essays of the Authoress." See Carretta, *Biography of a Genius in Bondage*, 213n41.

80. Phillis Wheatley, "Isaiah lxiii" in Carretta, *Complete Writings*, 34. Though the imagery is not as apparent as other revival poets' references to espousal imagery, the poem does transform the Psalm into a Eucharistic poem, according to Natasha Duquette, *Veiled Intent: Dissenting Women's Aesthetic Approach to Biblical Interpretation* (Eugene, OR: Pickwick, 2016), 106.

81. Phillis Wheatley, "To the University at Cambridge," in Carretta, *Complete Writings*, 11. Recent works on Wheatley's Miltonic influences are Reginald A. Wilburn, *Preaching the Gospel of Black Revolt: Appropriating Milton in Early African American Literature* (Pittsburgh: Duquesne University Press, 2014) and Paula Loscocco, *Phillis Wheatley's Miltonic Poetics* (New York: Palgrave Macmillan, 2014).

82. Duquette, *Veiled Intent*, 97–111.

83. Elizabeth Dillon, *The Gender of Freedom* (Oxford: Oxford University Press, 2004).

84. Samuel Davies, "Lord Thou Knowest All Things," *Miscellaneous Poems*, 5.

85. Davies, "Lord Thou Knowest All Things," 16.

86. Edmund Waller, "Of This Translation, and of the Use of Poetry," *Horace's Art of Poetry made English by the Earl of Roscommon* (London: Henry Herringman, 1680).

87. Phillis Wheatley, "On Recollection," in Carretta, *Complete Writings*, 35.

88. Given Wheatley's deep association with the Moorhead family, including a poem written to Mary Moorhead on the death of her father John Moorhead, and her interaction with other young women in the community, such as Ruth Barrell Andrews, it is quite plausible that A.M. is the other daughter of John and Sarah Moorhead—Agnes Ann Moorhead.

89. Jeffrey Bilbro, "Who Are Lost and How They're Found: Redemption and Theodicy in Wheatley, Newton, and Cowper," *Early American Literature* 47.3 (2012), 567, 583.

90. The book, which has not been examined by literary critics, contains decades of poetry of which the earliest pertains to the poetic circle within which Wheatley moved. Given that Mary Wheatley was close enough to Jane Tyler that Mary named a child after her, it makes sense that at least two poems seem to directly involve Phillis Wheatley. One poem titled "On Absence" dedicated to "Miss P.W." may be dedicated to her; the other entitled "On Recollection." Portia's "On Recollection" is not dated, but it is the second poem in the manuscript book, which was given to Tyler on July 3, 1773. Several pages later, a poem is dated July 1777. Jane Tyler Book, Royall Tyler Family Collection, Vermont Historical Society.

91. Gwendolyn Davies, "Researching Eighteenth-Century Maritime Women Writers: Deborah How Cottnam—A Case Study, in *Working in Women's Archives*, eds. Marlene Kadar and Helen M. Buss (Waterloo, ON: Wilfrid Laurier University Press, 2001). Jane Tyler's book is the earliest known appearance of Cottnam's poem "On Recollection."

92. Wheatley, "On Recollection," 121.

93. Portia, "On Recollection."

94. Wheatley, "On Recollection," 121.

95. Portia, "On Recollection."

96. Brooks.

97. Portia, "On Recollection."

98. Susan M. Stabile, *Memory's Daughters: The Material Culture of Remembrance in Eighteenth-Century America* (Ithaca, NY: Cornell University Press, 2004), 16.

99. John Andrews, Letter to William Barrell, September 22, 1772, Andrews-Eliot Manuscripts, 1772, Massachusetts Historical Society.

100. Britt Rusert, *Fugitive Science: Empiricism and Freedom in Early African American Culture* (New York: New York University Press, 2017), 74, 67.

101. Kyla Schuller, *The Biopolitics of Feeling: Race, Sex, and Science in the Nineteenth Century* (Durham, NC: Duke University Press, 2017).

102. Cahill, *Liberty of the Imagination*, 72.

103. Rowen Ricardo Phillips, *When Blackness Rhymes with Blackness* (Champaign, IL, and London: Dalkey Archive Press, 2010), 22.

104. Trica Lootens urges scholars to connect the poetess to the experience of Atlantic slavery in *The Political Poetess: Victorian Femininity, Race, and the Legacy of Separate Spheres* (Princeton, NJ: Princeton University Press, 2016).

Chapter 5

1. Susan Juster, *Disorderly Women: Sexual Politics and Evangelicalism in Revolutionary New England* (Ithaca, NY: Cornell University Press, 1994). This chapter draws on the work of Janet Moore Lindman and Jewel Spangler, who both detail the challenges to gender and patriarchy that Baptist conversion posed, as well as its limitations: Lindman, *Bodies of Belief: Baptist Community in Early America* (Philadelphia: University of Pennsylvania, 2008; Spangler, *Virginians Reborn* (Charlottesville: University of Virginia Press, 2008). Lindman provides a rigorous treatment of Ireland's narrative for its construction of an evangelical masculinity in response to Baptist life's perceived effeminacy by Southern men. My analysis adds to her work by emphasizing the impact of poetic culture. Lindman, "Acting the Manly Christian: White Evangelical Masculinity in Revolutionary Virginia," *The William and Mary Quarterly* 57 (2000), 393–416.

2. Gregory S. Jackson, *The Word and Its Witness: The Spiritualization of American Realism* (Chicago: University of Chicago Press, 2009). For recent work on the novel and evangelicalism, also see Dawn Coleman, *Preaching and the Rise of the American Novel* (Columbus: Ohio State University Press, 2013).

3. Ruttenburg, *Democratic Personality: Popular Voice and the Trial of American Authorship* (Stanford, CA: Stanford University Press, 1998), 431.

4. Gilbert Tennent, *The Danger of an Unconverted Ministry* (Philadelphia: Benjamin Franklin, 1740), 9.

5. Caleb Snow Papers, Diary, Massachusetts Historical Society.

6. David Benedict, *A General History of the Baptist Denomination in America: And Other Parts of the World* (Lincoln & Edmands, no. 53, Cornhill, 1813), 33, 479.

7. Brook Hollifield, *The Gentleman Theologians* (Durham, NC: Duke University Press, 1978), 24.

8. Lindman, *Bodies of Belief*, 156–178.

9. J. A. Leo Leman, "Richard Lewis and Augustan American Poetry," *PMLA* 83 (1968), 81.

10. David Shields, "Literature of the Colonial South," *Resources for American Literary Study* 19.2 (1993), 195; Richard Beale Davis, *Intellectual Life in the Colonial South, 1585–1763* (Knoxville: University of Tennessee Press, 1978); Richard Beale Davis and J. A. Leo Lemay, *Essays in Early Virginia Literature Honoring Richard Beale Davis* (New York: B. Franklin, 1977).

11. Robert Bolling, "A Bright Bay Horse," Advertisement, *Virginia Gazette*, October 17, 1766, sec. Advertisements: 1; Robert Bolling's poetry has been a particularly important site for understanding the construction of genteel identity. Kenneth A. Lockridge, "Colonial Self-Fashioning: Paradoxes and Pathologies in the Construction of Genteel Identity in Eighteenth-Century America," in *Through a Glass Darkly: Reflections on Personal Identity in Early America*, eds. Ronald Hoffman, Mechal Sobel, and Fredrika Teute (Chapel Hill: Published for the Omohundro Institute of Early American History & Culture by the University of North Carolina Press, 1997), 274–339.

12. Robert D. Arner, "The Muse of History: Robert Bolling's Verses on the Norfolk Inoculation Riots of 1768–1769," in *Early American Literature and Culture: Essays Honoring Harrison T. Meserole*, eds. Derounian-Stodola and Kathryn Zabelle (Newark: University of Delaware Press, 1992), 168–169.

13. Bolling, "Occlusion, or Final Poem If Ever My Compositions Be Published," "A Collection of Diverting Anecdotes Bons Mots and Other Trifling Pieces . . . 1764," Br[ock] 163, Huntington Library, 75.

14. Bolling, "Occlusion," 72.

15. Arner, "The Muse," 174.

16. Joseph Craig, "The History of Rev. Joseph Craig," in *Esteemed Reproach*, eds. Keith Harper and Martin Jacumin (Macon, GA: Mercer University Press, 2005), 44.

17. Joel Barlow, "The Hasty-Pudding," in *American Poetry: The Seventeenth and Eighteenth Centuries*, ed. David S. Shields (New York: Library of America, 2007), 806.

18. Ireland, "The Life of the Rev. James Ireland," in *Esteemed Reproach*, eds. Keith Harper and Martin Jacumin (Macon, GA: Mercer University Press, 2005), 40.

19. Ireland, "The Life," 21–22, 82.

20. David S. Shields, *Civil Tongues and Polite Letters in British America* (Chapel Hill: Published for the Institute of Early American History and Culture Williamsburg Virginia by University of North Carolina Press, 1997), 158.

21. Ireland, "The Life," 46.

22. Charles Wesley, "Yield to me now, for I am weak," 1742.

23. Shields, *Civil Tongues*, 168–173.

24. Ireland, "The Life," 48.

25. Baptists considered any spontaneous worship service, or prolonged religious gathering, a revival.

26. Ireland, "The Life," 49.

27. Ireland, "The Life," 49.

28. Ireland, "The Life," 49.

29. Ireland, "The Life," 50–51.

30. Ireland, "The Life," 49, 50–51.

31. Though he gives lip service to "embrac[ing] His truths by lively faith," the poem itself does not reach the pitch of emotion typical of those actually affected by such an enthusiastic faith. Only when fully within the throes of the new birth does Ireland compose a poem saturated with emotion and appeals for God's action.

32. Ireland, "The Life," 49–50.

33. Ralph Erskine, *Gospel Sonnets*, 1st American edition (London: printed; Philadelphia: reprinted: B. Franklin, 1740), 137.

34. Ireland, "The Life," 54.

35. Ireland, "The Life," 54.

36. Ireland, "The Life," 55.

37. Ireland, "The Life," 55.

38. Ireland, "The Life," 55.

39. Lindman writes extensively on the corporeal nature of Baptist conversions and ritual life. Lindman, *Bodies of Belief.*

40. Ireland, "The Life," 56.

41. William Huntting Howell, *Against Self-Reliance: The Arts of Dependence in the Early United States* (Philadelphia: University of Pennsylvania, 2015), 46–84.

42. Francis Jeffrey, "Wordsworth's Excursion," *Edinburgh Review, or Critical Journal* 47 (November 1814), 4.

43. John Stuart Mill, "Thoughts on Poetry and Its Varieties," in *The Collected Works of John Stuart Mill*, Volume I: *Autobiography and Literary Essays—Online Library of Liberty*, http://oll.libertyfund.org/titles/mill-the-collected-works-of-john-stuart-mill-volume-i-autobiography-and-literary-essays, 359.

44. Ireland, "The Life," 43.

45. Ireland, "The Life," 85–86.

46. Ireland, "The Life," 86.

47. Ireland, "The Life," 85–88.

48. Ireland, "The Life," 89.

49. Ireland, "The Life," 89.

50. Ireland, "The Life," 90.

51. Ireland, "The Life," 45.

52. Ireland, "The Life," 88.

53. Recent work on evangelicalism and its investments in art and sociability is beginning to correct this. Bruce Hindmarsh moves close in this direction by suggesting that scholars understand evangelical devotion as a kind of eighteenth-century school with particular investments in aesthetics and art. D. Bruce Hindmarsh, *The Spirit of Early Evangelicalism* (Oxford: Oxford University Press, 2018), 251.

54. Michael C. Cohen, *The Social Lives of Poems* (Philadelphia: University of Pennsylvania, 2015).

55. Jürgen Habermas, *The Structural Transformation of the Public Sphere*, trans. Thomas Burger (Cambridge: Blackwell Publishers, 1989).

56. The Countess of Huntingdon was one of the most famous patrons of Methodists. The ballad monger Plummer pursued his own local patron.

57. Joshua Marsden, "To the Reader," in *Leisure Hours* (New York: Paul & Thomas, 1812), 9–10.

58. Joseph Craig, "The History."

59. Joseph Thomas, *The Life of the Pilgrim* (Winchester, VA: Foster, 1817), 368.

60. Ireland, "The Life," 43.

61. Ireland, "The Life," 145.

62. Ireland, "The Life," 163.

63. Richard J. Mouw and Mark A. Noll, eds., *Wonderful Words of Life: Hymns in American Protestant History and Theology* (Grand Rapids, MI: W. B. Eerdmans, 2004), 4.

64. Ireland, "The Life," 164.

65. Ireland, "The Life," 166.

66. Christopher N. Phillips, *The Hymnal: A Reading History* (Baltimore, MD: Johns Hopkins University Press, 2018).

67. For scholarship on hymns, also see Mark Noll and Edith Waldvogel, eds., *"Sing Them Over Again to Me": Hymns and Hymnbooks in America* (Tucaloosa: University of Alabama Press, 2006).

68. Joshua Marsden, in *Grace Displayed*, writes, "Some may think that I have been too lavish of poetry; possibly this is the case—but it may be some atonement that it is original, extracted from a manuscript poem, which I intend to publish whenever it is in my power." Marsden, *Grace Displayed* (New York: Paul & Thomas for Griffin & Rudd, 1813), 2. Most directly pertinent to Ireland's practice is Simeon Crowell who, like Ireland, was a sailor and a poet who became a Baptist through writing his own poems. In his journal, in which he records both his conversion and poetry, he keeps several of the poems that he wrote before his conversion without editing them. Simeon Crowell Commonplace-book, 1790–1824, Massachusetts Historical Society. The *Memoirs of the Late Rev. Abraham Marshall* detail Marshall's Baptist conversion in 1770 and includes witty verse as well as elegies. Jabez P. Marshall, *Memoirs of the Late Rev. Abraham Marshall* (Mount Zion, Hancock, GA: Printed for the Author), 1824.

69. Ireland, "The Life," 45.

70. Ireland, "The Life," 88.

71. There is no independent verification for this claim. However, the poems do seem to progress from a less experiential relationship with God to one steeped in affective religion. The first poems promote a more active role in salvation, while the later poems become more dependent on God's all sufficient action. Regardless, even if Ireland did revise them, the fact that he claims not to would further underscore the point because it would reveal his deep desire that they function as historic markers of conversion, even as he struggled with the demands of literary expectation.

72. Gordon T. Smith, *Transforming Conversion: Rethinking the Language and Contours of Christian Initiation* (Grand Rapids, MI: Baker, 2010), 5.

73. W. R. Ward, *The Protestant Evangelical Awakening* (Cambridge: Cambridge University Press, 1992), 2.

74. I know of no other extended autobiography by a poet that focuses extensively on the role of poetic conversion.

75. Lindman, *Bodies of Belief*.

76. For example, the Virginian Baptist ministers Jeremiah Moore in Stafford County in 1771 and James Garnett near Blue Run Meeting House in Orange County in 1770 both attributed their conversions to a Watts hymn stuck in their minds. Garnett was

knocked to the ground by one line until a subsequent verse alleviated his guilt. James Barnett Taylor, *Virginia Baptist Ministers*, Volume I (Philadelphia: J. B. Lippincott, 1859), 218, 174.

77. Spangler, *Virginians Reborn*, 170.

78. Ireland, "The Life," 23.

79. Ireland, "The Life," 86.

80. When scholars reference Ireland's autobiography it is usually to emphasize his status as one of only two itinerants who left personal narratives about their persecution in Virginia. Ireland not only experienced violence at the hands of local community members, but was also jailed several times and poisoned. Scholars disagree on the exact reasons for Baptist persecution, though it included their illegal preaching (outdoors without state permits) and their relative degree of nonconformity with Anglican decorum and values. Though Presbyterians also fought for religious toleration, they did not experience the same level of persecution and moved into the mainstream fairly quickly.

81. John Leland, *The Writings of the Late Elder John Leland*, ed. Miss L. F. Greene (New York: G. W. Wood, 1845), 115.

82. Ireland, "The Life," 164.

83. Thomas, *Life of the Pilgrim*, 368.

84. David W. Music and Paul Akers Richardson, *"I Will Sing the Wondrous Story": A History of Baptist Hymnody in North America*, 1st edition (Macon, GA: Mercer University Press, 2008), 79–87.

85. Music and Richardson, *"I Will Sing the Wondrous Story,"* 127.

86. Music and Richardson, *"I Will Sing the Wondrous Story,"* 120.

87. John Gano, *Biographical Memoirs of the Late Rev. John Gano* (New York: Southwick and Hardcastle for J. Tiebout, 1806), 141.

88. The editor explains that "Mr. Gano was travelling, as an itinerant preacher, and as it was dangerous to travel without a pass, he requested Mr. Newman, who was a magistrate, to write him one. Mr. Newman with cheerfulness immediately complied" and sealed the poem with his ring. Gano, *Biographical Memoirs*, 142.

89. Critiques of skeptical readings include religious and post-secular critics, such as: Tracy Fessenden, *Culture and Redemption: Religion, the Secular, and American Literature* (Princeton, NJ: Princeton University Press, 2006) and John Lardas Modern, *Secularism and Antebellum America* (Chicago: Chicago University Press, 2011); as well as a cluster of associated approaches grouped together under reparative reading and surface reading: Eve Sedgwick, "Paranoid Reading and Reparative Reading," in *Touching Feeling* (Durham, NC: Duke University Press, 2002): 123–151; Stephen Best and Sharon Marcus, "Surface Reading: An Introduction," *Representations* 108 (2009): 1–22.

90. Fessenden, *Culture and Redemption*.

91. Jordana Rosenberg, *Critical Enthusiasm: Capital Accumulation and the Transformation of Religious Passion* (Oxford: Oxford University Press, 2011), 149.

92. John Marrant, *A Narrative of the Lord's Wonderful Dealings* (London: R. Hawes, 1785). For an important reading of Marrant and the public sphere, see Elizabeth

Maddock Dillon, "John Marrant Blows the French Horn," in *Early African American Print Culture*, eds. Lara Langer Cohen and Jordan Stein (Philadelphia: University of Pennsylvania Press, 2012): 318–339.

93. Michael Warner, "The Preacher's Footing" in *This Is Enlightenment*, ed. Clifford Siskin (University of Chicago Press, 2010), 382.

94. G. W. Hegel, *Aesthetics: Lectures on Fine Art*, trans. T. M. Knox (Oxford: Clarendon Press, 1975), 2:921.

95. Taylor, Charles, *A Secular Age* (Cambridge, MA: Harvard University Press, 2007), 27.

96. Virginia Jackson and Yopie Prins, eds., *The Lyric Theory Reader: A Critical Anthology* (Baltimore, MD: Johns Hopkins University Press, 2014), 4.

97. Jackson and Prins, *Lyric Theory Reader*, 3; John Stuart Mill, "Thoughts on Poetry and Its Varieties."

Chapter 6

1. James Claypool, *Original Poems* (Winchester, VA: J. Foster, 181), iii.

2. Claypool, *Original Poems*, 20–21.

3. Mark Hutchinson and John Wolffe, *A Short History of Global Evangelicalism* (Cambridge: Cambridge University Press, 2012), 277.

4. Benjamin Keach, "The Proem," in *The Glorious Lover, A Divine Poem Upon the Adorable Mystery of Sinners Redemption* (London: J. D., 1679).

5. Peletiah Chapin, *Evangelic Poetry. For the Purposes of Devotion, Excited by Spiritual Songs, and Conviction Urged by Gospel Truth* (Concord, NH: Geo. Hough, 1794).

6. Nathan Cole, "The Spiritual Travels of Nathan Cole," in *Early Evangelicalism: A Reader*, ed. Jonathan M. Yeager (Oxford: Oxford University Press, 2013), 73–75.

7. Joseph Croswell, *Sketches of the Life, and Extracts from the Journals, and Other Writings of the Late Joseph Croswell* (Boston: Lincoln and Edmands, 1809), 11.

8. Catherine Brekus, "Writing as a Protestant Practice: Devotional Diaries in Early New England," in *Practicing Protestants: Histories of Christian Life in America 1630–1965*, eds. Laurie F. Maffly-Kipp, Leigh E. Schmidt, and Mark Valeri (Baltimore, MD: Johns Hopkins University Press, 2016), 34.

9. Jane Dunlap, *Poems, Upon Several Sermons, Preached by the Rev'd, and Renowned, George Whitefield, While in Boston* (Boston: Ezekial Russell, 1771).

10. Joseph Thomas, *A Poetic Descant On the Primeval and Present State of Mankind; or, The Pilgrim's Muse* (Winchester, VA: J. Foster, 1816), vii.

11. William Marsh, *A Few Select Poems, Composed On Various Subjects, Especially On The Doctrine of Free Grace* (Bennington, VT: Anthony Haswell, 1797), 4.

12. Samuel C. Loveland, "The Wrestler," in *A Short Poem, Containing A Descant on the Universal Plan; Also, The Wrestler"* (Weathersfield, VT: Eddy and Patrick, 1814), 18.

13. "From the Mercury of Augt 14, 1740 copied in *The Rev. Wm Becket's Notices and Letters Concerning Incidents at Lewes Town from the years 1727 to 1735*, Historical Society of Pennsylvania.

14. T. Tristram, "To a Lady, With the Last Day," in *The Complaint: or, Night-Thoughts on Life, Death, and Immortality* (Philadelphia: Robert Bell, 1777).

15. Joshua Marsden, *Leisure Hours; or Poems, Moral, Religious, and Descriptive* (New York: Paul and Thomas, 1812), 11.
16. Benjamin Allen, *Urania, or the True Use of Poesy* (New York and Philadelphia: Inskeep, 1814), 12.
17. Allen, *Urania*, 15.
18. Allen, *Urania*, 15.
19. Allen, *Urania*, 15.
20. Allen, *Urania*, 16.
21. Asahel Nettleton, *Village Hymns for Social Worship: Selected and Original: Designed as a Supplement to Watts's Psalms and Hymns*, 2nd edition (Hartford, CT: Goodwin, 1824), v–vi.
22. John Pierpoint, *Airs of Palestine* (Boston: Wells and Lilly, 1817), vi.
23. John Peck, *A Poem, Containing a Descant on the Universal Plan* (Keene, NH: John Prentiss, 1801), 2.
24. Lydia Huntley Sigourney, "Religious Tracts," in *Zinzendorff, and Other Poems* (New York: Leavitt, Lord, 1835), 193.
25. Candy Gunther Brown in *The Word in the World*, the foundational study on nineteenth-century evangelical print culture, broaches some of the differences between evangelicals and Romantics at least until the second half of the nineteenth century. She emphasizes that for evangelicals "the Word *was* God, and the Holy Spirit really, not symbolically, operated through divine and human words in radically transformative ways." Brown, *The Word in the World: Evangelical Writing, Publishing, and Reading in America, 1789–1880* (Chapel Hill: University of North Carolina Press, 2004), 45.

Appendix B

1. Anne Dutton, "An HYMN Compos'd upon copying out something for the Press," *The Weekly History*, London, 69, July 31, 1742, 3. Also in Anne Dutton, *Letters on Spiritual Subjects, and Divers Occasions, Sent to Relations and Friends* (London: J. Hart, 1743), preface.
2. Sarah Moorhead, "A POEM, dedicated to the Reverend Mr RALPH ERSKINE, by a Lady in *New-England*, upon reading his Gospel-Sonnets in Ralph Erskine, *Gospel Sonnets*" (Edinburgh: John Gray and Gavin Alston, 1762). Of significance is also Ralph Erskine, *Gospel Sonnets*, 2nd American edition (Worcester: Isaiah Thomas, 1798).
3. Sarah Moorhead, "To the Rev. Mr. Gilbert Tennent, Upon Hearing Him Display Both the Terrors of the Law and Blessed Invitations of the Gospel, to Awaken Sinners, and Comfort Saints" in *General Magazine and Historical Chronicle* (Philadelphia: Franklin, 1741), Reproduced by The Facsimile Text Society (New York: Columbia University Press, 1938), 281–282. First printed in *New England Weekly Journal*, Number 726, March 17, 1741.

4. Sarah Moorhead, To the REVEREND Mr. *James Davenport* on his Departure from *Boston*, By Way of a DREAM (Boston: Charles Harrison, 1742). Original held at Boston Public Library.

5. Sarah Moorhead, "A POEM in Honour of the Reverend Mr. *Whitefield*: Composed upon hearing him preach with so much Flame the Truths of the blessed Gospel of the SON of GOD" (Boston: Kneeland and Green, 1744). Held at John Hay Library, Brown University and at The Newberry Library.

6. Sarah Moorhead, "*The* Spouse of CHRIST *returning to her first Love. An Hymn* compos'd (as 'tis tho't) by a LADY in *New-England*," *The Boston Gazette*, July 9, 1751.

7. Letter, Martha Brewster to Eleazer Wheelock, September 18, 1769, 769518, Papers of Eleazar Wheelock, Rauner Library, Dartmouth College.

Index

revival verse and, 101
sacred, 93–94
slaves and, 122
universal, 101, 104
See also evangelical harmony
Harris, Howell, 61, 70–71
Harrison, Charles, 73–74
Harte, Walter, 108
Hastings, Selina, 61. *See also* Countess of
   Huntingdon
heart religion, 6–7, 32–33, 37, 57–58, 84
heaven, aural pleasures of, 24
heavenly beings, invocations to, 73
heavenly choir, 24, 28, 29, 55, 57–58
heavenly language, responding to espousal
   to Christ, 57
heavenly song, prototype for, 57
Hegel, G. W., 200–1
Hemans, Felicia, 1–2, 44, 52–53, 88–89
Herbert, George, 9–10, 32–33, 44, 81–83,
   100, 205
heroic couplets, 18, 47
historical poetics, 199
History of Joseph, The (Rowe), 52, 56
Hollifield, Brook, 174–75
holy fairs, 33
homiletics, poetry and, 18
Hopkins, Samuel, 154–55, 158–59
Horae Lyricae (Watts), 4–5, 53–54,
   242n31, 242n34
"Hour of Death, The" (Hemans), 1–2
Howell, William Huntting, 129
Hudibras (Butler), 108–9
human race, singular event of, 124–25
Hume, David, 97, 129, 152, 204–5
Hunter, William, 93
Hutcheson, Francis, 55–56, 96, 97
hymnal-poetic tradition, 198–99
hymnbooks
   as accessories, 147
   culture surrounding, in white families, 166
"HYMN Compos'd upon copying
   something for the Press, A" (Dutton),
   61–62, 219–20
"Hymn to the Morning" (Leapor), 149
hymnody, 17–18
   history of, 8
   traditional history of, 198

hymns
   centrality of, to evangelical devotional
      life, 148
   conversion experience and, 195
   creation of, 5
   distinct from poetry, 4–6
   epic, 149
   experienced together with
      poems, 192–93
   included in church services, 17–18
   literary poetic tradition and, 198–99
   neoclassical vs. evangelical, 148–49
   paired with sermons, 61–62
   theological need for, 249n29
Hymns and Spiritual Songs (Watts), 4–5

ideal convert, pietistic verse and, 80–81
Imitatio Christi (Thomas a Kempis), 186
imitation, conversion and, 173
immanent rhyme, 44
Indian School (Dartmouth College), 73
*Inquiry into the Original of Our
   Ideas of Beauty and Virtue, An*
   (Hutcheson), 96
interracial sex, 112, 115–16
*Invitations to the Reverend Mr. Whitefield,
   from The Eastern Consociation of the
   County of Fairfield*, 79–80
Ireland, James, 14–15, 212
   activities of, 170
   becoming an outcast, 187–89
   conversion narrative of, 170–74, 182–
      85 (see also *Life of the Rev. James
      Ireland, The*)
   conversion by poetry, 199–200
   disinterested religiosity of, 184
   evangelical wit and, 201
   excluding other poets from
      narrative, 195–97
   gendering evangelical
      experience, 180–81
   heaven in poetry of, 182
   itinerancy of, and print production, 197
   itinerant community of, 197–98
   linking revision and poetic address to
      evangelical conversion, 171–72
   literary skill games and, 178–79,
      180, 192